D0464623

LCCC LIBRARY
DISCARD

Sisters in Spirit

Sisters in Spirit

Mormon Women in Historical and Cultural Perspective

EDITED BY

Maureen Ursenbach Beecher

AND

Lavina Fielding Anderson

With a Foreword by Jan Shipps

University of Illinois Press
Urbana and Chicago

© 1987 by the Board of Trustees of the University of Illinois
Manufactured in the United States of America
C 5 4 3 2 1

This book is printed on acid-free paper.

Library of Congress Cataloging-in-Publication Data

Sisters in spirit.
    Includes index.
    Contents: The redemption of Eve / Jolene Edmunds
Rockwood—Precedents for Mormon women from scriptures /
Melodie Moench Charles—The Mormon concept of a Mother
in Heaven / Linda P. Wilcox—[etc.]
    1. Women in the Mormon Church.   2. Mormon church—
Doctrines.   3. Church of Jesus Christ of Latter-day
Saints—Doctrines.   I. Beecher, Maureen Ursenbach.
II. Anderson, Lavina Fielding, 1944–
BX8641.S56   1987   289.3′088042   86-30757
ISBN 0-252-01411-1 (alk. paper)

Contents

Foreword

This book of essays about Mormon women, all written and edited by scholars who are themselves Mormon women, is a brave and important work. Readers will appreciate just how brave and important it really is, however, only if they can see how this work of historical theology fits into the history of historical writing about Mormon women, as well as how it fits into Mormon history itself. For that reason, that history will be reviewed ever so briefly here.

Throughout the nineteenth century, Mormons—women as well as men—were engaged in a *restoration* venture of monumental proportions. Believing that their movement was a restoration of primitive Christianity, the followers of Joseph Smith, their modern prophet, borrowed the term used in the New Testament to refer to members of early Christian communities, adopting the name Latter-day Saints. They conceived of the church they established in 1830 as the New Testament church, formed again in these latter days. Consequently, they went to great pains to structure their "Church of Jesus Christ" precisely as specified in revelations given through their prophet. As the century progressed, moreover, many of the Saints came to believe that the publication of the Book of Mormon and the development of the LDS (Latter-day Saint) movement signified something other than a simple restoration of primitive Christianity: it was "a restoration of all things," including the restoration of the kingdom of God essentially as it had existed in ancient times when David and Solomon ruled over Israel. While this expanded conception of restoration was by no means accepted by all the Saints, it stood at the heart of the Mormon culture that started to develop in Nauvoo, Illinois, in the final years of Joseph Smith's life and came into its own among the Saints who followed Brigham Young to the intermountain region of the western United States after Smith was murdered in 1844 and there established what they believed would be God's kingdom.

Although revelations set forth what might be thought of as blueprints for the LDS restoration of the kingdom of God, the actual day-by-day work of bringing the kingdom into being had to be carried out by the Saints who "gathered to Zion" on the American frontier. As certain as they were that they were divinely led, they had to make their own way across the plains and over the mountains—through the wilderness. Once they were settled in the valley of the Great Salt Lake, much LDS individual and communal effort was required before the desert started to "blossom as the rose." It was the believing Saints residing in the valleys of the mountains who had to learn to live in a "theo-democracy" which abrogated the separation of church and state in everything but name. They were the ones who had to contrive ways to make their livings inside a managed economy. And they had to accept the principle of restoration of *all* things and come to grips with the practice of plural marriage. Thus, as do all serious restoration projects, the building of the kingdom of God on the American frontier obviously required heroic effort.

This kingdom-building venture required the participation of all the Saints, women as well as men. Indeed, while that part of the story is not so often told, the contributions made by Mormon women were so important that the kingdom could never have been built without their assistance and cooperation.

With composure and courage, for example, Mormon sisters met the demands of forced immigration—from Ohio to Missouri, Missouri back to Illinois, and from Illinois to the Great Basin—establishing homes for their families time and time again. Under almost inconceivably difficult conditions, they welcomed the homeless to their firesides, cared for the sick, fed the hungry, and generally fulfilled the domestic responsibilities incumbent on women in an age when the world was divided into public and private, men's and women's, spheres. In addition, since revelation had convinced the Saints of the urgent necessity of carrying the LDS gospel to the nations, even as the kingdom was coming into being, many Mormon women had to assume positions as heads of households while their husbands were away on proselyting missions. They had to support themselves and their children, often with minimal help from the larger Mormon community. Then there was the matter of plural marriage. Not only were the women in the LDS world in many cases required to assist with (or even take the sole responsibility for) their livelihood and that of their children, but they were also asked to defy the conventions of Victorian America by marrying into "plurality." As a result, in far greater numbers than elsewhere in the Western world, women who lived in the LDS kingdom developed occupational and professional skills that turned them into virtually independent professional women.

As a consequence, perhaps, of their contributions to its restoration, the nineteenth-century Mormon kingdom provided for LDS women a situation that allowed them a fair measure of independence. They had their own newspaper, the *Woman's Exponent;* they worked for—and during much of the century exercised—suffrage; and, although they never held priesthood offices, they had direct access to the highest levels of ecclesiastical authority through their reasonably autonomous women's Relief Society. Yet the independence exercised by nineteenth-century sisters must not be misunderstood. The countless diaries and letters of such women extant reveal that the primary concern of LDS women was not personal independence. Documents such as those included in the recently published collection of Kenneth Godfrey, Audrey M. Godfrey, and Jill Mulvay Derr, *Women's Voices,* show that the lives of most Mormon women were dedicated, as were the lives of the men, first, last, and always to the success of Mormonism.

The Saints' success in building, inside the boundaries of the United States, a kingdom of God which operated according to ancient principles (especially insofar as polygamy and ecclesiastical control of politics and the economy were concerned) generated non-Mormon opposition. This opposition grew increasingly intense after the close of the Civil War. By the 1890s, it became so strong that, for self-protection, Mormonism shifted away from its restoration to what may be described as a preservation mode. Exchanging the political kingdom and the practice of plural marriage for Utah statehood, the Saints gave up their radical—the word is not too strong—restoration activities in favor of a more conservative method of operation, one that permitted them to preserve the kingdom *idea,* while waiting for the inauguration of a grander kingdom restored by the divine hand.

This shift from radicalism to conservatism, from working to create God's kingdom according to an Old Testament pattern to preserving an acceptable Victorian American status quo, was neither easily nor quickly accomplished, for it required major alterations in life style, if not in fundamental world view. Not the least of these alterations was the change that came about in the lives of Mormon women in the new situation. No longer required to go against the social and religious conventions of the larger culture and, as a result of more settled conditions and the ecclesiastical enforcement of monogamy, no longer required to take so much direct responsibility for themselves and their children, Mormon women gradually moved or were pushed back into the domestic sphere. For a while they held on to their newspaper and their autonomous auxiliary, and for a surprisingly long time they continued to work openly in Utah and all across the nation for women's rights. But things were not the same as they had been when LDS sisters lived "in the kingdom." As wives who had married into plurality grew old and as Mormonism made its peace with the larger culture, LDS women found their new places in the sun as the wives of LDS men who held the priesthood and ruled over home and church, and as the mothers of LDS sons who would hold the priesthood and start learning to exercise its authority as soon as they reached the age of twelve.

As the shift from the restoration to the preservation mode came about, a peculiar thing happened to keep the change from causing undue disruption of the Mormon world. The Saints in increasing numbers started writing narrative accounts of their own past. As they did this, the narrators read the changed situation back into the early and mid-nineteenth century. Klaus Hansen has shown how Andrew Love Neff, Leland Creer, and other historians transformed the radicalism of nineteenth-century Mormon politics into twentieth-century Americanism. But what happened to the story of nineteenth-century Mormon women? What had actually happened was not glossed over or transformed so much as it was simply ignored. When the stories of early LDS women found their ways into the faith-promoting literature, as they sometimes did, the changed conditions in which sisters now lived their lives were read back into the pioneer past. Of course the women were pictured as having been brave and faithful; but as plural marriage became something of an embarrassment and as activities for women outside the home were discouraged more and more, the stories of pioneer foremothers of twentieth-century Latter-day Saints presented them as domestic paragons whose lives revolved around hearth, home, and family.

Just as non-Mormon women of the recent past started to search for their feminine backgrounds as consciousnesses were raised by the women's movement, so LDS women started seriously looking backward in the early 1970s. An entire issue of the influential periodical *Dialogue: A Journal of Mormon Thought* was devoted to women, with most of the text written by LDS women. Two volumes dealing with LDS women's history followed rather quickly: *Mormon Sisters,* edited by Claudia L. Bushman, and *Sister Saints,* edited by Vicky Burgess-Olson. At approximately the same time, the women of the Boston Stake of the LDS church founded *Exponent II,* a quarterly issued in a newsprint format recalling the nineteenth-century *Woman's Exponent,* a connection made doubly clear by articles reprinted from the earlier journal interspersed among fiction, poetry, and essays of current interest. For Mormon women these various publications matched in importance the women's studies literature issuing from non-Mormon presses during the same decade. They celebrated the history of the female portion of the human race, providing a sense of identity and rootedness for women who had more or less suddenly discovered that history written in traditional language dealing with exclusively male exploits left them without a past of their own.

Even though the historical essays in *Mormon Sisters* and *Sister Saints* contained abundant evidence of the very real differences in the character of the lives of LDS women in the nineteenth and twentieth centuries, the dramatic contrast between the lives of women in the two eras was somewhat muted for several years by the adulatory attitudes of faithful Saints when they considered Mormons—men as well as women—who lived during Mormonism's "pioneer period," its apostolic age. Thus, the discovery of the history of Mormon women tended in the beginning to be reassuring and faith-promoting for most Mormon girls and women. Yet the contrast was there for all to see, and in time it started to bother LDS women whose lives were circumscribed in a community which mainly valued the domestic accomplishments of women and clearly disapproved of work outside the home. When the church's modern expectations for LDS women were measured against the experience of Mormon pioneer women, an attitude of concern started to manifest itself in various Mormon circles.

The open opposition of the LDS church to the passage of the Equal Rights Amendment exacerbated this concern, leading to widespread discussion within the community of Mormon sisters about their future in the church. When Sonia Johnson challenged the current situation for women in Mormondom, as well as the church's opposition to the ERA, some of the writings about LDS women started to exhibit enormous hostility to the church and most particularly hostility to the all-male church hierarchy. Johnson's autobiography, *From Housewife to Heretic,* and another work published earlier by Marilyn Warenski, *Patriarchs and Politics,* made an extended argument that the "plight of the Mormon women" could be blamed entirely on the Mormon men who made up the all-male authority structure of the church.

In *Sisters in Spirit,* the essayists reject the conspiracy theory that pervades the works of Johnson and Warenski. They avoid the "you done us in, you rascals you" attitude and seek not to assign blame for that which is unacceptable in the present situation so much as to understand the condition of Mormon women today. It has to be pointed out, however, that these scholars have not been satisfied to gather more and more evidence simply to produce a bigger and better volume in the "we were there" genre either. Instead, asking what Mormon women believed and how they expressed those beliefs, these scholars have re-examined the sources and written a work that holds up a mirror to the nineteenth-century Mormon world. Rather than finding early versions of themselves and their modern sisters there, they found a very different LDS female experience. Possibly without so intending, they managed to pull back the curtain to lay bare the difference for sister Saints then, when Mormonism operated in a radical restorationist mode, and now, when it operates in a conservative preservation mode.

This work concerns itself with the religious lives of Mormon women. The significance of the book is not that it engages in abstruse theological argument, however. It is significant because it documents in precise detail the difference between what Mormonism once meant for LDS women and what it means now. In essay after essay, a sense of movement from Point A to Point B carries the reader across a dramatic divide. This is accomplished not with angry argument, novelistic flourish, or fancy poetic footwork but with evidence, citations of chapter and verse, diary and record book, all documenting change.

Yet when the essays are taken together, they do raise a serious theological question, one far more important than questions about whether women should have been deprived of the right to give blessings to sick children or the right to carry on certain duties now reserved to the priesthood that finally are matters of liturgical practice. The exceedingly important theological question that these essays cast up is more fundamental; it is the question of the full extent of "free agency" in Mormonism.

A fundamental theological tenet that separates Mormonism from traditional Christianity is its rejection of the power of original sin. The LDS doctrine of individual salvation rests on a passage in the Book of Mormon which indicates that, since the atoning sacrifice of Christ redeemed the children of men from the fall, men are free forever, having the right to choose good over evil, liberty over captivity to sin and death, and so on. In a variety of ways, the essays in this book make it clear that while LDS men may be free so that in Adam's fall they did not all sin, LDS women continue to suffer the curse of Eve and consequently are consigned to all the tasks connected with eternal motherhood. During Mormonism's pioneer era, many Saints expected, these essays say, that Eve's curse would be lifted from women when the kingdom was restored and the millennium ushered in. But in this age of preservation, priesthood and motherhood seem forever balanced, leaving the curse of Eve intact. What implications does this have regarding the "agency" of LDS women?

Any book that can *in faith* raise such a theological conundrum is both brave and important. This one is a marvel. It deserves to be widely read.

JAN SHIPPS

Preface

In the early 1970s, an undefined collection of Mormon women began meeting for lunch on Wednesdays in or near the twenty-six-story general office building of the Church of Jesus Christ of Latter-day Saints. The location was convenient—most of us worked nearby—and the surroundings informed our discussions and shaped our talk. The tall office building, and those smaller but equally significant structures surrounding it, the Relief Society Building, the Church Administration Building, and the temple itself, formed a focus for our conversation. Often we ate in the enclosed garden of the Lion House, where the precedents of our gathering, the women of nineteenth-century Mormondom, entered our thoughts.

Mostly the discussions had to do with women and the church. The topic was not unique to us. It was a time of foment among women worldwide as social, economic, and political forces affecting women's lives were being examined to reveal the generally disadvantaged status of half the world's population. How these forces, and, dearer to us, the patterns of our own religion, were affecting our lives shaped our discussions.

Almost all of us were married, most of us career-oriented, many with children at home. All connected deeply to the church, we had reason to be concerned. We watched as outsiders accused Mormon culture of chauvinism, sometimes with justification; we observed how insiders defended the faith, sometimes with sophistries we could not accept. We recognized the joy of many Mormon women whose lives in the pattern of wife- and motherhood fulfilled them; we saw also the pain of others caught between the Scylla of poverty-level, stay-at-home mothering and the Charybdis of out-of-home employment. We saw our sisters serving energetically in church and community; we recognized that they were often pressed into unproductive roles when they had potential for dynamic leadership. We ourselves struggled to balance our family responsibilities with our community opportunities. We heard from friends and sisters of their successes in their homes, careers, and church and community service; we also heard of gender-based abuses, not only in the world of daily work, but within the church itself. The paradoxes mounted.

In our concern, we were part of a larger movement within the church itself. In New England, for example, a group of women searching for understanding of their own lives had turned to their Mormon past, and in their preparation to teach a course at the local Institute of Religion had discovered the *Woman's Exponent,* the semi-monthly newspaper which from 1872 to 1914 had held Mormon women together in faith and sisterhood. In their concern, these Massachusetts women met together regularly for long and serious talk; they wrote for the *Ensign,* the official organ of the church, and for other outlets. They created two publications of their own: the 1971 "pink" issue of *Dialogue,* and their own book, *Mormon Sisters,* published under their "Emmeline" imprimatur. Their stance was moderate; their editor recalled later that "I couldn't get those women in Boston to be radical enough." Their purpose was not reform but discovery, and their effect was widespread. As contemporary Mormon women came to know their nineteenth-century counterparts, they saw models of behavior which extended beyond their own perceived options. They began to question both their interpretations of the past and the possibilities of the present.

The *Relief Society Magazine,* long the official voice of the church to women, discontinued in 1970; the *Ensign,* which followed, aimed at too wide a readership to deal with women's separate issues. There was no effective forum for official female response to the questions raised. Relief Society materials came through Correlation procedures after long delays and many editings; seldom did they address current concerns. Books directed to women, written primarily by men and published through the quasi-official Deseret Book Company, seemed to some to be limited in focus, leaving women few options.

In 1972 the Equal Rights Amendment passed in Congress and went into the state-by-state ratification process. Many Mormon women saw in its declaration a protection from abuses they had experienced; others feared the damage its general coverage might do to a way of life they valued. Within two years, Barbara Bradshaw Smith, newly called general president of the Relief Society, would express for the church its opposition to that amendment, leaving those Mormon women who had initially supported it feeling torn between two loyalties.

Tension was in the air whenever women's issues were raised. Some of the voices became strident. Mormons for the ERA formed itself around Sonia Johnson in the East and spread westward. Beverly Campbell followed the movement, giving the counter arguments. Mormon women's stances became polarized; the middle ground seemed lost but for a few woman who had concern and credibility in both camps. With the federally sponsored state celebrations of the International Women's Year, the issues became tense and battle lines grew more pronounced. Those of us in the middle, who with equal intensity mourned the discord at IWY conferences and rejoiced in the reinstitution of church-sponsored women's conferences, felt deeply the need for moderating voices.

We knew we should be building bridges, that sisterhood was too significant to be lost in jangling discord. In 1978, as Marilyn Warenski's *Patriarchs and Politics: The Plight of the Mormon Woman* came off the press, we said to each other that "we should have written our own book!" Hers had raised significant questions, but its responses to the issues were irresponsible. Instead of realizing the richness of our heritage and the possibilities it suggested for future contributions of women, the book blamed a male patriarchy for trends which were rampant in the society as a whole. There was surely a better context into which our past could be set, we said to each other—one which, without tearing down, could build around the structures already set on the firm foundation of a restored gospel.

Elsewhere positive steps were being taken: women at Brigham Young University were sponsoring an annual women's conference; a Women's Research Institute was established there; the Harold B. Lee Library opened a women's history archives and initiated an annual symposium on the subject; Relief Societies in various regions were holding their own conventions, addressed by some of the most thoughtful women available; academic groups were encouraging scholarship in Mormon women's history—the Utah Women's History Association, the Logan-centered "Hands Across the Valley" conference, media productions on women's issues. *Exponent II* had a subscription list of over two thousand. All of these events involved participants in the Wednesday lunches and informed our discussions there.

So we talked, until our talking led to further researching and to discovering some of the routes by which Mormon women arrived at the point where we found ourselves. As we grew in our understanding, we also felt the need to share our findings with our sisters, in and out of Mormonism. And with our husbands and brothers, and with the scholars of history, of sociology, of women's studies, religion, anthropology, American studies, and other fields where a better understanding of Mormon women's experience might be useful.

Whatever the uniqueness of Mormon women in the American West among their American sisters generally or the similarities which remained to link them to their eastern United States and immigrant past, they are a significant group to study. Source materials are legion: diaries, letters, and autobiographies are collected in numbers in the archives of the area; documents of the culture itself—minute books, financial and business records, newspapers, ecclesiastical reports, sermons, educational materials—all are equally accessible. That essays of this nature could be written with such confidence, on such sure documentation, indicates how rich are the resources on which they are based. We set our hands to the task.

The women who wrote these essays were not neophytes to scholarly writing; neither were they seasoned academics. All presented their findings in various professional meetings, laid their conclusions on the table for the scrutiny of their colleagues, accepted criticism, researched further, and rewrote. Several of our pieces were published elsewhere and found warm reception from lay and academic readers alike.

As this work took hold, the National Endowment for the Humanities provided generous support for the project. We are grateful for its confidence and its awareness, with us, of the importance of these essays. We also appreciated the money.

As the book took shape, Jan Shipps, our friend and noted non-Mormon scholar of Mormon history, offered encouragement and advice. At our request, she consented to provide a foreword for the book, setting our efforts in the context of Mormonism's development as a whole and women's place in that development. And Maryann MacMurray, our poet at lunch, put into images some of the concepts we all were grappling with. Eliza Snow would have understood the need for the poetic form.

The essays, as they evolved through our cooperative process, drew on both shared understandings and individual interpretations. Not always was there total agreement among the authors and editors on all points, but we valued the diversity and let stand whatever contradictions we could not comfortably resolve on the basis of the documents available.

There was overlap as authors, each with a particular question in mind, drew insights from some of the same documents. While the editorial process attempted to diminish duplication of quoted references in the final essays, there remained some repetition necessary for the argument in each context.

Mormonism carries with it the intellectual and cultural traditions of the Judeo-Christian tradition, overlaid with the revelations of Joseph Smith and his successors. When, then, Jolene Edmunds Rockwood delineates the interpretations and uses of the Eden story in her chapter, "The Redemption of Eve," she is speaking about a major thread in the Mormon message to women. That that story plays itself out in the temple worship of Mormons and is thus reinforced in a particular interpretation to devout Mormon women gives it a power in popular Mormon doctrine beyond its significance to Christian thought generally. Rockwood's essay illustrates some uses to which the story has been put in the past and near past and then, to assess its pure meaning, returns to the original Hebrew text to examine the intent of the scriptural account. By means of structural analysis, elucidation of metaphors, and explication of Hebrew terms, she gives us a story which not only does not demean women, as its subsequent interpretations sometimes do, but which exalts them as sisters to the sons of Adam. In refutation to the "curse of Eve" which Mormon and other Christian women have long worn as albatrosses about their necks, she gives us an explication which shows the mortal Adam and Eve together subject to the human condition; only the serpent is cursed. In Mormon thought, Eve's redemption is as sure as is Adam's; the Mormon credo that "man will be punished for his own sins, and not for Adam's transgression" is equally applicable to woman.

The infusion of other Old Testament models into Mormon thought is traced next by Melodie Moench Charles, as she considers scriptural precedents for Mormon women. The books held by Mormons to be scriptural include the Bible, Old and New Testaments; the Book of Mormon, translated by Joseph Smith from metal plates; the Doctrine and Covenants, revelations received and dictated by Joseph Smith and later prophets; and the Pearl of Great Price. Charles finds in most of the Old Testament "a dismal view of women's worth, their rights, and the restrictions their religious society placed upon them." Yet in spite of this, the Israelites valued and relied upon the talents of some remarkable women. Like parts of the Old Testament, the Doctrine and Covenants reveals concern with priestly responsibilities and largely neglects those people who are not administratively empowered, women among them. Little there is addressed to women by more than implication. Similarly the Book of Mormon has little to say directly to women; even the much-loved King Benjamin address, Charles reminds us, is spoken to "my brethren," to "ye old men, and also ye young men, and you little children." Stories of women appear in both the Old Testament and Book of Mormon, but in less than significant proportion to the concern with men's issues. For Charles's purposes, the New Testament gospels provide the most positive portrayal and perception of women. She points out that, while the letters alternate between limiting or disparaging women and presuming that women serve, worship, and possess talents equally with men, Jesus throughout the gospels embodies nonsexist ideals that contrast with his Jewish culture. In Christ, Charles suggests, is woman restored to daughtership in the household of God.

That woman is daughter of an eternal Mother as well as Father in Heaven is a significant doctrine, enunciated in the first decade of Mormonism's dispensation. Not unique to Mormonism, it is made significant to Mormon women in establishing patterns of belief in eternal union of the sexes. Its history and impact on Mormon women are addressed in this volume by Linda P. Wilcox. Beyond the importance of the material of the essay itself is the significance it had in encouraging scholarship in the history of Mormon women. At its first public reading, in Salt Lake City in 1978, there began a celebration of scholarship which energized the movement and encouraged other academicians to study Mormon thought and history as it pertains to women.

Originating simultaneously with the Mother in Heaven doctrine in early Mormonism is the elaboration of the ceremonies of the temple as the "endowment" was extended to the Saints. Traced in the essay by Carol Cornwall Madsen, these ceremonies gave to women a stature generally denied them in nineteenth-century Christian thought. Madsen sees the empowering of women in the organization of their Relief Society as linked to the contemporaneous introduction of the high temple ritual, with its sense of the interdependence of women and men in God's plan of redemption and exaltation.

Nineteenth-century Mormon women also felt empowered, observes Linda King Newell in the next essay, to exercise their spiritual gifts for the good of their co-religionists. Tracing the practice of and official dicta concerning such manifestations as healing, speaking in and interpreting "tongues," and prophesying, she sees a trend away from full encouragement toward institutional discouragement in most overt expression of the gifts of the spirit. Like Madsen, she connects the women's practices with the temple and with Joseph Smith's words to the women in their Relief Society meetings.

How all of these threads wove a comforting blanket over the whole community of Mormon women is demonstrated in Jill Mulvay Derr's essay, " 'Strength in Our Union': The Making of Mormon Sisterhood." Approaching an interpretation of Spencer W. Kimball's 1979 paradigm which placed sisterhood as analogous to priesthood as fatherhood is analogous to motherhood, Derr shows the interweaving of the social and religious practices of the women and its strengthening effect on them singularly as well as cooperatively. The subsequent unravelling of that cloth is an issue not fully resolved.

Observers in and outside the church note the emphasis placed in this century on the mothering roles of women. And certainly, as the essays so far have suggested, that emphasis had firm roots in early Mormonism, as in the prevailing American culture. Linda Wilcox, in tracing chronologically the official church statements on the subject of motherhood, sees a continuation of nineteenth-century American values persisting long after the prevailing society had adapted itself to increasingly diverse patterns available to women. Indeed, that single stance had frequently been the center of our luncheon talk as we struggled, many of us, with demands for what seemed an overstrict adherence to the mother-in-the-home pattern. In stepping back historically, Wilcox lets us consider the root of the concept and see its development over the past century.

Because American Mormons are so like their American counterparts of other creeds, it is not difficult to find applicable studies to identify how Mormon women have actually worked out their mothering and other familial roles and to observe to what degree the injunctions traced by Wilcox have actually entered the practice of the faithful. Those aspects of Mormon thought which have created different modes of marriage interaction are suggested in Marybeth Raynes's contribution, "Mormon Marriages in an American Context." A marriage and family therapist by profession, Raynes draws on her own research as well as the research of others to identify patterns of interaction between marriage partners. She notes the similarities between Mormon and American marriage patterns, leading to the conclusion that Mormons are more like than unlike their Gentile sisters. She considers in depth Mormon responses to two significant aspects of marriage: decision-making, in the light of Mormon adherence to "patriarchal" family order; and sexual expression among people to whom, doctrinally, sexual sin is second only to murder in its seriousness.

Where, in all of this, does the matter of priesthood fit? In a period when every major Judeo-Christian denomination is considering or has resolved the question of exclusive male leadership, the Latter-day Saints stand firm on the doctrine that only worthy men are eligible to hold priesthood. That black men were initially denied priesthood, and then granted it in the light of a revelation announced in 1978, has suggested to some that it is only a matter of time, that "ripeness is all," that someday Mormon women, too, will be ordained. However that is organizationally resolved, they must come to some personal resolution which allows for the doctrine and must find ways of behaving appropriately under male priesthood direction. Grethe Ballif Peterson, looking for approaches of Mormon women to the subject usually addressed officially only by men, interviewed eight women, chosen for their experience in working at all levels of church administration and for their thoughtful approach to the meaning of priesthood. In a church which presents to the observer a sense of monolithic interpretation of doctrine, it is unusual to see the variety of views expressed on this one point. The personal responses reveal more than aspects of doctrine.

Thus, chronologically, from the beginning to the present, and in a continuum of point of view, from scholarly to personal, the book illuminates aspects of Mormon women's experience, present and past. In a church which holds as canon not only its scriptures but also the daily utterances of its leaders, there will always be change. That change will continue in the future, as it has in the past, to affect the lives of women.

To the greater understanding of those changes as they come, we submit this volume: may our past be preface to a continually enlightened future.

MAUREEN URSENBACH BEECHER

Acknowledgments

The whole group of women who participated, and still participate, in the Wednesday lunch discussions are to be acknowledged for the questions they raised and the approaches to answers which they suggested. Our mentors and colleagues deserve thanks for timely assistance: Leonard J. Arrington, Janath R. Cannon, D. Michael Quinn, and Laurel Thatcher Ulrich. They read the essays and critiqued them with an honesty which was sometimes painful but always appreciated. Nevertheless, we, the authors and editors, remain individually and collectively responsible for the points of view expressed here.

Permission to republish, in revised form, the essays by Linda King Newell and Linda P. Wilcox has been received from *Sunstone*. *Dialogue* granted permission to reprint the poems of Maryann MacMurray, originally published there under the pseudonym Brooke Elizabeth Smith.

The National Endowment for the Humanities assisted in the funding of the project; their support is acknowledged and appreciated.

Our typists for the project were Jennie Long and Marilyn Rish Parks. We appreciate their diligence. Finally, in the publication process we acknowledge with thanks the work of our editor, Cynthia Mitchell, and the patience and persistence of Elizabeth Dulany. We hope it was all worth waiting for.

Sisters in Spirit

JOLENE EDMUNDS ROCKWOOD

The Redemption of Eve

I am Eve, the wife of noble Adam; it was I who violated Jesus in the past; it was I who robbed my children of heaven; it is I by right who should have been crucified.

I had heaven at my command; evil the bad choice that shamed me; evil the punishment for my crime that has aged me; alas, my hand is not pure.

It was I who plucked the apple; it went past the narrow of my gullet; as long as they live in daylight women will not cease from folly on account of that.

There would be no ice in any place; there would be no bright windy winter; there would be no hell, there would be no grief, there would be no terror but for me.

Anonymous, Old Irish[1]

For over two thousand years, since the first commentary on Genesis was presented, Eve has been blamed for woes ranging from the origin of sin to the presumed inferiority of the female sex. Because of Eve, women have been cursed, their subordination to man has been justified, and their feminine weaknesses have been stereotyped. Much of this tradition has been so engrained in our Judeo-Christian culture that we are often unaware of its presence or its origin. Yet if it were possible to eradicate all our culturally induced prejudices about Eve and examine the original Hebrew text of the whole Eden account, we would find a story that actually says very little of what it has throughout the centuries been credited with saying. Let us first see how a few commentators have interpreted the Genesis 1–3 account in various time periods.[2] Then we will look at the Hebrew text of the Adam and Eve story. Finally we will compare this new perspective with other sources of particular relevance to Latter-day Saints.

Whatever meaning the Adam and Eve story had to Old Testament Israelites is unknown, for after Genesis 5 it is not referred to again throughout the rest of the Old Testament canon.[3] There is no indication, at least until post-exilic times, that the story had any major impact on Israelite customs or worship comparable to the exodus from Egypt, for instance, or God's covenant with Abraham. Unfortunately, no other contemporaneous records survive to illuminate the intent of the author at the time Genesis 1–3 was written. The earliest documents available after the Genesis account itself were early Jewish writings dating from about 400 B.C. to the latter part of the first Christian century.[4] The Midrash and Talmud (some of these early writings) established in Jewish culture the use of the Adam and Eve account of Genesis to justify the roles of men and women. At the time these were written, the Jews believed that Eve, because she was formed from Adam's rib, was a secondary creation, thus subject to and inferior to Adam.

Although in Judaism a woman was honored in her role as mother, she had little or no role in public worship. In the synagogues, men and women worshipped in separate chambers to prevent the women from "distracting" the men, a tradition referring back to the image of Eve as temptress. As woman was the cause of Adam's fall, so also a woman's voice in a religious meeting would tempt a man away from higher worship.[5] It was the woman's duty to listen but not respond or be seen.

Even some of the religious rituals a woman conducted in the home became her responsibility because of Eve's actions in the Garden of Eden. The woman, for example, was to light the candles to begin the Sabbath observance because it was woman who originally "extinguished the light of man's soul."[6] When she kneaded dough, it was her responsibility to separate out a "heave" offering (the best portions of the sacrificial animal which historically were set aside for Yahweh and the priests before the sacrifice was made) to make amends for Eve's defiling Adam, who was "the heave offering of the world."[7]

A woman "acquired merit" by encouraging her husband and sons to study the Torah, but "whoever teaches his daughter Torah is as though he taught her obscenity," and "let the words of the Torah rather be destroyed by fire than imparted to women," because "a woman has no learning except in the use of the spindle."[8]

The men were encouraged to leave their wives at home and "go into the marketplace and learn intelligence from other men," because women, by nature of their creation, were intellectually and physically inferior to men.[9] The Midrash records that God deliberated long in deciding which part of the body he would use to make the wife of Adam, but "in spite of the great caution used, woman has all the faults God tried to obviate"—including haughtiness, eavesdropping, wantonness, and jealousy. These characteristics were seen as evident not only in Eve but also in Sarah, "an eavesdropper in her own tent"; Miriam, "a talebearer" who accused Moses; Rachel, who was "envious" of Leah; and Dinah, who was "a gadabout."[10] At their first meeting Adam perceived these pernicious qualities in Eve and knew she would "seek to carry her point with man either by entreaties and tears, or flattery and caresses."[11]

The Midrash also derives other qualities of women from that primeval rib. For example, women need to use perfumes and men do not because "dust of the ground remains the same no matter how long it is kept; flesh, however, requires salt to keep it in good condition." Women's voices are high and "shrill" and men's are not because "when soft viands are cooked, no sound is heard, but let a bone be put in a pot, and at once it crackles." Women are rigid and not easily placated like men because "a few drops of water suffice to soften a clod of earth" but "a bone stays hard" and will not soften in water. It is the man who proposes marriage and not the woman because man lost his rib and must find a woman to retrieve it. And finally, "women precede men in a funeral cortege, because it was woman who brought death into the world."[12]

Jews prayed for sons and celebrated when they were born. No corresponding celebration marked the birth of a daughter. "The world cannot exist without males and females," a Rabbinical dictum states, "but happy is he whose children are sons and woe to him whose children are daughters."[13] "The Lord bless thee with sons and keep thee from daughters" were the words of the Priestly Benediction.[14]

According to Israelite law, after childbirth a woman must not touch any sacred relic or enter any sacred place until she was "purified." If her child was male, this period was forty days; for a daughter, purification required twice as long, eighty days. The pseudepigraphal book of Jubilees explained the discrepancy by maintaining that the creation of Adam and Eve took place in the first week, but Adam did not see Eve for two weeks. Adam entered Eden after forty days; Eve did not enter Eden for eighty days.[15]

And, finally, to be born male was itself reason to give thanks daily: "A man is obliged to offer three benedictions daily; that He has made me an Israelite, that He has not made me a woman, that He has not made me a boor."[16]

This bias against women reflected the theology that Eve was solely responsible for the transgression in Eden and that, because of her role in the Fall, all women were subjugated to men, who were held blameless as Adam. In the apocryphal book of Sirach, probably written sometime between 300 and 275 B.C., we read the following scathing treatise on the nature of a wicked woman:

> Any wound, only not a heart-wound!
>   Any wickedness, only not the wickedness of a woman! . . .
> There is no poison above the poison of a serpent,
>   And there is no wrath above the wrath of a woman. . . .
> I would rather dwell with a lion and a dragon,
>   Than keep house with a wicked woman. . . .

(There is but) little malice like the malice of a woman,
    May the lot of the wicked fall upon her! . . .
From a woman did sin originate,
    And because of her we all must die.[17]

The author thus blames Eve as the ultimate source for a woman's wickedness but sees Adam far differently: "above every living thing was the beauteous glory of Adam."[18] The view is not atypical. The book of Jubilees refers to Adam as a great patriarch linked with Enoch and Noah. So does 1 Enoch. The "Apocalypsis Mosis" and "Vita Adae et Evae" in "The Books of Adam and Eve" and 2 Enoch all suggest that in Eden Eve transgressed sexually with the serpent then seduced Adam, the innocent victim of Eve's deception.[19]

Thus, in the Jewish writings which emerged between the end of the Old Testament period and the first centuries after Christ, the Genesis Adam and Eve account was used by many commentators to justify cultural practices, explain, or even create, sexual characteristics, and define roles of men and women.

The Midrash, Talmud, and apocryphal and pseudepigraphal literature were all in use by the Jews at the time of Christ and shaped the society into which he was born. His mother took him to the temple after her days of purification. He studied the Torah along with other boys. The four Gospel accounts of his ministry depict him as having a thorough knowledge of the scriptures and the law of Moses as found in such Jewish works as the Talmud and Midrash. Yet in none of the Gospels is Jesus seen using the Adam and Eve story as an explanation for either the origin of sin or the respective roles of men and women. On the contrary, he taught that people were not punished for the previous sins of parents or any ancestors[20] and demonstrated in his actions his respect for women. Many women were numbered among his closest associates, including Mary Magdalene, Joanna, Susanna, and others.[21] His gospel was one in which women could fully participate. Martha reprimands her sister Mary for listening to Jesus rather than helping with the serving, but Jesus answers that Mary had "chosen that good part, which shall not be taken away from her," thus expanding dramatically the structured role of a righteous Jewish woman by enabling her to study the scriptures as a man would do.[22]

Jesus seems to have deliberately paired men-women examples in his teachings, as if to make sure that women also saw his teachings as relevant. For example, it is a male shepherd who leaves the ninety and nine to find a lost sheep and a woman who loses a coin and searches her home until she finds it. Both rejoice in the finding.[23] The point of both stories is the same: that the worth of every individual, male or female, is great. Yet they are told sequentially in the text. Christ heals the centurion's male servant and immediately afterward raises the widow's son. He likens the kingdom of heaven first to a grain of mustard seed which a man plants in his garden and second to some leaven which a woman puts in her dough.[24] Other examples of pairing are found throughout the four Gospels; Luke, more than the other evangelists, groups them together.[25] Christ includes women as well as men in his gospel, his conversations, and his healings. Christian doctrine which made women full participants in worship must have caused problems for the early converts of the young church Christ left behind at his death, for all the first converts to Christianity were Jewish, presumably burdened with the traditional attitudes about women. With the conversion of non-Jews to Christianity came the necessity of determining which of the traditions of the past were compatible with the new faith and which were not.[26]

The apostle Paul was particularly sympathetic to the problems involved in separating Jewish culture from Christian doctrine. He had been a devout defender of Judaism against Christianity. Raised as a Pharisee, he had been trained under the renowned Jewish scholar Gamaliel and was, by his own description, a "perfect" observer of the Jewish law. After having observed the stoning of the Christian disciple Stephen, Paul was prevented by a miraculous conversion from further persecuting the Christians. By the time he wrote those epistles now preserved in the New Testament, he knew both Judaism and Christianity thoroughly.[27]

It is in the epistles of Paul or in letters attributed to him that the status and conduct of women is most discussed and that the Adam and Eve account is once again used out of its context to illustrate a point. These communications with different units of the church contained advice, doctrine, and answers to any questions which had caused conflicts within individual units. Paul's advice on issues involving women was usually a mixture of Christian principles boldly sprinkled with Jewish customs. For example, he tells the Corinthians that he approves of women praying and prophesying in the church (Christian principle), as long as they cover their heads (Jewish tradition).[28] The veil or head covering served as a sign upon all women of the shame of Eve for bringing sin into the world and also protected women, with their weaker wills, from the influence of evil angels.[29] To justify his reasoning, Paul states that man "is the image and glory of God: but the woman is the glory of man. For the man is not of the woman; but the woman of the man. Neither was the man created for the woman; but the woman for the man" and, for this reason, "ought the woman to have power on her head because of the angels." In many Bible translations, including the Revised Standard Version, *power* is translated *veil*. Thus Paul presents the classic Jewish interpretation of the rib creation story in Genesis 2 and uses it to support his claim that women should cover their heads, not men, as in Jewish tradition.

Paul then seemingly undoes his argument with an afterthought: "Nevertheless neither is the man without the woman, neither the woman without the man, in the Lord. For as the woman is of the man, even so is the man also by the woman; but all things of God" (Christian principle). He then stopped giving his opinion and threw the question back to his audience to answer for themselves. "Judge in yourselves: is it comely that a woman pray unto God uncovered? Doth not even nature itself teach you, that, if a man have long hair, it is a shame unto him? But if a woman have long hair, it is a glory to her: for her hair is given her for a covering."[30] But without additional information to help them avoid interpreting the question from within their culture, the questions would, more than likely, simply be heard as rhetorical.

In 2 Corinthians Paul uses the example of Eve once again to make a point. In chastising the members in Corinth for following after every false prophet who entered into their midst with a new and persuasive doctrine, he compares them with Eve, who, being gullible, was easily "beguiled" by the serpent. Here a problem of contemporary Christians was illuminated for the Jewish converts by referring to their traditional view of Eve.[31]

In 1 Timothy Eve is again used, this time to encourage women to "adorn themselves in modest apparel, with shamefacedness and sobriety" and to "learn in silence with all subjection." Paul explains: "I suffer not a woman to teach, nor to usurp authority over the man, but to be in silence. For Adam was first formed, then Eve. And Adam was not deceived, but the woman being deceived was in the transgression. Notwithstanding she shall be saved in childbearing, if they continue in faith and charity and holiness with sobriety."[32] These verses are laden with Jewish tradition. "Shamefacedness and sobriety" were considered appropriate facial demeanor because of the disgrace of Eve's actions in the Garden of Eden. This shame could be overcome by bearing and raising children in the Jewish faith. Likewise, because Adam was superior by virtue of being formed first and because Eve caused the fall of innocent Adam, women should not attempt to teach men or exercise authority over men but be silent. Some New Testament scholars believe that this passage was written by someone else in Paul's name.[33] Possible support for this interpretation is that Paul in Romans attributes the Fall to Adam, not Eve: "Wherefore, as by one man sin entered into the world, and death by sin; and so death passed upon all men, for that all have sinned."[34]

The line separating Judaism from Christianity in its early years was often fine. The epistles make numerous references to the Mosaic law and many passages seem to echo the Midrash and Talmud. Following the persecution by the Romans and the deaths of the apostles, we see that early church fathers and Catholic theologians use the Adam and Eve story to define emerging Catholic doctrines. These statements are numerous and stretch all the way from the second Christian century to the nineteenth century. Only a few relevant examples will be dealt with here.

One obvious doctrinal connection with Eve was the origin of sin and evil in the world. Catholic explorations echoed much of the apocryphal and pseudepigraphal literature already in existence. Irenaeus (died c. A.D. 200) wrote that evil and death entered the world through Eve, who then led the innocent Adam into sin, hardly an original observation.[35] Clement (c. 150-215) denounced women's jewelry by referring to Eve's role in the fall: "Yet, these women do not blush when they wear such conspicuous symbols of wickedness. Just as the serpent deceived Eve, so, too, the enticing golden ornament in the shape of a serpent enkindles a mad frenzy in the hearts of the rest of womankind, leading them to have images made of lampreys and snakes as decorations."[36] This view of Eve, and thus of all women, as inherently seductive and weak-willed was important in ascribing to Eve sole responsibility for sin in the world.

When Origen (185-253) made one of the first references to the practice of infant baptism and the doctrine of original sin, he perceived the fall as a sexual sin, the serpent's seduction of Eve.[37] Thus, because lust and the sexual act brought about sin, the woman became unclean and anything born of her consequently in need of baptism.

Tertullian (A.D. 155-220), like Origen, proposed that since Adam was blameless Cain must actually have been the son of Satan, who, as the serpent, had intercourse with Eve in the Garden of Eden. He even attributed the blame for Christ's death to Eve and all women: "And do you not know that you are (each) an Eve? The sentence of God on this sex of yours lives in this age: the guilt must of necessity live too. You are the devil's gateway; you are the unsealer of that (forbidden) tree: you are the first deserter of the divine law: you are she who persuaded him whom the devil was not valiant enough to attack. You destroyed so easily God's image, man. On account of your desert—that is death—even the Son of God had to die."[38]

During the medieval period, theologians provided women with another alternative than hapless identification with an evil Eve. Virginity, celebrated as the highest ideal of Christian life, would preserve women from the sin of lust as well as from the inherent evil of the sexual act. Some orders of nuns not only preserved virginity but remained silent to atone for Eve's guilty conversation in the Garden of Eden.[39] Eve's example was used repeatedly as the reason for mistrusting women in the marriage relationship. She was, after all, the originator of sin and the seducer of Adam in the garden.[40] However, Thomas Aquinas (1225-74) ascribes guilt in the fall to Adam as well as to Eve; but because Adam's mental abilities and intelligence were far superior to Eve's, he must accept more responsibility though Eve's sin was more serious.[41]

With the Protestant Reformation, marriage was no longer seen as a poor second choice, and thus the views of Adam and Eve changed. Martin Luther wrote that the married state was not sinful but rather to be desired and that women were not to be despised for the sexual sin of Eve, for sin was common to both sexes. Even though women were weaker than men and possessed "several vices" of mind and body, they were redeemed by "the womb and birth," because Eve's role in life was to give birth.[42]

The Protestant Reformation also created a hitherto unknown diversity of beliefs within Christianity which has increased and intensified throughout the nineteenth and twentieth centuries.[43] For example, the beginnings of the woman suffrage movement in the nineteenth century brought a feminist perspective to the Adam and Eve account. In this quotation from the *Woman's Bible* by Elizabeth Cady Stanton, Eve is depicted as heroic and Adam as an inferior dupe:

> Note the significant fact that we always hear of the "fall of man," not the fall of woman, showing that the consensus of human thought has been more unerring than masculine interpretation. Reading this narrative carefully, it is amazing that any set of men ever claimed that the dogma of the inferiority of woman is here set forth. The conduct of Eve from the beginning to the end is so superior to that of Adam. . . . Then the woman fearless of death if she can gain wisdom takes of the fruit; and all this time Adam standing beside her interposes no word of objection. "Her husband with her" are the words of V.6. Had he been the representative of the divinely appointed head in married life, he assuredly would have taken upon himself the burden of the discussion with the serpent, but no, he is silent in this crisis of their fate. Having had the command from God himself he interposes no word of warning or remonstrance, but takes the fruit from the hand of his wife without a protest. It takes six verses to describe the "fall" of woman, the fall of man is contemptuously dismissed in a line and a half.
>
> The subsequent conduct of Adam was to the last degree dastardly. When the awful time of reckoning comes, and the Jehovah God appears to demand why his command has been disobeyed, Adam endeavors to shield himself behind the gentle being he has declared to be so dear. "The woman thou gavest to be with me, she gave me and I did eat," he whines—trying to shield himself at his wife's expense! Again we are amazed that upon such a story men have built up a theory of their superiority![44]

In summary, then, the history of the Adam and Eve story is a record of its interpretation both as shaped by cultures and as shaping them. Sadly enough, those cultural messages have often supported a negative view of women, seeing Eve as weak, sinful, seductive, and unrestrained.

Nineteenth- and twentieth-century Mormon theologians were not immune to the effects of culture. They, too, used the Adam and Eve story to support issues relevant to the times in which they lived. In the nineteenth century, one of the major issues in the Church of Jesus Christ of Latter-day Saints was polygamy. George Q. Cannon, a member of the First Presidency, stated in 1869 that its "correct practice" would "redeem woman from the effects of [Eve's] curse," which he specified as "thy desire shall be to thy husband, and he shall rule over thee." He postulated that many more women than men would be admitted to the celestial kingdom because women "are not held accountable to the same extent as men are." They are cursed with "yearning after the other sex," while men are "strong" and will be held "responsible for the use of the influence [they] exercise . . . over [women]." He felt that polygamy would help relieve women of their "jealousy" and thus make them able to overcome Eve's curse.[45] Brigham Young was less explicit in defining the curse of Eve but linked the Garden of Eden closely to plural marriage in teaching that Eve was "one of [Adam's] wives" in the premortal existence.[46] During the polygamy era, General Authorities frequently cited 1 Timothy, which states that Eve, not Adam, was "deceived," to support a woman's subjection to her husband.[47] My sense is that the use of this scripture in general conference addresses declined considerably after the polygamy era.

Nineteenth-century Mormon women evidently also believed that they were cursed because of Eve, but they were confident that through obedience they could become equals with men. Some felt this equality, fostered by the woman suffrage movement, could be attained in the near future. The *Utah Woman Suffrage Songbook* declares:

> Woman, 'rise, thy penance o'er,
> Sit thou in the dust no more;'
> Seize the sceptre, hold the van,
> Equal with thy brother, man.[48]

An essay in the 1895 *Woman's Exponent* showed similar sentiment: "Ever since Eve partook of the forbidden fruit, which certainly showed her pluck, women have been blamed for all the ills that flesh is heir to; there has been a woman at the bottom of everything that savored of ill repute, but in the future there will be a woman at the bottom of everything good, not excluding good governments. Men have not been slow to lay their burdens upon us, but they have been so afraid we should find it out."[49]

Other Mormon women felt that equality for women would occur during the millennium or in the after-life. Eliza R. Snow, regarded by Mormon women as "prophetess" and "presidentess," wrote:

> What we experience here, is but a school
> Wherein the ruled will be prepared to rule.
> · · · · · · · · · · · · · · · ·
> Clothed with the beauties purity reflects
> Th' acknowledged glory of the other sex,
> From life's crude dross and rubbish, will come forth,
> By weight of character—by strength of worth;
> And thro' obedience, Woman will obtain
> The *power of reigning, and the right to reign.*[50]

Another essay in the *Woman's Exponent,* dated 1 February 1889, described the curse as a blessing in disguise which would be removed at the millennium:

> Since the days of Eve her daughters have lived under the curse of social inferiority to her brother man. In this generation the irksomeness of this condition has been displayed by the woman's movement for equal rights, This movement has met with slurs and opposition at every step, just as every truth has always been opposed by its adversary; . . . God, who made us all, and who is no respecter of persons, intended that woman should in every way be equal to man in dignity; but He also knew the station in which she would be placed while on earth, that her child-bearing and child-rearing sphere would curtail other aspirations, which man would have the opportunity to follow. Of the two He knew that the former would be of the greater importance to the world, and therefore in the guise of a curse, bestowed upon her the *blessing* to be subject to man, that she might the better fulfill her mission, . . . To me it seems like one of the latter day signs, that women are becoming restless beneath their oppressed situation. The world's record will soon be finished . . . and when the millennium shall set in, and the curse be removed. . . . I write with confidence, for I firmly believe that our Heavenly Father loves His daughters just as well as he loves His sons, and that He does not desire the glorification of one at the sacrifice of the happiness of the other.[51]

That God's judgment on Eve after the fall was a curse and that this curse was visited upon all women seems to have been commonly accepted by both men and women in the early Mormon church.

In the early twentieth century after polygamy ceased to be a major issue, the Adam and Eve story was used to support more current emphases. Apostle James E. Talmage in 1913 maintained that premortal Adam knew "all the essentials of the Word of Wisdom" and that the fall was the result of "the eating of things unfit."[52] Rudger Clawson in 1918 and Orson F. Whitney in 1925, both apostles, gave conference addresses against evolution in which they cited the Adam and Eve story.[53]

Recent Mormon commentators, in an age of increased interest in women's rights and sexual equality, have chosen to ignore the more controversial aspects of the Adam and Eve story. Marion G. Romney, a member of the First Presidency, in a presentation before the Relief Society Conference in 1967 gave an entire address about Eve without once referring to either the rib story or the curse upon Eve in Genesis 2. Rather, he emphasized her role as a "noble woman" and her essential unity with Adam.[54] Spencer W. Kimball, president of the church during the 1970s, described the relationship between Adam and Eve as a "partnership" and praised her understanding of her "responsibility of bearing and nurturing children." In a context that included the Adam and Eve story, he encouraged Mormon women to become "contributing and full partners," rather than "silent" or "limited" partners, in their marriages. He admonished women to become "scholars of the scriptures as well as our men" and urged women to "set your goals ... to make you reach and strain." He emphasized that the story of the rib is figurative, defined God's fiat "let us make man" to mean "a complete man, which is husband and wife," stressed the joyful aspects of the fall and reiterated a simultaneous creation (mankind = male *and* female).[55] Furthermore, he repeated the same message to Mormon men in a general priesthood meeting: "The sisters in this dispensation include many of the most noble daughters of our Heavenly Father.... Our sisters do not wish to be indulged or to be treated condescendingly; they desire to be respected and revered as our sisters and our equals. I mention all these things, my brethren, not because the doctrines or the teachings of the church regarding women are in any doubt, but because in some situations our behavior is of doubtful quality."[56]

This survey of views of the Adam and Eve story is admittedly sketchy and selective rather than comprehensive. Still, it demonstrates how some commentators in different epochs have used the story almost at will to justify a particular cultural role for women and a theological explanation for the origin of sin. The original story seems protean, plastic, infinitely malleable. But if we put aside the commentaries, it becomes most instructive to examine the text itself, analyzing its structure and language for meaning and perspective.

Internal textual evidence shows that the Genesis account of the creation, temptation, and fall of Adam and Eve is most appropriately viewed as a piece of Hebrew poetry rather than as a literal historical account. During periods when literal biblical interpretation was the norm, the creation-and-fall account inevitably posed problems that diminish when its poetic nature is understood. In addition, consideration of the poetic aspects of such writings reveals dimensions of truth and meaning unavailable when only principles of prose are considered. Classical Hebrew poetry generally does not use rhyme but rather relies on sound, rhythm, and repetition of ideas through parallel thoughts to convey its meaning. It uses a great deal of imagery, symbolism, and multi-leveled meaning. As is characteristic of this literary form, the Genesis Eden account is a tightly woven, symmetrical unit in which the meaning of the story is conveyed through imagery and parallelism.[57] It is interesting that the author of Genesis chose to present this story in poetical language whereas other sections of Genesis use different literary styles. We may conjecture that the author was emphasizing a poetic reality that transcended the historical facts.

Jewish historian Flavius Josephus (A.D. 37–100) commented in the first century after Christ that Moses, while writing Genesis, used three different literary modes to express his thoughts: direct or plain words, philosophical or allegorical words, and enigmatical expressions. The translator notes that

Josephus has Moses describe the creation (Gen. 1-2:4) in direct language, then shift to the philosophical (or allegorical) mode to relate the formation of man, a section which includes the rib story in Genesis 2:4-22.[58] Modern commentators have concurred with Josephus' view. One twentieth-century biblical scholar, G. E. Mendenhall, classified that section with the classical Hebrew poetry books of Psalms, Proverbs, and Ecclesiastes.[59]

Since the account is related in poetic language, we must interpret it figuratively rather than historically; and each half of a parallel unit, whether two lines or whole sections, must be interpreted in light of the other half. Because each parallel unit consists of a single idea repeated, or two ideas contrasted, each is dependent on the other for full meaning. By the same token, we cannot view one half of a symmetrical story without the other. Many commentators who have used only portions of the Adam and Eve story have thus, inevitably, quoted out of context without considering how that portion fits with the whole.

Let us then read the Adam and Eve story as a symmetrical unit, emphasizing the parallel elements to be sure that the interpretation of one section of the story is consistent with interpretations of other sections and of the story as a whole. We will also note such poetic elements as imagery, symmetry, and other aspects of Hebrew poetry. We will deal with the Genesis account in three sections: the creation (Gen. 1:26-2:25), the temptation and fall (Gen. 3:1-7), and the trial and judgment (Gen. 3:8-24).

The Creation (1:26-2:25)

We begin with Genesis 1:26-28 because the entire Adam and Eve account, including the Cain and Abel story, is bracketed between two almost identical scriptural passages: Genesis 1:26-27 and Genesis 5:1-2. Our view of the text sees it as poetically and purposefully constructed.[60] Why has the author repeated these verses? Genesis 1:26-28 suggests the purpose of mortality in a few short verses: man and woman were created in the image of God to replenish the earth. All things on the earth were given them for life, and they were given dominion or stewardship over the earth together, unified as man and woman. So also the concluding statement in Genesis 5:1-2 summarizes the whole of mortality. Man and woman were created in the image of God. Blessed as a good creation, they replenished the earth. Genesis 5 continues by telling how this was done. We could say that the author of Genesis used 1:26-28 as an introduction and 5:1-2 as a final summary; between the two, all other parts of the story of Adam and Eve are contained. This view becomes even more likely when we consider that the story is not mentioned or referred to again anywhere else in the Old Testament. (See note 2.)

It is interesting that the word translated as *man* is the Hebrew *'adam*, meaning "humankind," or man in a collective sense. It is used throughout most of the story rather than the more specific Hebrew noun *'iš*, meaning "one man," or husband. In English, *'adam* could have several different meanings, an ambiguity leading to inconsistency in English translations of Genesis. If *'adam* appears alone without the Hebrew definitive article *ha-* preceding it, it could mean either "man" as a collective (humankind, humanity) or "Adam" as a proper name. There are only two places in the text where it definitely occurs this way, and in both places the context dictates translation as a collective humankind.[61] *Ha-'adam* means "the human," or collective man. This form is used almost exclusively.[62] Its use of *them* indicates the plural sense of *ha-'adam* in "Let us make *man* in our image . . . and let *them* have dominion. . . . So God created *man* . . . male and female created he *them*."[63]

After the introduction in 1:26–28, the author describes the creation in figurative language. The mystical formation of the human being is described symbolically. The author clearly says that a human is formed by a union between elements from the earth (physical body) and an element from God (spiritual body); together, body and spirit constitute the soul. This verse parallels Genesis 3:19, in which the Lord points out that because of the fall man is subject to death and would "return unto the ground; for out of it wast thou taken: for dust thou art, and unto dust shalt thou return." The dust of Genesis 2:7, however, is a ground that yields easily to man and provides trees that are pleasant to the sight and have everything good for food. The dust of 3:19 is a fallen world that has been "cursed." It produces thistles and thorns spontaneously, and man must work it by the sweat of his brow.

The symmetry is important. In the beginning, the human and the earth are united and mutually dependent one upon the other. In 2:5 it is seen as negative that there is no human to till or serve the ground. In 2:7, when the human is formed from the ground, he is given dominion over the ground but will also serve it. In Hebrew, this dependency and unity is stated in the form of an epigram—almost a pun, as the words for earth and man are almost identical: mankind (*ha-'adam*) takes its existence from the earth (*ha-'adamah*).[64]

In 2:8 the garden is prepared; in 2:15 man is placed within to "dress it and to keep it." Food and water are supplied by God. The harmony with the earth is continued. The human and the plant kingdoms are characterized by mutual dependency and unity. Man's dependency on and unity with the animal kingdom follows in Genesis 2:19–20, where all living creatures are formed (also from the ground) and brought to the human to be named. In verses 16 and 17 God has issued in poetical imagery a warning to the human that if he partakes of the fruit of the tree of knowledge of good and evil, which was planted in the garden, he will die. Knowledge of good and evil, and death are the results of the mortal condition. The fruit and the tree symbolize whatever of his actions will cause the human and his world to become mortal.

God then states, "It is not good that the man [collective] should be alone; I will make him an help meet for him."[65] In other words, neither the plant kingdom nor the animal kingdom contains a creation fit for mankind. This phrase "help meet" (Hebrew `ezer kənegdo`) is an interesting one. `Ezer,` which in this context is translated as "help" (meaning "helper"), has the unfortunate English connotation of an assistant of lesser status, a subordinate or inferior—for instance, a willing but not very competent child.[66] In Hebrew, however, the word describes an equal, if not a superior. The other usages of `ezer` in the Old Testament show that in most cases God is an `ezer` to human beings,[67] a fact which makes us question whether "helper" is an accurate translation in *any* of the instances it is used. A more accurate translation in this context would be "strength" or "power." Evidence indicates that the word `ezer` originally had two roots, both beginning with different gutteral sounds.[68] Over time, the two gutterals were merged into one word, but the two meanings, "to save" and "to be strong," remained. Later, the meanings also merged into one word, "to help." Therefore, if we use the more archaic meanings of `ezer` and translate `ezer` as either "savior" or "strength," it clarifies not only the context we are discussing but also the other passages in the Old Testament where `ezer` is used, especially where `ezer` refers to God in his relationship with humankind.

`Ezer` translated as "strength" or "power" also fits in nicely with the second word in the phrase, *kənegdo,* which has traditionally been translated as "meet for" or "fit for." Because *kənegdo* only appears this one time in the Old Testament, earlier translators had little upon which to base translations. An important clue to the meaning of this word is found in its usage in Mishnaic Hebrew, where the root means "equal." *Kənegdo* then, means "equal to" and the entire phrase `ezer kənegdo` means "power or strength equal to." Thus, when God makes *ha-'adam* into two beings, he creates woman, a power or strength equal to man.

The King James translation of *kənegdo* as "meet for" is based on the actual seventeenth-century meaning of *meet,* "worthy of," which is no longer used in English. This archaic translation has allowed confused readers to hyphenate the noun and adjective as *help-meet,* detach the sense of "meet for," and then develop the neologism *help-mate,* a term that never existed either in the original Hebrew or in the King James version. The phrase has, however, become so much a part of the Christian vernacular that references are commonly heard to wives as help-meets and help-mates.

The Lord then removes a "rib" from which he forms man's companion.[69] The Hebrew *şela`* is used more than forty times in the Old Testament, but only here has it been translated as "rib." Only two other usages refer to a human being: Job 18:12, where it is translated as "side" ("destruction shall be ready at his side"), and Jeremiah 20:10, which has uncertain meaning ("all my familiars [friends] watched for *my halting,*" [KJV], "for my *fall*" [RSV], or, "at my *side*"). The word refers to the side of a hill in 2 Samuel 16:13, but every other usage gives construction details for the tabernacle or temple (i.e., *side* of the tabernacle, *side* of the altar, etc.).[70]

Ṣela` in Genesis 1:21–22 thus should be similarly read as construction information, though the object being constructed is a life form. The Lord, as master builder, takes the "side" (*ṣela`*) of the human and uses it to "build" (*banah*) another person. Reading *ṣela`* as "side" rather than "rib" also better dramatizes the unity of the man and the woman, enhances the phrase "power equal to him," and makes the man's later characterization of woman as "bone of my bone and flesh of my flesh" even more meaningful. Thus, when God causes the human to sleep, he takes one of his sides and creates two beings out of one.

This section of the text is so symbolic that some early writings, the Nag Hammadi documents and early legends of the Jews among them, have maintained that the author was describing an androgynous creation that was later split into male and female parts.[71] However, since we are treating the story as symbolic, it is more realistically seen as a symbolic representation of the unity of the first couple.

The creation of man as two individuals appears to be presented symbolically as simultaneous, rather than sequential.[72] "No specific purpose is stated as it was with the animals, who were brought to the human to be named." The two are presented to one another as companions, and the man seems to react with surprise and delight:[73] "This is now bone of my bones, and flesh of my flesh: she shall be called Woman, because she was taken out of Man." Up to this point, the human has been *ha-'adam*. Now the words *man* (*'is*) and *woman* (*'issah*) are used for the first time. These are definite nouns which signify man and woman as separate individuals with definite gender. In addition, the man uses the feminine *zo't* ("this is now bone of my bones") for the first time.[74] However, the man at this point is not naming the woman. *'Issah* is not a name; it is a common noun which designates gender. It also appears in the previous verse before the man uses it. The man is actually making a pun on the origin of woman. As the human (*ha-'adam*) received his existence from the earth (*ha-'adamah*), now the man (*'is*) has been used to form the woman (*'issah*).[75] We see this difference even more clearly when we look more closely at the episode where *ha-'adam* names the animals. He uses a Hebrew naming formula: the verb *to call* (*qara'*) followed by the word *name* (*šem*) or "calling the name." Cain "builded a city, and *called* the *name* of the city, after the name of his son"; and "Adam knew his wife again, and she bare a son, and *called* his *name* Seth."[76] It is interesting that the man does not employ this formula for the woman until after the Fall when he "calls her name Eve," but even in this instance he is calling her by a title.

It is significant that the man calls the woman "bone of my bone and flesh of my flesh," a statement he could not have made about the animals. In Hebrew, these phrases indicate a closeness, a blood relationship between the two parties, and in this case a unified companionship between the man and the woman. But the phrases are also used in other places in the Old Testament to describe two parties who are not necessarily blood relatives but who have made a covenant with each other, such as when the northern tribes of Israel made a covenant with David, their new king, and confirmed: "Behold, we are thy bone and thy flesh." David makes a similar covenant with the elders of Judah: "Ye are my brethren, ye are my bones and my flesh." Some of the participants may have been related, but the phrase refers to a mutual covenant the two parties have made with each other.[77]

Bone in Hebrew symbolizes power, and *flesh* weakness. "Bone of my bones and flesh of my flesh" thus becomes a ritual pledge to be bound in the best of circumstances (power) as well as the worst (weakness). The man's use of this phrase here implies a covenant similar to a marriage agreement and is, in fact, reminiscent of the phrase "for better or for worse" used in marriage vows. Thus it would be a mistake to read this verse as an expression of Eve's "subordination" (totally "derived" from Adam) or as an expression of Adam's possessiveness (she is "his" because she is part of him). Instead it acknowledges a total union of two creatures who have both strength and weakness.

Genesis 2:24 summarizes the covenant and the whole episode: "Therefore shall a man leave his father and his mother, and shall cleave unto his wife: and they shall be one flesh." The man and the woman have just been created and have no physical father or mother in the story. But they are symbolic representations of all men and women, and thus the covenant episode symbolically represents the relationship between all men and women. Male and female were created from one flesh to become separate individuals who are companions to one another and who strive to again become as one in their relationship. As one scholar put it, "From one comes two; from wholeness comes differentiation. Now, at the conclusion of the episode this differentiation returns to wholeness" as two become one flesh.[78] It is interesting that man is commanded to leave his parents and cleave unto his woman. In view of the patriarchal society in which this was written, one would instead expect to see the woman leave her parents and cleave unto her husband. It seems as though the author of this summary statement is trying to make three points: the woman is an independent and equal creation; marriage does not make her the possession of the man; and achieving oneness should be the common goal of both.

The last verse in Genesis 2 indicates that the man and the woman are "naked and not ashamed." The lack of shame is a metaphor for innocence — not necessarily a negative condition except as it is coupled with nakedness, which in Hebrew is often used to mean defenselessness.[79] Living in a state of perfection and oneness and having no knowledge of opposition or evil, they have no appreciation of good. The author thus sets the stage for the episode that follows:

The Temptation and Fall (3:1-7)

This episode and the final one are symmetrically juxtaposed with the beginning episode. Whereas the three levels of creation are unified and dependent on one another in the first scene, now they are all participants in their own fall: the animal kingdom provides the temptation (serpent), the plant kingdom the mode for the fall (fruit and tree), and the humans the agents of the deed. In the first part, God tells the couple they will die if they eat the fruit; in the second, the serpent says they will not die. In the first, they are naked and not ashamed; in the second their eyes are opened and they know they are naked and make aprons.

Until the woman and the man actually partake of the fruit, however, the language of the text indicates a union in their actions. Furthermore, the text does not say that the two are separated at the time of the temptation but actually suggests the opposite. The serpent addresses the woman with the plural Hebrew *you* form and she replies with the plural *we* and *us*: "And he [the serpent] said unto the woman, Yea, hath God said, *Ye* [plural Hebrew] shall not eat of every tree of the garden? And the woman said unto the serpent, *We* may eat of the fruit of the trees of the garden: But of the fruit of the tree which is in the midst of the garden, God hath said, *Ye* [Hebrew plural] shall not eat of it, neither shall *ye* touch it, lest *ye* [Hebrew plural] die. And the serpent said unto the woman, *Ye* [Hebrew plural] shall not surely die." When she partook of the fruit she then gave some to "her man" (King James Version *husband*) who was "with her."[80]

If we take the view that they were separated at the time of the temptation, implied in 1 Timothy 2:13-14, then we can say that the woman was presented with a set of deceptive and incomplete facts and concluded through her own perception what the results of her actions would be. Thus, she made a more difficult choice. She then presented the situation to the man in a clear and rational manner which enabled him to perceive his alternatives accurately and, hence, the course he should take. The text does not say that the serpent first tempted the man alone and, after he refused, went to the woman; it says only that he tempted the woman, who then gave the fruit to "her man and he did eat." There is no tempting or coercing on the part of the woman and apparently no hesitation on the part of the man. They became mutually responsible for the transgression.

Because the story is symbolic, however, it does not matter whether they were separate or apart, or in what order they were tempted. At this point the author uses the plural pronouns *you, we,* and *us* and the phrases "her man" and, "[who was] with her," thus implying that they are still united in thought and action. We can infer, consequently, that whatever action one would take, the other would take also.

The Trial and Judgment (3:8–24)

In this section of the story, the unity of the man and woman becomes sudden separateness. They use the first person singular for the first time in the narrative as the Lord confronts them: "*I* heard thy voice in the garden, and *I* was afraid, because *I* was naked; and *I* hid *myself*," explains Adam, speaking only for himself. The man's comments are even more interesting when we realize that *both* the man and the woman heard God's voice, *both* were afraid, and *both* of them hid. Though performing the same actions, their unity is ruptured. The woman also uses the first person singular to answer the Lord's question: "The serpent beguiled *me*, and *I* did eat."[81]

Not only is their unity gone, but their self-possession and sense of responsibility has also eroded. The man first blames the Lord ("The woman whom thou gavest to be with me") and then blames the woman ("she gave me of the tree") before admitting that he had in fact partaken of the fruit. Even though he blames her, he does not say that she tempted or cajoled him, only that she gave it to him and he ate. Similarly, the woman blames the serpent (he "beguiled me") before admitting her part.[82]

God then pronounces what have traditionally been called the curse of Adam and the curse of Eve. The serpent, however, is the only agent who is directly cursed and then, apparently, for usurping the role of deity and reversing the words of the deity. In the first episode, God tells man not to eat of the tree because he will die. In the second episode, the serpent tells man to eat of the tree and he will not die. His dishonesty is planned, deliberate, and deadly, for the actions of Adam and Eve bring death, as God has promised. The serpent is cursed for his part in blasphemy and disobedience by being relegated to the bottom of animal creation, his loathsome lowliness symbolized by the dust he is condemned to "eat all the days of thy life." He is also prevented from gaining any power over mortals through future deceit by the hatred set between the serpent and humankind. The serpent shall have the power to "bruise" the heel of the seed of the woman, but that seed shall ultimately triumph and shall bruise the serpent's head.

This judgment is obviously expressed in figurative language. The author uses a serpent as a symbol to represent the source of evil which tempted the first couple. The language is opaque, apparently deliberately obscure, and certainly seems to have more than one level of meaning.

The judgments God pronounces upon the man and the woman seem to be different from the curse upon the serpent. In fact, when we view the text of that section as a structural element of the story, these judgments are shown to be statements of cause and effect which describe the result of the mortal condition. God's descriptions of mortality parallel the earlier warning in 2:17 that mortality will result in a knowledge of good and evil (thus a loss of innocence), and death. Here he instructs them more about their new state: the man must now labor by the sweat of his brow to survive. This is so because not only the man but all orders of creation fell to a mortal existence. The earth is now cursed (fallen) and will no longer automatically supply the man with all his needs. The plant kingdom will provide not fruitful trees but thistles and thorns. Subject to death, he is told "unto dust shalt thou return."[83] Likewise, the woman has become mortal and must suffer the hardship and pain of bearing children. The phrase "thy desire shall be to thy husband" may indicate three things: (1) the results of her sexual desire will produce children, which will cause her sorrow and pain; (2) because of her childbearing, she will also desire her husband's protection against the real dangers of a fallen world; (3) and perhaps some of her desire refers to the second part of her judgment—that her husband "will rule over" her. Perhaps she desires her husband to return her to her former state of equality rather than to rule over her.[84]

It is not clear in this context whether rule connotes unrighteous or righteous dominion on the part of the male. It appears most often in the Old Testament to indicate unrighteous dominion, such as Pharoah's unrighteous rule over the Israelites, but it also appears benignly: the sun is created to "rule the day, and the [moon is] to rule the night."[85] But whether the man's rule is righteous or unrighteous in mortality, the fact that it is mentioned at all presupposes that man did not rule over woman before the fall. No elements of the judgments are in existence in the prefallen state. Fallen man must work an unyielding earth by the sweat of his brow; before the fall he was not subject to death. Fallen woman must bear children in pain; before the fall she could not understand pain nor have children. Fallen man rules over fallen woman; before the fall, they were equal companions.

As before Adam made a covenant with her, now he gives her a title of great honor: "Life, the mother of all living." This is not a mere naming. It signifies that a great event has taken place, and a title commensurate with the event is bestowed upon the woman. It is also similar to the Near Eastern formula for titles given to goddesses.[86]

The author does not accuse or blame the couple for their transgression. In fact, he seems to imply that the choice they made is good, for the paralleling sequence now is reminiscent of the Genesis 1:26-28 statement of the purpose of the creation: to "multiply and replenish the earth." In the prefallen state, the man and the woman were innocent and sterile. Now they have knowledge and are fertile.

The Lord then provides clothing for the couple and sends them out of the garden. With this act, the symmetry of the story becomes complete. In

the first episode, unity and perfection characterize all of the orders of creation. In the second episode, all orders of creation participate in their own
fall, which brings separateness and conflict in episode three. Yet the author
introduces the story with a statement that celebrates the fall from immortality to mortality and ends it in the same way. The symmetry of the story is,
in fact, one of contrasts. In episode one there is unity and perfection but
there is no joy, for they know neither good nor evil. They have no knowledge. Their very innocence leaves them defenseless. In episode two, they
gain knowledge, realize they are naked, and attempt to conceal their guilt
from God. Their very guilt, however, means that they have gained knowledge, the knowledge of good and evil. With knowledge they can cover their
"nakedness," thus acquiring a defense against evil. The experience is com-
pounded of both bitter and sweet. Episode three presents a final contrast.
Because they are mortal, they will now experience pain and hardship. They
will be separated from deity. Yet, paradoxically, they will only now be able to
know joy. They are sent away from the garden, but it is for their own good,
for they are imperfect and could no longer live in the presence of perfection.
Nor could they gain experience in an environment where their needs are
automatically supplied. The Lord provides them with clothing (shields of
knowledge) to cover their nakedness (defenselessness). They can now defend themselves against evil. His final response is thus an act of compassion,
not punishment. Reading the entire account as a poetical unit thus resolves
many of the individual elements; they are symbols, symmetrically paired to
reveal the layers of contrast in the story as a whole.

After this close reading of the Hebrew text, it is instructive to sample the
impressive amount of Latter-day Saint commentary on the creation and fall.
This survey is by no means comprehensive, but it makes an effort to be
representative of those sources which support the overall interpretation of
the Hebrew text discussed above.

For example, from the early days of the Mormon church to the present,
Latter-day Saints have quite consistently taught that the text is figurative
rather than literal. The location of a real Garden of Eden, the existence of
deity, the actual existence of the first parents, and the fall to mortality have
all been seen as historical events. But the exact creation of the man and the
woman—especially the rib story—and the mode of the fall (the serpent and
the fruit) have been interpreted as symbols of a much more complex historical actuality. Spencer W. Kimball, as president of the church, stated that the
rib story "of course is figurative."[87] Brigham Young went so far as to call it a
"baby" story.[88] He also maintained, as did Joseph Smith, Joseph Fielding
Smith, and others, that Adam and Eve's bodies were engendered and born
by natural sexual functioning and that they were placed in Eden as adult
beings.[89]

As a second important resemblance, church leaders have generally affirmed that the Genesis account describes the first couple as united in their actions in Eden. Most have recognized 'aḏam as a plural word representing both the man and the woman. For example, Erastus Snow, a member of the Quorum of the Twelve, said in 1878: "Male and female created he them and called their name Adam, which in the original, in which these Scriptures were written by Moses, signifies 'the first man.' There was no effort at distinguishing between the one half and the other, and calling one man and the other woman. This was an after distinction, but the explanation of it is—one man, one being, and he called their name Adam."[90] Spencer W. Kimball made a similar scriptural gloss in 1976:

> "And I, God, blessed them [Man here is always in the plural. It was plural from the beginning] (Moses 2:28).
> "And I, God said unto mine Only Begotten, which was with me from the beginning: Let us make man [not a separate man, but a complete man, which is husband and wife] in our image. (Moses 2:26).
> "Male and female created he them; and blessed them, and called their name Adam" [Mr. and Mrs. Adam, I suppose, or Brother and Sister Adam] (Gen. 5:12).[91]

Joseph Smith, Mormonism's founder, included Eve in the mystical description of the formation of humankind from the dust of the earth in Genesis 2:7: "The 7th verse of 2nd chapter of Genesis ought to read—God breathed into Adam his spirit [i.e., Adam's spirit] or breath of life; but when the word 'rauch' applies to Eve, it should be translated lives."[92]

Throughout Latter-day Saint scriptures, the word *man* can also mean humankind. In 2 Nephi 9:6 in the Book of Mormon, *man* is used as a plural for the first couple, just as in the Hebrew version of Genesis: "And because man became fallen, they were cut off from the presence of the Lord."

Latter-day Saint theologians have also persistently taught that Adam and Eve were sealed by an eternal marriage covenant, paralleling the Hebrew sense of the phrase "bone of my bones." Orson Pratt, an apostle, in 1875 preached that God himself officiated in a "marriage for eternity" linking Adam and Eve.[93] Spencer W. Kimball reiterated the concept in 1975: "What a beautiful partnership! Adam and Eve were married for eternity by the Lord. Such a marriage extends beyond the grave." In the same discourse he amplifies on the quality of that relationship: " 'Therefore shall a man leave his father and his mother, and shall cleave unto his wife: and they shall be one flesh,' (Gen. 2:24). Do you note that? She, the woman, occupies the first place. She is preeminent, even above the parents who are so dear to all of us. Even the children must take their proper but significant place."[94]

Because Latter-day Saint doctrine sees the fall to mortality as an essential part of the premortal plan and finds the first parents "sacrificing" their immortality that mankind might be, both the man and the woman have been treated as equally responsible for the transgression. Brigham Young and others taught that Adam had a knowledge of the plan of salvation dating to his premortal existence as a spirit without a body and was foreordained to partake of the fruit as the "design of the Lord."[95] Eve must have also been foreordained; as we have seen, they acted in unison. Orson Pratt, among others, attributes transgression evenly to "one man and woman."[96] Throughout the Book of Mormon, the transgression is almost always referred to as Adam's, suggesting that *'adam* was probably used in the Hebrew sense to designate the first couple as a unit.[97] In 2 Nephi 2:18–26, Eve is singled out, but as the object of temptation by Satan, to whom the guilt is assigned.

The vehicle of temptation (the serpent) and the mode (the fruit) have been viewed as symbols, just as the creation of Adam and Eve was seen as figurative. Orson Pratt suggested that the pair were tempted on numerous occasions, not only by the serpent, but by other "beings" who had been "angels of light and truth" in the premortal existence but had then become followers of Satan.[98] The book of Revelation identifies the serpent as Satan or Lucifer, who "was cast into the earth" for rebellion against God, a scripture Mormons interpret as referring to the premortal existence.[99]

Mormon theologians also taught that Adam and Eve became mortal by eating a substance which was poisonous to their immortal systems. One apostle, Erastus Snow, for example, said in 1878:

> Death passed upon our first parents, Adam and Eve, through their partaking of the fruits of the earth, their systems become [*sic*] infected by it, and the blood formed in their veins, and composed of the elements of the earth, which they partook, and these contain the seeds of dissolution and decay. And this blood, circulating in their veins, which was made up of the fruits of the earth—those things of which they partook—that formed their flesh, and made the deposits that constituted their muscle, and their bones, arteries and nerves, and every part of the body, became mortal and this circulating fluid in their systems produced friction which ultimately wore out the machinery of their organism, and brought it to decay, that it became no longer tenable for their spirits to inhabit, and death ensued.[100]

The tree and the fruit, then, have been seen in Mormon thought as symbols which represent the process by which the fall came about.

There is no evidence in Mormon scriptures to suggest that Adam and Eve were apart at the time of the fall or that Adam was tempted first and refused. The book of Moses uses the same wording as the King James version and the Hebrew text: She "also gave unto her husband [who was] *with her.*"[101] The Doctrine and Covenants, a collection of Joseph Smith's revelations, even states that "*Adam* [was] tempted of the devil" and "partook of the forbidden fruit,"[102] which may be either another indication that the name is being used as a collective word for Adam and Eve as a unit or that Adam and Eve *were* together at the time of the temptation.

As for the judgments placed upon the man and the woman in the third episode, we have already seen that nineteenth-century Mormons seemed to believe that Eve's judgment was a curse on all women. But the curse of Eve on all women is seldom mentioned any more in general conference addresses or articles written about women. Even the land, which, along with the serpent, was the only thing actually cursed in the Hebrew text, seems to have been redeemed as part of the restoration of the gospel by Joseph Smith, according to a revelation he recorded in 1831: "And, as I, the Lord, in the beginning cursed the land, even so in the last days have I blessed it, in its time, for the use of my saints, that they may partake of the fatness thereof" (Doctrine and Covenants 61:17).

Mormon specialist in ancient scriptures Hugh Nibley recently called the judgments "curses" but maintained that the man and the woman received identical curses:

> Now a curse was placed on Eve, and it looked as if she would have to pay a high price for taking the initiative in the search for knowledge. To our surprise the *identical* curse was placed on Adam also. For Eve, God "will greatly multiply thy sorrow and thy conception. In sorrow shalt thou bring forth children." The key is the word for sorrow, *tsavadh*, meaning to labor, to toil, to sweat, to do something very hard. To *multiply* does not mean to add or increase but to repeat over and over again; the word in the Septuagint is *plethynomai*, as in the multiplying of words in the repetitious prayers of the ancients. Both the conception and the labor of Eve will be multiple; she will have many children. Then the Lord says to Adam, "In *sorrow* shalt thou eat of it all the days of thy life" (i.e., the bread which his labor must bring forth from the earth). The identical word is used in both cases, the root meaning is to work hard at cutting or digging; both the man and the woman must sorrow and both must labor. (The septuagint word is *lype*, meaning bodily or mental strain, discomfort, or affliction.) It means not to be sorry, but to have a hard time. If Eve must labor to bring forth, so too must Adam labor (Genesis 3:17; Moses 4:23) to quicken the earth so it shall bring forth. Both of them bring forth life with sweat and tears, and Adam is not the favored party. If his labor is not as severe as hers, it is more protracted. For Eve's life will be spared long after her childbearing—"nevertheless thy life will be spared"—while Adam's toil must go on to the end of his days: "In sorrow shalt thou eat of it *all* the days of thy life!" Even retirement is no escape from that sorrow. The thing to notice is that Adam is not let off lightly as a privileged character; he is as bound to Mother Earth as she [Eve] is to the law of her husband. And why not? If he was willing to follow her, he was also willing to suffer with her, for this affliction was imposed on Adam expressly "because thou hast hearkened unto thy wife and hast partaken of the fruit."[103]

The "curse" for both the man and the woman, then, simply amounts to feeling the results of mortality, which made them imperfect, "carnal," and subject to temptation and sin. Many scriptures from the Book of Mormon state this same philosophy: that with mortality came sin. Such statements usually continue with a way to overcome the effects of sin. In Mosiah 3:19 we read: "For the natural man is an enemy to God, and has been from the fall of Adam, and will be, forever and ever, unless he yields to the enticings of the Holy Spirit, and putteth off the natural man and becometh a saint through the atonement of Christ the Lord." That verse continues, enumerating the characteristics of the redeemed person: he or she "becometh as a child, submissive, meek, humble, patient, full of love, willing to submit to all things which the Lord seeth fit to inflict upon him [or her], even as a child doth submit to his [or her] father." The "natural" or fallen person does not spontaneously have these traits, for with mortality comes inequality in our relationships, pride, a tendency toward selfishness, arrogance, suspicion, and self-seeking rather than love.

Needless to say, all of these traits tend to create differences where there were none, to magnify small differences into great differences, and to reinforce the tendency toward hierarchy, division, and the rule of the "superior" over the perceived inferior. Any relationship in which one member "rules" over the other seems to be associated more with the fallen state than with the redeemed state.

Spencer W. Kimball, in discussing Genesis 3:16, redefined it: "I have a question about the word *rule*. It gives the wrong impression. I would prefer to use the word *preside* because that's what he does. A righteous husband presides over his wife and family."[104] Unfortunately he did not take the next step and define *preside*. A man using business organization models, or even some church organizations that he might have observed, might well be puzzled by a distinction between *rule* and *preside*.

Some light is shed on this question by Doctrine and Covenants 121, an oft-quoted charter for the use of priesthood. Even though the context of this revelation, received by Joseph Smith in 1839, does not specify marriage or family setting, contemporary usage gives it a broad application to any situation in which a priesthood holder might be presumed to have some authority, whether ecclesiastically, maritally, paternally, or socially. This section begins with a warning: "We have learned by sad experience that it is the nature and disposition of almost all men, as soon as they get a little authority, as they suppose, they will immediately begin to exercise unrighteous dominion." The contrasting "righteous dominion" is described a few verses later:

> No power or influence can or ought to be maintained by virtue of the priesthood, only by persuasion, by long-suffering, by gentleness and meekness, and by love unfeigned;
> By kindness, and pure knowledge, which shall greatly enlarge the soul without hypocrisy, and without guile. . . .
> Let thy bowels also be full of charity towards all men, and to the household

of faith, and let virtue garnish thy thoughts unceasingly; then shall thy confidence wax strong in the presence of God; and the doctrine of the priesthood shall distill upon thy soul as the dews from heaven.

The Holy Ghost shall be thy constant companion, and thy scepter an unchanging scepter of righteousness and truth; and thy dominion shall be an everlasting dominion, and without compulsory means it shall flow unto thee forever and ever.[105]

Dominion based on "righteousness and truth . . . *without compulsory means*" does not describe a relationship of subordination. The goal of mortality is to overcome such "carnal" tendencies as unrighteous dominion and to strive for oneness in relationships with others and with God. This sense of oneness has permeated Latter-day Saint doctrine since the beginning: from the oneness of the celestialized Father and Mother in Heaven, to the oneness of the Godhead, to the oneness that must exist among the Saints before Zion can be established prior to the second coming of Christ: "And the Lord called his people ZION because they were of one heart and one mind, and dwelt in righteousness."[106]

Ida Smith, then director of Brigham Young University's Women's Research Institute, speaking at BYU's Women's Conference in 1980, said that a relationship in which inequality exists cannot be a celestial relationship: "A just God would not require the yoking of two unequal beings for eternity. . . . It is important for a woman to learn in this life her eternal role so that when she is sealed [a temple ceremony of marriage] she will be prepared and ready—with all her heart—to function in and glorify that role. That means being ready and prepared to function as a full partner in a celestial team—without having to look *up* because of any feeling of inferiority, or look *down* because of any feeling of superiority, but look *across* into the eyes of an equally prepared, equally magnificent eternal mate." She maintained that the gospel of Christ should free men and women from the sexual stereotypes we sometimes attach to one another in mortality and pointed out that Christ openly displayed traits which have often been thought of as "feminine": he embraced children, he openly wept, he was gentle and compassionate. And likewise, we have many examples of intelligence, wisdom, and initiative in the great women of the church.[107] Carolyn J. Rasmus, administrative assistant to the president of BYU, in another address given at the same conference, corroborated: "The differences between men and women are designed to be complementary and unifying, not divisive and separating. The ultimate plan is for achievement of a perfect balance, with neither sex to be unduly emphasized."[108]

In discussing the creation episode of the Hebrew text, we suggested that Genesis 2:24 ("Therefore shall a man leave his father and mother") summarized the meaning of the figurative rib story which preceded it: that man and woman were symbolically created from one being, split into two, and married so that they could strive in their relationship to again become sym-bolically one. The book of Moses, another creation account recorded by Joseph Smith in June 1830, gives more details about Adam and Eve's life after they were sent from the Garden of Eden. Regarded as scripture by Mormons, this account shows that Adam and Eve apparently understood that the goal of their relationship was to reestablish this oneness which they had before the fall. In Moses 5:1 we see Eve working alongside Adam in the fields; likewise in 5:12 we see Adam participating in the child rearing. The text further states that they prayed together, had children together, rejoiced for revelations, and grieved for their disobedient children together. Neither is silent; both speak freely. Neither blames the other for the transgression, but both share a view of the fall as a great blessing: "Blessed be the name of God," rejoices Adam, "for because of my [not Eve's] transgression my eyes are opened, and in this life I shall have joy, and again in the flesh I shall see God. And Eve, his wife, heard all these things and was glad, saying: Were it not for our transgression we never should have had seed, and never should have known good and evil, and the joy of our redemption, and the eternal life which God giveth unto all the obedient."[109]

This variant text helps explain why Adam, in Genesis 3:20, followed God's judgments by naming Eve positively as "the mother of all living." Adam and Eve did not feel cursed; they recognized that the greatest bless-ing of mortality, the ability to produce children, was theirs. Adam's joyous honoring of Eve as Life itself shows a forward-looking expectation to ful-filling the commandment to "replenish" that was also the reason for their creation. *Eve* (Life) is an honorific and descriptive title; in Latter-day Saint doctrine, so is *Adam*. This same book of Moses includes an appearance of God to Moses during which he states: "And worlds without number have I created. . . . And the first man of all men have I called Adam, which is *many*." Later, in a summary of the creation story, the account records: "Adam called his wife's name Eve, because she was the mother of all living; for thus have I, the Lord God, called the first of all women, which are *many*."[110] *Adam* and *Eve* appear to be general titles which have been used numerous times by the Creator to signify the first parents of a world. Adam, then, did not name Eve. He was calling her by her title, previously conferred by God. In the book of Moses, Moses calls the woman Eve even before Adam does.[111]

In conclusion, then, the Adam and Eve account in Genesis 1–3 must be viewed as a symbolic representation rather than as a historical account. Before the fall the man and woman are united in equal status before their creator. The rib (or side) story is symbolic of the completeness and per-fection of their union. This context allows no sense of subjugation or in-equality, only parity and oneness. The serpent symbolizes the source of the temptation. Whether this agent was Satan in person, a fallen angel, or an actual serpent endowed with speech is irrelevant to the story, for this episode is again symbolic. The details of how the couple was tempted, partook of the fruit, and fell to mortality have been left to the imagination of commentators over the ages. The fruit symbolizes the process by which man and woman became mortal. Whether it was some kind of fruit, the concept of willful disobedience itself, or some kind of poisonous substance which caused the fluid within the pre-fall bodies to become mortal blood again is irrelevant to the story.

The judgments pronounced by the Lord were not curses but statements which symbolized the essential characteristics of mortality for all humanity. To say that because of Eve all women are cursed is not only a misunderstanding of the intent of the Genesis story but also a misunderstanding of the eternal doctrine of free agency and personal reponsibility. As a literal tenet of Latter-day Saint faith, Mormons "believe that men [and women] will be punished for their own sins, and not for Adam's [and Eve's] transgression."[112] Women and men feel the results of that transgression in that they are mortal and subject to imperfections of the flesh—sin, illness, fatigue, pain, etc. If we conclude that the judgments enumerated in Genesis 3:4-20 are results of the mortal condition, the implications are that we, like Adam and Eve, can strive to overcome these judgments while still in mortality by an understanding of Christ's atonement and by obedience to his commandments. The promise is that we will eventually be able to return to a state of unity and oneness with God, with others, and with ourselves like that possessed by Adam and Eve before the fall.

It is fitting, then, that we finally redeem Eve from the misconceptions about the curse that have clouded our understanding of her role these many years. For only when we understand the real purpose and significance of the events in Eden can we truly appreciate the magnitude of the opportunity and challenge Jesus Christ gave to the sons and daughters of Adam and Eve when he commanded: "I say unto you, be one; and if ye are not one ye are not mine."[113]

NOTES

1. As quoted in Marina Warner, *Alone of All Her Sex: The Myth and the Cult of the Virgin Mary* (New York: Vintage Books, 1983), p. 50.

2. An exhaustive examination of all uses of the Adam and Eve story from antiquity to the present would be impossible in a work of this length. Rather, I have chosen a few examples of how the account was used out of context to reinforce cultural standards of certain time periods. My choice of commentators, also, does not indicate that all others in the same age or time period were in agreement with the view quoted. Diversity in belief can be found in all ages.

3. There are possible allusions in Ezek. 28:13-19, Job 31:33, and Isa. 43:27. The

first does not refer to either Adam or Eve by name; the latter two refer only to Adam as transgressor but say nothing about Eve.

4. These include the Midrash, Mishna, and Talmud, which were commentaries on the Old Testament canon and interpretations on specific parts of the Torah (the Mosaic law), written by scribes and rabbis. These commentaries were supplemented by the Apocrypha and Pseudepigrapha, most of which were probably written from 200 B.C. to A.D. 200. Some were ascribed to famous figures like Enoch or Ezra; others were anonymous. But the Council of Jamnia (ca. A.D. 90) judged that all were written too late to be included in the Old Testament canon. Recent discoveries of documents such as the Dead Sea Scrolls and the Nag Hammadi Libraries would also be included in this category.

5. Ber 24a and Meg 23a, Talmud, as cited in Constance F. Parvey, "The Theology and Leadership of Women," in *Religion and Sexism: Images of Women in the Jewish and Christian Traditions,* ed. Rosemary Radford Ruether (New York: Simon and Schuster, Touchstone, 1974), p. 129.

6. Louis Ginzberg, *The Legends of the Jews,* 12th ed., 7 vols. (1909; Philadelphia: Jewish Publication Society of America, 1937) 1:67.

7. Ibid.

8. A. Cohen, *Everyman's Talmud* (New York: Schocken Books, 1975), pp. 160, 179.

9. Ibid., p. 161.

10. Ginzberg, *Legends* 1:66.

11. Ibid. 1:68.

12. Ibid. 1:67.

13. Cohen, *Everyman's Talmud,* p. 171.

14. Ibid., p. 172.

15. Jubilees 3:8–13, in R. H. Charles, ed., *The Apocrypha and Pseudepigrapha of the Old Testament,* 7th ed., 2 vols. (Oxford: Clarendon Press, 1973) 2:16.

16. Cohen, *Everyman's Talmud,* p. 159.

17. Sirach 25:13, 15, 16, 19, 24, in Charles, *The Apocrypha* 1:401–2.

18. Ibid. 49:16, in Charles, *The Apocrypha* 1:506.

19. Jubilees 19:24–27; 22:13, and 1 Enoch 37:1 in Charles, *Pseudepigrapha* 2:41, 42, 45, 46, 208. For other divergent views concerning Adam and Eve throughout the Apochrypha and Pseudepigrapha see 1 Enoch 32:6; 69:6, in Charles 2:207, 233; 2 Baruch 23; 54:15–19; 56:5–6, in Charles 2:495, 511–13; 4 Ezra 3:21; 4:30; 7:11, 116–118, in Charles 2:563, 566, 580, 591, among others. References to Eve's seduction appear in "Apocalypsis Mosis" 19:1–3 and "Vita Adae et Evae" 16:4 in "The Books of Adam and Eve" and in 2 Enoch 31:6 in Charles, *Pseudepigrapha* 2:146, 137, 451.

20. John 9:2–3.

21. Luke 8:1–3.

22. Luke 10:38–42.

23. Luke 15:3–10.

24. Luke 7:2–18; Matt. 13:31–33; Luke 13:18–21.

25. See Luke 10:29–37 and 38:42 (he teaches a man, then a woman); 13:10–16 and 14:2–6; (Jesus heals first a woman, then a man on the Sabbath); 17:35 and 36 (one man shall be taken from two who are in the field; one woman shall be

taken from two who are grinding); Mark 7:24-30 and 31-37 (he heals a Gentile's daughter, then a deaf man); Matt. 9:20-22, 23-26 and 27-34 (he heals a woman, raises a girl from the dead, and then heals two blind men). For a commentary, see Parvey, "Theology and Leadership," pp. 138-42.

26. See Acts 10, 15.

27. See Acts 7:58; 8:1; 22:3-5.

28. See 1 Cor. 11:3-15. This statement by Paul would seem to be in direct opposition to his statement three chapters later in 1 Cor. 14:34-35: "Let your women keep silence in the churches: for it is not permitted unto them to speak; but they are commanded to be under obedience, as also saith the law. And if they will learn anything, let them ask their husbands at home: for it is a shame for women to speak in the church." L. R. Iannaccone in "Let the Women Be Silent," *Sunstone* 7 (May-June 1982): 39-45, presents convincing evidence that in 1 Cor. 14:34-35 Paul is quoting from the original letter he received from Corinth, rather than offering his own opinion.

29. Ginzberg, *Legends* 1:67; Parvey, "Theology and Leadership," p. 126.

30. 1 Cor. 11:7-15.

31. 2 Cor. 11:3.

32. 1 Tim. 2:9-15.

33. See George Arthur Buttrick, ed., *The Interpreter's Dictionary of the Bible*, 4 vols. (Nashville, Tenn: Abingdon Press, 1962) 3:683 and 4:651.

34. Rom. 5:12. See also I Cor. 15:22.

35. Irenaeus, *Adversus Haereses* 3, 22, 4; 3, 23, 5; 4, Preface, 4; 4, 38, 1-4; 4, 39, 2; 5, 19, 1; 5, 23, 1; as used in Bernard P. Prusak, "Woman: Seductive Siren and Source of Sin?" in Ruether, *Religion and Sexism,* pp. 100-101.

36. Clement, *Paedagogus* 2, 12, as cited in Prusak, "Woman," p. 101.

37. Origen, *Leviticum homiliae* 12:4; 8:3; *Lucam homilae* 14; *Contra Celsum* 7, 50, as used in Prusak, "Woman," pp. 103-4.

38. Tertullian, *De Patientia 5; De Carne Christ 17; De Cultu Feminarium* 1, 1 as cited in Prusak, "Woman," pp. 104-5.

39. Eleanor Commo McLaughlin, "Equality of Souls, Inequality of Sexes: Women in Medieval Theology," in Ruether, *Religion and Sexism,* p. 244. Some male monastic orders also practiced the discipline of silence for different reasons.

40. Ibid., p. 253.

41. Thomas Aquinas, *Summa Theologica* II-II, 165, 2, ad 1; II-II 163, 4, concl.; I-II, 81, 5, ad 2 in McLaughlin, "Equality," pp. 218-19.

42. Martin Luther, *E narrationes in 1 Mose,* as used in Jane Dempsey Douglass, "Women and the Continental Reformation," in Ruether, *Religion and Sexism,* p. 297.

43. The reader may note here that I have left several hundred years of biblical commentary untouched. Covering the rich and varied views that emerged from about A.D. 200 to the present day would greatly overtax this one simple chapter, even though I know many significant contributions were made to the subject by Protestant writers like Calvin as well as by radical reformers like George Fox and Ann Lee. Rather, I have chosen to sample the early Jewish and Christian documents, including the Old and New Testaments, because they played such a critical role in establishing modern-day Judeo-Christian standards.

For an interesting and detailed tracing of the role and nature of Eve in Protestant

New England from 1650-1750, see Laurel Thatcher Ulrich, *Good Wives: Image and Reality in the Lives of Women in Northern New England 1650-1750* (New York: Oxford University Press, 1982).

44. Elizabeth Cady Stanton et al., *The Woman's Bible* (Seattle: Coalition Task Force on Women and Religion, 1974), pp. 26-27.

45. George Q. Cannon, 9 October 1869, *Journal of Discourses*, 26 vols. (Liverpool: Franklin D. Richards, 1855-86) 13:207, hereafter cited as *JD*, with speaker and date.

46. Brigham Young, 9 April 1852, *JD* 1:50; see also 20 April 1856, *JD* 3:319.

47. 1 Tim. 2:14. Among nineteenth-century citations in *JD* see Brigham Young, 27 December 1857, 6:145; Orson Pratt, 18 July 1880, 21:288-89; Wilford Woodruff, 14 May 1882, 23:125, George Q. Cannon, 28 September 1884, 26:188-89.

48. *The Utah Woman Suffrage Songbook* (Salt Lake City: Woman's Exponent, n.d.).

49. R.M.F., "Lecture on Suffrage," *Woman's Exponent* 24 (15 August 1895): 41.

50. Eliza R. Snow, "Woman," in *Poems Religious, Historical and Political*, 2 vols. (Salt Lake City: LDS Printing and Publishing Establishment, 1877) 2:178. Italics hers.

51. Ruby Lamont, "The Woman's Movement," *Woman's Exponent* 17 (1 February 1889): 129.

52. James E. Talmage, *Eighty-Fourth Semi-Annual Conference Report of the Church of Jesus Christ of Latter-day Saints*, October 1913, p. 118. Although the view that Adam and Eve's bodies were changed from divine to mortal through the eating of earthly fruits was taught by Brigham Young and others years previous to this, here in this context we see it used as a supportive example in a talk on the Word of Wisdom.

53. Orson F. Whitney in *Ninety-Sixth Annual Conference Report*, October 1925, pp. 100-102; Rudger Clawson, *Eighty-Sixth Annual Conference Report*, April 1918, pp. 32-33.

54. Marion G. Romney, "Mother Eve, A Worthy Exemplar," *Relief Society Magazine* 55 (February 1968): 84-89.

55. Spencer W. Kimball, "Privileges and Responsibilities of Sisters," Women's Fireside, 16 September 1978, *Ensign* 8 (November 1978): 102-6; also, Spencer W. Kimball, "The Blessings and Responsibilities of Womanhood," *Ensign* 6 (March 1976): 70-71.

56. Spencer W. Kimball, "Our Sisters in the Church," 6 October 1979, *Ensign* 9 (November 1979): 48-49, reprinted in *Blueprints for Living*, ed. Maren M. Mouritsen (Provo, Utah: Brigham Young University Press, 1980), pp. 1-3; see also Spencer W. Kimball, "The Role of Righteous Women," *Ensign* 9 (November 1979): 102-4.

57. A comprehensive examination of Gen. 1-3 as a poetical work is found in Phyllis Trible, *God and the Rhetoric of Sexuality* (Philadelphia: Fortress Press, 1978), ch. 4, "A Love Story Gone Awry," pp. 72-143. Many of the ideas contained in this section of the paper were extracted from this work. See also Jerome T. Walsh, "Genesis 2:4b-3:24: A Synchronic Approach," *Journal of Biblical Literature* 96 (1977): 161-77; and Edwin M. Good, *Irony in the Old Testament* (Philadelphia: Westminster Press, 1965), pp. 81-84.

58. *Josephus: Complete Works*, trans. William Whiston (Grand Rapids, Mich: Kregal Publications, 1960), pp. 24, 25n.

59. Mendenhall also felt the story was a parable. See George E. Mendenhall, "The

Shady Side of Wisdom: The Date and Purpose of Gen. 3," in *A Light Unto My Path: O.T. Studies in Honor of Jacob M. Myers,* ed. Howard N. Bream et al. (Philadelphia: Temple University Press, 1974), pp. 319-34.

60. Many scholars have traditionally believed that Gen. 1:26-28 and Gen. 2:4-22 were two different accounts of the creation of man, written by two different authors, P (priestly writer), and J (Yahwist writer). Although this view has less support today than it once did, in this essay it is not relevant whether the accounts were authored by one or two persons. The editor or compiler of Genesis evidently thought both accounts were important enough to include in the final manuscript. See Good, *Irony in the Old Testament,* p. 82.

61. One is in Gen. 1:27 where *'adam* is used with a plural pronoun "them," and the other is in Gen. 2:5: "there was not a man to till the ground." The presence of the negative before *'adam* would make translation of *'adam* as a proper name nonsensical: "there was no Adam to till the ground." Three other places in the text are uncertain because the word *'adam* is preceded by a preposition which in Hebrew would eliminate the *ha*: 2:20, 3:17, and 3:21. See John Ellington, "Man and Adam in Genesis 1-5," *The Bible Translator* 30 (April 1979): 201-5; Gerhard Von Rad, *Genesis,* 2nd ed. (Philadelphia: Westminster Press, 1974), p. 57; and Ernest Lussier, "*'Adam* in Gen. 1, 1-4, 24," *Catholic Biblical Quarterly* 18 (1956): 137-39.

62. The King James translation has inconsistently translated *ha-'adam* most often as a proper name, Adam. See Lussier, "*'Adam* in Genesis 1, 1-4, 24": 137-39.

63. Gen. 1:26-27, italics added.

64. Trible, *God and the Rhetoric of Sexuality,* pp. 79-80; also John L. McKenzie, "The Literary Characteristics of Genesis 2-3," *Theological Studies* 15 (1954): 556.

65. Genesis 2:18.

66. Trible, *God and the Rhetoric of Sexuality,* p. 90; also McKenzie, "The Literary Characteristics of Genesis 2-3": 559; Clarence J. Voz, *Woman in Old Testament Worship* (Amsterdam: N.V. Verenigde Drukkerijen Judels & Brinkman-Delft, n.d.), p. 16.

67. From Voz, *Woman in Old Testament Worship,* p. 16: "Besides Gen. 2:18, 20, this word [*'ezer*] appears in the Old Testament nineteen times. Of these it is used once in a question. (Ps. 121:1—the answer to the question is given in the following verse in which it is said that one's help comes from the Lord.) It is used three times of man as a help, (Is. 30:5; Ezk. 12:14; Dn. 11:34), but in each instance it is clear that man's help is not effectual. (Dn. 11:34 could refer to God); fifteen times it is used of God as the one who brings succor to the needy and desperate. Thus, if one excluded Gen. 2:18, 20 it could be said that only God gives effectual help (*'ezer*) to man.... Viewing woman as created to be a subordinate assistant to man finds no basis in the word (*'ezer*)." See also Jean Higgins, "Anastasius Sinaita and the Superiority of the Woman," *Journal of Biblical Literature* 97, no. 2 (1978): 255: "Of forty-five occurrences of the word in the LXX, [Septuagint], forty-two unmistakably refer to help from a stronger one."

68. R. David Freedman, "Woman, A Power Equal to Man," *Biblical Archaeology Review* 9 (January-February 1983): 56-58.

69. Gen. 2:21-22.

70. A complete listing of usages is found in George V. Wigram, *The Englishman's Hebrew and Chaldee Concordance of the Old Testament,* 5th ed. (Grand Rapids, Mich:

Zondervan Publishing House, 1980), pp. 1073-74; see also Walter Brueggemann, "Of the Same Flesh and Bone (Gn. 2, 23a)" *Catholic Biblical Quarterly* 32 (1970): 532-42.

71. Trible, *God and the Rhetoric of Sexuality*, pp. 98-99.

72. Ibid., p. 98.

73. James N. Robinson, ed., "The Apochryphan of John" and "The Gospel of Philip," in *The Nag Hammadi Library* (San Francisco: Harper & Row, 1977), pp. 110, 141; Ginzberg, *Legends of the Jews* 1:66.

74. Gen. 2:23; Trible, *God and the Rhetoric of Sexuality*, p. 97; John A. Bailey, "Initiation and the Primal Woman in Gilgamesh and Genesis 2-3," *Journal of Biblical Literature* 89 (1970): 142-43.

75. Trible, *God and the Rhetoric of Sexuality*, pp. 98, 100; McKenzie, "The Literary Characteristics of Genesis 2-3": 556-59.

76. Gen. 4:17, 25; Trible, *God and the Rhetoric of Sexuality*, pp. 99-100, italics added.

77. 2 Sam. 5:1; 19:12; Brueggemann, "Of the Same Flesh and Bone (Gen. 2, 23a)": 532-42.

78. Trible, *God and the Rhetoric of Sexuality*, p. 104.

79. Good, *Irony in the Old Testament*, pp. 83-84; Trible, *God and the Rhetoric of Sexuality*, p. 108.

80. Gen. 3:1-6; Trible, *God and the Rhetoric of Sexuality*, pp. 112-13; Jean M. Higgins, "The Myth of Eve: The Temptress," *Journal of the American Academy of Religion* 44 (1976): 645-47.

81. Gen. 3:10, 13, italics added.

82. Gen. 3:12-13; Trible, *God and the Rhetoric of Sexuality*, p. 118; A. Williams, "The Relationship of Gen. 3:20 to the Serpent," *Zeitschrift für die Alttestamentliche Wissenschaft* 89 (1977): 357-74.

83. Gen. 3:19.

84. See Voz, *Woman in Old Testament Worship*, pp. 24-25; Trible, *God and the Rhetoric of Sexuality*, p. 128.

85. Gen. 1:16.

86. Isaac M. Kikawada, "Two Notes on Eve," *Journal of Biblical Literature* 91 (1972): 33-37.

87. Kimball, "Blessings and Responsibilities": 71.

88. Brigham Young, 23 October 1853, *JD* 2:6.

89. Idem, 9 April 1852, *JD* 1:50; 20 April 1856, *JD* 3:319; 9 October 1859, *JD* 7:285; Orson Pratt, 13 April 1856, *JD* 3:344; Joseph Fielding Smith, *Doctrines of Salvation*, comp. Bruce R. McConkie, 3 vols. (Salt Lake City, Utah: Bookcraft, 1954-56) 1:97. The reader may note here and in many following instances that teachings in the doctrine of the church and the accounts given in the books of Moses, Abraham, and Genesis differ from the depiction of the creation and fall in the temple ceremony. The intent of the temple ceremony seems to be much the same as the intent of the Genesis account: to present ideas through symbols and figurative language which have many layers of meaning. It is perhaps appropriate that the creation story in the temple is presented in a symbolic fashion, as the rest of the endowment is highly ritualistic and has numerous levels of meaning. To interpret the visual (film) depiction of the creation and fall as only history rather than also as a

figurative representation of underlying truths would deviate from the intent of the temple experience as a whole. One part cannot be interpreted as strictly symbolic and another as strictly historical. (See Boyd K. Packer, *The Holy Temple* [Salt Lake City, Utah: Bookcraft, 1980], pp. 38-41, on the symbolic nature of temple instruction.) Hyrum Andrus, in noting the difference between the temple portrayal and the books of Abraham and Moses said: "A study of the problem suggests that the temple ceremony gives merely a general *portrayal* and not an actual *account* of the creation. ... Letters written by Brigham Young concerning the nature and organization of the temple ceremony, on file in the St. George Temple, support the view that Joseph Smith did not dictate the temple ceremony as he did the revelations and translations which he committed to writing." Andrus felt that Joseph Smith obtained the basic endowment from the writings of Abraham, which he later gave to Brigham Young, who added such instructional portions as the creation account. See L. John Nuttal, Diary, 7 February 1877, as quoted in Hyrum Andrus, *God, Man and the Universe*, 2nd ed. 4 vols. (Salt Lake City, Utah: Bookcraft, 1970) 1:333-34, footnote. This footnote does not appear in later editions. Whether or not Brigham Young ever produced a written script is unknown, but in 1877 he requested Wilford Woodruff (assisted by George Q. Cannon) to write a standardized script for the endowment ceremony. Upon completion of this script Brigham Young said, "Now you have ... an ensample to carry on the endowments in all the temples until the Coming of the Son of Man." Packer, *The Holy Temple*, pp. 191-94; see also John K. Edmunds, *Through Temple Doors*, 4th ed. (Salt Lake City, Utah: Bookcraft, 1979), pp. 73-74. Since that time, wording in the script and the dramatization of the script of the instructional part of the temple ceremony has been altered from time to time for clarification.

90. Erastus Snow, 3 March 1878, *JD* 19:269.

91. Kimball, "Blessings and Responsibilities," p. 71, bracketed interpolations his.

92. *Teachings of the Prophet Joseph Smith*, sel. Joseph Fielding Smith (Salt Lake City, Utah: Deseret Book Co., 1972), p. 301, bracketed interpolations his. Joseph Smith is probably referring to the Hebrew word *ruah*, which means "spirit" or "soul." This word, however, does not appear in Genesis 2:7. The phrase *nišmat hayyim*, which means literally "breath of life," is used.

93. Orson Pratt, 11 July 1875, JD 18:48; see also Joseph Fielding Smith, *Doctrines of Salvation* 1:115.

94. Kimball, "Blessings and Responsibilities": 72.

95. Brigham Young, 3 June 1855, *JD* 2:302; Edward W. Tullidge, *The Women of Mormondom* (New York: Tullidge and Crandall, 1877), pp. 197-99, stated that Mother Eve chose to be the first to partake of the fruit to symbolize the great maternal sacrifice.

96. Orson Pratt, 7 October 1867, *JD* 19:317; see also Erastus Snow, 3 March 1878, *JD* 19:269-72, 274.

97. See, for example, Mosiah 3:11, 19; 4:7; Alma 12:21-23; 22:12-14; 42:2-4; Helaman 14:16-17; Mormon 9:12. In some of these references, Adam and Eve are mentioned together as the first parents. See also 1 Nephi 5:11; Mosiah 16:3-4.

98. Orson Pratt, 22 November 1873, *JD* 16:318.

99. Rev. 12:7-9; see also Moses 4:3-4.

100. Erastus Snow, 3 March 1878, *JD* 19:271-72.

101. Moses 4:12, italics added.

102. Doctrine and Covenants 29:36, 40; italics added.

103. Hugh Nibley, "Patriarchy and Matriarchy," in Mouritsen, *Blueprints for Living,* pp. 45-46. *The Holy Scriptures According to the Masoretic Text,* 47th ed. (Philadelphia: Jewish Publication Society of America, 1964), states a similar meaning in its translation of Gen. 3:16, 17: "Unto the woman He said: I will greatly multiply thy pain and thy travail; in pain thou shalt bring forth children . . . And unto Adam He said . . . cursed is the ground for thy sake; in toil thou shalt eat of it."

104. Kimball, "Blessings and Responsibilities": 72.

105. Doctrine and Covenants 121:39, 41-42, 45-46.

106. Moses 7:18.

107. Ida Smith, "The Lord as a Role Model for Men and Women," BYU Women's Conference, 2 February 1980, *Ensign* 10 (August 1980): 66-67.

108. Carolyn J. Rasmus, "Mormon Women: A Convert's Perspective," BYU Women's Conference, 1 February 1980, *Ensign* 10 (August 1980): 69.

109. Moses 5:2, 4, 10-11, 16, 27.

110. Ibid. 1:33-34; 4:26, italics added.

111. Ibid. 4:6.

112. "The Articles of Faith of the Church of Jesus Christ of Latter-day Saints," no. 2, in The Pearl of Great Price.

113. Doctrine and Covenants 38:27.

MELODIE MOENCH CHARLES

Precedents for Mormon Women from Scriptures

In claiming to believe "the Bible to be the word of God," Mormonism acknowledges the truthfulness, usefulness, and normative value of books accepted as scripture by religious communities worldwide. But Mormonism also asserts that wicked connivers have intentionally perverted the original clarity and truth of the Bible. Therefore, Mormon acceptance of the Bible is a qualified acceptance. In claiming to believe the Bible to be the word of God "as far as it is translated correctly" (which can be interpreted broadly), Mormonism is able to reject biblical teachings, practices, and history that do not accord with its views of the gospel of Christ and of God's dealings with people. Furthermore, a basic tenet of Mormonism is that God has revealed his will since the closing of the biblical canon and will continue to do so any time it suits his purposes.[1] Scriptures that are uniquely Mormon, the Book of Mormon, Doctrine and Covenants, and Pearl of Great Price, supercede the Bible any time they conflict with it. They too can be superceded by modern revelation, whether canonized as scripture or not. Mormonism has a healthy respect for scriptural precedents for practice and belief, and a healthy ability to set them aside as inadequate, inappropriate, or irrelevant for the current situation.

Each scripture except the Doctrine and Covenants contains narratives which tell the religious history of a particular group of people. Each scripture contains instruction from God through prophets for that group of people and, often, for people generally. Because the material within each scripture comes from the different viewpoints, concerns, and cultural circumstances of more than one author, none of the scriptures presents just one view of anything. They all disclose a variety of attitudes, practices, and doctrines concerning women to which religious people in earlier ages subscribed.

Of particular interest are scriptural statements that describe and prescribe proper behavior for women and proper treatment of them. In addition to examining such statements, this essay will explore what is inadvertently said about women through the scripture's overwhelming focus on men. It will consider outstanding individual women in the scriptures and will try to ascertain what patterns provided by scripture have been incorporated into the Latter-day Saint view of women, past and present.

While women are not glaringly omitted from the Pearl of Great Price, they are mentioned only in passing as it concentrates on stories about Moses, Enoch, Noah, Abraham, and Joseph Smith. They do not figure in the revision of Matthew 24 nor in the belief statements which comprise the Articles of Faith. Only the creation story's concern with Eve comments directly about women. Since this material is covered in "The Redemption of Eve," it will not be dealt with here.

A largely unidentifiable collection of authors wrote the Old Testament over more than a thousand years' time. Because these authors had different social, political, geographic, cultural, and religious backgrounds, their writings reflect their different views and purposes. The Old Testament contains historical narratives, myths, legends, court records, declarations from deity, prophetic speeches, prayers, law codes, priestly instruction, poetry, philosophizing, visions, and more. In its concerns with the public and domestic lives of significant individuals in Israel's history and with regulating social intercourse and religious activity, it is naturally concerned with women, although the authors generally devote far less attention to women than to men.

Much of the Old Testament presents a dismal view of women's worth, their rights, and the restrictions their religious society placed upon them. Women are often shown in subservient positions as the appendages of males. Economic, religious, social, and legal conditions, regardless of intent, in fact subjugated women. Israelite society was not structured to promote equality among its members. It had a priesthood hierarchy, a distinction between slave and free, and a social unit based on a family with a patriarch at its head. It is unlikely that there was any conscious effort to deny rights to women; rather, because the male head of the house was the focus of religious and social concern, children and adult females had no rights which would conflict with the patriarch's best interests. A father had absolute authority; all others in his household were his possessions, inescapably tied to him.[2]

A woman was considered to be the property of her father, her husband, or even her brother.[3] For example, woman is listed in the tenth commandment as one of man's possessions: "you shall not covet your neighbor's house . . . *wife* . . . manservant . . . maidservant . . . ox . . . ass . . . or anything that is your neighbor's." The wife is not given a primary or unique position among these possessions: her position in the sequence does not suggest that she is more significant than a man's house or his ox.[4] Further, the law permitted a father to sell his daughter as a slave.[5] The context interprets this action as a way to alleviate severe financial difficulty rather than a way to get rich, and it would not be without benefit to the daughter of a poor man. It could assure her of a financial stability her father could not provide and might win her a wealthier husband than she could otherwise hope to attract.[6] Deuteronomy 24:1-3 grants a husband the right to divorce a wife who dissatisfies him. It does not establish criteria for determining acceptable reasons nor does it obligate the husband to provide for his former wife's maintenance. In contrast, the law contains no provision for a wife to divorce her husband.[7]

The laws in Numbers 30 regulating vows allow women to enter into contracts but stipulate that any contract a woman might make could be made void by the male who has familial authority over her. A woman's husband or father could nullify her "thoughtless utterance," presumably in order to protect her from her own incompetence or to protect himself from a bargain not to his advantage.[8] A widow or divorcee had more legal autonomy; because no male could be held responsible for her, no man could reverse her agreement. Yet the widow and the divorcee were in a very awkward position. Because a woman left her father's family to become part of her husband's household, property would stay with a family if it were passed on through the males but not if it were passed on through the females. Therefore, wives and daughters of a deceased man typically received no inheritance. (Numbers 27:1-11 allows inheritance by daughters of a man without male heirs.) This feature of the law, the dispossession of widows and orphans, provides background for a recurring theme of the prophets: all Israelites should relieve the burdens of the widows and orphans.

A woman's chastity was protected by law, though not necessarily because her chastity had intrinsic value. Because she was the property of her husband or father, her chastity was important for preserving their honor.[9] No similar value was attached to the chastity of men. If a man and a single woman committed fornication, a crime against the woman's father, the offending man could make restitution by marrying her or paying her father a set sum if the father refused the marriage offer.[10] Even if the male were already married, polygyny, a man's being allowed to have more than one living wife, made this solution possible. However, when a man and a married woman committed adultery, they violated the husband's property and his honor. No restitution to the husband was possible, and both adulterers were required to suffer death.[11]

The law is addressed to males rather than people,[12] freeing women from some religious obligations but denying them full participation in communal worship. For males, circumcision was a rite of initiation into the religious community.[13] Because no comparable rite was available to women, even to initiate a girl into the society of women, women were forever outsiders.

Further deterrents to religious participation were the rules prescribing ritual purity. On their surface, they applied equally to men and women. Anyone who had anything other than urine issuing from her or his genitals was unfit to participate in religious rituals and was unfit for any social contact until the situation cleared. Because men were unclean for the rest of the day anytime they had an emission of semen, they were occasionally unclean. In contrast, women were unclean for at least a quarter of their childbearing years, and some could be unclean almost all of the time. They were unclean whenever they had menstrual periods (which, by definition, lasted at least seven days); they were unclean for the rest of the day whenever they participated in sexual intercourse; they were unclean if they had an unusual showing of blood and for seven days after the showing had stopped; they were unclean after they gave birth. If her newborn were male, a mother was ritually unclean for forty days, but the time doubled to eighty days if her newborn were female, implying that bearing male children was less contaminating than bearing female children.[14]

Women were not totally without status, though. To the extent that they worked to promote their husbands' interests, they were honored. A woman's main function was to bear children for her husband. If a man had no progeny he was forgettable, not "immortal" at all. Childbirth was thus the key to a woman's worth, and infertility was always seen as caused by a defect in a wife, never in a husband. Even though a man might already have children by another wife, a wife who was barren still felt a desperate need to provide her husband with children. The stories of Sarah, Rachael, Samson's mother, and Hannah all manifest the stigma and disgrace associated with barrenness. The jealousy of Sarah toward Hagar, of Rachael toward Leah, and the pride of Hagar and Leah in their own fertility, show that women evaluated themselves and each other by their ability to bear children.

This idea that a man's honor continues after him through his children is the basis of Levirate marriage, regulated in Deuteronomy 25:6. In this form of marriage a man provided seed for his dead brother's childless widow: "The first son whom she bears shall succeed to the name of his brother who is dead, that his name may not be blotted out in Israel." The story of Judah and his widowed daughter-in-law, Tamar, in Genesis 38 demonstrates the importance of a woman's fulfilling this duty. Judah's two oldest sons successively married Tamar but died without children. Judah sent Tamar home to her father's house, telling her to wait until Judah's last son, Shelah, achieved maturity. Judah had no intention of allowing a third marriage for he wanted to save Shelah from the fate of the first two sons. When it became clear to Tamar that Judah would not carry out the requirements of the law, she masqueraded as a prostitute and Judah procured her services. Later, when she was discovered to be pregnant, he wanted her burned for her sin, but when she proved that the child was his, he understood that she was fulfilling her duty to provide her dead husband with an heir. Tamar's prostitution and duplicity, though wrong in other circumstances, were judged as acceptable means to accomplish this virtuous and overriding end of providing children for her husband. Judah declared, "She was more righteous than I, inasmuch as I did not give her to my son." Neither the author nor anyone in the story even hints that Judah merits punishment or condemnation for engaging the services of someone he thought was a prostitute.

The story of Jephthah's daughter illustrates the power of a patriarch over the people in his household and the importance of a woman's being able to bear children. Even more, it is the story of a remarkable young woman.

While Jephthah is defending Israel from the Ammonites he makes an unnecessary vow to God, which is certain to be disastrous: he vows that if the Lord will give him victory, he will sacrifice to the Lord "whoever comes forth from the doors of my house to meet me, when I return victorious." The vow is unnecessary because the Spirit of the Lord, which presumably will allow him to achieve victory, has already come upon him. The vow will certainly be disastrous because anyone who comes to meet him will be someone who cares about him.

When he returns victorious and is met by his daughter, his only child, his thoughts are only of himself. Instead of berating himself for making such a vow, instead of apologizing for what his vow has done to her, he condemns her for bringing him low and becoming the cause of trouble to him. In contrast, she does not condemn him for his thoughtlessness in making a vow that will end her life, nor does she ask for an apology or even pity. With no apparent horror, dismay, or reluctance she offers herself to him so that he may fulfill his vow; she asks only for two months in which to "bewail her virginity" with her friends. After her father sacrifices her, Israelite women mourn her death each year (Judg. 11:29-40). Showing the male-centeredness of historical memory, the Bible says no more about this courageous daughter but remembers rash, cruel, self-centered Jephthah for his faith (Heb. 11:32-33).[15]

In contrast to the restricted, confined role for women that much of the Old Testament presents is a picture of independent, talented women who are accepted and appreciated by their society. This picture indicates that the confined role did not prevail in all periods and that it was at times more theory than fact. Proverbs 31 describes the virtuous woman. This woman is no mere producer of progeny and tender of the home. She shows tremendous initiative and has complete freedom to execute her own independently conceived business ventures. But while the author lauds her accomplishments, he is really praising her not for being an amazing woman but rather for being an amazing wife. The chief reason her attributes and actions are praiseworthy is that, in everything she does, she promotes her husband's interests. "The heart of her husband trusts in her, and he will have no lack of gain. She does him good and not harm all the days of her life." She appears to do all the work of the household to free him for the higher duty and privilege of sitting with the elders at the gates of the city. Certainly most people would be delighted to have such a person working in their behalf; however, being that woman who "rises while it is yet night" and whose "lamp does not go out at night," who is the sole source of the family's economic and physical well-being, seems a little less appealing. Even in this most positive of presentations is the notion that women are appreciated to the extent that they benefit men.

Many of the narratives in the Old Testament present stories of individual women who were significant figures in Israel's history and were not noticeably subordinate to their husbands or to men generally. Through the patriarchal narratives in Genesis runs a thread of successful and acceptable deception: the person who can best outwit someone else wins. While the person deceived resents the deceiver, neither the author nor the culture seems to find such deception religiously unacceptable. Abraham and Isaac passing off their wives as their single, marriageable sisters, Jacob stealing Esau's birthright, and Jacob and Laban stealing from and cheating each other are examples of this thread. The wives of the patriarchs played this game just as well as their husbands.

When Rebekah decided that her favorite son, Jacob, ought to have her husband's final blessing intended for his favorite son, Esau, she defrauded Esau by exploiting her husband's blindness and substituting one son for the other.[16] Her act, not one to be admired nor emulated, completely changed the future lives of her two sons and, perhaps, the future of all Israel.

Rachael, after having been cheated with her husband by her own father, Laban, used his methods and Israel's customs in her own behalf. She stole his household gods (which probably had significant property as well as religious value) and prevented his finding them by sitting on them and claiming that she was menstruating.[17] Though the laws of ritual purity were not codified until much later there was almost certainly a customary taboo about contact with menstruating women which prevented his moving her to search where she sat. These women's influence on the history of Israel came primarily through their changing the lives of key male figures in Israelite history—their husbands and sons. Yet although these women, along with Sarah and Bathsheba, are primarily characters in their husbands' and sons' stories rather than protagonists in their own stories, they are depicted as real, multifaceted people rather than as stereotypes or merely as foils for the men.

There are also women who are the main characters in their own stories—not satellites to any male—who influenced Israel's history directly. In this society with its strong male bias, two women, Ruth and Esther, were upheld as examples, each with a book of scripture bearing her name and devoted to her story. It is remarkable that the authors of these books tell their stories matter-of-factly, without editorializing about or apologizing for the gender of the heroic protagonists. Ruth's widowhood gave her the opportunity to prove the loyalty and devotion for which she is so revered. Her insistence upon accompanying Naomi is both remarkable and foolhardy. Phyllis Trible explains that "one female has chosen another female in a world where life depends upon men. There is no more radical decision in the memories of Israel."[18] Though not so bold as Tamar, she too initiated the relationship which would allow her to provide her dead husband with children. Esther saved the lives of all the Jews in Babylon by her amazing courage. (Although the author did not, modern feminists prefer Esther's predecessor, Vashti, to Esther. In a time when disobeying one's husband was unthinkable, especially if he were king, Vashti refused to obey the unreasonable and demeaning command of her husband. The author and his characters reject Vashti's example as bad and dangerous and promote Esther's submission as the proper model for wives to follow.)

Certain women had unique abilities and talents which men willingly employed. When Joab wanted to influence David to recall his banished son, Absalom, he sent a woman known for her wisdom. She accomplished Joab's purpose.[19] When King Josiah commanded his servants to find out if the Lord intended to impose on Israel a punishment threatened for violators of the law, his servants consulted Huldah, a prophetess, who accurately foretold the future.[20]

Following a long tradition of males uncomfortable with a female prophet, today's LDS church tends to minimize or ignore Huldah.[21] The *Old Testament Student Manual* prepared by the Church Education System in 1981 says that "all we can infer from the fact that the king sent to her is that she was highly distinguished on account of prophetical renown, *and that none of the prophets of renown, such as Jeremiah and Zephaniah, were at that time in Jerusalem.*"[22] The LDS-authored dictionary in the church's newly published Bible completely omits Huldah, even though the Cambridge Bible Dictionary on which it is based included her and called her a prophetess.[23]

Needing to be inconspicuous in Jericho, Joshua's spies lodged with Rahab, a harlot, where they could hide their real purpose in Jericho as they pretended to be there merely as her customers. Rahab saved the spies' lives and shrewdly preserved the lives of her family as well. The New Testament commends her faith and declares her "justified" by her works.[24]

Because Deborah held the position of legal judge, Israelites turned to her to decide legal controversies and resolve disputes.[25] In addition, she filled another role called "judge" by being a military leader whom God empowered to restore Israel to a state of peace and righteousness.[26] The Bible records no other woman who filled either role of judge nor does it tell of any other person, male or female, who held these positions simultaneously.

In addition to being a judge, Deborah was also a prophetess who foretold future events.[27] As military leader, Deborah gave her fellow commander, Barak, instructions on how to conquer Israel's enemies. Barak's response indicates Deborah's power: he refused to go to battle unless Deborah accompanied him. She agreed and prophesied victory but added that Barak's lack of courage would result in a woman's receiving the honor for the victory, not him. This prophecy reflects the culture's assumption that it was disgraceful to be outshone by a woman.

Deborah's role and accomplishments, like Huldah's, have bothered men. Male commentators have tried to diminish her importance by attacking her character, by claiming that God used her only to embarrass unworthy men, by claiming that there were no worthy men available, or by ignoring what she did. With their great reverence for the text, the rabbis in the Talmud were unable to deny what she did, yet because she was female they were unable to tolerate her having done it. She is condemned for being haughty and for boasting. Rabbi Nahman's proof for this was that rather than going to Barak she sent for him to come to her.[28] With no textual basis, Calvin said of her prophesying: "We know that the gift of prophecy is sometimes though rarely allowed to women, and there is no doubt that female prophets existed whenever God wished to brand men with a mark of ignominy as strongly as possible. . . . When Deborah and Huldah discharged the prophetic office . . . God doubtless wished to raise them on high to shame the men and obliquely to show them their slothfulness."[29]

Like these commentators, the LDS church has been unable to grant that Deborah judged Israel and prophesied simply because she was talented and was endowed with God's spirit, and that her doing so reflected on no one but herself. While not specifically addressing the subject of Deborah, Brigham Young's comments about women's leadership are applicable: "When the servants of God in any age have consented to follow a woman for their leader, either in a public or in a family capacity, they have sunk beneath the standard their organization has fitted them for; when a people of God submit to that, their Priesthood is taken from them, and they become as any other people."[30]

Using a series of claims that at best have no textual support and at worst contradict the text, the Old Testament manual produced by the Church Educational System in 1980 has a section titled "How Was It That a Woman, Deborah, Led Israel?" It explains that "Israel was sorely lacking in leadership at this time. The regular priesthood leadership was not in effect because the covenant had been broken. Deborah did not direct Israel in any official sense; she was a prophetess. . . . She was blessed with spiritual insight and leadership qualities that were not being put to use by any man."[31] Because current church doctrine links priesthood power (something that a female obviously could not have had) with being a community's prophet, the new LDS Bible Dictionary pretends that Deborah never functioned as a prophet. It calls her "a famous woman who judged Israel," a deliberate change from its predecessor, which called her "a famous prophetess who judged Israel."[32]

Although Old Testament law shows an Israelite culture which restricted women to being dependents and appendages, some of the Old Testament narratives show women significantly affecting their society, not merely as the wives or mothers of important males but on the merits of their own wisdom, spiritual endowments, courage, shrewdness, and military ability. In spite of a restrictive society, these women rose to prominence and were respected for their talents.

Because the Doctrine and Covenants had primarily one author (God mediated through the prophet, Joseph Smith), one genre (revelation), and for the most part a very limited span of time (about fifteen years), it has almost none of the diversity apparent in the Old Testament. Instead, it reflects the developing theology and ecclesiastical system of a new church defining itself. The handful of letters, visions, prophetic expositions, and official declarations from Joseph Smith and other Mormon prophets down to 1978 do not significantly affect the book's unity. As the only Mormon scripture that directly addresses the church that Joseph Smith began, it influences the thoughts and practices that are unique to the Mormon church today more than any other scripture does. Even though the Doctrine and Covenants is very concerned with people's accepting and spreading the gospel of Christ, it is similar to the Old Testament in its portrayal of a nationalistic God who can be vengeful, in its concern with priesthood rights and duties, in its authorizing of polygyny, and in the view of women which accompanies such a practice.

The Doctrine and Covenants often echoes the tendency of Old Testament writers to consciously or unconsciously assume that women are insignificant —or at least less significant than men. Like the Old Testament, it expects women to promote their husbands' interests, and one important way to do this is to bear their children. Unlike the Old Testament, the Doctrine and Covenants contains no historical narratives showing women acting independently to balance against this assumption.

Like the Old Testament law, the Doctrine and Covenants is generally addressed to "men" or assumes an all-male audience.[33] Section 123, for example, instructs "the saints" to publish the true account of their persecutions, yet verse 7 talks of the duty "we owe to God, to angels . . . to ourselves, to *our wives* and children." Verses 16-17 apparently equate "saints" with "brethren." A canonized letter from Joseph Smith to the church which begins with "My dearly beloved *brethren and sisters*" closes with only "Brethren."[34]

Section 42 verses 18-26 presents a series of "thou shalt not's" addressed to "the church." Because they include "thou shalt love *thy wife*," "he that looketh upon *a woman* to lust after *her*," and "*he* that committeth adultery," it is clear that the author of the text presumes adult males are the significant members of "the church." However, verses 74–77 strangely switch to "persons" and the prohibitions against adultery in the earlier portion are re-addressed with awkward carefulness to both men and women: if *a man or a woman* does X, then *he or she* shall Y, and if *thy brother or sister* does X, Y shall be done to *him or her*. Apparently somewhere in the middle of section 42 someone realized that women could be considered exempt unless the nouns and pronouns of address were broadened. This explicitly inclusive form was used only fleetingly, though; subsequent sections are again directed only to men though they have no exclusively male content.[35]

Judging by the fact that eight verses in section 42 alone as well as others elsewhere are devoted to the issue of adultery, we can assume that it was a burning issue. Adulterers are to be forgiven if they repent and severed from the church if they do not. A church court will judge offenders, but the penalty is the vague one of being "dealt with according to the law of God." These penalties apply equally to offenders of both sexes, but Section 132 introduces new penalties for adultery which do not. A woman married in "the new and everlasting covenant" who commits adultery should be destroyed (v. 41), while a man married in "the new and everlasting covenant" who commits adultery suffers only the much softer penalty of having his betrayed wife bestowed on another man (v. 44). The imbalance continues. The punishment for the adulterous man seems to require that the wife has remained faithful; thus, his incurring a penalty is as dependent upon his wife's actions as upon his own. Yet the adulteress's penalty apparently comes automatically on the heels of her sin. Moreover, the innocent wife whose husband has been unfaithful is not consulted about her fate. She is simply transferred from an unworthy man to a worthy one, "for he shall be made a ruler over many" (v. 44).[36]

Sections 131 and 132 introduce "the new and everlasting covenant of marriage" as an essential ordinance of salvation. Although females are obviously involved, the texts focus on males. Section 131:1–4 states: "In the celestial glory there are three heavens or degrees; And in order to obtain the highest, a man must enter into this order of the priesthood [meaning the new and everlasting covenant of marriage]; And if he does not, he cannot obtain it. He may enter into the other, but that is the end of his kingdom; he cannot have an increase."

Section 132 reveals that this new style of marriage is polygyny, the most obvious echo of the Old Testament in the Doctrine and Covenants. While verses 19 and 20 promise the same exaltation to godhood for both women and men who participate, the rest of this section talks about women as if they were merely the instruments which aid men to fulfill their mortal religious obligations and enable them to produce kingdoms to rule over in heaven. Abraham's concubines "were given unto him" so that he could fulfill God's law (v. 37). Women have been given to Joseph Smith, presumably so that he can be ruler over "many things" (v. 53).[37] These teachings view women as property rather than as individuals with inherent importance. A man with many wives "cannot commit adultery [with them] for they belong to him, and they are given unto him" (v. 62) so that he can obey the commandment to multiply and replenish the earth. Women are given to him "for their exaltation in the eternal worlds" so that "they may bear the souls of men" (v. 63).

Examples of nineteenth-century Mormon men who lost their wives as punishment[38] and of men who were tested by being asked to give up their wives[39] show that this scriptural view of women as property of their husbands, as instruments for men to use to fulfill their religious obligations, was incorporated into Mormon practice. Brigham Young's adaptation of the New Testament's parable of the talents shows that not only was polygamy to be practiced after this life, the accompanying notion of females as vehicles for men's exaltation was to continue then too: The man who would not take more than one wife "will perhaps be saved in the celestial kingdom; but when he gets there he will not find himself in possession of any wife at all. He has had a talent that he has given up. He will come forward and say, 'Here is that which thou gavest me, I have not wasted it, and here is the one talent,' and he will not enjoy it, but it will be taken and given to those who have improved the talents they received, and he will find himself without any wife, and he will remain single forever."[40]

Wilford Woodruff's Manifesto theoretically ended the Mormon practice of polygyny in the United States in 1890, although the church actually continued to allow the contracting of polygynous marriages for almost fifteen more years. Nor has it rejected polygyny as a valid principle. Therefore, some Mormon women in the 1980s remain haunted by it. They are apprehensive —probably unrealistically—that, if the political climate were to allow it again, the church might reinstitute the practice; and they dread the heavenly polygyny that has never disappeared from the church's theology.

Section 132 also exhibits a preoccupation with female virginity. Verses 61-63, which discuss a man's taking more than one wife, refer to women as "virgins," possibly a misnomer, for verse 63 continues to use the term even after the women are married. Perhaps *virgin* is used only by analogy with the parable in Matthew 25 of the ten virgins, meaning marriageable women, and is not to be understood literally. However, if the term is meant literally, these verses use sexual inexperience as the sole criterion of women's suitability to participate in "the new covenant of marriage." They theoretically disqualify a virtuous widow or divorcee of excellent moral character while allowing a woman who has not experienced sexual intercourse regardless of her moral character. There is no corresponding concern for the virginity of men.

Comparing the five times that women are addressed by name in the Doctrine and Covenants with the more than 400 times men are addressed by name again demonstrates the book's presumption that only men are religiously significant. In only three sections are specific women addressed. One section gives a certain Vienna Jacques instructions on moving to Missouri, but more noteworthy are two sections dealing with Joseph Smith's wife Emma.

The tone of section 25 is loving, positive, uplifting, and accepting. It praises Emma, forgives her sins, gives her the unique assignment to compile a hymnbook, and assigns her a task which only a few of the most trusted males had—to be Joseph Smith's scribe. The revelation promises blessings in return for righteousness and faithfulness. Emma is promised to "be ordained . . . to expound scriptures, and to exhort the church," a rare privilege for a woman. Whether it was intended to, in practice "the church" here meant "the female members of the church." As president of the Female Relief Society Emma did expound scriptures and exhort, but only at the meetings of this women's organization, not for the benefit of male as well as female church members.

The tone of the second revelation to Emma, section 132:52–56, is radically different. Here she is warned to support Joseph in practicing polygyny "for I am the Lord . . . and will destroy her if she will not obey my law." Furthermore, if she does not accept polygyny willingly she will have to endure Joseph's receiving the blessing of "an hundred-fold in this world, of . . . wives." This threat gave Emma no options; she could accept more wives willingly or she could have them forced upon her. The message would have been bitter in any case, but it has an added tang when one remembers that this revelation from God was transmitted through Emma's husband rather than some less involved person; in essence, her husband, speaking for God, required Emma to accept a situation morally repugnant to her and to forgive Joseph's sins.

Though not explicitly stated, underlying the Doctrine and Covenants is a presumption that only males can hold the priesthood. Unlike the Old Testament priesthood, which was limited to only a select group of males, the Mormon priesthood could admit any worthy male. And yet, consistent with traditional Christian views of priesthood, those who exercise the Mormon priesthood are to manifest what have typically been considered feminine virtues. Section 121 dealing with priesthood downplays controlling others, completely condemns coercive power, and states that priesthood power and influence can be maintained "only by persuasion, by long-suffering, by gentleness and meekness, and by love unfeigned; by kindness, and pure knowledge, which shall greatly enlarge the soul without hypocrisy, and without guile." Priesthood holders are to show "charity towards all men, and to the household of faith" and they should "let virtue garnish [their] thoughts unceasingly."

Section 20 outlines the government of the church. Since it is governed by priesthood-holders, the church is run by men. Only priesthood-holders officiate at meetings. Only priesthood-holders have the duty to preach and teach. Only priesthood-holders can officiate in the ordinances of baptism, conferring the Holy Ghost, and administering the sacrament. Yet these essential ordinances are restricted only in who may perform them. Each church member, female or male, must be baptized, must receive the Holy Ghost, and may receive the sacrament (18:42; 20:73-74).

Generally accepted laws of ethical behavior, such as not lying, stealing, or doing "any manner of iniquity," are the standard for all people. Parents, not just mothers nor just fathers, are responsible for teaching their children to be righteous and to rely on the Lord (68:25-28). Whatever the penalty, all married people are to remain faithful to their spouses, and all single people are to avoid fornication. The Doctrine and Covenants presents no ordinances as steps to salvation that are forbidden to females. God "created man male and female . . . and he gave unto them commandments that they should love and serve him, the only living and true God, and that he should be the only being whom they should worship."[41]

The Book of Mormon is an account of a group of Israelites who migrated from Palestine to inhabit the American continents. Unlike the Israelites portrayed in the Old Testament, the Book of Mormon Israelites are primarily Christians or apostate Christians from their beginnings in about 600 B.C. until their demise in A.D. 421. Although the righteous Book of Mormon people observed the law of Moses until Christ appeared to them in A.D. 34, with the exception of a handful of references to offering sacrifices to show gratitude to God, the Book of Mormon gives no detail about its people's observance of the particulars of the Old Testament law. Therefore, it neither states nor presumes any religious practices or laws similar to those in the Old Testament which affect women differently than men. Its male priesthood seems to be restricted to a limited group of men. As in the Doctrine and Covenants, the Christian ordinances of baptism, conferring the Holy Ghost, and administering the sacrament, which priesthood-holders perform, are available to every church member, male or female.

Still, the Book of Mormon shares with the Old Testament and the Doctrine and Covenants the assumption that women are less significant than men. The book was written by males; and because it focuses on religious leaders, civic leaders, and battles, it primarily records the actions, speeches, and thoughts of males. Even when it focuses on the private lives of these leaders rather than their public works, it concentrates on relationships that men have with each other.

Only six women in the Book of Mormon are referred to by name. Most of the rest are identified as some man's wife, some man's sister, or some man's mother. Their most frequently recorded actions seem to be worrying for their families in peril or mourning for their families after disaster.[42] Three of the named women, Eve, Mary, and Sarah, are biblical characters who are only mentioned and do not participate in the Book of Mormon action. Only three named women do participate. Sariah of 1 Nephi is a very human wife and mother who complains in trying moments but is generally faithful to God, loyal to her husband, and always concerned for her children's welfare. Isabel is a harlot who is merely a vehicle for male degeneracy. The sixth named woman, a Lamanite named Abish, is significant by herself. Her story is also the story of the unnamed queen she serves. Both women are portrayed as being exemplary. When King Lamoni swoons because of the power of the gospel message, the queen sends for the prophet. She believes the prophet's assurance that the king is not dead and he praises her: "Blessed art thou because of thy exceeding faith; I say unto thee, woman, there has not been such great faith among all the people of the Nephites."[43] When the king awakens as the prophet promised, all present except Abish, who is already a believer, swoon because of the power of God. Abish then gathers everyone else to see the miracle. The crowd misunderstands and becomes hostile toward the "enemy" prophet but disaster is averted when Abish, by exercising her faith, is able to rouse her queen.

Alma 22 records a similar circumstance wherein another Book of Mormon queen whose husband is in a religious swoon initially reacts negatively but is later converted with her whole household. A third Book of Mormon queen is the unwitting pawn of a usurper who, in the tradition of Absalom and Adonijah, acquires the kingdom by acquiring the queen. Her story suggests that a kingdom could have passed to a widowed queen rather than to a male heir, though no queen was ever regent in the Book of Mormon.[44]

Groups of women in the Book of Mormon are portrayed as being worthy of emulation. The mothers of Helaman's two thousand young warriors taught their sons that "if they did not doubt, God would deliver them." The sons had faith in their mothers' faith. Some women are shown heroically facing martyrdom with their children for their beliefs. In extreme cases, women in the Book of Mormon were armed and prepared for war, and once they actually fought.[45]

This is not an impressive tally for a book of 400 pages. Furthermore, other clues further suggest that Book of Mormon authors considered women less significant than men. Just as in the tenth commandment in the Old Testament, where "wife" is not given a primary or unique place in the list of a man's possessions, the Book of Mormon contains at least six similar lists in which women or wives are mentioned after flocks, seeds, lands, church, homes, etc. For example, the blessing in Alma 7:27 says, "May the peace of God rest upon you, and upon your houses and lands, and upon your flocks and herds, and all that you possess, your *women* and your children."[46] In Lehi's dream of the tree of life he mentions his concern for his family, specifying only his wife, his righteous sons, and his wicked sons. His son Nephi consistently divides his siblings into the "righteous" Sam, Joseph, and Jacob and the "wicked" Laman and Lemuel. Yet in 2 Nephi 5, Nephi reveals that he also had sisters. When Nephi reports that "*we* did go down into the ship . . . everyone according to *his* age; wherefore *we* did *all* go down into the ship, with *our wives* and our children," he assumes that the important family members are male; women and children are only appendages.[47]

Many speeches in the Book of Mormon are addressed to "brethren," "beloved brethren," or "sons," though the substance of those speeches is almost always a universal message with no specific male content. Such an example of obliviousness to women is the otherwise humanitarian and inspiring speech of King Benjamin in Mosiah 2–4. King Benjamin decrees that all should gather to hear his address. They congregate, "every man according to his family, consisting of his wife, and his sons, and his daughters" (2:5). King Benjamin addresses his group as "my *brethren,* all ye that have assembled yourselves together" (2:9), "my *brethren*" (2:20, 31, 36; 3:1), and "my friends and my *brethren,* my kindred and my people" (4:4). He tells the group that if a sinner does not repent "mercy hath no claim on that *man*" (2:38–39). Listing his audience to stress that his instructions apply to absolutely everyone, he addresses "all ye *old men,* and also ye *young men,* and you *little children* who can understand my words." Throughout the speech he totally ignores the adult female portion of his audience, while specifically addressing all other groups, even children.

A similar omission occurs in Jacob's chastizing speech in Jacob 2 and 3. He addresses the people of Nephi as "my beloved *brethren.*" He talks about "your *wives* and your children" and tells them that each of them is to have only one wife and no concubines. His "you," spoken to a group of men, women, and children, acknowledges only the adult males. However, unlike other sermons addressed only to the men, this message actually is meant for them only. He accuses them of behaving abominably, being unfaithful to their wives, causing them terrible distress and pain, breaking their hearts and destroying their confidence. Jacob characterizes the women, with the children, as innocents, "exceedingly tender and chaste and delicate before God" (2:7), and expresses concern that his words will wound them as if their souls and "delicate minds" were pierced with daggers (2:9). He says that many of the women's and children's hearts "have died" (2:35). We may assume, however, that if these men have been unfaithful to their wives in having illicit relationships with other women, then some of these women in his audience whom he characterizes as "tender and chaste and delicate" must be those "other women," considerably less innocent than he paints them.

Although much of the narrative of the Book of Mormon, like most of the

Doctrine and Covenants, seems oblivious to women, the most important teachings show that salvation is available equally to all. When Nephi says that Christ died for all men, he adds "*women* and children." Echoing Galatians, he also claims that all can come to the Lord, "black and white, bond and free, male and *female*." Those who are obedient and who believe can become Christ's "sons and *daughters*." All humankind, "men and *women* ... must be born again" to be redeemed by God.[48] The same salvation awaits all righteous people, and all people's righteousness is measured by the same criteria.

In the hundred or so years in which the New Testament was written, because Christ's followers' initial expectation of his imminent second coming disappeared as Jerusalem was crushed by the Romans, they began to establish an institution to facilitate spreading and preaching the gospel, worship, and unified Christian communities. The New Testament writers experienced the emergence of Christianity from a small Jewish sect concentrated in Palestine to a religion distinct from Judaism, made up of Jews and Gentiles spread throughout the eastern Mediterranean. The New Testament writings reflect and helped shape this changing religious, political, geographical, and cultural environment. Through miracle stories, sermons, parables, and more, the historical narratives of the Gospels and Acts tell of the life, teachings, and salvation of Jesus and the events in the lives of his earliest followers. Like the Doctrine and Covenants, the letters from early Christian leaders define a new theology and the beginnings of an ecclesiastical system. While the male Jesus, his life, his teachings, and the salvation available through him are the main concern of the New Testament, his life story as recorded is directed to women as well as men, and his salvation is offered to women as well as men.

The Old Testament laws and practices that affected women differently from men are in the background in the New Testament, as are even more stringent customs and practices later adopted by the Jews. Among these are men avoiding speaking to women, even their wives, in public; men not teaching women the scriptures or religion generally; and only men concerning themselves with religious affairs while women concerned themselves with household affairs at home.[49] Particularly in the gospels, these are more important in being superceded than observed. There were women among the crowds who listened to Jesus, even some who followed him from town to town.[50] He taught women, gave others teachings through women, and cultivated friendships with women. Though some of Jesus' male disciples seemed less generous toward women than did Jesus himself, apparently they accepted women in their group.[51] In contrast to the Old Testament culture's valuing of women principally for their ability to give birth, Jesus and his New Testament followers valued women on the same basis that they valued men: for their belief in Christ and their commitment to his teachings.

While some of Jesus' teachings are cast in a form which addresses only males, some which address males are balanced by reciprocal directives to women, e.g., "whoever divorces *his wife* and marries another, commits adultery against *her*; and if *she* divorces *her husband* and marries another, *she* commits adultery."[52] The Mary and Martha story of Luke 10:38-42 demonstrates that Jesus felt it appropriate to teach women. Jesus commends Mary's choosing to listen to his teaching. Obviously Jesus did not feel that women should be barred or excused from dealing with religious concerns. He viewed no activity as more important for this woman than learning the religious truths he had to teach. His actions and words rejected the assumption that all women should be concerned only with what has been typically considered "women's work." This story, and that of Jesus restoring Lazarus to life (John 11-12:8), suggests that Jesus not only taught women but thought of them as friends. Mary and Martha were not merely the women in the household of Jesus' friend, Lazarus. Luke's record puts Jesus in the home of Mary and Martha, not mentioning Lazarus. John records that Jesus loved these women along with their brother (11:5) and was deeply pained at Mary's sorrow over Lazarus' death (11:33). Jesus ignored his society's norms in his close friendship with these women.

Jesus also acknowledged women in that many of his significant teachings came through encounters with women. One of these teachings was the proper relationship of ethical law and ritual law. As Jesus responded to a plea to go to Jarius' daughter to restore her life, "a woman who had suffered from a hemorrhage for twelve years came up behind him and touched the fringe of his garment." The woman's behavior was clearly improper, for Levitical proscription said that a woman with a discharge of blood made everything and everyone she touched unclean. Jesus stopped; but rather than recoiling or rebuking her, he made her well. He supported the woman's boldness in defying the law to achieve something greater than ritual obedience.[53] At Jarius' house, he took the dead daughter "by the hand and the girl arose." Though Old Testament law stipulated that anyone touching a corpse was unclean for seven days, Jesus was not deterred.[54] Twice in one day he taught through women that observing the ritual law was less important than the ethical act of helping someone.

When Jesus taught the Samaritan woman at the well (John 4), he breached propriety by talking to a woman at all and, even worse, to a woman who was a Samaritan. Using metaphors she would find meaningful, he taught her that the living water he could give would satisfy the spiritual thirst of a lifetime. Through prophecy he proved to her that he had abilities beyond those of mere mortals. He revealed to her that he was the Messiah. Excited by what she had learned, she returned and told others, who "believed in him because of the woman's testimony" (4:39).

Jesus demonstrated to women as well as to men that he had the power and authority to forgive sins. As he ate at a Pharisee's house, a "woman . . . who was a sinner" came to the house, "wet his feet with her tears, and wiped them with the hair of her head, and kissed his feet and anointed them with ointment." He taught the Pharisee and his guests that, despite her sins, her love was far greater than theirs and told the woman: "Your sins are forgiven. . . . Your faith has saved you; go in peace."[55] He treated her as a person worthy of his attention and through her taught a useful lesson to others.

Knowledge of the resurrection came first to women who were instructed to share it with men. From Luke, the women who went to Jesus' tomb to anoint his body were told by angels that "he is not here, but is risen." Remembering Jesus' own statement that he would rise, they told the rest of the disciples what they witnessed. In John's version, though male disciples were also at the tomb, it was to Mary Magdalene that Jesus revealed himself, commissioning her to tell the disciples that he was ascending to his Father. All of the gospels show the resurrected Jesus revealing himself first to women and show women being commanded to tell others that he had been resurrected.[56]

In addition to Old Testament and Jewish tradition, contact with the Greco-Roman world in which women had quite a bit of freedom and respect is also background for the New Testament. This freedom is reflected in the letters as women are shown as leaders as well as participants in religious communities. The letters also seem to react against this freedom, withdrawing rights that the women had already assumed and refusing other rights before women could claim them. Although the letters sometimes commend women for their involvement, they also sharply remind women that they are subordinate to men in the hierarchies of church and home.[57] While the letters sometimes acknowledge the duties of Christian men and women to be the same, they also suggest that women are morally and spiritually weaker than men. Thus, the letters' message about the worth of women is far more ambiguous than the gospels' messages.

Romans 16 presents some remarkable information about women's participation in the leadership of the early Christian churches. In verses 1-2 Paul praises Phoebe for being a minister or servant (*diakonos* or deacon) and for being a helper, protector, or patroness (*prostatis*) of many, including Paul himself. While *diakonos* at this point (c. A.D. 55) probably described more a function than an office in a priesthood hierarchy, the function evolved into an office soon after.[58] It is unjustified to translate *diakonos*, which appears in Paul's letters twenty-two times, as "servant" solely in the case of Phoebe.[59] The noun *prostatis* has no other biblical attestation, but its corresponding verb (*proistanai*) denotes "leading" or governing. Therefore, the translations that call Phoebe merely a "helper," "good friend," or "succorer" are substantially weaker than the Greek original.[60]

In verses 3-4 Paul calls the married couple Prisca and Aquilla "my fellow workers in Christ Jesus who risked their necks for my life, to whom not only I but also all the churches of the Gentiles give thanks." In verse 6 he acknowledges "Mary who has worked hard among you."

Although verse 7 is ambiguous, it probably praises a woman, Junia, for her service as an apostle. While someone "eminent among the apostles" could be understood as someone esteemed by the apostles, it is far more likely that it denotes an apostle whom other people held in esteem.[61] Virtually all modern translators and commentators who deal with this verse presume that *Iounian* was a male name, Junias,[62] often explaining it as a short, endearing form of a longer Latin name. However, Junias has no attestation till long after the New Testament period, and endearing forms of Latin names are long, not short. Virtually all who commented on this verse before about 1300 presumed that *Iounian* was a female name, Junia, a common name in the New Testament period. Bernadette Brooten explains the modern scholars' reasoning: "A woman could not have been called an apostle. Because a woman could not be an apostle, the woman who is here called an apostle could not have been a woman."[63] Though hardly apparent to readers of modern translations, women apparently performed significant leadership roles in the emerging hierarchy of the early New Testament church.

Apparently women as well as men manifested spiritual gifts in New Testament churches. Paul instructs women to cover their heads when they prophesy and all members to exercise faith, wisdom, healing, and the ability to work miracles; to prophesy, speak in and interpret tongues when moved by the spirit; and not to stifle the gifts of others.[64] Yet despite this obvious involvement of women, Paul's letters were largely written as if their intended audiences were male. Paul typically addresses or talks about his "brethren" in Christ. In contrast, the authors of 1 John and Jude use the sexually neutral, very loving designations of "beloved" or "little children," addresses which easily admit females as part of the intended audience.

More like these sexually neutral addresses are the instructions Paul gives equally to men and women. In 1 Corinthians 7 he outlines acceptable sexual behavior. Wives may not withhold sexual relations from their husbands, but Paul gives the same instructions to husbands about their wives. Abstinence should be only by agreement (7:3-5). The same chapter says that both single males and single females can give more attention to the Lord than married persons can (7:32-34). In promoting a single state as being more conducive to serving the Lord than a married state (a teaching Mormonism emphatically rejects), Paul expands righteous options for women.

In 1 Corinthians 12 he develops a beautiful metaphor comparing the company of believers to the body of Christ. Just as each part of the body— the foot, the hand, the eye—is necessary for the body to function properly, each member of the congregation is as vital as any other. This metaphor values all believers regardless of their gender or ecclesiastical position. This metaphor, coupled with the universality of the ordinance of baptism, grants women the status of membership in the congregation, a major improvement from their condition in Judaism of their time.

However, while Paul gives with one hand, he takes with the other. The same Paul who grants women membership status and teaches that each member is as significant as the next preaches the subordination of wives to their husbands. He alludes to the creation accounts of both Genesis 1 and 2 in claiming man was created in the image of God (implying that woman was not)[65] and that because woman was created from man, for man, she should be subordinate to him. This in part explains how "the head of every man is Christ and the head of a woman is her husband, and the head of Christ is God."[66] Although most Christians have not recognized it because Paul's use of these creation accounts imposes meanings on the texts that are not inherent in them, the theology he bases on his interpretations of these texts has limited value.[67]

The author of 1 Peter counsels women that wifely subordination is an excellent way to convert by example. Wives should submit to their husbands "so that some . . . may be won without a word by the behavior of their wives, when they see your reverent and chaste behavior." He too turns to the Old Testament for support: "Sarah obeyed Abraham calling him Lord."[68] In addition, wifely submission will ensure "that the word of God may not be discredited."[69] This submissive relationship does not mean bowing to ruthless tyranny nor does it suggest a property-owner relationship as the Old Testament does. Husbands are admonished to love their wives and wives their husbands.[70]

Beyond hierarchy in marriage, the letters preach that all women are to be subordinate to all men. A woman is to "learn in silence with all submissiveness. I permit no woman to teach or to have authority over men; she is to keep silent." Again the Old Testament is used to justify this view: "Adam was formed first, then Eve, and Adam was not deceived, but the woman was deceived and became a transgressor."[71] Although elsewhere he gave women directives on how to pray and prophesy (presumably in church), Paul definitively states that "as in all the churches of the saints, the women should keep silence in the churches. For they are not permitted to speak, but should be subordinate, even as the law says. If there is anything they desire to know, let them ask their husbands at home. For it is shameful for a woman to speak in church."[72]

Early Mormons accepted these biblical teachings about wives being subordinate to their husbands and women being subordinate to men. Annie Clark Tanner remembered that for Mormons in the 1800s "It was a man's place to create conditions, and a woman's place to accept them."[73] Some implied that this subordination was proof of female inferiority. Brigham

Young preached that Mormon women were to submit to the rule of their husbands as God's curse upon Eve demanded and that he, Brigham, ruled over his wives by virtue of his "superior intelligence." "Let our wives be the weaker vessels, and the men be men, and show the women by their superior ability that God gives husbands wisdom and ability to lead their wives into their presence."[74] Heber C. Kimball described women as "those made to be led and counseled and directed."[75] Erastus Snow taught that husbands were lords over their wives and should be treated accordingly.[76]

Using the term "the Priesthood" to denote men who hold the Mormon priesthood, Parley P. Pratt taught that Mormon women were never to presume to have any kind of authority over "the Priesthood." At the same time he made an attempt to elevate those activities allowed to women (routine household chores) by calling them "privileges":

> It is not the privilege of the sisters to teach the brethren or usurp authority over them, and especially over the Priesthood. . . . It is their privilege and duty to warn all. . . . It is a very different thing to warn the world, professors and non-professors to repent, and invite them to the ordinances of God's house, from what it is to teach the Church (or those who have obeyed the gospel) and to usurp authority over those to whom they should be in subjection. Women may pray, testify, speak in tongues, and prophesy in the Church, when liberty is given by the elders but *not* for the *instruction* of the Elders in their duties. . . . Women may vote in the Church, and yet keep silence — It is their privilege to make and mend, and wash, and cook for the Saints; and lodge strangers; and wash the saints' feet . . . and we rejoice that the sisters esteem it a privilege thus to minister to our necessities, and it is their privilege, in all such things, to labour with us in the gospel.[77]

Subordination and inferiority of women is no longer explicitly preached in the Mormon church. The current message is that wives and husbands are in partnership. Yet when former church president Spencer W. Kimball urged wives in a 1978 women's conference to be "full partners"—contributing, not silent—he was not announcing equal status or authority with men in the church; for the priesthood, and therefore most of the hierarchy is still open only to men; and husbands, with input from their wives, are still expected to be the authority figures in their homes. As full partners, wives should be performing challenging and fulfilling roles at home, "creating the environment in which a child can grow and develop."[78] Partnership in marriage thus is still a hierarchy in which each person assumes her or his proper and essential role. While asserting that men and women are equally important before the Lord, the official statement from the church presidency in 1978 also insisted women and men each had proper roles that were different from each other.[79]

In the New Testament, this recurring emphasis on a hierarchical order in which women are lower than men is balanced by many concepts, teachings, and practices that apply equally to all. Jesus never preaches that women have certain roles and men have others; instead he preaches ethical behavior for everyone, calls all to follow him, and teaches whoever is willing to listen. He offers salvation to anyone who loves him, loves his Father, and is willing to keep his commandments. Neither he nor his followers in the early period establish an institution with a hierarchy that reserves all positions of authority, power, and importance to men. And Paul says, "For as many of you as were baptized into Christ have put on Christ. There is neither Jew nor Greek, there is neither slave nor free, there is neither male nor female; for you are all one in Christ Jesus."[80] This precept obliterates rank and status.

Mormons are not alone in giving less serious attention to what the New Testament presents about equality among believers than to what it presents about hierarchies and restrictions on women's behavior. As the early Christians struggled to become a united church, one line of thought came to be promoted as orthodox while others were branded as heretical. Because equality for women often accompanied other teachings deemed dangerous and anarchistic, equality for women soon was identified as heresy and expunged from the orthodox church.[81] This tendency to limit rather than broaden women's options has characterized most Christian churches throughout history, in spite of the more generous teachings in some letters and the gospels.

The scriptures here discussed have documented a variety of patterns for women's behavior and for the treatment of women. Mormonism has adopted many of these patterns and has rejected and abandoned others in its changing teachings concerning women. Because baptism is open to and required of everyone, women have always been considered participating members in Mormonism, just as in the New Testament church. However, from its beginning, Mormonism has had a hierarchy based on a male-only priesthood. It has consistently defined women's roles as different from men's.

The teachings of the LDS church today show a positive evolution from the earlier LDS teachings of female subordination and inferiority, and the assumption that females were less significant than males. All of these teachings had scriptural antecedents. There is no reason to believe that the future will not bring further modification to Mormon perceptions of women's place in the temporal and eternal scheme. Even though negative, restrictive, scriptural perceptions of women adopted by Mormonism must have seemed eternal to those who held them, many of these views did not withstand the passage of time and the changing environment.

The most attractive scriptural concepts of women have yet to be incorporated into Mormonism. Some people in the Old and New Testaments simply assumed that women or men endowed with God's spirit could lead a people, prophesy, or preach. Rather than promoting roles for each sex, Jesus and Old Testament prophets preached the same message to women and to men: all should love God and be compassionate to their neighbors. Perhaps the time will come when only these unrestrictive attitudes and expectations will define the role of a Mormon woman and a Mormon man. Perhaps the time will come when opportunities for service in the church will be based on talent rather than on gender.

NOTES

1. Eighth and ninth Articles of Faith, The Pearl of Great Price.

2. See Numb. 16 and Josh. 7, where the sin of the head of the house extends to a man's whole family, so that when he is punished with death, his entire household (meaning all of his moveable property including servants, children, and wives) dies with him. There is no record of a woman committing a sin with such far-reaching consequences.

3. Gen. 24:29-60.

4. Exod. 20:17. Because it is easy to understand and is almost always accurate to the best manuscripts available, the Revised Standard Version is the Bible used in this essay. Unless otherwise noted, all italics in quotations are the author's.

5. The absence of a provision for selling a son is logical in a society in which a bridegroom pays his bride's father a "bride-price" and married daughters become part of their husbands' families, while sons incorporate their wives into their father's families.

6. Exod. 21:7-11. Roland De Vaux, *Ancient Israel,* 2 vols. (New York: McGraw-Hill Book Co., 1965), 1:27, 86.

7. There were only two circumstances under which a man could not divorce his wife: if he falsely accused her of not being virginal when he married her or if he married her because they were guilty of fornication (Deut. 23:19, 29).

8. Whether women's contractual promises could be nullified by their husbands was still a live legal issue in the United States into the 1920s. See *American Law Reports* 18:1542-47, and Supp. 71:744-49.

9. When Abraham and Isaac have their wives pose as their unmarried sisters to rulers who might find them attractive, they show no concern about threatening their wives' chastity with their expedient deceptions (Genesis 12, 20, and 26). It is impossible to tell from Genesis 34 whether the extremely violent reaction of Simeon and Levi to the rape of their sister Dinah was because she had suffered appalling indignity or because they, as her family, had. See especially verses 7 and 31.

10. Exod. 22:16-17; Deut. 22:28-29.

11. Exod. 20:14; Lev. 20:10; Deut. 22:22. Adultery in the Old Testament is "sexual intercourse between a married woman and any man other than her husband." *Universal Jewish Encyclopedia s.v.* "adultery." Phyllis Bird in "Images of Women in the Old Testament," in *Religion and Sexism*, ed. Rosemary Radford Ruether (New York: Simon and Schuster, 1974), p. 51, uses these examples to show that women were thought of as property.

12. The law was recorded as either "*thou* shalt not," using the second-person masculine singular address, or as "if a *man* does X," using the specifically male word, not the generic word for humankind.

13. "Circumcision appears throughout the entire OT and NT as a token of membership in Israel and of association with the covenant." John L. McKenzie, *Dictionary of the Bible* (New York: Macmillan Co., 1965), p. 137.

14. Lev. 12–16. The psychological effect on women to have been so often considered ritually unclean, impure, unacceptable to God must have been profound. A menstruating woman made everything and everyone she touched impure. At the end of a period of unusual uncleanness, and after giving birth, she had to offer a sacrifice to atone for her impure condition.

15. Phyllis Trible, "A Daughter's Death: Feminism, Literary Criticism, and the Bible," *Michigan Quarterly Review* 22 (Summer 1983): 176–89.

16. Gen. 27.

17. Gen. 31:19–35.

18. Phyllis Trible, as cited in Katherine Doob Sakenfeld, "Loyalty and Love: The Language of Human Interconnections in the Hebrew Bible," *Michigan Quarterly Review* 22 (Summer 1983): 202.

19. 2 Sam. 14.

20. 2 Kings 22:11–20.

21. James Hurley, *Man and Woman in Biblical Perspective: A Study in Role Relationships and Authority* (Leicester, England: Inter-Varsity Press, 1981), p. 70, says that rabbis had trouble explaining Huldah's functioning in a time when male prophets, particularly Jeremiah, lived. Rabbi Nahman said that Huldah, along with Deborah, was haughty and that her name (literally meaning weasel) was hateful, just as Deborah's (literally meaning hornet) was.

22. *Old Testament Student Manual: I Kings-Malachi*, prepared by the Church Educational System (Salt Lake City: Church of Jesus Christ of Latter-day Saints, 1981), p. 214.

23. Noted by Nadine Hansen, "Women and the Priesthood," *Dialogue* 14 (Winter 1981): 50.

24. Heb. 11:31; James 2:25.

25. Francis Brown, S. R. Driver, C. A. Briggs, *A Hebrew and English Lexicon of the Old Testament* (Oxford: Clarendon Press, 1978), pp. 1047–49; George Arthur Buttrick, ed., *The Interpreter's Dictionary of the Bible*, 4 vols. and supp. (Nashville, Tenn.: Abingdon Press, 1962) 2:1017.

26. Though it is not recorded in Deborah's story that her position and ability as a military judge came from God, the introduction to the book of Judges says that the Lord raised up judges to save Israel and that the Lord was with those judges whom he raised up (Judg. 2:16–18).

27. Judg. 4:4–5.

28. Hurley, *Man and Woman*, p. 70.

29. From John Calvin, *Corpus Reformatum*, quoted in Susan T. Foh, *Women and the Word of God: A Response to Biblical Feminism* (Phillipsburg, N.J.: Presbyterian and Reformed Publishing, 1979), p. 84.

30. Brigham Young, 15 June 1862, *Journal of Discourses*, 26 vols. (Liverpool: F. D. Richards, 1855–86) 9:307, hereafter cited as *JD*, with speaker and date.

31. *Old Testament Student Manual: Genesis-2 Samuel*, prepared by the Church Educational System (Salt Lake City: Church of Jesus Christ of Latter-day Saints, 1981), p. 254.

32. Hansen, "Women and the Priesthood," pp. 49–50.

33. See, for example, Doctrine and Covenants 76:69–75 (hereafter cited as D&C), which describes "the men" who will be saved and the realms of glory in which they will dwell.

34. D&C 128:15, 25.

35. See D&C 43:81.

36. The direct object is not specified, but context suggests that a man could rule over "many wives," "many families," or "many kingdoms," which the wife would help him provide.

37. An entire family is theoretically reduced to the status of "things" when Joseph Smith is blessed that he will be given "an hundred-fold in this world of fathers and mothers, brothers and sisters, wives and children."

38. Juanita Brooks, *John D. Lee* (Glendale, Calif.: Arthur H. Clark Co., 1973), pp. 122–23.

39. Jedediah M. Grant, February 19, 1854, *JD* 2:14, said, "Did the Prophet Joseph want every man's wife he asked for? He did not. . . . The grand object in view was to try the people of God." The story of Heber C. Kimball being asked to give his wife, Vilate, may be apocryphal, but its wide distribution as lore among Mormons suggests how thoroughly its tellers accepted its premise: that Vilate was Heber's to give.

40. Brigham Young, 31 August 1873, *JD* 16:66.

41. D&C 18:42; 20:18–19, 73–74; 42:74–93; 63:14–19; 132:26, 41–44.

42. See Marjorie Meads Spencer, "My Book of Mormon Sisters," *Ensign* 7 (September 1977): 66–71, for greater detail about the women in the Book of Mormon.

43. Alma 19:10.

44. 2 Sam. 16:20–22; 1 Kings 2:17–25; Alma 47:35.

45. Alma 56; 14:11–18; Ether 15:14–15.

46. Alma 43:9, 45; 48:3; Ether 1:41; 14:12.

47. 1 Nephi 18:6.

48. 2 Nephi 9:21, 26:33; Mosiah 5:7; Ether 3:14; Mosiah 27:25.

49. Leonard Swidler, *Women in Judaism* (Metuchen, N.J.: Scarecrow Press, 1976), pp. 93–96, 120–23. See also Evelyn and Frank Stagg, *Women in the World of Jesus* (Philadelphia: Westminster Press, 1978), pp. 51–53.

50. Matt. 27:55–56; Luke 11:27; 23:49, 55; 24:22.

51. See the response of Jesus' male disciples when they found him talking with the woman at the well (John 4:27) and their refusal to believe the testimony the women bore of the risen Christ (Luke 24:10–11). However, in Luke 24:22 they refer to the women as "women of our company."

52. Mark 10:10–11. Note that it is not a typical feature of Greek to distinguish between masculine and feminine verb or pronoun forms. Jesus' teachings are usually addressed to people rather than to males or females.

53. Matt. 9:18–22; Lev. 15:19–30.

54. Matt. 9:25; Num. 19:11–22.

55. Luke 7:37–38, 48–50.

56. This is particularly significant because with rare exceptions Jewish law did not accept testimony given by women as valid. Judith Hauptman, "Images of Women in the Talmud" in Ruether, *Religion and Sexism,* p. 194, and Swidler, *Women in Judaism,*

p. 115. The apostles (Luke 24:10-11) and "those who had been with him" (Mark 16:10-11) refused to believe the women's testimonies.

57. Constance F. Parvey, "The Theology and Leadership of Women in the New Testament," in Ruether, *Religion and Sexism*, pp. 118-32. Very possibly the authors of the letters saw this female involvement as excessive, as something that threatened the stability and harmony of the new Christian communities.

58. Charles R. Meyer, *Man of God: A Study of the Priesthood* (Garden City: Doubleday, 1974), p. 60; and Anthony A. Hutchinson, "Women and Ordination: Introduction to the Biblical Context," *Dialogue* 14 (Winter 1981): 65. Compare Phil. 1:1 and 1 Tim. 3:8-12.

59. Andre Dumas, "Biblical Anthropology and the Participation of Women in the Ministry of the Church," *Concerning the Ordination of Women* (N.p.: The World Council of Churches, [1963]), p. 20.

60. Dumas, p. 20; and Hurley, *Man and Woman*, p. 122.

61. *Jerome Biblical Commentary*, 2 vols., Raymond E. Brown, Joseph A. Fitzmeyer, Roland E. Murphy, eds. (Englewood Cliffs, N. J.: Prentice-Hall, 1968) 2:330; and Hutchinson, "Women and Ordination": 65-66.

62. Dumas, p. 20.

63. Bernadette Brooten, "Junia . . . Outstanding among the Apostles," in *Women Priests: A Catholic Commentary on the Vatican Declaration*, ed. L. and A. Swidler (New York: Paulist Press, 1977), pp. 141-42.

64. 1 Cor. 11:5; 12:8-10; 1 Thess. 5:19-20.

65. Here is the reasoning on which this interpretation of Genesis 1:27 is based: "God created man in his own image; in the image of God created he him" refers only to male persons. This was all that God created in his image. "Male and female created he them" simply continues the list of things which God created. Rosemary Radford Ruether, "Mysogynism and Virginal Feminism in the Fathers of the Church," in *Religion and Sexism*, pp. 154-56.

66. 1 Cor. 11. This same hierarchy appears in Eph. 5:21-33 and Col. 3:18.

67. The Hebrew *'adam* (man) used in Genesis 1:27 is the generic word for humans. Therefore, in creating man in his own image, God created human beings in his own image, not specifically and not only males in his own image. Although Genesis 2 portrays woman as being created from the man, after him, and as a helper to him, this method, order, and purpose of creation cannot fairly be said to imply subordinate status. In 16 of the 21 times the Hebrew word `*ezer* (helper) is used in the Old Testament, it denotes a super-ordinate helper (most often the Lord), not subordinate helper. Though Genesis 2 has been used to provide a rationale for the subordination of women, that clearly was not the author's intent. See Emily C. Hewitt and Suzanne R. Hiatt, *Woman Priests: Yes or No?* (New York: Seabury Press, 1973), p. 52.

68. 1 Pet. 3-6.

69. Tit. 2:4-5.

70. Eph. 5:25-33; Col. 3:19; Tit. 2:4.

71. 1 Tim. 2:11-14.

72. 1 Cor. 14:33-35.

73. Annie Clark Tanner, *A Mormon Mother* (1969; rpt., Salt Lake City: University of Utah Library/Tanner Trust Fund, 1976), p. 29.

74. Brigham Young, 21 September 1856, *JD* 4:57; 15 June 1862, *JD* 9:307.

75. Heber C. Kimball, 12 July 1857, *JD* 5:29.

76. Erastus Snow, 4 October 1857, *JD* 5:291.

77. *LDS Millennial Star* 1 (August 1840): 100-101.

78. Spencer W. Kimball, "Privileges and Responsibilities of Sisters," *Ensign* 8 (November 1978): 106.

79. *Salt Lake Tribune,* 27 August 1978, B1.

80. Gal. 3:26-28.

81. This is reflected in the emphasis in the pseudo-Pauline epistles (1 and 2 Timothy and Titus) on church government and their tendency to bar women from it (Parvey, "Theology and Church Government," pp. 136-37). The Gnostic writings often present a parity of men and women along with other notions which disappeared as the official church disapproved of them. Elaine Pagels, *The Gnostic Gospels* (New York: Random House, 1979), pp. 48-69. The writings of the early church fathers granted the status of orthodoxy to the notion that women were subordinate to men. Ruether, "Mysogynism," pp. 150-83.

LINDA P. WILCOX

The Mormon Concept of a Mother in Heaven

The idea of a Mother in Heaven is a shadowy and elusive one floating around the edges of Mormon consciousness. Mormons who grow up singing "O My Father" are familiar with the concept of a Heavenly Mother, but few hear much else about her. She exists, apparently, but has not been very evident in Mormon meetings or writings; and little if any "theology" has been developed to elucidate her nature and characterize our relationship to her.

While nearly all world religions have had female divinities and feminine symbolism, the god of Western Judeo-Christian culture and scripture has been almost unremittingly masculine.[1] Still, the idea of a Heavenly Mother or a female counterpart to the male father-god is not unknown in Christianity. Recently discovered Gnostic texts from the first century after Christ reveal doctrinal teachings about a divine mother as well as father. In some texts God is conceived of as a dyad, both male and female. There is also a body of writings which identifies the divine mother as the Holy Spirit, the third member of the Trinity, which then becomes a family group—the Father, Mother, and Son.[2]

Christianity has also had the elevation of Mary in Catholicism. From first being the Mother of God, Mary eventually became the mother of everyone as she took on a mediating function and became a divine presence to whom prayers could be addressed. This feminization of the divine made possible some further theological developments such as the fourteenth-century epiphany of Dame Julian of Norwich, who experienced the mother-hood as well as fatherhood of God and ecstatically expressed Christ in mother images.[3]

The nineteenth-century American milieu from which Mormonism sprang had some prototypes for a female deity as well. Ann Lee in the late 1700s had proclaimed herself to be the feminine incarnation of the Messiah, as Christ had been the male incarnation—a necessary balance in her system since she described a god which was both male and female, father and mother. The Father-Mother God of the Shakers and Christian Scientists included both sexes in a form of divine androgyny, as in this nineteenth-century prayer by Mary Baker Eddy:

Father-Mother God
Loving Me
Guard me while I sleep
Guide my little feet up to Thee.[4]

By the end of the century Elizabeth Cady Stanton in her *Woman's Bible* was explaining Genesis 1:26-28 ("And God said, Let us make man in our image, after our likeness") as implying the "simultaneous creation of both sexes, in the image of God. It is evident from the language," she writes, "that the masculine and feminine elements were equally represented" in the Godhead which planned the peopling of the earth. To her, as in the Gnostic texts, a trinity of Father, Mother, and Son was more rational, and she called for "the recognition by the rising generation of an ideal Heavenly Mother, to whom their prayers should be addressed, as well as to a Father."[5]

Half a century before Mrs. Stanton's *Woman's Bible,* the Mormon religion had begun to develop a doctrine of just such a Heavenly Mother—a glorified goddess, spouse to an actual Heavenly Father, and therefore the literal mother of mortal spirits. While the need for a divine feminine element in religion is perhaps universal, the form it took in Mormonism was particularly well suited to other aspects of Mormon theology. The Mother in Heaven concept was a logical and natural extension of a theology which posited both an anthropomorphic God who had once been a man and the possibility of eternal procreation of spirit children.

The origins of the Heavenly Mother concept in Mormonism are shadowy. The best known exposition is, of course, Eliza R. Snow's poem, "O My Father," or—the title it was known by earlier—"Invocation, or the Eternal Father and Mother." When the poem was first published in the *Times and Seasons,* it carried the notation "City of Joseph, Oct. 1845," but the actual date of composition is not known. It does not appear in Eliza's notebook/diary for the years 1842-44.[6]

Although President Wilford Woodruff gave Eliza R. Snow credit for originating the idea—"That hymn is a revelation, though it was given unto us by a woman."[7]—it is more likely that Joseph Smith was the first to expound the doctrine of a Mother in Heaven. Joseph F. Smith claimed that "God revealed that principle that we have a mother as well as a father in heaven to Joseph Smith; Joseph Smith revealed it to Eliza Snow Smith, his wife; and Eliza Snow was inspired, being a poet, to put it into verse."[8]

Other incidents tend to confirm this latter view. Susa Young Gates told of Joseph's consoling Zina Diantha Huntington on the death of her mother in

1839 by telling her that not only would she know her mother again on the other side but, "more than that, you will meet and become acquainted with your eternal Mother, the wife of your Father in Heaven." Gates went on to say that about this same time Eliza R. Snow "learned the same glorious truth from the same inspired lips: and was then moved to put this truth into verse."[9] Since Zina Huntington and Eliza were close friends as well, it was also a likely possibility that Zina might have spoken of this idea to Eliza.[10] David McKay recorded that during a buggy ride on which he accompanied Eliza R. Snow he asked her if the Lord had revealed the Mother in Heaven doctrine to her. She replied no, that "I got my inspiration from the Prophets teachings all that I was required to do was to use my Poetical gift and give that Eternal principal in Poetry."[11]

Women were not the only ones to have had some acquaintance with the idea of a Mother in Heaven during the lifetime of Joseph Smith. There is a third-hand account of an experience related by Zebedee Coltrin: "One day the Prophet Joseph asked him and Sidney Rigdon to accompany him into the woods to pray. When they had reached a secluded spot Joseph laid down on his back and stretched out his arms. He told the brethren to lie one on each arm, and then shut their eyes. After they had prayed he told them to open their eyes. They did so and saw a brilliant light surrounding a pedestal which seemed to rest on the earth. They closed their eyes and again prayed. They then saw, on opening them, the Father seated upon a throne; they prayed again and on looking saw the Mother also; after praying and looking the fourth time they saw the Savior added to the group."[12]

Church leaders of the nineteenth century, though they did not speak much about a Mother in Heaven, seemed to accept the idea as a common-sense one, that for God to be a father implied the existence of a mother as well. Brigham Young said that God "created man, as we create our children; for there is no other process of creation in heaven, on the earth, in the earth, or under the earth, or in all the eternities, that is, that were, or that ever will be"—an indirect reference to the necessity of a mother for the process of creation.[13] He also quoted Heber C. Kimball's recollection of Joseph Smith's saying "that he would not worship a God who had not a Father and I do not know that he would if he had not a mother; the one would be as absurd as the other."[14]

Apostle Erastus Snow also used indirect inference in explaining the logic of the Heavenly Mother concept. "Now, it is not said in so many words in the Scriptures, that we have a Mother in heaven as well as a Father," he admitted. "It is left for us to infer this from what we see and know of all living things in the earth including man. The male and female principle is united and both necessary to the accomplishment of the object of their being, and if this be not the case with our Father in heaven after whose image we are created, then it is an anomaly in nature. But to our minds the idea of a Father suggests that of a Mother."[15]

Snow was somewhat distinct from other Mormon leaders in that he described God as a unity of male and female elements, much like the Shakers' Father-Mother God. " 'What,' says one, 'do you mean we should understand that Deity consists of man and woman?' Most certainly I do. If I believe anything that God has ever said about himself, and anything pertaining to the creation and organization of man upon the earth, I must believe that Deity consists of man and woman . . . there can be no God except he is composed of the man and woman united, and there is not in all the eternities that exist, nor ever will be, a God in any other way. . . . There never was a God, and there never will be in all eternities, except they are made of these two component parts; a man and a woman; the male and the female." [16] To Erastus Snow, God was not a male personage, with a Heavenly Mother being a second divine personage; both of them together constituted God.

This development of theology by means of inference and commonsense extension of ordinary earth-life experience continued on into the twentieth century. In fact, it is the primary approach taken by most of those who have made mention of a Mother in Heaven. Apostle Bruce R. McConkie in *Mormon Doctrine,* for example, said that "an exalted and glorified Man of Holiness (Moses 6:57) could not be a Father unless a Woman of like glory, perfection, and holiness was associated with him as a Mother. The begetting of children makes a man a father and a woman a mother whether we are dealing with man in his mortal or immortal state." [17] And Hugh B. Brown, then a member of the First Presidency, noted in 1961 that, "some have questioned our concept of a mother in heaven, but no home, no church, no heaven would be complete without a mother there." [18]

One reason why little theology was developed about a Heavenly Mother is that the scriptural basis for the doctrine was very slim. But Joseph Fielding Smith noted that "the fact that there is no reference to a mother in heaven either in the Bible, Book of Mormon or Doctrine and Covenants, is not sufficient proof that no such thing as a mother did exist there." [19] One possible reason for this gap in the scriptures is offered by a twentieth-century LDS Seminary teacher: "Considering the way man has profaned the name of God, the Father, and His Son, Jesus Christ, is it any wonder that the name of our Mother in Heaven has been withheld, not to mention the fact that the mention of Her is practically nil in scripture?" [20]

In looking at statements by church leaders in the twentieth century, I concentrate on three time periods: the first decade of the century, the 1920s and 1930s, and the 1960s and 1970s. Some themes are apparent in these time periods which may be illustrative of developments in the larger society as well. The examples presented here are not exhaustive, and I suspect that similar ideas on the subject turn up at other times throughout the century.

For example, right after the turn of the century one noticeable thread which ran through several comments about the Mother in Heaven was an association of that doctrine with the movement for women's rights—a major issue in the last years of the nineteenth century, especially in Utah. Apostle James E. Talmage, discussing the status and mission of women, spoke of the early granting of the franchise to women in Utah and the Mormon church's claim that woman is man's equal. In this context, he went on: "The Church is bold enough to go so far as to declare that man has an Eternal Mother in the Heavens as well as an Eternal Father, and in the same sense 'we look upon woman as a being, essential in every particular to the carrying out of God's purposes in respect to mankind.' "[21] An article in the *Deseret News* noted that the truthfulness of the doctrine of a Mother in Heaven would eventually be accepted by the world—that "it is a truth from which, when fully realized, the perfect 'emancipation' and ennobling of woman will result."[22] To many, the concept of a Mother in Heaven was a fitting expression of a larger movement which aimed at raising the status of women and expanding their rights and opportunities.

Another theme, evident elsewhere in American thought as well as in Mormonism, was the yearning for a female divinity—the need for a nurturing presence in the universe. A Mother in Heaven thus exemplified and embodied all those maternal qualities which men had experienced as so warm and soul-filling in their own mothers (or which they perhaps had not experienced and so now desperately wanted) and which were generally absent in a male god that perhaps reflected a stern and rigid image of Victorian manhood. A national article excerpted in the *Deseret News* said that the world was coming to accept the idea of a Mother in Heaven. It spoke of the tendency for human beings to crave, especially in times of grief and anguish, the tenderness, gentleness, and sympathy of a mother-figure which must in some way "be resident in the divine Being."[23] And in the *Millennial Star* an article noted how not only small children but also adults need and want a mother figure as a divine personage. "The heart of man craves this faith and has from time immemorial demanded the deification of woman."[24]

But also in that first decade the Mormon church's teaching of the Mother in Heaven doctrine was criticized and challenged by the Salt Lake Ministerial Association in 1907 as being unchristian.[25] B. H. Roberts, one of the members of the Council of Seventy, responded by claiming that the ministers were inconsistent. They object to the idea of Jesus having a literal Heavenly Father, he said, but then they also complain because "we believe that we have for our spirits a heavenly mother as well as a heavenly father! Now observe the peculiar position of these critics," Roberts continued. "It is all right for Jesus to have a mother; but it is all wrong for him to have a father. On the other hand, it is all right for men's spirits to have a Father in heaven, but our reviewers object to our doctrine of their having a mother there."[26]

Two years later the First Presidency of the Mormon church issued a statement entitled "The Origin of Man." Although much of this message was concerned with explicating a Mormon view of man's (and woman's) earthly origins, the statement also took up the question of man's (and woman's) spiritual beginnings. While couching the doctrine partly in abstract generalities such as that "man, as a spirit, was begotten and born of heavenly parents," the statement also made a clear and explicit reference to a Mother in Heaven: "All men and women are in the similitude of the universal Father and Mother and are literally the sons and daughters of Deity."[27] By 1909, then, if not before, the Mother in Heaven was an official part of Mormon belief. Joseph Fielding Smith described this as one of (presumably several) "official and authoritative statements" about this doctrine.[28]

In the 1920s and 1930s, there seemed to be an emphasis on the idea of "eternal" motherhood or "everlasting" motherhood, with several sermons or articles having titles of this sort or dealing with this theme. Somehow it seemed important to emphasize that motherhood was as ongoing and eternal as was godhood. Apostle John A. Widtsoe, for example, found a "radiant warmth" in the "thought that among the exalted beings in the world to come we shall find a mother who possesses the attributes of Godhood. Such conceptions raise motherhood to a high position. They explain the generous provision made for women in the Church of Christ. To be a mother is to engage in the eternal work of God."[29]

Melvin J. Ballard carried on the theme of everlasting motherhood when he noted that "motherhood is eternal with Godhood, and there is no such thing as eternal or endless life without the eternal and endless continuation of motherhood." With more fervor than accuracy, Ballard claimed that there was not one single life form on earth without a mother; hence "there is no life in the realms that are above and beyond us, unless there also is a mother." Perhaps unaware of other strains of Christian thought—not to mention other cultures and religions which worshipped female deities— Ballard called the Mother in Heaven concept a "startling doctrine" which was "so far as I know, never taught before in the history of the world." He also emphasized the noble, goddess-like aspects of the Heavenly Mother. She stands side by side with the Heavenly Father "in all her glory, a glory like unto his . . . a companion, the Mother of his children." She is "a glorified, exalted, ennobled Mother."[30]

German Ellsworth, who served as president of the Northern States Mission during this period, also stressed the theme of "eternal motherhood" and noted that finally, after eighty years, the world was coming to accept the doctrine that if we had a Heavenly Father we must have had a Heavenly Mother as well. Ellsworth linked this doctrine specifically to the "true mission of women" on the earth, which was to be mothers. In particular, "the women of Zion can rejoice and take heart in the great calling given to them, in being privileged to be the earthly mothers of the elect sons of our Heavenly Father." The Mother in Heaven concept seems important to Ellsworth mainly as a role model for women, who were to help achieve the (by then dying) Progressive ideal by wanting to become mothers and seeking "to build up a better race—to successfully do their part in peopling the earth with a noble and intelligent class of citizens."[31] These examples share an attempt to raise the status of the mothering role, or of women specifically as mothers, by pointing out that the role of the Mother in Heaven is as important and eternal as that of God.

In the more recent period of the 1960s and 1970s we can see some widening out, with a greater variety of images presented by General Authorities who speak about a Mother in Heaven. Apostle and later church president Joseph Fielding Smith, much like Elizabeth Cady Stanton, quotes Genesis 1:26—"Let *us* make man in *our* image after our likeness" [*italics his*]—and suggests, "Is it not feasible to believe that female spirits were created in the image of a 'Mother in Heaven'?"[32] His emphasis implies that a female goddess was involved in the planning and decision making, was part of whatever group of exalted beings decided to create earthly men and women.

H. Burke Peterson of the Presiding Bishopric in 1974 emphasized the Heavenly Mother's role as producer of spirit offspring. In asking church members to count the cost of a mother working outside the home, he warned about the danger of becoming "a mother whose energy is so sapped that she is sometimes neglecting her call from the Lord, a call that will one day prepare her to become an eternal mother—a cocreator of spiritual offspring."[33] One supposes that by "her call" Bishop Peterson means the care of her children and is suggesting that the complex responsibility of nurturing and guiding one's children is the most valuable preparation for eventually becoming an exalted goddess-mother.

In 1978 then President Spencer W. Kimball expressed a view of the Mother in Heaven as "the ultimate in maternal modesty" and "restrained, queenly elegance." He also emphasized her great influence on us: "Knowing how profoundly our mortal mothers have shaped us here," he said, "do we suppose her influence on us as individuals to be less if we live so as to return there?"[34] Here we have maternal nurturing attributes and also a recognition of an exalted goddess quality in the Mother in Heaven.

At the same conference, Neal A. Maxwell, then a member of the First Quorum of the Seventy, presented this version of the role and activities of our Heavenly Mother: "When we return to our real home, it will be with the 'mutual approbation' of those who reign in the 'royal courts on high.' There we will find beauty such as mortal 'eye hath not seen'; we will hear sounds of surpassing music which mortal 'ear hath not heard.' Could such a regal homecoming be possible without the anticipatory arrangements of a Heavenly Mother?"[35]

"We honor woman when we acknowledge Godhood in her eternal Prototype," says an article in the 1910 *Millennial Star*.[36] This brief survey of some of the images which have been expressed about a less-than-well-defined entity suggest that one's concept of a Mother in Heaven may reflect one's views about real women and their roles. Those who see women as basically producers of babies might tend to emphasize the feminine deity's role as producer of spirit children. Those who consider women to be more refined and spiritual than men may emphasize the Heavenly Mother's nobility and queenly attributes—and so forth.

What seems to be happening currently in the development of the Mother in Heaven concept is an increasing awareness of and attention to the idea at the grass-roots level in the church—particularly among women and in informal ways.

A sampling of the poems submitted to the 1980 Eliza R. Snow Poetry contest sponsored by the Relief Society illustrates one strain of such thought. In the memory of one of the judges, that year was the first in which there were several poems submitted dealing with the subject of a Heavenly Mother. Collectively, these poems picture a Mother in Heaven who is the quintessence of femininity and nurturing motherhood. She has a "radiant face," a "soft firm voice." She is usually smiling although often her "gentle eyes fill with tears." Her spirit children learn wisdom at her knee. She gives tender goodbye kisses to her daughters as they leave for their earth missions. She advises them to set goals, overcome discouragement, take time to appreciate beauty—and in times of despair to call upon their Heavenly Father and Elder Brother for help and comfort. She is "the Father's cherished half" who "surely must merit His eternal love." She is described as a "Goddess, a Priestess, and a loving companion" and enough of a noble presence in the celestial realms that perhaps "the heavenly flowers bend with adoration" and "the animals await [her] caress."

There is considerable speculation in these poems about the Mother in Heaven's role in sending spirit children to earth. One poem has her announcing and justifying the departure times for various spirits. Another, in contrast, has a daughter running to tell the Mother the news of her impending departure. There is also speculation about what the Mother in Heaven's previous earth-life experience was like and the supposition that it was very much like our own.

Also evident in these poems is a vague sense of not really knowing enough to feel as close as one would like to the Heavenly Mother—wondering about her name and how we might react to it were we to know it, transferring the Father's attributes to her, yet realizing that she can only be apprehended "darkly" with a resultant feeling of unease and incompletion.

Although the content and style of these poems seem traditional or conventional as regards the Mother in Heaven role, the poems themselves are indicative of a wider interest in the concept of a Heavenly Mother among mainstream church members than has perhaps been usual.[37]

A recent cartoon circulating in manuscript shows a wife asking her husband, "What do you think Heavenly Mother's attitudes are about polygamy, Frank?" to which the husband responds, "Which Heavenly Mother?" A question to which there is as yet no definitive answer—but much speculation —is whether there is more than one Mother in Heaven. The Mormon church's doctrinal commitment to plural marriage as well as the exigencies of producing at least billions of spirit children suggest the probability— some believe necessity—of more than one Mother in Heaven. Apostle John Taylor, writing in answer to a question supposedly raised by a woman in the church, said in 1857 in the columns of a newspaper he was publishing in New York City: "Knowest thou not that eternities ago thy spirit, pure and holy, dwelt in thy Heavenly Father's bosom, and in his presence, and with thy mother, one of the Queens of heaven, surrounded by thy brother and sister spirits in the spirit world, among the Gods?"[38] The implication is that there is one Heavenly Father but several "Queens." More recently, a Department of Seminaries and Institutes student manual also hints at the possibility of multiple heavenly mothers. In a diagram entitled "Becoming a Spirit Child of Heavenly Parents," the individual person (male) is depicted with upward lines to his heavenly parents, the one parent labeled "Heavenly Father" (caps), the other labeled "A heavenly mother" (lower case).[39]

Lately there has also been increased discussion and speculation about how we can or do relate to our Heavenly Mother (or possibly Mothers?). Orson Pratt, an apostle called by Joseph Smith, taught that we are not to worship the mother of our spirits although we worship the father, "for the Father of our spirit is the head of His household, and His wives and children are required to yield the most perfect obedience to their great Head. It is lawful for the children to worship the King of heaven, but not the 'Queen of heaven.'" Pratt went on to point out that "Jesus prayed to His father, and taught His disciples to do likewise; but we are nowhere taught that Jesus prayed to His Heavenly Mother."[40] In 1910 Apostle Rudger Clawson, however, pointed out that men as well as women and children crave a Mother in Heaven to worship and "yearn to adore her." He said, "It doesn't take from our worship of the Eternal Father, to adore our Eternal Mother, any more than it diminishes the love we bear our earthly fathers, to include our earthly mothers in our affections."[41] Currently there is no encouragement on the part of Mormon church leaders to pray to a Heavenly Mother. Whether one can worship or adore her without the mechanism of prayer and/or meditation is an open question.

Still, there has been recently a more evident desire to reach out to Mother in Heaven in some way. A letter to the editor of *Dialogue* in 1974 told of a Mormon woman spending preparatory time in meditation, kneeling privately to pray, and then calling out for the first time, "'Mother in Heaven. I believe you may exist. Are you there? We know the Father and the Son, but why have you not revealed yourself?' And a wondrous voice clearly answered,

'Good daughter. Until this time, no one asked. The men have not thought to ask.' ”[42]

More women are now wondering and asking. In *Exponent II* Lisa Bolin Hawkins expressed in a poem a prayerful reaching out to ask Heavenly Mother to reveal herself and provide women with an adequate role model of goddesshood:

Another Prayer

Why are you silent, Mother? How can I
Become a goddess when the patterns here
Are those of gods? I struggle, and I try
To mold my womanself to something near
Their goodness. I need you, who gave me birth
In your own image, to reveal your ways:
A rich example of thy daughters' worth;
Pillar of Womanhood to guide our days;
Fire of power and grace to guide my night
When I am lost.
My brothers question me,
And wonder why I seek this added light.
No one can answer all my pain but Thee,
Ordain me to my womanhood, and share
The light that Queens and Priestesses must bear.[43]

This poem expresses the need which a Heavenly Mother can fill that a male deity cannot and suggests attributes of both nurturance and spiritual power, as in the concept of "ordaining" her daughters and sharing special spiritual light with them.

Other current expressions extend the image of a Heavenly Mother even further. Linda Sillitoe's recent poem is a good example:

Song of Creation

Who made the world, my child?
Father made the rain
silver and forever.
Mother's hand
drew riverbeds and hollowed seas,
drew riverbeds and hollowed seas
to bring the rain home.

Father bridled winds, my child,
to keep the world new.
Mother clashed
fire free from stones
and breathed it strong and dancing,
and breathed it strong and dancing
the color of her hair.

He armed the thunderclouds
rolled out of heaven;
Her fingers flickered
hummingbirds
weaving the delicate white snow,
weaving the delicate white snow,
a waterfall of flowers.

And if you live long, my child,
you'll see snow burst
from thunderclouds
and lightning in the snow;
listen to Mother and Father laughing,
listen to Mother and Father laughing
behind the locked door.[44]

Here is a Heavenly Mother who is a full partner and cocreator with the Father (of something other than babies), making riverbeds and seas for the rain he makes, creating fire and other elements on an equal basis with him—a competent, productive female figure who is also a sexual being, even outside of the context of bearing spirit children. Images such as this of a Heavenly Mother, reflecting strength, competence, sexuality, and mutuality, are still rare.

So what can be said about Mormon theology concerning a Heavenly Mother? At present the nineteenth-century generalized image of a female counterpart to a literal male father-god is receiving increased attention and expansion and is becoming more personalized and individualized. The widening "theology" which is developing is more of a "folk," or at least speculative, theology than a systematic development by theologians or a set of definitive pronouncements from ecclesiastical leaders. For the moment, Mother in Heaven can be almost whatever an individual Mormon envisions her to be. Perhaps ironically, we thus set her up, despite herself, to fill the most basic maternal role of all—that of meeting the deepest needs of her children, whatever they might be.

NOTES

1. There are a few instances of feminine imagery of God in Christian scripture, such as Isaiah 66:13 ("As one whom his mother comforteth, so will I comfort you; and ye shall be comforted in Jerusalem") and Matthew 23:37 ("how often would I have gathered thy children together, even as a hen gathereth her chickens under her wings, and ye would not!"). These verses were brought to my attention by Melodie Moench Charles.

2. See Elaine H. Pagels, "What Became of God the Mother? Conflicting Images of God in Early Christianty," *Signs* (Winter 1976): 293–303.

3. See Elizabeth Clark and Herbert Richardson, "Dame Julian of Norwich and

Margery Kempe: Divine Motherhood and Human Sisterhood," in *Women and Religion: A Feminist Sourcebook of Christian Thought* (New York: Harper & Row, 1977), pp. 102-12.

4. Ibid., p. 164.

5. Elizabeth Cady Stanton, *The Woman's Bible*, pt. 1 (1895-98; reprint ed., New York: Arno Press, 1972), p. 218.

6. Maureen Ursenbach Beecher, "The Eliza Enigma: The Life and Legend of Eliza R. Snow," in *Essays on the American West, 1974-75*, ed. Thomas G. Alexander, Charles Redd Monographs on Western History, no. 6 (Provo, Utah: Brigham Young University Press, 1976), p. 34; *Times and Seasons* 6 (15 November 1845): 1039.

7. Wilford Woodruff, "Discourse," 1893, *Millennial Star* 56 (April 1894): 229.

8. Joseph F. Smith, "Discourse," *Deseret Evening News*, 9 February 1895. I am indebted to Maureen Ursenbach Beecher for much information regarding Eliza R. Snow and the Mother in Heaven doctrine. As Boyd Kirtland has noted, a number of sources suggest that Eliza R. Snow and Brigham Young believed Eve to be the Mother in Heaven. Letter to the editor, *Sunstone* 6 (March-April 1981): 4-5.

9. Susa Young Gates, *History of the Young Ladies' Mutual Improvement Association* (Salt Lake City: General Board of the YLMIA, 1911), pp. 15-16.

10. The debate has continued, however. B. H. Roberts spoke of "that splendid hymn of ours on heavenly motherhood, the great throbbing hunger of woman's soul, and which was given to this world through the inspired mind of Eliza R. Snow." Perhaps, however, he was referring only to the poem, not the doctrine. *Answer to Ministerial Association Review,* delivered at two meetings of M.I.A. Conference, 9 June 1907 (Salt Lake City: Church of Jesus Christ of Latter-day Saints, 1907), p. 18. Melvin J. Ballard, however, considered the Mother in Heaven concept a revelation given by Jesus Christ through Joseph Smith. Mother's Day address in Tabernacle, 8 May 1921, Journal History, typescript, Historical Department Archives of the Church of Jesus Christ of Latter-day Saints, Salt Lake City, hereafter cited as LDS Church Archives, same date, pp. 1-3. Apostle Milton R. Hunter in 1945 claimed that the doctrine of a Mother in Heaven originated with Joseph Smith, ascribing to him revelations by which "a more complete understanding of man— especially regarding his personal relationship to Deity—was received than could be found in all of the holy scriptures combined." Among such new understandings was the "stupendous truth of the existence of a Heavenly Mother" and the "complete realization that we are the offspring of Heavenly Parents." Hunter said that these ideas became "established facts in Mormon theology" and an "integral part of Mormon philosophy." *The Gospel Through the Ages* (Salt Lake City: Stevens and Wallis, Inc., 1945), pp. 98-99.

11. David McKay to Mrs. James Hood, 16 March 1916, photocopy of holograph in the files of Maureen Ursenbach Beecher, courtesy of Shirley Bailey.

12. Abraham H. Cannon, Journal, 25 August 1980, LDS Church Archives.

13. Brigham Young, 18 June 1865, *Journal of Discourses*, 26 vols. (Liverpool: Franklin D. Richards et al., 1855-86), 11:122, hereafter cited as *JD,* with speaker and date.

14. Idem., 23 February 1862, *JD* 9:286.

15. Erastus Snow, 31 May 1885, *JD* 26:214.

16. Idem., 3 March 1878, *JD* 19:269-70.

17. Bruce R. McConkie, *Mormon Doctrine* (Salt Lake City: Bookcraft, 1966), p. 516. Also, Doctrine and Covenants 132 states that one cannot be a god without entering into the holy order of marriage and this implies both a father and a mother god.

18. Hugh B. Brown, "Relief Society—An Extension of the Home," address delivered at the general session of the Relief Society Annual Conference, 27 September 1961, *Relief Society Magazine* 48 (December 1961): 814.

19. Joseph Fielding Smith, *Answers to Gospel Questions*, 5 vols. (Salt Lake City: Deseret Book, 1960) 3:142.

20. Melvin R. Brooks, *LDS Reference Encyclopedia* (Salt Lake City: Bookcraft, 1960), pp. 309-10.

21. James E. Talmage, speech in Tabernacle on 27 April 1902, *Deseret News,* 28 April 1902.

22. "The Divine Feminine," *Deseret News,* 4 February 1905.

23. George Barlow, "On the Dual Nature of Deity," *Contemporary Review* 87 (January 1905): 83, excerpted in "The Divine Feminine," *Deseret News,* 4 February 1905.

24. "Our Mother in Heaven," *LDS Millennial Star* 72 (29 September 1910): 619.

25. "Ministerial Association's Review of Mormon Address to the World," from text in the *Salt Lake Herald,* 4 June 1907, p. 8.

26. B. H. Roberts, "Answer to Ministerial Association Review," delivered at MIA Conference, Salt Lake City, 9 June 1907, in *An Address: The Church of Jesus Christ of Latter-day Saints to the World* (Salt Lake City: Church of Jesus Christ of Latter-day Saints, 1907), pp. 18-19.

27. First Presidency (Joseph F. Smith, John R. Winder, Anthon H. Lund), "The Origin of Man," *Improvement Era* 13 (November 1909): 80.

28. Joseph Fielding Smith, "Mothers in Israel," address delivered at the general session of Relief Society Annual Conference, 30 September 1970, *Relief Society Magazine* 57 (December 1970): 884.

29. John A. Widtsoe, "Everlasting Motherhood," *LDS Millennial Star* 90 (10 May 1928): 298.

30. Melvin J. Ballard, address in Tabernacle, 8 May 1921, Journal History, LDS Church Archives, same date, pp. 1-3.

31. German E. Ellsworth, "Eternal Motherhood," *Deseret News,* 7 May 1932, Journal History, same date, p. 5.

32. Smith, *Answers to Gospel Questions* 3:144.

33. H. Burke Peterson, General Conference address, 5 April 1974, *Ensign* 4 (May 1974): 32.

34. Spencer W. Kimball, General Conference address, 1 April 1978, *Ensign* 8 (May 1978): 6.

35. Neal A. Maxwell, General Conference address, 1 April 1978, *Ensign* 8 (May 1978): 11.

36. "Our Mother in Heaven," *LDS Millennial Star* 72 (29 September 1910): 620.

37. Direct quotes are from the following poems: Sydney Lee Harmer, "My Heavenly Mother"; Nancy Anderson, "Heavenly Mother"; Janet E. Nichols, "The Farewell." General comments are based on the above poems plus two others: Lynda Jacobs Gardner, "My Heavenly Mother," and Patricia Michell Sylvestre, "My

Mother in Heaven." A somewhat similar picture of a heavenly Mother as she nurtures, teaches, comforts, and plays with her daughter Eve in her spirit childhood appears in Marsha Newman's *Reflections of Eve and Her Daughters* (Concord, Calif.: Wellspring, 1981). In these writings, however, the Mother plays no part either in Eve's creation or in the special blessing and assignment given her as she is sent to earth; the Father is the only parent involved in and responsible for these landmark events.

38. [John Taylor], "Origin, Object, and Destiny of Women," *The Mormon*, 29 August 1857.

39. *Book of Mormon Student Manual*, 2 vols. (Salt Lake City: Church Educational System, 1976) 1:218.

40. Orson Pratt, "Celestial Marriage," *The Seer* 1 (October 1853): 159.

41. Rudger Clawson was the editor and publisher at the time and so was probably responsible for the unsigned article, "Our Mother in Heaven," *LDS Millennial Star* 72 (29 September 1910): 619–20.

42. Letter to the editor, *Dialogue: A Journal of Mormon Thought* 7 (Autumn 1974): 7.

43. Lisa Bolin Hawkins, "Another Prayer," *Exponent II* 6 (Winter 1980): 16.

44. Linda Sillitoe, "Song of Creation," *Dialogue: A Journal of Mormon Thought* 12 (Winter 1979): 95.

MARYANN MACMURRAY

Oil upon Oil

Like the sound of laying the warp, whispered names
resonate within the grained, muraled, marble
and curtain walls of this holy place, and veil
the light and air with your form, hands
and face. Mother, sister, friend, I look for you here and hear
your voice in the water's cool promise of oil.

Innocence and experience rainbow in the slow oil,
palmed from the silver ladle, the small bowl. Names,
like holiness, converge to the center place; I hear
them and see your image layered on the marble
partitions; for years now, neither light nor hands
have removed that shadow. Look, you still veil

this place: diaphanous or opaque, the veil
of yourself is warm and scented yet with the oil.
Looking down the rows, I recognize your hands,
or ahead in the lines following Eve, whose names
I breathe, I see the lines of your marble
gestures; if you only whispered, I would hear

our conversations interlacing the covenants we hear,
counterpointing the ordinances we veil.
Fleshed and robed, names rustle toward the curtain of marble
questions, the altars of profound intention, the oil
of the inner sanctuary, and who seals the promise and names
the unspeakable in the true tent made with hands—

before us, the High Priest entered One made without hands;
A lamp mirrors the gold horn and the water we hear
splashing a bead upon the Silences who name:
Is not this a brand plucked from the burning, who veil:

the tree of life in the mount of granite and the oil
of victory. I will watch here at the marble

wall. I will wait for you to ascend the marble
stair; I will not vision other-world hands
or another day to do this: to taste the oil;
I, too, will not be comforted until I hear:
The day of the righteous is come. I cannot veil:
Here is the last place, now the last time, and ours the last names.

Emma, Joseph, Sarah, Abraham, whose hands part this veil,
whose ears hear the New Song, who soften with oil
the bruised hands and marble feet and wrestle for the Names.

Reprinted with permission from *Dialogue* 17 (Autumn 1984): 156-57.

CAROL CORNWALL MADSEN

Mormon Women and the Temple: Toward a New Understanding

On 28 April 1842 Joseph Smith attended the sixth meeting of the newly organized Female Relief Society in Nauvoo, Illinois. To the women assembled in the lodge room on the second floor of his store, all selected by unanimous vote, he presented a sermon on the priesthood, showing how the sisters would come in possession of its privileges, blessings, and gifts.[1] Twice during the sermon he prophetically announced that "they would not long have him to instruct them" and that he was about to give to them, as well as to the elders and the church, the keys of the kingdom "that they would be able to detect every thing false." He also said that he was going to instruct the women how to conduct themselves so that they might act according to the will of God. "I now turn the key to you in the name of God," he further declared, "and this society shall rejoice and knowledge and intelligence shall flow down from this time — this is the beginning of better days to this Society."[2]

Joseph Smith's charge to the women was twofold. Turning the key to them was a delegation of "a portion of the keys of the kingdom," Apostle Bruce R. McConkie explained in 1950, by which the officers were authorized to direct, control, and govern the affairs of the society. They thus became "legal administrators holding the keys of presidency."[3] The other delegation of keys that day, however, was of broader significance. The "keys of the kingdom" he was soon to give them would open the way to their salvation and eventual exaltation. That day they received an intimation of what would be theirs when the fulness of the gospel was finally and completely restored. Reynolds Cahoon confirmed Joseph's intent in an 1843 sermon to the Relief Society: "You knew no doubt [that] this society is raisd [sic] by the Lord to prepare us for the great blessings which are for us in the House of the Lord in the Temple."[4] The women of the church soon learned about "the great blessings" awaiting them in the temple but not wholly through the Relief Society. Only the promise of what he would yet reveal to them did Joseph give during his few visits to the new society in 1842.

Mormon women were already aware of the importance of the temple in Mormon theology. Although they did not receive any of the special "endowments of power" or ordinances given in the Kirtland Temple several years before, they had contributed to its furnishings by their own handiwork and had participated in the outpourings of the spirit manifest at its dedication in 1836. The ordinances performed there were primarily to empower the elders of the church in connection with their proselyting and ecclesiastical callings. In 1853 Brigham Young, Joseph Smith's successor, explained the differences between those and later temple ordinances: "Though accompanied by the ministrations of angels and the presence of the Lord Jesus they [the ordinances] were but a faint similitude of the ordinances of the House of the Lord in their fulness."[5] Orson Pratt, a member of the Quorum of the Twelve under both Joseph Smith and Brigham Young, also sought to clarify the distinction between Kirtland Temple ordinances and later ones: "When the [Kirtland] temple was built, the Lord did not see proper to reveal all the ordinances of the Endowment, such as we now understand. He revealed little by little. No rooms were prepared for washings; no special place prepared for the anointings, such as you understand, and such as you comprehend at this period of the history of the Church! Neither did we know the necessity of the washings, such as we now receive."[6] As Apostle George A. Smith explained in 1855, it was necessary for the Saints to be properly prepared before receiving knowledge of the saving ordinances; he added that Joseph Smith would have revealed more during the Kirtland period if the people had been sufficiently receptive to his teachings.[7]

Besides their peripheral involvement with the Kirtland Temple, Mormon women, along with all members of the church, were taught in the early days in Nauvoo a major principle of temple worship by Joseph Smith—vicarious work, by which living persons could perform essential ordinances on behalf of the dead. Teaching them the purpose and necessity of baptism for the dead, he opened doors for the spiritual reunion of families that had lost members to death or, as was common among early converts, had been estranged when loved ones joined the church, never to meet again in life. Baptism for the dead, followed by vicarious endowments and sealings, made possible the reuniting of families for eternity. One of the first to use this principle was Jane Newman, who was baptized for her dead son Cyrus just a month after the introduction of this ordinance. Emma Smith was baptized for her father, Isaac Hale, in 1841, and Emmeline Wells was baptized for her dead father.[8] At first no gender distinctions were made in the performance of vicarious ordinances, but in 1845 Brigham Young explained that "all men must be redeemed by men, that are found worthy and the women are to be redeemed, women acting for and in their behalf."[9]

The principle of vicarious work and the extended role of the Saints as "saviours on Mount Zion" brought hope and reassurance to those who recognized that now salvation was available not only to long-dead progenitors but, of more immediate concern, to deceased wives, husbands, and children. Sally Randall was one of those who gratefully received the new doctrine. Her eldest son had died soon after the family arrived in Nauvoo from their home in New England, and the knowledge that he could receive baptism, with her husband acting as proxy, was joyously reassuring to her. She eagerly shared her happiness with her non-Mormon mother in New England: "What a glorious thing it is that we believe and receive the fulness of the gospel as it is preached now and can be baptized for all our dead friends and save them as far back as we can get any knowledge of them. . . . O mother, if we are so happy as to have a part in the first resurrection, we shall have our children just as we laid them down in their graves."[10]

In the absence of baptismal fonts, all baptisms for the living and for the dead were performed in rivers and lakes. But in January 1841, when Joseph Smith announced the revelation on temple work, he made clear that, except in the "days of your poverty," baptisms for the dead were acceptable only in the Lord's house. Nevertheless, he explained, baptisms in natural fonts would continue to be valid until the temple was completed. Moreover, it is evident from this revelation that all of the saving ordinances were to be restored at this time, "even the fulness of the priesthood." Significantly, these ordinances this time were to be available to both women and men: "And verily I say unto you, let this house be built unto my name, that I may reveal mine ordinances unto my people; for I deign to reveal unto my church, things which have been kept hid from before the foundation of the world; things that pertain to the dispensation of the fulness of times."[11]

The cornerstone of the Nauvoo Temple was laid on 6 April 1841 and construction began immediately. As with the Kirtland Temple, women became involved at the outset. Mercy Fielding Thompson sought inspiration to know how she could assist. "Try to get the Sisters to subscribe one Cent per Week for the purpose of buying glass and nails for the Temple," was the answer which came to her. She went immediately to Joseph Smith and told him "what seemed to be the whispering of the still small voice." He told her to follow that prompting. She received assistance from her sister, Mary Fielding, and Mary's husband, Hyrum Smith, Joseph's brother, who "did all in his power to encourage and help by speaking to the Sisters on the subject . . . promising them that they should receive their blessings in that Temple." Mercy also enlisted the aid of female church members in England through a notice in the *Millennial Star* in June 1844. Twenty English pounds were raised and forwarded to Nauvoo.[12] The names of all who subscribed were recorded in the "Book of the Law of the Lord," and notwithstanding the poverty of the people at that time, Mercy and Mary were able to accumulate nearly $1000.[13]

As the temple neared completion toward the end of 1845, women made cushions and upholstery, laid carpet, and prepared the rooms for the endowment.[14] Sarah Kimball's interest in contributing to the temple cause found a novel expression. Three days after the birth of her infant son she asked her husband, Hiram, a well-to-do merchant and non-Mormon, what he thought the child was worth. When he did not readily respond she suggested the sum of a thousand dollars. "More than that if he lives," the loving father agreed. "And half of him is mine?" He agreed again. "Then I have something to help on the Temple . . . and I think of turning my share right in as tithing." Some days later, Hiram related the conversation to Joseph Smith. "I accept all such donations," Joseph promptly answered, "and from this day the boy shall stand recorded, *Church property.*" Then he added, "You now have the privilege of paying $500 and retaining possession, or receiving $500 and giving possession." Hiram Kimball readily deeded to Joseph a piece of property well worth the $500, thereby gaining title to his child and closing the transaction.[15] Sarah was pleased.

Joseph Smith had contemplated at great length the blessings that would come to the church when the temple was completed. Early in January 1842, two months before the Relief Society was organized, he wrote of his expectations for the coming year:

> The Saints seem to be influenced by a kind and indulgent Providence in their dispositions and [blessed] with means to rear the Temple of the Most High God, anxiously looking forth to the completion thereof as an event of the greatest importance to the Church and the world. . . . Truly this is a day long to be remembered by the Saints of the last days,—a day in which the God of heaven has begun to restore the ancient order of His kingdom unto His servants and His people,—a day in which all things are concurring to bring about the completion of the fulness of the Gospel, a fulness of the dispensation of dispensations, even the fulness of times . . . to prepare the earth for the return of His glory, even a celestial glory, and a kingdom of Priests and kings to God and the Lamb, forever, on Mount Zion.[16]

Thus, by the time the Relief Society was organized in March 1842, the women of the church were well acquainted with the significance of temple work and anticipated the completion of the temple in Nauvoo, where they would be able to receive the saving ordinances of the gospel and perform them for their deceased loved ones. While these ordinances were applicable to both men and women and promised the same level of exaltation to both, they had particular significance to women. They opened up a new concept of spiritual participation relating to the "privileges, blessings and gifts of the priesthood" which not only enhanced their position in the church but offered limitless potential in the hereafter.

It is evident from several of the Prophet's messages to the Relief Society during his nine visits in 1842 that its organization was but another step toward preparing the women of the church to receive the fulness of the gospel. At the 30 March meeting, he instructed the women that "none should be received into the Society but those who were worthy." He "propos'd that the Society go into a close examination of every candidate—that they were going too fast—that the Society should grow up by degrees—should commence with a few individuals—thus have a select Society of the virtuous and those who will walk circumspectly."[17] At that time the Society had indeed grown—from twenty to seventy-six members in less than two weeks—and would continue to grow in spite of Joseph Smith's urging for restraint. His concluding remarks at that meeting are a direct reference to the imminent introduction of the temple ordinances. He told the women that "the Society should move according to the ancient Priesthood, hence there should be a select Society separate from all the evils of the world, choice, virtuous, and holy." Then, drawing upon the very words he had written two months earlier, he told the sisters that he "was going to make of this Society a 'kingdom of priests' as in Enoch's day—as in Paul's day."[18] Years later, Bathsheba W. Smith, an original member and later fourth general president of the Relief Society, remarked on that sermon: "The sisters flocked to our meetings every week, and the prophet Joseph met with us as long as he could. . . . He said he had given the sisters instructions that they could administer to the sick and he wanted to make us, as the women were in Paul's day, 'A kingdom of priestesses.' We have the ceremony in our endowments as Joseph taught."[19] Mercy Thompson also recalled Joseph's teachings to the Relief Society: "I have been present at meetings of the Relief Society and heard him give directions and counsels to the sisters, calculated to inspire them to efforts which would lead to celestial glory and exaltation, and oh! how my heart rejoiced."[20] By the time Joseph Smith met with the Relief Society for the sixth time, on 28 April 1842 when he spoke of giving them the keys of the kingdom, it was clear that he was exhorting them to put their lives in order to receive the "knowledge and intelligence" that he would soon reveal to them.

Less than two weeks later, 4 May 1842, Joseph Smith gave some of that "knowledge and intelligence" to nine selected men who met with him in the upper room of his store, where he instructed them in the "principles and order of the Priesthood." During that meeting he attended to "washings, anointings, endowments and the communications of keys pertaining to the Aaronic Priesthood, and so on to the highest order of the Melchizedek Priesthood, setting forth the order pertaining to the Ancient of Days, and all those plans and principles by which any one is enabled to secure the fulness of those blessings which have been prepared for the Church of the First Born, and come up and abide in the presence of the Eloheim in the eternal worlds. In this council was instituted the ancient order of things for the first time in these last days."[21]

He explained on that occasion that such things were spiritual and to be received only by the spiritually minded and that these things would be made known to all the Saints as soon as they were prepared to receive them and a proper place established to communicate them. This gathering was the first of several meetings of the "Holy Order" or "Quorum of the Anointed," as the group came to be known by its members.[22] It was the formal beginning of the administration of temple ordinances performed in Mormon temples throughout the world today, the initiation of the ritual of the endowment.

Three weeks later, on 27 May 1842, Bishop Newel K. Whitney, one of the nine men who received this knowledge from Joseph Smith, exuberantly addressed the Relief Society about the blessings that awaited them. The secretary recorded that he "rejoic'd at the formation of the society that we might improve our talents and to prepare for those blessings which God is soon to bestow upon us." Then he explained:

> In the beginning God created man male and female and bestow'd upon man certain blessings peculiar to a man of God, of which woman partook, so that without the female all things cannot be restor'd to the earth—it takes all to restore the Priesthood. It [this restoration] is the interest of the Society, [that] by humility and faithfulness, in connexion with husbands [they may be] found worthy, Rejoice while contemplating the blessing which will be pour'd out on the heads of the saints. God has many precious things to bestow, even to our astonishment if we are faithful. . . . I rejoice that God has given us means whereby we may get intelligence and instruction. It is our privilege to stand in an attitude to get testimony for ourselves—it is as much our privilege as that of the ancient saints. I tell you there are blessings [ahead] to be confer'd as soon as our hearts are prepar'd to receive them.[23]

While the syntax is not always complete, the message was very clear: women were as essential to the restoration of all things as were men and both would experience the promised blessings of the temple ordinances.

On 28 September 1843 Emma Smith, wife of the Prophet Joseph, received her endowment in the Holy Order, the first woman in this dispensation to receive it. In the ensuing months, additional women as well as men joined the Holy Order and received their temple endowments, membership in the Holy Order eventually reaching approximately sixty-five before the Prophet's death in June 1844.[24] The endowment group was deliberately kept small, Joseph Smith explained, in order to restrict the knowledge of these sacred ordinances until the temple was completed and all worthy members could receive them in a properly dedicated edifice.[25]

Even before receiving their endowments, some members of the Holy

Order had been introduced to the covenant of eternal marriage. The earliest account of a "sealing," or marriage for eternity, is that of Heber and Vilate Kimball. In 1841, as the doctrine of polygamy was beginning to be privately taught and practiced, Joseph Smith had requested that Heber give him Vilate as a plural wife. After three agonizing days of prayer and fasting, Heber took Vilate to Joseph. The Prophet wept at this demonstration of obedience and faith, then sealed Heber and Vilate together for time and eternity.[26] Newel K. and Elizabeth Ann Whitney were sealed in eternal marriage in August 1842. Joseph and Emma Smith were sealed in May 1843, and several other couples were sealed the following day. Other members of the Holy Order were sealed in marriage after receiving their endowments.[27]

Acting with the sealing powers conferred upon him in the Kirtland Temple,[28] Joseph Smith both performed sealings and delegated the sealing power to others before the completion of the Nauvoo Temple. Thus, before the revelation on eternal marriage was put in written form in July 1843, a small group of Mormon couples not only knew of the principle but had actually been sealed in marriage for eternity.

In the fall of 1843 Elizabeth Ann Whitney, wife of Bishop Newel K. Whitney and a member of the Holy Order with her husband, became the second woman to receive her endowments. On 17 January 1844 she gave birth to the first child, a girl whom the Prophet named Mary, born "heir to the Holy Priesthood and in the New and Everlasting Covenant in this dispensation."[29] Having been "sealed" or married to her husband for eternity in 1842, Elizabeth could also claim an eternal relationship with her children. At a time of high infant mortality, the principle of an eternal familial bond was a coveted blessing.

When women began to join the Holy Order, Emma Smith, as the first woman to receive the temple ordinances and as wife of the Prophet, presided over both the Relief Society and those women ordained to perform temple ordinances. Had the temple been completed before her husband's death in June 1844, she and Joseph may well have presided there as president and presidentess, a commonly used nineteenth-century term for the position now known as temple matron. Three other women would also preside simultaneously over the Relief Society and the female temple ordinance workers: Eliza R. Snow (1866–87), Zina D. H. Young (1888–1901), and Bathsheba W. Smith (1901–10).

The opportunity to meet in the Holy Order, to gain instruction from the Prophet himself in these sacred matters, and to receive the temple ordinances under his personal direction and authority was highly prized by this select group of faithful Saints. Mercy Fielding Thompson remembered the Prophet Joseph telling her at the time she received her endowment that "this will bring you out of darkness into marvellous light."[30] Bathsheba W. Smith recalled her first attendance at the Holy Order meetings in December 1843.

"I received the ordinance of anointing in a room in Sister Emma Smith's house in Nauvoo," she recalled, "and the same day, in company with my husband, I received my endowment in the upper room over the Prophet Joseph Smith's store. The endowments were given under the direction of the Prophet Joseph Smith, who afterwards gave us a lecture or instructions in regard to the endowment ceremonies." She frequently referred to her experiences in the Holy Order and the great opportunity it was to be "led and taught . . . by the Prophet himself who explained and enlarged wonderfully upon every point as they passed along the way."[31]

Joseph Smith's sense of impending death, expressed to the Relief Society and on other occasions to members of the Twelve, undoubtedly compelled him to reveal these saving ordinances before the Nauvoo Temple was completed. Praying with the Holy Order that "his days might be prolonged until his mission on the earth [was] accomplished,"[32] he insured fulfillment of this prayer by giving this chosen group all of the final, necessary elements of the gospel.

The deaths of Joseph and Hyrum Smith in June 1844 did not terminate the meetings of the Holy Order. In fact, additional members were invited to join the group and receive their ordinances from Brigham Young, who had been given the sealing powers by Joseph Smith.[33] On Sunday, 7 December 1845, the attic story of the temple was sufficiently completed for the first meeting of the Holy Order in the temple itself. Forty-two members met on a snowy winter morning to sing, pray, and partake of the sacrament, the holy eucharist. Several of the brethren spoke and the group decided to meet each Sunday morning in the temple for a sacrament meeting. "Great solemnity rested upon the brethren and sisters," wrote Heber C. Kimball. There was "great union in our meeting."[34]

The Sunday assembly grew rapidly as newly endowed members were invited to attend. It was soon obvious that as temple ordinances became available to all worthy church members in the completed temple there was no longer a need for a select Holy Order, and it met only four times in the temple. During this period all of the still-faithful members of that group who had previously received their endowments under Joseph Smith or Brigham Young repeated them in the temple. Mary Ann Young (Brigham's wife), Vilate Kimball (Heber's wife), and Elizabeth Ann Whitney (Newel K.'s wife) were the first women both to receive and perform the initiatory rites in the Nauvoo Temple, officiating in the ordinances for one another. Lucy Mack Smith, mother of the Prophet Joseph, also "went through the Holy Ordinances" in the Nauvoo Temple, a repetition of her previous endowment in October 1843.[35] In the brief period of three months from December 1845 to February 1846, more than five thousand endowments were performed and nearly three thousand sealings for the living. Among the thirty-six women who officiated as "priestesses" in that temple were some of the original members of the Holy Order such as Mercy Fielding Thompson, Elizabeth Ann Whitney, Bathsheba W. Smith, Mary Ann Young, and Vilate Kimball.

Thus the introduction of temple ordinances in Nauvoo opened not only to the privileged few of the Holy Order but to all worthy Mormon women a new understanding of their place in the plan of salvation and in the church. They joyously received temple ordinances for the new dimension of spiritual life and hope they offered. They accepted the opportunity to participate in temple work as an honor and cherished the sacredness of their temple experiences.

"O Praise the Lord for all his goodness, y[ea] his mercies endureth forever. Exalt his holy name for he hath no end. He hath established his work upon the Earth no more to be throne down. He will r[em]ember all his covenants to fulfill them in there times. O Praise the Lord Forever more, Amen." [36] Thus did Zina D. Huntington Young offer her own psalm of thanksgiving to the Lord for the restoration of the gospel. It was 24 May 1845 and on that day, she recorded, "the last stone was lade on the Temple with shouts of Hosanah to God and the Lamb." With the other Saints of Nauvoo she had looked forward to the completion of the temple, so that every faithful member of the church would be able to receive its saving ordinances. There, according to promise, they would be endowed with power from on high, "a power," John A. Widtsoe later explained, "based on enlarged knowledge and intelligence . . . of a quality with God's own power." [37] The temple, as many Saints already knew, would be a place where their baptisms for the dead would be performed, indeed, "where the keys of the priesthood would be committed in abundance." [38] Joseph Smith had already taught the Saints in 1832 that the priesthood was central to the administration of temple ordinances. "This greater priesthood [Melchizedek] administereth the gospel and holdeth the keys of the mysteries of the kingdom, even the key of the knowledge of God," [39] he had explained, and only through the ordinances of this priesthood, they learned, could they hope to regain the presence of God.

When he explained the nature of priesthood to his apostles in 1839 before they began their ministry abroad, Joseph reaffirmed the inseparability of priesthood and ordinance: "If there is no change of ordinances, there is no change of Priesthood. Wherever the ordinances of the Gospel are administered, there is the Priesthood." [40] Later, he identified patriarchal authority as a specific kind of priesthood related to the temple. "Go to and finish the temple," he promised "and God will fill it with power, and you will then receive more knowledge concerning this [patriarchal] Priesthood." [41] Patriarchal authority, associated with the sealing powers delivered to Joseph Smith by Elijah in the Kirtland Temple, is the authority that links generation to generation in an eternal priesthood bond.

As the message of the temple became clearer, the Saints came to understand that it was not enough to live Christ-like lives and to develop their own private relationship with the Savior. As meritorious as this life pattern might be, it alone could not assure them a place in the celestial kingdom, the dwelling place of the Father. However, accompanied by the saving ordinances of the gospel, it promised a meaningful life here and eternal life hereafter. Thus in Mormon doctrine the temple is the heart and core of the gospel, and all else derives meaning and purpose from it. Yet not all were ready to receive this saving knowledge. "There are a great many wise men and women too in our midst," Joseph Smith lamented, "who are too wise to be taught; therefore they must die in their ignorance, and in the resurrection they will find their mistake. Many seal up the door to heaven by saying, So far God may reveal and I will believe."[42] Had the Saints been more spiritually prepared, Joseph explained, he could have revealed more to them sooner than he did.[43] Although he did not live to see the completion of the Nauvoo Temple, where these priesthood ordinances would be appropriately performed, Joseph Smith left behind both the authority for and the knowledge of every element of temple work. As Zina Young had exclaimed in 1845: "He hath established his work uppon the Earth no more to be throne down."

The ordinances and rites of the temple are held sacred by Latter-day Saints and are thus guarded by vows of secrecy. Yet much has been publicly written and spoken about them in an effort to provide understanding of their significance in the lives of church members. John A. Widtsoe has given one of the most explicit descriptions of the temple ceremony: "The Temple Endowment relates the story of man's eternal journey; sets forth the conditions upon which progress in the eternal journey depends; requires covenants or agreements of those participating, to accept and use the laws of progress; gives tests by which our willingness and fitness for righteousness may be known, and finally points out the ultimate destiny of those who love truth and live by it."[44]

Temple covenants, James E. Talmage explains, are obligations "to observe the law of strict virtue and chastity, to be charitable, benevolent, tolerant and pure; to devote both talent and material means to the spread of truth and the uplifting of the race; to maintain devotion to the cause of truth; and to seek in every way to contribute to the great preparation that the earth may be made ready to receive her King—the Lord Jesus Christ."[45]

Brigham Young had earlier defined the temple rites as a process of receiving that knowledge which is necessary for an individual "to walk back to the presence of the Father, passing the angels who stand as sentinels, being enabled to give them the key words, the signs and tokens, pertaining to the Holy Priesthood, and gain [their] exaltation."[46] Those who have the privilege of going to the temple, he continued, were "those who are counted worthy to dwell with the Father and the Son" for they have "received an education fitting them for that society; they have been made fully acquainted with every pass-word, token and sign which have enabled them to pass by the porters through the doors into the celestial kingdom."[47]

According to Latter-day Saint teachings, temple ordinances, essential to salvation, were first revealed to Adam, and some form of temple worship has been found in religions in almost every age throughout history. Those who understand the eternal nature of the gospel, John A. Widtsoe said, "understand clearly why all history seems to revolve about the building and use of temples."[48] Temple worship is not indigenous to this dispensation. Joseph Smith expressly stated that the "keys of the kingdom" which he revealed to the Holy Order were the restoration of the "ancient order of things."

Since 1843 women have worked side by side with men in temple work, both essential to the performance of temple ordinances. Two years after the completion of the St. George, Utah, Temple in 1877, President John Taylor addressed a Relief Society conference in Juab Stake, confirming this mutual responsibility: "Our sisters should be prepared to take their position in Zion. Our sisters are really one with us, and when the brethren go into the Temples to officiate for the males, the sisters will go for the females; we operate together for the good of the whole, that we may be united together for time and all eternity."[49]

In early days, women who officiated in the temple were frequently called priestesses. Eliza R. Snow, for example, bore many titles in her work among the early sisters of the church, but none was of more significance to her than those related to the temple. "Thanks be to God," she wrote in a letter to Phebe Snow, "for the holy ordinances of His house and how cheerfully grateful we ought to be that we are the happy participants of these great blessings."[50] A sketch of Eliza Snow's association with the Nauvoo Temple explains the significance given to such titles: "The Temple, which had been in process of erection at the time of the death of the prophet, was at length finished; and woman was called upon to take her part in administering therein, officiating in the character of priestess. Sister Eliza then began another era in her peculiar life; and she ministered in the Temple in the holy rites that pertain to the house of the Lord as priestess and Mother in Israel to hundreds of her sex."[51] Frequently she was referred to as "high priestess" of the temple, as were the others who served, like her, as head of the women temple workers.

From baptism to the final saving ordinances, the requirements and blessings of each covenant and each ordinance are ultimately the same for women and men. James E. Talmage explains: "It is a precept of the Church that women of the Church share the authority of the Priesthood with their husbands, actual or prospective; and therefore women, whether taking the endowment for themselves or for the dead, are not ordained to specific rank in the Priesthood. Nevertheless, there is no grade, rank, or phase of the temple endowment to which women are not eligible on an equality with man."[52]

The ordinances of washing and anointing, which comprise the initiatory rites of the temple, are "mostly symbolic in nature," Apostle Boyd K. Packer explained, "but promising definite, immediate blessings as well as future blessings." Church president John Taylor explained some of these future blessings to the Juab Stake Relief Society on 20 April 1879: "The Saints," he said, "were only on the verge of the greatness that awaited them, and while the men would be Kings and Priests, the women would be Queens and Priestesses, all acting mutually, through the ordinances of the Gospel, as saviours upon Mount Zion." Eliza R. Snow counseled the women of the church to remain faithful so that they could "become Queens of Queens and Priestesses unto the Most High God." She reminded them frequently that "God has put the means in your hands to become queens and priestesses in his kingdom if you only live for it." All of these royal titles apply to the hereafter and suggest an exalted place in God's kingdom.[53] Women receive the initiatory rites from other women who, like Emma Smith, the first so authorized, have been set apart and given authority to perform them.

For many years, baptisms and washings and anointings were administered not just as saving ordinances but also as healing ordinances. Third Relief Society general president Zina D. H. Young was one of many who attested to the efficacy of rebaptism for the purpose of healing and frequently participated in this ordinance. Mary Ann Freeze, president of the Salt Lake Stake Young Ladies Mutual Improvement Association, was rebaptized for her health in the newly dedicated Salt Lake Temple.[54] Baptisms for healing, along with the laying on of hands for the same purpose, were often performed in the temple, though not as part of the official temple ceremony. Numerous diaries relate healings that resulted from blessings given by women in the temple or from a special washing and anointing. Eliza R. Snow, Zina D. H. Young, Lucy B. Young, and many other long-time women temple workers are known to have given hundreds of such blessings in the temple to distressed or ailing sisters.

They also performed these ordinances outside the temple for the same purposes.[55] One of the earliest accounts of washing and anointing for health outside a temple occurred in Nauvoo. Abigail Leonard tells of moving to Nauvoo with her husband: "As soon as we were located we were all seized with sickness, and scarcely had I recovered, when there came into our midst some brethren from England, who were homeless, and our people took them in with their own families. One of the families we took to live with us. The woman was sick, and we sent for the elders to heal her, but their endeavors were not successful, and I told the husband of the sick woman that but one thing was left to be done, which was to send for the sisters. The sisters came, washed, anointed, and administered to her. . . . In three days she sat up and had her hair combed and soon recovered."[56] The practice followed the church westward and spread wherever faithful women settled, supported and encouraged by the Relief Society. In 1895, for example, a crippled boy in Cardston, Canada, was healed through this kind of administration by his mother's Relief Society sisters.[57]

While there are numerous allusions to the practice of using this ordinance for healing, it was primarily administered to women approaching childbirth. One who received this blessing was Lula Greene Richards, who had lost her first two daughters soon after their births. While expecting her third child she was washed and anointed by Emmeline B. Wells, Zina D. H. Young, and Eliza R. Snow and was subsequently delivered of a healthy son.[58] These washings and anointings performed for expectant mothers, even those done in the temple for them, were distinct from the washings and anointings that are associated with the endowment. The latter are priesthood ordinances but the former rely on the power of faith and prayer, a distinction made by Wilford Woodruff in 1888. Moreover, he explained, outside the temple they may be performed by anyone of faith, endowed or not.[59] The practice soon declined, however, as Linda Newell's essay outlines, and was officially discouraged in 1946 by Apostle Joseph Fielding Smith.

The temple endowment, according to Apostle James E. Talmage, "comprises instruction relating to the significance and sequence of past dispensations, and the importance of the present as the greatest and grandest era in human history. This course of instruction includes a recital of the most prominent events of the creative period, the condition of our first parents in the Garden of Eden, their disobedience and consequent expulsion from that blissful abode, their condition in the lone and dreary world when doomed to live by labor and sweat, the plan of redemption by which the great transgression may be atoned, the period of the great apostasy, the restoration of the gospel with all its ancient powers and privileges, the absolute and indispensable condition of personal purity and devotion to the right in present life, and a strict compliance with Gospel requirements."[60]

For women, this instruction centers on the person of Eve, who, as the first woman, is symbolic of all women who must pass through mortality to be eventually reunited with the Father. Punished for her disobedience in the garden, she is destined to suffer pain and sorrow in childbirth, just as Adam was condemned to work by the sweat of his brow all the days of his life. Eve is further instructed that she must henceforth render obedience to Adam.[61] More significantly, both are banished from the presence of God and told they will experience temporal death, as will all their posterity. This punishment reflects the change in their condition, in Mormon terms, from terrestrial to telestial. Nevertheless, just as Christ overcame death, brought into the world by Adam and Eve's transgression, so did he atone for their sins, as he does for the sins of all repentant women and men. Through his sufferings he overcame the effects of the Fall. Moreover, Eve, though punished for telestializing the world, is exalted for leading the way toward the eventual celestializing of her posterity. Her sorrow in childbirth and subjection to Adam, like his mortal toil, are conditions of a telestial life, their punishment presupposing a different condition and relationship before the Fall.

It is by the atoning power of Christ that mortal beings can progress beyond the telestial condition imposed on them by the Edenic transgression. It is logical to assume that this atoning power will ultimately restore the equitable relationship between Adam and Eve that existed before the Fall, a process that began when Joseph Smith turned the key to women, early Mormon women believed. That the restoration of the church in its fulness includes the restoration of equality was suggested by church president Spencer W. Kimball in 1979: "We had full equality as his [the Lord's] spirit children." Then, quoting John A. Widtsoe, he continued: "The place of women in the Church is to walk beside the man, not in front of him nor behind him. In the Church [gospel] there is full equality between man and woman. The gospel, which is the only concern of the Church, was devised by the Lord for men and women alike."[62]

One feature of the endowment in both ancient and modern temple worship is the prayer circle. Prayer meetings and circles were characteristic of a number of religious groups as early as 1815. Many women "formed themselves into praying societies and obtained in the discharge of duty—comfort to themselves, and light, and direction to others."[63] Revivalism provided the impetus for increased gatherings of women where they could share the sense of sisterhood that their common religious conversions had given them.[64] Prayer meetings were thus familiar to some Mormon converts who had associated with the revivalist movement. The addition of priesthood in this procedure, however, and the connection of prayer circles with temple worship gave it a particularly sacred significance to Mormons.[65]

In 1872 Bathsheba W. Smith related her first experience in a prayer circle: "Once when speaking in one of our general fast meetings, he [Joseph] said that we did not know how to pray to have our prayers answered. But when I and my husband had our endowments in February, 1844, Joseph Smith presiding, he taught us the order of prayer."[66] She also remembered meeting "many times with Brother Joseph and others who had received their endowments in company with my husband in an upper room dedicated for that purpose and prayed with them repeatedly in these meetings."[67] The continued repetitions not only entrenched the form in which prayer circles were to be conducted but allowed the group to unite in prayer in behalf of the church.

In later years requirements and instructions for prayer circles were outlined for participants: "Get Close to the Lord, Spirits drawn out to God and His Son, Hearts Humble, contrite and at peace, Soften hearts of participants and draws them near to God, Perfect love and harmony, PRAY FOR THE SICK, Pray for the advance of the Lord's work with his blessings upon the people and His leaders."[68]

When the Nauvoo Temple was completed and the Holy Order was discontinued, prayer meetings continued. Unlike the brief period before Joseph Smith's death when women and men met together frequently in the Holy Order to pray, however, after 1845 women were inexplicably seldom included in these special prayer circles. Nor were they allowed to conduct their own. Heber C. Kimball instructed them that "they ought not to gather together in schools to pray unless their husbands or some man be with them."[69] Evidence exists, however, that for a number of years female prayer meetings were held, though such meetings may not have included prayer circles as conducted in the temple. Eliza R. Snow makes reference to special gatherings for prayer which seemed to be different from the usual prayers offered in camp during the trek west. For example on 15 June 1847 she records: "This afternoon several of the sis. met in a little circle on the prairie in front of our wagons." On this occasion two men met with them, Brother Robert Peirce and Father John Smith. On 17 August of that year she recorded: "The men go in search of the cattle. The sis[ters] meet in the grove for prayer—we have a time not to be forgotten. Bless the Lord, O my soul, yea, I do praise him for the gift of his holy spirit." After reaching the valley, the sisters met frequently in informal gatherings; a meeting on 6 April 1848 honored the anniversary of the founding of the church "in prayer for the Saints in Winter Quarters and elsewhere."[70]

There were occasions when women were permitted to hold prayer circles in the temple. Mary Ann Freeze described a prayer circle assembled in her behalf: "The sisters, quite a number, came to have a prayer meeting, so bro. [John R.] Winder [a member of the temple presidency] took us up to the Elders room where there was an altar around which we knelt, Aunt Zina [Young] being mouth and the rest repeating after her. I was then [re]baptized, Frank Armstrong officiating."[71] It is likely that other such female prayer circles were held for similar purposes in the various temples at that time.

In 1895 a large prayer circle was held in a private home in Cardston, Canada, by a group of Relief Society sisters. The minutes describe the event:

> Sister Zina Card requested that we all kneel with our faces toward the Temple [in Utah]. As our President Wilford Woodruff had promised the Saints when they desired any Special blessing from the Lord if they should do so, it would be granted unto them. Our Sister who we had come to bless lead in prayer her humble petition called down from heaven the Holy influence that ran from heart to heart, and She was followed by Zina Y. Card, [and others]. Singing

Come, come Ye Saints, after which the ordinance of washing and anointing was done by Sisters Sarah B. Daines and Rhoda Hinman sen. the Sisters 27 in number gathered around placing their hands upon Sister Steed. sister Zina Young Card sealed the anointing promising her life and health and strength and that She would be an example for her Sisters and that her children should rise up and call her blessed. the Spirit of God rested upon us insomuch that every one present rose and bore their testimony and all felt that She would recover.[72]

Hannah Adeline Savage enjoyed the blessings of a prayer circle in her behalf on 7 May 1896. After years of persistent illness, she decided to be baptized for her health. She was immersed seven times and then reconfirmed for the reception of the Holy Ghost. "We then attended a prayer meeting in the afternoon of the Relief Society. all the sisters [who] are members of our society was present at this meeting but one member all of us fasting that day. and part of us having kept our fast for two days that the Lord would here our prayers. . . . We knelt in three different prayer circles. Then I offered up a prayer by myself. I felt if the Lord would heal me I would devote the remainder of my days to His service, with His aid and after I arose to my feet the Spirit of the Lord seemed to fill my soul and I felt I was healed. Indeed the whole room was filled with the spirit of the Lord it was as a penticost to us."[73]

Evidently such prayer meetings were held frequently enough to reach the attention of church authorities. In 1896, while not prohibiting gatherings for prayer, a new policy in effect reestablished Heber C. Kimball's original ban against women meeting in prayer circles outside the temple:

The subject of permission to the sisters to meet in prayer circles was discussed, as the question had been asked whether it would be right or whether they could be permitted to meet with their husbands in a prayer circle, seeing that sisters had been admitted to prayer circles in the Nauvoo Temple. It was shown, however, that on such occasions it was for the purpose of teaching the order of prayer as it is now the custom in the Temples. It was decided that if the sisters desired to meet for prayer they could do so as members and officers of the Relief Societies in their regular places of meeting, but that it would not be advisable for them to meet at circles or to participate in prayer circle meetings.[74]

Like the ordinances of baptism and washing and anointing, prayer circles had been used outside the temple as a particular means of supplication for the restoration of health, for knowledge, and for other blessings. The use of the first two ordinances for these purposes was discontinued in the early part of this century, but men's prayer circles persisted until 1978, when they too were discontinued by a directive from the First Presidency.[75] Those few occasions when women met together in prayer circles appear to have been sporadic outcroppings of a practice once enjoyed but soon denied outside its temple setting. The additional prohibition of women participating with their husbands in prayer circles is unclear; but the purpose of prayer circles, now administered to men and women together exclusively within the temple, has not changed: "Great things can be accomplished through the power of prayer and the exercise of faith in the right way," George Q. Cannon observed in 1881.[76]

In ancient times, as in the present, temple worship included a designated place of the highest or holiest order. It is separated from the other parts of the temple, usually by a veil. In ancient Israel the high priest passed through the veil of the temple into the Holy of Holies once each year as part of the sacrificial rites performed in similitude of the Messiah's coming sacrifice. Now that Christ has made that sacrifice, Mormon thought continues, the law is fulfilled. Apostle Bruce R. McConkie explained the symbolism of this passage through the veil: "The Holy of Holies is now open to all, and all, through the atoning blood of the Lamb, can now enter into the highest and holiest of all places, that kingdom where eternal life is found. Paul, in expressive language (Heb. 9 and 10), shows how the ordinances performed through the veil of the ancient temple were in similitude of what Christ was to do, which he now having done, all men [and women] become eligible to pass through the veil into the presence of the Lord to inherit full exaltation."[77]

When one approaches the veil of the temple, he or she is symbolically at the threshold of the Lord's presence, as Elder McConkie has suggested. Covenants have been made, obligations assumed, and knowledge received that will permit the individual to pass through the veil and on to exaltation. The procedure is exactly the same for men and women. The "conversations received at this holy place" exact the same information of and offer the same promises to both.[78] Both are received on the other side of the veil by one who stands in the place of the Lord into whose presence they have symbolically been admitted, for "the keeper of the gate," the Book of Mormon explains, "is the Holy One of Israel; *and he employeth no servant there*; and there is none other way save it be by the gate; for he cannot be deceived, for the Lord God is his name."[79] There are, in other words, no intermediaries between the Savior and the members of his kingdom at this holy juncture. All who come to the veil are accountable directly to the Lord (whom the person at the veil represents) for the information which has been given to them through the ordinances. As the scriptures explain, "Except ye abide my law ye cannot attain to this glory. For strait is the gate, and narrow the way that leadeth unto the exaltation and continuation of the lives, and few there be that find it, because ye receive me not in the world neither do ye know me."[80]

Exaltation, the goal of temple worship, is explained as a "fulness and a continuation of the seeds forever and ever."[81] It is eternal life, an inheritance of the highest heaven in the celestial sphere. It is to receive "all that the

Father hath" and to become like him. The sealing ordinance of marriage, like all of the other saving ordinances, is absolutely essential to exaltation. President Joseph Fielding Smith explains: "There can be no exaltation to the fulness of the celestial kingdom outside of the marriage relationship. . . . Each must have a companion to share the honors and blessings of this great exaltation, by which *his [God's] children become his heirs*, into whose hands he gives all things."[82] The ancient apostle Paul expressed this essential interdependence: "Neither is man without the woman, neither the woman without the man, in the Lord."[83] Marriage was ordained of God to be an eternal relationship. This was not a common doctrine at the time Joseph Smith taught it to his apostles, nor was it easily accepted. In 1855 George A. Smith told the Latter-day Saints in Utah that Joseph was unable to reveal this particular doctrine, along with many others, as early as he would have liked because the Saints were not ready to receive it:

> Now if the Lord had considered it wisdom, on the day of the Kirtland endowment and great solemn assembly, to come forward and reveal to the children of men the facts that are laid down plainly in the Bible, and had told them that, without the law of sealing, no man could be exalted to a throne in the celestial kingdom, that is, without he had a woman by his side; and that no woman could be exalted in the celestial world, without she was exalted with a man at her head, . . . had He revealed this simple sentiment, up would have jumped some man, saying, "What! got to have a woman sealed to me in order to be saved, in order to be exalted to thrones, dominions, and eternal increase?" "Yes." "I do not believe a word of it, I cannot stand that, for I never intended to get married, I do not believe in any of this nonsense."[84]

Life after death and the hope of seeing loved ones again in heaven were not original to Mormon doctrine. But the eternity of marriage and family relationships and the necessity of specific temporal works to insure such eternal relationships were new doctrines.[85] By the time of this preaching, apparently, the Saints were quite comfortable with the concept; now it is an oft-repeated core doctrine.

In the temple a couple is sealed together for time and eternity by a specific priesthood authority. Only the anointed prophet holds the keys of the sealing power and thus only specifically designated individuals to whom the prophet has delegated those keys can perform temple marriages. The power of the Melchizedek Priesthood alone is not sufficient to seal men and women together for eternity. The keys of the sealing power or "last key of the priesthood," "the most sacred of all," is essential. It "pertains exclusively to the first presidency of the church, without whose sanction and approval or authority, no sealing blessings shall be administered pertaining to things of the resurrection and the life to come."[86] Thus, by that specially delegated sealing authority, a man and woman are married, both promising to keep similar covenants, both promised in return the same blessings of exaltation upon their faithfulness to those covenants. One is not subordinate to the other in this marriage covenant, which leads the couple back into the relationship with each other which existed before the fall—a *full* partnership, as President Kimball characterized it.[87] Emmeline B. Wells, fifth general president of the Relief Society, explained this principle in a Relief Society handbook in 1902: "As sure as the Scriptures are true, and they *are true,* so sure woman must be instrumental in bringing about the restoration of that equality which existed when the world was created. . . . Perfect equality then and so it must be when all things are restored as they were in the beginning."[88]

Through the marriage covenant and all of the other covenants and ordinances of the temple, a couple is given a higher or celestial law by which to conduct their lives. They are, in effect, beginning their eternal relationship. "The married state," Elder Talmage has explained, "is regarded as sacred, sanctified, and holy in all temple procedure; and within the House of the Lord the woman is the equal of and the help-meet to the man."[89] Moreover, no worthy women or men will be denied the blessing of exaltation, though circumstances beyond their control may withhold marriage. Nor will a worthy married woman or man be denied exaltation though the marriage partner may live unworthily. "*No one can be deprived of exaltation who remains faithful,*" explained Bruce R. McConkie and confirmed President Kimball in 1978.[90] Faithful single women and men may avail themselves of the spiritual support of temple worship, though marriage to a worthy partner for some may be deferred.

Thus in Mormon thought marriage unlocks the gate to the highest portion of the celestial realm. A couple married in the new and everlasting covenant "by him who is anointed, unto whom I have appointed this power and the keys of this priesthood," states the Doctrine and Covenants, "shall inherit thrones, kingdoms, principalities, and powers, dominions, all heights and depths . . . and they shall pass by the angels, and the gods, which are set there, to their exaltation and glory in all things." To them both, the woman and the man alike, the Lord promises all that He has to give: "Then shall *they* be gods, because they have no end; therefore shall they be from everlasting to everlasting, because they continue; then shall *they* be above all, because all things are subject unto them. Then shall *they* be gods, because *they* have all power, and the angels are subject unto them."[91]

When women and men therefore attain this glorified state, they will, in the words of James E. Talmage, "administer in their respective stations, seeing and understanding alike, and cooperating to the full in the government of their family kingdom." Recognizing the inequities that followed from Eve's subordination in Eden, he continued: "Then shall woman be recompensed in rich measure for all the injustice that womanhood has endured in mortality. Then shall woman reign by Divine right, a queen in the resplendent realm of her glorified state, even as exalted man shall stand, priest and king unto the Most High God."[92] Apostle Joseph Fielding Smith also affirmed women's potential as "priestesses and queens in the kingdom of God" and concluded that "they will be given authority."[93] Thus, the scriptural promise of "thrones, kingdoms, principalities, powers, and dominions" is given in full measure to both marriage partners. If modern scripture is correct, a woman's godhood, which, like a man's, is "above all" and encompasses "all power," is neither limited nor subservient. No distinctions are made as to the dimensions of male and female godhood.

Early members of the church seemed to understand this bestowal of God's power or priesthood through the endowment and other temple ordinances as all encompassing, embracing both men and women. When Joseph Smith addressed the Relief Society on 28 April 1842, he indicated he would show the sisters how they would come into the "gifts, privileges and blessings of the priesthood." Sarah Melissa Granger Kimball, who first suggested the idea of a woman's organization in Nauvoo, confirmed this: "We had some by-laws written out by Sister E. R. Snow, and we showed them to President Joseph Smith, and he said he was glad to have the opportunity of organizing the women, as a part of the priesthood belonged to them." The Relief Society itself as an organization within the church was empowered with priesthood as well. Joseph Smith explained his purpose in organizing the women: "I have desired to organize the Sisters in the order of the Priesthood. I now have the key by which I can do it. . . . I will organize you in the Order of the Priesthood after the pattern of the Church."[94] The principle of jointly held priesthood power was confirmed by Brigham Young. In urging women and men to uphold their marriage covenants, he said, "Now, brethren, the man that honors his Priesthood, the woman that honors her Priesthood, will receive an everlasting inheritance in the kingdom of God."[95] Bishop Edward Hunter acknowledged the same joint possession. In 1878 he complimented the Relief Societies for "doing much good; they have saved much suffering, and have been a great help to the Bishops. They have the Priesthood," he said, "a portion of the priesthood rests upon the sisters."[96]

Joseph Smith's intent to bestow the "privileges, blessings, and gifts of the priesthood" on women thus found expression in his organizing the Relief Society in the "order of the Priesthood" but more specifically in the temple ordinances, an intention deeply internalized by early Mormon women and publicly recognized by many early church leaders.

In 1888 Apostle Franklin D. Richards elucidated the conferral of priesthood on women through the temple ordinances:

> I ask any and everybody present who have received their endowments, whether he be a brother Apostle, Bishop, High Priest, Elder, or whatever office he may hold in the Church, What blessings did you receive, what ordinance, what power, intelligence, sanctification or grace did you receive that your wife did not partake of with you? I will answer, that there was one thing that our wives

were not made special partakers of, and that was the ordination to the various orders of the priesthood which were conferred upon us. Aside from that, our sisters share with us any and all of the ordinances of the holy anointing, endowments, sealings, sanctifications and blessings that we have been made partakers of.

Now, I ask you: Is it possible that we have the holy priesthood and our wives have none of it? Do you not see, by what I have read, that Joseph desired to confer these keys of power upon them in connection with their husbands? I hold that a faithful wife has certain gifts and blessings and promises with her husband, which she cannot be deprived of except by transgression of the holy order of God. They shall enjoy what God said they should. And these signs shall follow them if they believe.[97]

The ambiguity that came to surround the relationship of women and the priesthood seemed to center on the extent to which women shared or held the priesthood in connection with their husbands, the distinction between "sharing" and "holding," and the manner in which the investiture of priesthood was to be manifest in a woman's life.

While there was no consensus on the answer to the first question, most of the church leaders who addressed the issue agreed that an investiture of priesthood power was given to women in the temple in relationship with their husbands. To the second question attempts were made to distinguish between the two terms, but the issue never seemed to move beyond a problem of semantics. In recent times Apostle Boyd K. Packer utilized the two terms without offering a distinction between them in relationship to women: "We who hold the priesthood," he told a church-wide fireside audience, "can hold it and at once share it with our wives."[98] The extent to which a wife "shares" it with her husband still remains ambiguous. To the third question, it was generally agreed that husbands and wives could exercise the priesthood together in behalf of their families but that women did not have authority to administer in ecclesiastical affairs, except through their own organizations (Relief Society, YWMIA, and the Primary) and as temple workers.

Time seemed to ease the urgency to define the exact relationship of women and priesthood until very recently, but to the women of an earlier generation, access to the priesthood, or God's authority, through participation in the temple was an acknowledged and valued spiritual blessing.

For many women the debate to define the parameters of female priesthood power seemed inconsequential as they participated in both its blessings and privileges, as Joseph Smith had promised. Their sense of possession was continually reinforced by their participation in priesthood ordinances as both candidates and officiators in the temple, by their membership and responsibilities in the Relief Society, and in their administration of the personal and spiritual concerns of their families. Lucy Meserve Smith, for example, when threatened by evil spirits, immediately invoked the power of the "Holy Priesthood conferred upon [her] in common with my companion in the Temple of our God" and was instantly relieved of their influence.[99] Other women through their patriarchal blessings were expressly instructed that they then had or would receive that power. For example, Leonora Taylor was told by Hyrum Smith in 1843: "You shall be blest with your portion of the Priesthood which belongeth unto you, that you may be set apart for your Anointing & your induement [endowment]." After the death of her first husband, Zina Y. Card was given a blessing which promised that she would have power over the adversary, over evil spirits and wicked influences, as well as over diseases and all manner of sicknesses, and that she would stand firm, full of the spirit of the Father. "These blessings are yours," Patriarch Joseph Young went on to say, "the blessings and the power according to the holy Melchisedek Priesthood, you received in your Endowments, and you shall have them."[100]

As with all of the other saving ordinances, the eternal promises given to those who enter the Mormon covenant of marriage are made conditional upon continued faithfulness. And unwavering valiance in righteousness carries the possibility for an individual to receive assurance *in this life* of his or her salvation. As Joseph Smith explained to the Saints: "It is one thing to receive knowledge by the voice of God (this is my beloved Son, etc) & another to Know that you yourself will be saved, to have a positive promise of your own Salvation is making your Calling and Election sure. [namely] the voice of Jesus saying My Beloved thou shalt have eternal life."[101] When an individual has complied with all of the commandments, he further explained, "hungering and thirsting after righteousness, and living by every word of God . . . the Lord will soon say unto him, Son, thou shalt be exalted . . . then the man will find *his calling and his election sure.*"[102] This means, in another phrase significant to Mormons, that that individual— man or woman—has, during mortality, been "sealed up unto eternal life."[103] The promises given in the temple are no longer conditional, for the offerings, sacrifices, and faithfulness of the individual have been accepted of the Lord during the candidate's mortal life. The day of judgment has in effect been moved forward, as Bruce R. McConkie explained; the assurance of eternal life, exaltation, and eventual godhood has replaced its promise.[104]

Making one's calling and election sure is not an unearned blessing. While the Lord has declared that his work and his glory are to bring about the eternal life and exaltation of his children, it is necessary for his children to merit that reward. Peter anciently enumerated the steps that lead to making one's calling and election sure and receiving the "more sure word of prophecy" which the Prophet Joseph defined as knowing that one has been "sealed up unto eternal life, by revelation and the spirit of prophecy, through the power of the Holy Priesthood."[105] All faithful Saints are candidates for receiving this "more sure word of prophecy," this witness of acceptance by the Lord. Joseph Smith exhorted the Saints to "go on and continue to call upon God until you make your calling and election sure for yourselves by obtaining this more sure word of prophecy, and wait patiently for the promise until you obtain it."[106]

Along with the assurance of eternal life, making one's calling and election sure also implies ultimate godhood. Joseph Smith explained the process: "Here, then, is eternal life—to know the only wise and true God; and you have got to learn how to be gods yourselves, and to be kings and priests of God . . . by going from one small degree to another, and from a small capacity to a great one."[107] These steps are not all taken in this life. Learning the principles of exaltation is a long continuous process that will extend "even beyond the grave," he explained. "It will be a great while after you have passed through the veil before you will have learned them."[108]

The early Saints were urged to become worthy of such a blessing, for it also gave them the privilege of receiving the Second Comforter, which is Christ himself. Faith, repentance, baptism qualify an individual to receive the Holy Ghost, or the first comforter, Joseph Smith explained. But when an individual has so lived as to make his or her calling and election sure, "then it will be his [or her] privilege to receive the other Comforter, which the Lord hath promised the Saints as recorded in the testimony of St. John, in the 14th chapter, from the 12th to the 27th verses."[109]

Through the priesthood, an ordinance confirming one's calling and election is given in the temple. Many of the members of the Holy Order in Nauvoo received this special ordinance from the Prophet Joseph.[110] Sometimes referred to as the second endowment, second anointing, or more precisely the fulness of the priesthood, it is the highest of temple ordinances and is given only upon recommendation by the living prophet. It is always given to a couple, since it is an assurance of exaltation which can never be attained alone. As James E. Talmage explained, "There are certain of the higher ordinances to which an unmarried woman cannot be admitted, but the rule is equally in force as to a bachelor." Through the second anointing, a woman and man are ordained equally "to the highest order of the priesthood."[111]

No longer promised only "to *become* queens and priestesses," women of the early church who received this final ordinance valued its added spiritual dimension in their lives. Eliza R. Snow expressed this realization of the unique blessings available to Mormon women. "They occupy a more important position than is occupied by any other women on the earth, . . . associated, as they are, with apostles and prophets . . . with them sharing in the gifts and powers of the holy Priesthood . . . participating in those sacred ordinances, without which, we could never be prepared to dwell in the presence of the Holy Ones."[112]

A "kingdom of priestesses" had indeed been established as Joseph had prophesied, not as an organization but by virtue of the numbers of women so anointed in the early days of the church. At the funeral of Mary Ann Freeze, Joseph F. Smith, recalling the service she had rendered as a temple worker, indicated that she and her sister workers "had been set apart, ordained to the work, called to it, [and] authorized by the authority of the Holy Priesthood to minister to their sex, in the House of God for the living and for the dead." He then told the congregation, "Some of you will understand when I tell you that some of these good women who have passed beyond have actually been anointed queens and priestesses unto God and unto their husbands."[113]

While such an anointing did not entail specific ecclesiastical functions, it greatly expanded the spiritual horizons of those so ordained. Though Joseph Smith had explained to the Relief Society that "elect lady" meant "to preside," the term, along with "daughter of God," "priestess," and "Mother in Israel" carried deep significance to an earlier generation of Mormon women, for these titles were most frequently applied to those women who had received the fulness of the sealing power. Eliza R. Snow's appraisal of Mormon women came from knowledge of the full implication of temple worship in their lives.

For some women, conversion meant the fulfillment of religious yearnings, while for others it was a discovery of religious faith that brought a new sense of conviction and commitment. But it was in the temple experience that they felt the divine call of the elect. More than just a witness to their spirit that God's grace had been extended to them, the temple provided a clearly marked, step-by-step progression toward exaltation, placing its achievement in their own hands. Making their calling and election sure with its confirming ordinance, a possibility for all members, changed hope to knowledge and promise to fulfillment. Literally endowed with power from on high, that first generation of Mormon women radiated a sense of divine grace and approbation that perceptibly set them apart from the women of the world. Their vision of the eternities implied more than sweet rest in the bosom of Christ. It was an assurance that they would become *like him.* Like an "anchor to the soul," this knowledge gave them the strength to endure the physical and emotional sacrifices that their religion demanded of them. "Though the thunders might roll and lightnings flash, and earthquakes bellow, and wars gather thick around, yet this hope and knowledge would support the soul in every hour of trial, trouble and tribulation," Joseph had promised.[114]

Remembering that Joseph Smith had prophesied that "they should have power to command queens" and hearing repeatedly from Eliza R. Snow that "we are at the head of all the women of the world," they recognized that they were in the vanguard of a new dispensation for women.[115] It was not hyperbole with which the Kanab Relief Society officers welcomed Eliza R. Snow and her companion, Zina D. H. Young, in 1881, but sincere expression of belief: "We welcome sister Eliza and Zina as our Elect Lady and her counselor, and as Presidents of all the feminine portion of the human race, although comparatively few recognize their right to this authority. Yet, we know they have been set apart as leading Priestesses of this dispensation. As such we honor them."[116]

Winter Quarters, the 1846–47 layover between Illinois and the Salt Lake Valley for the migrating Mormons, seasoned this spiritual power. Meeting frequently together, often in the absence of husbands, sons, and fathers, some of the women there magnified their spiritual strength by exercising it repeatedly in behalf of one another. Blessing, prophesying, speaking in tongues, praying, and administering to the sick, they carried the spirit of the temple with them during their sojourn in the wilderness. Eliza R. Snow left with the second company for the Salt Lake Valley. On leaving Winter Quarters she wrote in her diary the simple words: "Bade farewell to many who seemed dearer to me than life."[117] After reaching the valley she sent a poem back to Mary Ann Young, Vilate Kimball, and Elizabeth Ann Whitney, her associates in the Relief Society and in the temple. It concludes:

> All is well, is well in Zion —
> Zion is the pure in heart:
> Come along, *you holy women,*
> And your blessings here impart.[118]

It was not just their isolation, their practice of polygamy, their monolithic social, economic, and political systems that made Mormons "a peculiar people." Temple worship, far more than these conditions, differentiated them from "Babylon" and set them apart from other sects. While the railroad eventually destroyed their isolation, the federal government outlawed their plural marriages, and eventual statehood decimated their unity, their temple worship remained essentially untouched. Whatever the changes a new century has made in Mormon women's dependence on spiritual power for healing, on spiritual bonds for sisterhood, or on spiritual truths for direction, the meaning of the temple is undiminished. Its power, its purpose, and its promises for women are unchanged.

NOTES

1. Joseph Smith, *History of the Church of Jesus Christ of Latter-day Saints*, 2nd ed., rev., 7 vols. (Salt Lake City: Church of Jesus Christ of Latter-day Saints, 1949) 4:602, hereafter cited as *HC*.

2. "A Record of the Organization, and Proceedings of the Female Relief Society of Nauvoo, 17 March 1842–16 March 1844," 28 April 1842, Archives, Historical

Dept., Church of Jesus Christ of Latter-day Saints, Salt Lake City, Utah, hereafter referred to as LDS Church Archives. Hereafter cited as Nauvoo Relief Society Minutes.

3. Bruce R. McConkie, "The Relief Society and the Keys of the Kingdom," *Relief Society Magazine* 37 (March 1950): 151.

4. Nauvoo Relief Society Minutes, 13 August 1843.

5. Brigham Young, sermon delivered 6 April 1853, *Journal of Discourses*, 20 vols. (Liverpool: F. D. Richards et al., 1855-86) 2:31-32, hereafter cited as *JD*, with speaker, date, volume, and page.

6. Orson Pratt, 20 May 1877, *JD* 19:160.

7. George A. Smith, 18 March 1855, *JD* 2:214-15.

8. "Baptisms for the Dead, Book A," MS, Salt Lake Temple Vaults, and "Supplementary Record, Nauvoo Temple, Endowments, 10 December 1845 to 7 February 1846," p. 85, Salt Lake Temple Vaults, as cited in Ileen Ann Waspe LeCheminant, "The Status of Women in the Philosophy of Mormonism, 1830-1845" (Master's thesis, Brigham Young University, 1942), p. 128. See also Emmeline B. Wells, address, Minutes of First Genealogical Convention, 7 April 1914, Salt Lake City, Utah, LDS Church Archives.

9. Brigham Young, Minutes and General Record of the First Council of Seventies, 1844-1847, 10 February 1845, p. 66, LDS Church Archives.

10. Sally Randall, letters from Nauvoo, April 1844, Sally Randall Papers, LDS Church Archives.

11. Doctrine and Covenants 124:40-41, hereafter D&C.

12. *LDS Millennial Star* 5 (June 1844): 15, and 8 (8 November 1846): 141.

13. See *Times and Seasons* 6 (15 March 1845): 847; Susa Young Gates, "Mother in Israel," *Relief Society Magazine* 3 (March 1916): 129; *HC* 6:298; "Reminiscences of Mercy Fielding Thompson, 20 December 1880," p. 3, LDS Church Archives.

14. Helen Mar Whitney, "Scenes from Nauvoo, and Incidents from Heber C. Kimball's Journal," *Woman's Exponent* 12 (1 October 1883): 71, and Nauvoo Endowment Record, p. 1.

15. Augusta Joyce Crocheron, comp., *Representative Women of Deseret: A Book of Biographical Sketches* (Salt Lake City: J. C. Graham & Co., 1884), pp. 25-26.

16. *HC* 4:492-93.

17. Nauvoo Relief Society Minutes, 30 March 1842.

18. Ibid.; see also *HC* 4:570.

19. Bathsheba W. Smith, *Woman's Exponent* 34 (July, August 1906): 14.

20. Mercy Fielding Thompson, "Recollections of the Prophet Joseph Smith," *Juvenile Instructor* 27 (1 July 1892): 398.

21. *HC* 5:1-2. See also Brigham Young, "Autobiography," 4 May 1842, p. 53, as cited in LeCheminant, "The Status of Women," pp. 129-30.

22. See D. Michael Quinn, "Latter-day Saint Prayer Circles," *BYU Studies* 19 (Fall 1978): 85.

23. Newel K. Whitney, Nauvoo Relief Society Minutes, 27 May 1842. See also *Woman's Exponent* 20 (15 April 1892): 149-50.

24. Andrew F. Ehat, "Joseph Smith's Introduction of Temple Ordinances and the 1844 Mormon Succession Question," (Master's thesis, Brigham Young University, 1981), p. 107.

25. Joseph Fielding, Journal, 1843–59, entry for ca. Fall 1844, as quoted in Quinn, "Prayer Circles," p. 88.

26. Orson F. Whitney, *Life of Heber C. Kimball* (Salt Lake City: Kimball Family, 1888), pp. 334–39.

27. Ehat, "Introduction of Temple Ordinances," pp. 63–64.

28. D&C 110 and *HC* 2:435–6.

29. *The Utah Genealogical and Historical Magazine* 28 (April 1937): 66; "A Leaf from an Autobiography," *Woman's Exponent* 7 (15 February 1879): 191; and *Woman's Exponent* 10 (15 March 1882): 154.

30. Thompson, "Recollections of the Prophet Joseph Smith," p. 400.

31. Bathsheba W. Smith, Diary, typescript, LDS Church Archives. She also made a number of public statements about her involvement in the Holy Order. Some can be found in Joseph F. Smith, *Blood Atonement and the Origin of Plural Marriage* (Independence: Zion's Printing and Publishing Co., n.d.), pp. 87–88; N. B. Lundwall, *Temples of the Most High* (Salt Lake City: Bookcraft, 1941), p. 246; "Latter-day Temples," *Relief Society Magazine* 4 (April 1917): 185–86; Crocheron, *Representative Women,* p. 42.

32. *HC* 6:39.

33. *Millennial Star* 5 (March 1845): 151.

34. Helen Mar Whitney, *Woman's Exponent* 12 (15 June 1883): 10.

35. Ibid. 12 (1 July 1883): 18.

36. Zina D. H. Young, Nauvoo Diary, 24 May 1845, LDS Church Archives.

37. John A. Widtsoe, "Symbolism in the Temple," in *Saviors on Mount Zion,* Archibald F. Bennett, ed. Advanced Senior Department Course of Study (Salt Lake City: Deseret Sunday School Union Board, 1950), p. 164.

38. Ibid. See also Joseph Fielding Smith, comp., *Teachings of the Prophet Joseph Smith* (1938; Salt Lake City: Deseret News Press, 1951), pp. 362–63.

39. D&C 84:19.

40. *HC* 3:387.

41. *HC* 5:555.

42. Smith, ed., *Teachings of the Prophet Joseph Smith,* p. 309.

43. *HC* 2:309–10, 426. George A. Smith told a congregation of Saints in Salt Lake City in 1855 that, at the time of the completion of the Kirtland Temple, had the Lord "revealed one single sentiment more, or went one step further to reveal more fully the law of redemption, I believe He would have upset the whole of us. The fact was, He dare not, on that very account, reveal to us a single principle further than He had done, for He had tried, over and over again, to do it." 18 March 1855, *JD* 2:215.

44. John A. Widtsoe, *Priesthood and Church Government* (Salt Lake City: Deseret Book Co., 1939), p. 351.

45. James E. Talmage, *The House of the Lord* (Salt Lake City: Church of Jesus Christ of Latter-day Saints, 1912), p. 100.

46. As successor to Joseph Smith, Brigham Young held the sealing power for the church, having been ordained to this authority by Joseph Smith before his death. See *LDS Millennial Star* 5 (March 1845): 151; D&C 132:7; and Widtsoe, *Priesthood,* p. 351.

47. Brigham Young, 6 April 1853, *JD* 2:31, and Doctrine and Covenants 132:18, 19; 24 May 1863, *JD* 10:172.

48. Widtsoe, "Symbolism in the Temple," p. 163: See also Hugh Nibley, "The Idea of the Temple in History," *LDS Millennial Star* 120 (August 1958): 237; and Joseph Fielding Smith, "Temples and the Sacred Rites Therein," *Utah Genealogical and Historical Magazine* 21 (April 1930): 53.

49. John Taylor, "Relief Society Conference, Juab Stake," *Woman's Exponent* 8 (1 June 1879): 2.

50. Eliza R. Snow to Phebe Snow, 6 April 1868, Eliza R. Snow Papers, LDS Church Archives.

51. Emmeline B. Wells, "Pen Sketch of an Illustrious Woman," *Woman's Exponent* 9 (15 October 1880): 74.

52. Talmage, *The House of the Lord*, p. 94.

53. Boyd K. Packer, *The Holy Temple* (Salt Lake City: Bookcraft, 1980), p. 154; Juab Stake Manuscript History, 20 April 1879; *LDS Millennial Star* 36 (13 January 1874): 21; *Woman's Exponent* 9 (1 April 1881): 166; Rev. 1:6; cf. Joseph Smith Translation Rev. 5:10; D&C 76:56 and 132:19.

54. *Young Woman's Journal* 4 (April 1893): 294, and Mary Ann Freeze, Diary, 18 September 1893, Harold B. Lee Library, Brigham Young University, Provo, Utah.

55. See Linda King Newell, "A Gift Given, A Gift Taken: Washing, Anointing, and Blessing the Sick among Mormon Women," *Sunstone* 6 (September–October 1981): 16–25. See also p. 122–25 in this volume.

56. Edward W. Tullidge, *The Women of Mormondom* (New York: Tullidge & Crandall, 1877), p. 169.

57. Minutes of a Special Meeting Held at Sister Elizabeth Hammer's Residence, n.d. [sometime between 21 March and 22 May 1895], Cardston Ward Relief Society Historical Record, Book A, 1890–1898, LDS Church Archives.

58. Louisa Greene Richards, Journal no. 2, 9 June 1878, LDS Church Archives.

59. Wilford Woodruff to Emmeline B. Wells, 27 April 1888, LDS Church Archives.

60. Talmage, *The House of the Lord*, pp. 99, 100.

61. Genesis 3:16–19; Moses 4:22–25.

62. Spencer W. Kimball, " 'Be Thou an Example,' " in idem., *My Beloved Sisters* (Salt Lake City: Deseret Book, 1979), pp. 35–45; see also *Improvement Era* 45 (March 1942): 161.

63. "Narrative of the State of Religion within the Bounds of the General Assembly of the Presbyterian Church . . . ," *Religious Intelligencer* (New Haven, Conn.), 15 June 1816, p. 45, reprinted in Keith E. Melder, *Beginnings of Sisterhood: The American Woman's Rights Movement, 1800–1850* (New York: Schocken Books, 1977), p. 38.

64. Prayer meetings continued through this period to be a frequent form of female association even among the young. One group of young women attending the Ipswich Seminary in 1831 met in prayer circles in their respective homes each Sunday morning, breaking into smaller groups for prayer during the week. Maria Cowles to Rev. Henry Cowles, 14 July 1831, typed copy, Mount Holyoke College Archives, in Melder, *Beginnings of Sisterhood*, p. 39. Ironically, when revivalist Charles Finney introduced "mixed" prayer meetings and testimonial meetings, he was at-

tacked for encouraging immorality and lax discipline. But such procedures continued. As one enthusiastic participant recorded: "Our prayer meetings have been one of the greatest means of the conversion of souls, especially those in which brothers and sisters have prayed together. If God has honored any meetings amongst us, it has been these." *A Narrative of the Revival of Religion in the County of Oneida Particularly in the Bounds of the Presbytery of Oneida, in the year 1826* (Utica, N.Y., 1826), p. 30, quoted in ibid., p. 38.

65. Quinn, "Prayer Circles," pp. 79-105 traces the history of prayer circles in the LDS church. See also Hugh Nibley, "The Early Christian Prayer Circle," *BYU Studies* 19 (Fall 1978): 41-78.

66. Bathsheba W. Smith, "Recollections of the Prophet Joseph Smith," *Juvenile Instructor* 27 (1 June 1892): 345.

67. B. W. Smith, Diary, typescript copy, LDS Church Archives.

68. "Requirements and Instructions for Setting up Prayer Circles," Church History Department, as cited in Quinn, "Prayer Circles," p. 104, emphasis in the original.

69. Heber C. Kimball, Journal, 1845-46, 21 December 1845, LDS Church Archives.

70. *Eliza R. Snow, An Immortal* (Salt Lake City: Nicholas G. Morgan Foundation, 1957), pp. 324, 339, 363-64.

71. Mary Ann Burnham Freeze, Diary, 19 September 1893.

72. Minutes of a Special Meeting held at the Residence of Sister Elizabeth Hammer, 14 February 1895, Cardston Ward Relief Society Historical Record Book A, 1890-1898, MS, LDS Church Archives.

73. Hannah Adaline Hatch Savage, Journal, 1894-1915, LDS Church Archives.

74. Journal History of the Church, 30 January 1896, p. 2, LDS Church Archives.

75. Spencer W. Kimball, Nathan Eldon Tanner, Marion G. Romney to All Stake Presidents and Bishops, 3 May 1978.

76. George Q. Cannon, 27 June 1881, *JD* 22:289.

77. Bruce R. McConkie, in *Doctrinal New Testament Commentary*, 3 vols. (Salt Lake City: Bookcraft, 1973) 1:829-30.

78. See D&C 124:39; Parley P. Pratt, *JD* 2:46, as reprinted in Widtsoe, *Priesthood and Church Government*, p. 350.

79. 2 Nephi 9:41, italics added.

80. D&C 132:21-23.

81. D&C 132:19.

82. Joseph Fielding Smith, *Doctrines of Salvation*, 3 vols. (Salt Lake City: Bookcraft, 1955) 2:65.

83. 1 Cor. 11:11.

84. George A. Smith, 18 March 1855, *JD* 2:216. Interestingly, Emma Smith's 1835 edition of the hymn book, before Joseph publicly taught the doctrine of eternal marriage, includes a hymn relating to the eternal marriage of Adam and Eve by an unknown author. The last verses read:

> Go, multiply, — replenish
> And fill the earth with men,
> That all your vast creation,

May come to God again:—
And dwell amid perfection
In Zion's wide domains,
Where union is eternal,
And Jesus ever reigns.

85. In the late 1860s Elizabeth Stuart Phelps began a series of consolation novels which describe a "domestic" heaven in which not only familial relationships endure but all the accoutrements of middle-class life surround the family with a comfortable hearthside ambiance. See also Mary Ann Meyers, "Gates Ajar: Death in Mormon Thought and Practice," in *Death in America*, ed. by David E. Stannard (Philadelphia: University of Pennsylvania Press, 1975).

86. Talmage, *House of the Lord*, p. 100.

87. Spencer W. Kimball, "Privileges and Responsibilities of Sisters," Women's Fireside Address, *Ensign* 8 (November 1978): 106.

88. *The General Relief Society, Officers, Objects and Status* (Salt Lake City: [General Board of the Relief Society], 1902), pp. 74-75.

89. Talmage, *House of the Lord*, p. 94.

90. Joseph Fielding Smith, *Doctrines of Salvation*, Bruce R. McConkie, ed., 3 vols. (Salt Lake City: Bookcraft, 1954-56), 2:65; see also Kimball, "The Role of Righteous Women," Women's Fireside Address, *Ensign* 9 (November 1979): 102.

91. D&C 132:20, italics added.

92. James E. Talmage, "The Eternity of Sex," *Young Woman's Journal* 25 (October 1914): 602-3.

93. *Doctrines of Salvation*, 3:178.

94. *Woman's Exponent* 7 (1 July 1878): 18; Minutes of Relief Society Central Board 17 March 1882 in Salt Lake Stake Relief Society Record, 1880-1892, LDS Church Archives.

95. Brigham Young, sermon, 28 June 1874, *JD* 17:119.

96. Edward Hunter, *Woman's Exponent* 6 (1 December 1877): 102.

97. Franklin D. Richards, *Woman's Exponent* 17 (1 September 1888): 54.

98. Boyd K. Packer, "Come, All Ye Sons of God," *Ensign* 13 (August 1983): 68.

99. Lucy Meserve Smith, Historical Sketch, 12 June 1889, "Historical Sketches of My Great Grandfather," LDS Church Archives.

100. Patriarchal Blessing, Nauvoo, Ill., 28 July 1843; Patriarchal Blessing, 28 May 1878, Zina Y. Card Papers, Harold B. Lee Library, Brigham Young University.

101. Joseph Smith, 21 May 1843, Howard and Martha Corey Notebook, in Andrew F. Ehat and Lyndon W. Cook, eds., *The Words of Joseph Smith* (Provo: Religious Studies Center, 1980), p. 208. See also *HC* 5:402-3; Smith, *Teachings of the Prophet Joseph Smith*, p. 306.

102. *HC* 3:379-81.

103. D&C 131:5.

104. *Doctrinal New Testament Commentary* 3:330-31; see also Roy W. Doxey, "Accepted of the Lord," *Ensign* 6 (July 1976): 50-53.

105. 2 Peter 1:5-10, 16-19; D&C 131:5.

106. Smith, *Teachings of the Prophet Joseph Smith*, p. 299.

107. Ibid., pp. 346-47.

108. Ibid., p. 348. Brigham Young saw eternal value in the most mundane knowledge. When Eliza R. Snow attempted to recruit women to manage women's commission stores as a means of promoting home industry, she told the sisters: "President Young thinks the Sisters are quite capable of keeping the store, he says how are we to become Queens unless we are able to conduct business." Minutes, Thirteenth Ward Relief Society, 26 September 1876, p. 266, LDS Church Archives.

109. Smith, *Teachings of the Prophet Joseph Smith*, p. 150.

110. Ehat, "Introduction of Temple Ordinances," pp. 95–96, 102–3, 121–22. See also LeCheminant, "Status of Women," pp. 133, 135.

111. Talmage, *House of the Lord*, p. 94; Quinn, "Prayer Circles," p. 87.

112. Eliza R. Snow, "Position and Duties," *Woman's Exponent* 3 (15 July 1874): 28.

113. Joseph F. Smith, *Gospel Doctrine* (Salt Lake City: Deseret Book Co., 1919), p. 461. Inasmuch as the sealing of individuals through the generations follows a patriarchal line and a woman is sealed into her husband's line, it is possible that in that sense she becomes a queen and priestess "unto him" as well as "unto God."

114. Smith, *Teachings of the Prophet Joseph Smith*, p. 298.

115. Snow, Nauvoo Relief Society Minutes, 28 April 1842; Smithfield Ward, Cache Stake Relief Society Minutes, 1868–78, 12 May 1878, p. 486, LDS Church Archives.

116. *Woman's Exponent* 9 (1 April 1881): 165.

117. Snow, Diary, 12 June 1847, reprinted in *Eliza R. Snow, An Immortal*, p. 324.

118. Eliza R. Snow, "Come to the Valley," *Poems, Religious, Historical, and Political*, 2 vols. (Liverpool: F. D. Richards, 1856) 1:188.

LINDA KING NEWELL

Gifts of the Spirit: Women's Share

And these signs shall follow them that believe; In my name shall they cast out devils; they shall speak with new tongues . . . they shall lay hands on the sick, and they shall recover.[1]

On an October evening in 1833 in a home where the Mormon prophet Joseph Smith was staying, a small group gathered to hear him preach. As they listened intently to the young religious leader, Joseph said, "If one of you will rise up and open your mouth it shall be filled, and you shall speak in tongues." Lydia Bailey, who later became the wife of Newel Knight, felt every eye turn to her as her companions voiced almost in unison, "Sister Lydia, rise up!" "And then the great glory of God was manifested to this weak but trusting girl. She was enveloped as with a flame, and unable longer to retain her seat, she arose and her mouth was filled with the praises of God and his glory. The spirit of tongues was upon her."[2]

Fourteen years later at Winter Quarters, Nebraska, Patty Sessions waited with the other Latter-day Saints for her time to start for the valley of the Great Salt Lake. On Wednesday, 17 March 1847, she matter-of-factly recorded in her diary: "She [Mary Peirce] was buried. I went to the funeral. Brigham [Young] preached. I then visited the sick. Mr Sessions and I went and laid hands on the widow Holmon's step-daughter. She was healed."[3]

In Cache Valley, Utah, a 1910 Relief Society meeting records testimonies of healing at least half a dozen women. "Sister Neddo spoke of her experience in washing and anointing the sick and they had been blessed & healed." As the meeting progressed, several other women bore similar testimony. "Sister Moench . . . Related an experience in blessing a child who had been given up by the doc[tor] and it got well."[4]

To the casual observer of Mormon history these three occasions, separated in time by nearly eighty years, may seem like rare jewels set in a chain of historical events. Jewels, yes; rare, no. They are only selected examples from the records of countless Mormon women who experienced these and other gifts of the spirit. While such powers and gifts exercised by women were not uncommon in earlier periods of the church, they are seldom spoken of among LDS women today.[5]

As we trace the development of spiritual gifts among women in the church, it soon becomes apparent that there was initially little difference between women and men as recipients of these gifts. When Joseph Smith reported a revelation on 3 March 1831, affirming the gifts of the spirit as recorded by the Apostle Paul to the Corinthian saints,[6] he formalized practices that had already been manifest within the church. The list recorded as Doctrine and Covenants section 46 included the supreme and crowning gift, the testimony of Jesus and his atonement. But it also named "the differences of administration, the word of wisdom, the word of knowledge, faith to be healed, faith to heal, the working of miracles, prophecy, the discerning of spirits, tongues and the interpretation of tongues."[7] In short, the latter-day restoration of all things now officially encompassed the restoration of these signs of the Holy Spirit according to the faith of the members. These gifts came ungendered. They were gifts of the household of faith, given to "the children of God," male and female. Women as well as men prophesied. The testimony of the Savior was given to both women and men who enthusiastically bore witness to others. Miracles, discernment, knowledge, and wisdom appear to have been bestowed evenhandedly. Only two of the gifts, tongues and healing, seem problematic to twentieth-century Latter-day Saints—and then in different ways for different reasons.

The practice of tongues and interpretation common in other religious groups initially appeared among the Latter-day Saints in one of the Pennsylvania branches. Joseph Smith first heard the gift used by Brigham Young in Kirtland in September 1832 and pronounced the strange language "pure Adamic," as spoken by Adam and Eve in the Garden of Eden.[8] Now, neither men or women practice glossolalia or interpretation in any regular or public way.

At first the gift of healing, like faith, wisdom, and discernment, was available for any worthy member of the church. Women were as likely to heal or be healed as were men. But during the early twentieth century, healing was increasingly regarded as a priesthood function, and hence the exclusive prerogative of men, since Mormon women are not ordained to priesthood offices. How the practice of healing and the exercise of glossolalia evolved in the Mormon experience to their present accepted form is the focus of this study.

Although there are scattered references to spiritual gifts during the New York period of LDS history (1829–31), it was in Kirtland, Ohio (1832–37), that they first flourished. At no time were they more in evidence than at the completion of the Kirtland Temple.[9] The women of the church had worked to build the temple and they attended public gatherings there, but they were not allowed to participate in the promised endowment. George A. Smith, reminiscing later as a member of the First Presidency, recalled that some of the women were "right huffy" as a consequence.[10]

Perhaps the women compensated through the exercise of tongues, although it was an accepted practice in public meetings for both men and women. One woman, Presendia Huntington, told of a fast meeting in the temple "during which a Brother McCarter rose and sang a song of Zion in tongues; I arose and sang simultaneously with him the same tune and words, beginning and ending each verse in perfect unison, without varying a word. It was just as though we had sung it together a thousand times."[11] Mary Fielding Smith, writing to her sister Mercy, described another meeting in the temple: "Many spake in tongues and others prophesied and interpreted. . . . Some of the sisters while engaged in conversing in tongues their countenances beaming with joy, clasped each other's hands . . . in the most affectionate manner. . . . A brite light shone across the house [temple] and rested upon some of the congregation."[12]

About twenty years later, Wilford Woodruff, the future third president of the church, reminisced with Elizabeth Ann Whitney and Eliza R. Snow about "the days of Kirtland" and heard again Elizabeth's gift of singing in tongues in the "pure language which Adam & Eve made use of in the garden of Eden." This gift, Woodruff recorded, "was obtained while in Kirtland through the promise of Joseph. He told her if she would rise upon her feet (while in the meeting) she should have the pure Language. She done so and immediately commenced singing in that language. It was as near heavenly music as any thing I ever herd."[13]

Kirtland was also where the "blessing meetings" were instituted. These were evening gatherings where Joseph Smith's father as patriarch to the church pronounced prophecies and blessings upon the heads of the faithful. Sometimes several families assembled for the occasion. These gatherings were especially significant to the women; they relished them and left many detailed accounts. Caroline Barnes Crosby wrote of her and her husband, Jonathan, receiving their patriarchal blessings: "These blessings cheered and rejoiced our hearts exceedingly. I truly felt humble before the Lord. . . . They led me to search into my heart, to see if there was any sin concealed there, and if so, to repent, and ask God to make me clean, and pure, in very deed. . . . Mother [Lucy Mack] Smith was in the room. She added her blessing or confirmed what we had already received."[14]

Sarah Studevant Leavitt remembered a spiritual blessing of another sort during this period. Sarah, praying to the Lord for her seriously ill daughter Louisa, saw an angel who told her to get the girl out of bed, lay "hands upon her head in the name of Jesus Christ and administer to her and she should recover." Sarah awakened her husband and told him to prepare

Louisa for the blessing. Though it was near midnight and she was weak, Louisa arose from her bed and Sarah administered to her. Louisa was soon "up and about."[15]

Sarah's experience may be the first recorded instance in the church of a healing blessing by a woman, but Joseph Smith, Sr., church patriarch, gave Eda Rogers a blessing in 1837 that clearly endorsed such spiritual powers: "In the absence of thy husband thou must pray with thy family. When they are sick thou shalt lay hands on them, and they shall recover. Sickness shall stand back."[16]

There came times, however, when Joseph Smith's cautions about abuse of the spiritual gifts were needed. In Kirtland a woman by the name of Hubble testified to the truthfulness of the Book of Mormon and "professed to be a prophetess of the Lord, and . . . have many revelations" and "deceived some, who were not able to detect her in her hypocrasy" until Joseph Smith announced a revelation instructing the people to "receive commandments and revelations . . . through him whom I [the Lord] have appointed," namely, Joseph Smith himself.[17] On 10 October 1833 Frederick G. Williams recorded a remarkable prophecy, apparently given by Elizabeth Ann Whitney, concerning the Indians. He warned, however, that "no prophecy spoken in tongues should be made public for this reason: — Many who pretend to have the gift of interpretation are liable to be mistaken, and do not give the true interpretation of what is spoken; but if any speak in tongues a word of exhortation, or doctrine, or the principles of the Gospel etc. let it be interpreted for the edification of the church."[18]

That same year, Joseph Smith also wrote to the church in Missouri: "Be careful, lest in this you be deceived. . . . Satan will no doubt trouble you about the gift of tongues, unless you are careful."[19] Later he added, "Do not indulge too much in the exercise of the gift of tongues, or the devil will take advantage of the innocent and unwary. . . . Be not so curious about tongues."[20] And finally, "I lay this down for a rule, that if anything is taught by the gift of tongues, it is not to be received for doctrine."[21]

In Nauvoo, Illinois, Joseph Smith not only formed the Female Relief Society as an essential part of the church, but he also introduced the ceremony of the temple endowment, the most elevated ritual among the Mormons. In the Relief Society, the women had an organization through which they could attend to the needs of the poor and also manifest the gifts of the spirit. Of this period, Susa Young Gates, a daughter of Brigham Young, wrote: "The privileges and powers outlined by the Prophet in those first meetings [of the Relief Society] have never been granted to women in full even yet." Then Susa asked, "Did those women, do you and I, live so well as to be worthy of them all?"[22]

What were these privileges and powers of which Susa spoke? The Nauvoo Relief Society minutes, carefully kept by Eliza R. Snow, tell us much. The

Prophet suggested "that the Sisters elect a presiding officer to preside over them, and let that presiding officer choose two Counsellors to assist in the duties of her office that he would ordain them to preside over the Society and let them preside just as the Presidency preside over the church; and if they need his instruction—ask him—he will give it from time to time.... If any officers are wanted to carry out the designs of the Institution, let them be appointed and act apart, as Deacons, Teachers &c. are among us."[23]

The women did elect their own president and Emma Smith, Joseph's wife, was the inevitable choice for president. After her two counselors were also elected by a vote of the women, Joseph Smith "ratified" the selection by explaining that Emma "was ordained at the time the [Elect Lady] Revelation was given,[24] to expound the Scriptures to all, and to teach the female part of the community." John Taylor, one of the twelve apostles, then "ordained" Sarah Cleveland and Elizabeth Ann Whitney as Emma's counselors. Susa Young Gates later stressed "not only set apart, but ordained."[25] Elizabeth Ann Whitney, in her own reminiscence, echoes that language: "I was also ordained and set apart under the hand of Joseph Smith the Prophet to administer to the sick and comfort the sorrowful. Several other sisters were also ordained and set apart to administer in these holy ordinances."[26]

The use of *ordain* seems to link these accounts to priesthood powers, although none of the women ever claimed they were ordained to the priesthood. Still, Joseph Smith's continued instructions to the Relief Society contain a confirmatory echo. On 30 March 1842 he told the women that "the Society should move according to the ancient Priesthood, hence there should be a select Society ... choice, virtuous and holy—[Joseph] Said he was going to make of this Society a kingdom of priests as in Enoch's day—as in Paul's day."[27] A month later, Joseph Smith told the women in a Relief Society meeting that he had come "to make observations respecting the Priesthood.... This Society is to get instruction thro' the order which God has established, thro' the medium of those appointed to lead." He further told the women, "and I now turn the key to you in the name of God and this Society shall rejoice and knowledge and intelligence shall flow down from this time—this is the beginning of better days to this Society."[28]

The phrase "I now turn the key to you" is significant. Contemporary Mormon women are familiar with the expression "I turn the key *in your behalf*," a variant that appears in the official *History of the Church*.[29] The change can be traced to George A. Smith, who in 1854 was given the task of completing Joseph Smith's history. In working on the manuscript covering the period from 1 April 1840 to 1 March 1842—including the Relief Society minutes in question—he revised and corrected the already compiled history, using "reports of sermons of Joseph Smith and others from minutes or sketches taken at the time in long hand." He mentioned using Eliza R. Snow's writings as well and said he had taken "the greatest care ... to convey the ideas in the prophet's style as near as possible; and in no case has the sentiment been varied that I know of."[30] He did not, however, comment on this particular passage from the minutes or explain his reasons for changing "I turn the key to you" to "I now turn the key in your behalf." George A. Smith's version has generally stood in church publications from that time to the present.

What did Joseph Smith mean by turning the key *to* women? A possible clue lies in the expansive view of women and their role in the church propounded by Newel K. Whitney in a meeting on 27 May 1842: "In the beginning God created man, male and female and bestowed upon man certain blessings peculiar to a man of God, which woman partook, so that without the female all things cannot be restored to the earth, it takes all to restore the Priesthood."[31] He may have been making an oblique reference to the endowment ceremony, a rite associated with the Nauvoo Temple, then moving toward completion. Joseph Smith had introduced him and a small circle of trusted friends to a form of it only two weeks earlier.[32] Alternatively, he may have felt that women had received an authority that paralleled and companioned the priesthood. At the very least, it is clear that the early Relief Society was not considered an "auxiliary" in the church as the Primary for children, Sunday School, and Mutual Improvement Association for adolescents would later be. Whatever the intent, the continued references to priesthood in relation to the women in Relief Society meetings left questions that would continue to surface.

In 1850 Zina Huntington Young, a plural wife first of Joseph Smith and later of Brigham Young, received a patriarchal blessing from John Smith, Joseph's uncle, which stated: "the Priesthood in fullness is & Shall be Conferd upon you."[33] When she, as president, addressed the first General Conference of the Relief Society on 6 April 1889, she reviewed the history of that organization and specified: "The Relief Society . . . was first organized . . . by the Prophet Joseph Smith; after the pattern of the Holy Priesthood, and under its direction."[34] Sarah M. Kimball, whose idea it was to organize the women of Nauvoo, had used the priesthood structure as a pattern for the Relief Society in her ward, complete with deaconesses and teachers.[35] However, John Taylor, who had originally ordained those first officers in March 1842, explained thirty-eight years later that "some of the sisters have thought that these sisters mentioned were, in this ordination, ordained to the priesthood. And for the information of all interested in this subject I will say, it is not the calling of these sisters to hold the Priesthood, only in connection with their husbands, they being one with their husbands."[36] His 1880 statement has stood as the official interpretation; however, the existing evidence signals an initially different role for the Relief Society than the one which ultimately developed. Joseph Smith may well have envisioned the Relief Society as an independent organization for women parallel to the priesthood organization for men.

Certainly the women saw their organization as more than a charitable society. In their meetings they not only discussed spiritual gifts such as speaking in tongues and healing the sick, but they openly practiced them. With Joseph Smith's approval, Emma Smith and her counselors laid hands on their sick sisters and blessed them that they might be healed. The fifth time the Relief Society convened, Sarah Cleveland invited the women to speak freely. A Sister Durfee "bore testimony to the great blessing she received when administered to after the close of the last meeting by Prest. E. Smith and [her] Councilors Cleveland and Whitney, she said she never realized more benefit thro' any administration," for she had "been healed and thought the sisters had more faith than the brethren." After that meeting, Sarah Cleveland and Elizabeth Whitney administered to another Relief Society member, Abigail Leonard, "for the restoration of health." [37]

In the intervening week, someone apparently reported to Joseph Smith that women were laying their hands on the sick in blessing and questioned the propriety of such acts. The Mormon leader addressed his answer directly to the women in the next meeting: "There could be no devil in it, if God gave his sanction by healing . . . there could be no more sin in any female laying hands on the sick than in wetting the face with water." He also indicated that there were women who were ordained to heal the sick and it was their privilege to do so. "If the sisters should have faith to heal the sick," he said, "let all hold their tongues." [38]

Healing was not the only spiritual gift recorded in the Relief Society minutes. Sarah Cleveland told the women that she often "felt in her heart what she could not express in our own language." She then expressed a desire "to speak in the gift of tongues, which she did in a powerful manner." [39] Joseph, however, reiterated his previous cautions on the proper use of their gifts of tongues. "If any have a matter to reveal," he told the women, "let it be in your own tongue. . . . You may speak in tongues for your own comfort, but . . . if anything is taught by the gift of tongues, it is not to be received for doctrine." [40]

By the end of the Nauvoo period of the church's history, vital links had been established between the Relief Society, the exercise of spiritual gifts, and the temple. The question of the relationship of the Relief Society to priesthood authority was a question that would persist through the nineteenth century and into the twentieth as the church organization itself changed and developed.

Ensuing events forced the disbanding of the Relief Society; the last Nauvoo minutes are dated April 1844. In March 1845 Brigham Young rather curtly announced that "when I want Sisters or the Wives of the members of the church to get up Relief Society I will summon them to my aid but until that time let them stay at home." [41] The Relief Society would endure a twelve years' hiatus before its official reinstatement, but the "blessing meetings" that had been a feature of both Kirtland and Nauvoo life continued. Years later, Presendia Lathrop Young recalled a meeting held at Winter Quarters: "Sister Eliza Snow walked the floor to keep her breath. All felt the distress and agony that awaited the nation. . . . and Sister Eliza Snow spoke afterwards in the pure language of Adam, with great power, and the interpretation was given."[42]

Eliza R. Snow's own diary contains numerous references to similar occasions during the same period. On 1 January 1847 she wrote of receiving a blessing "thro' our belov'd mother Chase and sis[ter] Clarissa [Decker] by the gift of tongues," adding "to describe the scene . . . would be beyond my power." Poetically she asserted

> Let not a gift be buried low
> That with a proper care
> And cultivation will bestow
> Celestial pleasure there.

On March 14, she records spending an evening "with Mother Chase & [Patty] Sessions. Father [Heber C.] Kimb[all] called in and gave us much beautiful instruction, after which we had some glorious communications of the spirit of God both by way of prophecy and the gift of tongues, and our hearts were made to rejoice and praise the name of God."[43]

The women participated with the men as equals in those informal and unstructured meetings. As the era ended, Presendia Lathrop Young observed, "There were not many brethren left [in Winter Quarters] and the sisters had to assist in many ways, both temporal and spiritual,"[44] indicating that, despite the promises of Joseph Smith, some women saw the exercise of spiritual gifts as a priesthood right for men, but only a privilege for women. Other evenings and afternoons of speaking in tongues, of blessing each other, and of uttering prophecy followed at short intervals. During these sessions, a bonding occurred that left these Saints, the women especially, intensely involved with each other and eloquent in expressing their feelings for each other and their commitments to the faith. This little group would teach the next several generations of Mormon women about spiritual gifts. The earlier association of these women with the Relief Society in Nauvoo made that particular identification even stronger.[45]

There were, however, those who continued to question the "propriety" of women's exercise of the gifts, and the two strands of confidence and doubt about the women's practice of spiritual gifts run through the rest of the nineteenth century. These same attitudes were also expressed about certain ordinances the Saints had received in the Nauvoo Temple. The ritual washing and anointing combined with the blessing of the sick became a common practice among church members, particularly women.

Mary Ellen Kimball records visiting a sick widow in company with Presendia Huntington, now her sister wife. They washed and anointed the woman, cooked her dinner, and watched her "eat pork and potatoes" with a gratifying appetite. After rejoicing with the healed woman, they returned home. Mary Ellen's journal continues: "I thought of the instructions I had received from time to time that the priesthood was not bestowed upon woman. I accordingly asked Mr. [Heber C.] Kimball [her husband] if woman had a right to wash and anoint the sick for the recovery of their health or is it mockery in them to do so. He replied inasmuch as they are obedient to their husbands they have a right to administer in that way in the name of the Lord Jesus Christ but not by authority of the priesthood invested in them for that authority is not given to woman. He also said they might administer by the authority given to their husbands in as much as they were one with their husband."[46] Mary Ellen's conclusion was the kind of argument that would calm women's apprehensions for the next four decades.

On other occasions, the concept of women holding the priesthood in connection with their husbands was reinforced when husbands and wives joined together in blessings. When Wilford Woodruff's namesake son, just ordained a priest, was about to begin his duties, the senior Woodruff summoned his household together, then recorded in third person, "His father and mother laid hands upon him and blessed him and dedicated him unto the Lord."[47] In 1875 George Goddard recorded that on the sixteenth birthday of his son, Brigham H., "his Mother and Myself, put our hands upon his head and pronounced a parents blessing upon him."[48]

At this time, church leaders strongly encouraged women to develop and use their spiritual powers. Brigham Young, speaking in the Tabernacle on 14 November 1869, asked, "Why do you not live so as to rebuke disease? . . . it is the privilege of a mother to have faith and to administer to her child; this she can do herself, as well as sending for the Elders."[49] The year before, in Cache Valley, Apostle Ezra T. Benson had called on the women who had been "ordained" and held "the power to rebuke diseases" to do so, and urged all the women to gain "the same power" by "exercis[ing] faith."[50] The record does not specify who the ordained women were or who ordained them, implying that they were well known in the community.

Spiritual gifts other than healing were also manifest among the women. Emmeline B. Wells was praised as "prophetic as well as poetical."[51] Apostle Orson Pratt, addressing the Saints in a general meeting, used women's exercise of the gift of prophecy to prove the authenticity of the church, for, he said, "there never was a genuine Christian Church unless it had Prophets and Prophetesses."[52] Eliza Snow, particularly in connection with her duties in the temple, frequently gave blessings which included prophecy. In 1857, when Guy Messiah Keysor was sealed to another wife in the endowment house, Eliza Snow laid her hands on his wife's head, "prophesied that she should live yet many days should receive her washings and anointings and health and things should come to pass according to her faith." She also prophesied in behalf of at least two more members of the party.[53] Emmeline Wells and Eliza Snow maintained, however, a jurisdictional distinction: they delivered prophetic utterances for individuals, but not for the church—a prerogative of the First Presidency.

As Eliza R. Snow's roles became more official, her duties may have encouraged women to feel that her spiritual gifts were attached to her calling. She, Zina D. Huntington Young, and other women who had shared the Winter Quarters experience, frequently encouraged the use of the gift of tongues in public gatherings, and we find records of occurrences of glossalalia in locales as far separated as Arizona and Canada.[54]

Men were often present at meetings where women exercised spiritual powers, indicating that they approved of the women's actions. Eliza R. Snow told a Santa Clara Relief Society meeting that "if the congregation would lift there hearts to God she would bless them in tongues, which she did with power and the Holy Ghost, then said if the people would lift there hearts to God Sister Zina would interpret, Sister Zina D. Smith [Young] then arose and said Sister Eliza first prayed for the Bretheren and sisters on the stand then the choir then the congragation . . . she said if they repent of there sins and turn to God they should be blessed." She was followed, the minutes note, by four brethren who testified to the truthfulness of the blessing.[55] The next year, while meeting in Orderville with the "young folks associations," Eliza again "Spoke in tongs. Interpreted by Sister Zina D. Young. We had a very good meeting."[56] Frederick Kesler's diary notes on 14 May 1875 that, "after urging," Elizabeth Ann Whitney spoke in tongues with fluid ease for some five minutes. Eliza R. Snow affirmed that it was the "pure tongue of Adam."[57] The diaries of Jens Christian Anderson Weibye tell of public meetings in Manti where women and men spoke in tongues and interpreted these utterances.[58]

But uneasiness about the use of tongues is also apparent. Emily Partridge Young records that at a tea party in 1874 Eliza R. Snow "insisted on my speaking in tongues so I complied, but I am not in favor of making much use of that gift." She wrote further: "The devil is apt to poke his nose in where there is tongues, especially among the inexperienced. And I do hope the sisters will be wise and not suffere themselves to get into a muddle, but seek those gifts that are most profitable to all. When we speak in our own tongue, we know what we say." And her last phrase gives both sides of this cherished but dubious coin: "Yet the gift of tongues is one of the gifts of the gospel, but should not be trifled with."[59]

Still, healing by women caused the most confusion. This quiet, routine practice occasionally raised questions which, when answered publicly by church leaders or the Relief Society, started a ripple of uneasiness. Zina Huntington Young's journal for 1881 mentions several healings. On Joseph

Smith's birthday, she washed and anointed one woman "for her health" and administered to another "for her hearing." Remembering the Prophet's birthday, she reminisced about the days in Nauvoo when she was one of his plural wives: "I have practiced much with My Sister Presendia Kimball while in Nauvoo & ever since before Joseph Smith's death. He blest Sisters to bless the sick." Three months later: "I went to see Chariton [her son] & administered to him, felt so sad to see him suffer." The next year she notes with satisfaction hearing an address by Bishop Whitney in the Eighteenth Ward wherein he "blest the Sisters in having faith to administer to there own families in humble faith not saying by the Authority of the Holy Priesthood but in the name of Jesus Christ."[60] Helen Mar Whitney, writing in 1877, reports being administered to by Eliza Snow and Margaret Smoot after a winter of illness and depression: "My health & spirits revived."[61] And Amy Brown Lyman in the 1942 *Relief Society Magazine* recalled the exciting visits of Eliza R. Snow and Zina D. H. Young to her town when she was a girl, and an administration they performed there: "They came to our home on several occasions to bless and comfort my semi-invalid mother. On one occasion we children were permitted in the room and were allowed to kneel in prayer with these sisters, and later to hear their fervent appeals for mother's recovery. They placed their hands upon her head and promised that through our united faith she would be spared to her family. This was an impressive spiritual experience for us, and the fulfillment of this promise, a testimony."[62]

While these private blessings continued, church leaders issued cautions about them. In an 1878 stake conference, Angus Cannon, president of the Salt Lake Stake, answered a question in stake conference about women holding the priesthood: "Women could only hold the priesthood in connection with their husbands; man held the priesthood independent of woman. The sisters have a right to anoint the sick, and pray the Father to heal them, and to exercise that faith that will prevail with God; but women must be careful how they use the authority of the priesthood in administering to the sick."[63] Two years later, in 8 August 1880, John Taylor's address "The Order and Duties of the Priesthood" reaffirmed that women "hold the Priesthood, only in connection with their husbands, they being one with their husbands."[64]

Meanwhile the administrative autonomy of Relief Society leaders was clarified. A circular letter sent from the First Presidency in October 1880 "to all the authorities of the Priesthood and Latter-day Saints" described the Relief Society, its composition, its purposes, the qualifications for its officers, and their duties. This document for the first time specified that Relief Society general officers should get the approval of stake presidents and bishops before holding meetings. The officers were not selected by local priesthood authorities but by the Relief Society general officers, then "sanctioned by the majority vote of the ladies present." After that process they were "blessed and set apart" by the stake president or bishop. The directive also stated that women "should not be ordained to any office in the Priesthood; but they may be appointed as Helps, and Assistants, and Presidents, among their own sex, to instruct, to exhort, to strengthen and to build up a holy people unto the Lord." The circular letter included a section called "The Sick and Afflicted": "It is the privilege of all faithful women and lay members of the church, who believe in Christ, to administer to all the sick or afflicted in their respective families, either by the laying on of hands, or by the anointing with oil in the name of the Lord: but they should administer in these sacred ordinances, not by virtue and authority of the priesthood, but by virtue of their faith in Christ, and the promises made to believers: and thus they should do in all their ministrations."[65] The First Presidency clarified that anointing and blessing the sick were not official functions of the Relief Society since any faithful church member might perform the actions. However, by specifying women's right to administer to the sick "in their respective families," the church leaders raised another question: What about administering to those outside the family circle? They gave no answer, although the practice of calling for the elders or calling for the sisters had certainly been established.

Several other church documents addressed related questions in that next decade, indicating increasing confusion. Answering queries "very frequently" received, Eliza R. Snow used the columns of the *Woman's Exponent* in 1884 to answer two questions. The first was: "Should members of the Relief Society go to the Bishops for counsel?" She replied:

> The Relief Society is designed to be a self-governing organization: to relieve the Bishops as well as to relieve the poor, to deal with its members, correct abuses, etc. If difficulties arise between members of a branch which they cannot settle between the members themselves, aided by the teachers, instead of troubling the Bishop, the matter should be referred to their president and her counselors. If the branch board cannot decide satisfactorily, an appeal to the stake board is next in order; if that fails to settle the question, the next step brings it before the general board, from which the only resort is to the Priesthood; but, if possible, we should relieve the Bishops instead of adding to their multitudinous labors.

No doubt Eliza R. Snow saw the Relief Society as a remarkably autonomous organization. She probably would not have questioned the language of the official circular letter—that the Relief Society leaders were set apart as presidents, assistants, and helps—but her language places such "helps" to priesthood leaders as coming from women as colleagues and equals, not as subordinates.

The second question also bears on the topic: "Is it necessary for sisters to be set apart to officiate in the sacred ordinances of washing, anointing, and laying on of hands in administering to the sick?" Here Eliza Snow was even more emphatic:

> It certainly is not. Any and all sisters who honor their holy endowments, not only have the right, but should feel it a duty, whenever called upon to administer to our sisters in these ordinances, which God has graciously committed to His daughters as well as to His sons; and we testify that when administered and received in faith and humility they are accompanied with all mighty power.
>
> Inasmuch as God our Father has revealed these sacred ordinances and committed them to His Saints, it is not only our privilege but our imperative duty to apply them for the relief of human suffering.

Thus did Eliza Snow in 1884 echo Joseph Smith's 28 April 1842 instruction to the Relief Society: "Thousands can testify that God has sanctioned the administration of these ordinances [of healing the sick] by our sisters with the manifestations of His healing influence."[66]

The washings and anointings to which Eliza Snow referred were done in connection with "administering to the sick." Although these rites certainly grew out of the temple ordinances in Nauvoo, their practice by women occurred outside the temple. Even after the establishment of the Endowment House in Salt Lake in 1855 and later the dedication of the St. George, Manti, and Logan temples, the ordinances took place both within those sacred structures and inside the privacy of individual homes. The wording took different forms as the occasion demanded. One of the most common uses of the washing and anointing blessing came as women administered to each other prior to childbirth.

Two differing points of view were now in print. Eliza Snow and the First Presidency agreed that the Relief Society had no monopoly on the ordinance of administration by and for women. The First Presidency, however, implied that the ordinance should now be limited to the woman's family without specifying any requirement but faithfulness. Eliza Snow, on the other hand, said nothing of limiting administrations to the family—indeed, the implication is clear that anyone in need of a blessing should receive it—but said that only women who had been endowed may officiate.

A Relief Society conference in the Logan Tabernacle in 1886 heard Sister Tenn Young urge the women: "I wish to speak of the great privilege given to us to wash and anoint the sick and suffering of our sex. I would counsel everyone who expects to become a Mother to have this ordinance administered by some good faithful sister." The secretary adds, "She later gave instructions how it should be done." Her counsel was endorsed by Mary Ann Freeze, who "said she attended to this and the curse to bring forth in sorrow was almost taken away."[67] And at the other end of the Utah territory, in St. George, Lucy B. Young, a wife of Brigham Young, had won the confidence of the Saints in administering to both the living and the dead. Her name led the roll of workers as soon as the St. George Temple was dedicated in 1877: "How many times the sick and suffering have come upon beds to that temple, and at once Sister Young would be called to take the afflicted one under immediate charge, as all knew the mighty power she had gained through long years of fastings and prayers in the exercise of her special gift. When her hands are upon the head of another in blessing, the words of inspiration and personal prophecy that flow from her lips are like a stream of living fire. One sister who had not walked for twelve years was brought, and under the cheering faith of Sister Young she went through the day's ordinance and was perfectly healed of her affliction."[68] When the Manti and Logan temples were dedicated, Sister Young went to both to train ordinance workers. In so doing, she must have strengthened the link between temple ceremonies and administrations for healing.

This link with the temple is also evident in an undated account of Catherine Jane Cottam Romney, grandmother of Camilla Eyring Kimball. Catherine had "special callings" in the Mormon communities of Arizona and Mexico. When a friend told Catherine's daughter that she had been blessed and healed by her mother and to "please thank her," the daughter asked her mother about the nature of the blessing. "Catherine explained that since there was no Temple there, that she and another Sister had been set apart to give washings and anointings to women sent to them by the Brethren. She said it was a very sacred calling and was not to be talked about."[69]

But doubts surfaced among women who desired approval from their presiding brethren and inevitably raised questions about propriety. Answers varied, however, depending on who provided them. In 1881 Emmeline B. Wells, editor of the *Woman's Exponent* and soon to be president of the Relief Society, sent Wilford Woodruff a list of questions on the topic of washing and anointings. Her questions and his response follow:

> First: Are sisters justified in administering the ordinance of washing and anointing previous to confinements to those who have received their endowments and have married men outside of the Church?
> Second: Can anyone who has not had their endowments be thus administered to by the sisters if she is a faithful Saint in good standing and has not yet had the opportunity of going to the temple for the ordinances?
> [Answer:] To begin with I desire to say that the *ordinance* of washing and anointing is one that should only be administered in Temples or other holy places which are dedicated for the purpose of giving endowments to the Saints. That *ordinance* might not be administered to any one whether she has received or has not received her endowments, in any other place or under any other circumstances.
> But I imagine from your question that you refer to a practice that has grown up among the sisters of washing and anointing sisters who are approaching their confinement. If so, this is not, strictly speaking, an ordinance, unless it be

done under the direction of the priesthood and in connection with the ordinance of laying on of hands for the restoration of the sick.

There is no impropriety in sisters washing and anointing their sisters in this way, under the circumstances you describe; but it should be understood that they do this, not as members of the priesthood, but as members of the Church, exercising faith for, and asking the blessings of the Lord upon, their sisters, just as they, and every member of the Church, might do in behalf of the members of their families.[70]

President Woodruff's careful distinctions between the temple ordinance of washing and anointing, the church member's practice of washing and anointing, and the priesthood ordinance of anointing in connection with a healing blessing do not directly address the position Eliza R. Snow had taken earlier that only endowed women should administer to others. The issue became more confused. When precisely the same act was performed and very nearly the same words were used among women in the temple, among women outside the temple, and among men administering to women, the distinction—in the average mind—became shadowy indeed.

In 1889 Zina D. H. Young, addressing a general conference of the Relief Society, gave the sisters advice on a variety of topics. Between wheat storage and silk culture came this paragraph: "It is the privilege of the sisters, who are faithful in the discharge of their duties, and have received their endowments and blessings in the house of the Lord, to administer to their sisters, and to the little ones, in time of sickness, in meekness and humility, ever being careful to ask in the name of Jesus, and to give God the glory."[71] Although she does not specify exactly what is meant by "to administer," she reaffirms that it is not exclusively a priesthood ordinance. She also reiterates Eliza Snow's position that it is a privilege of the endowed.

In 1895 Torkel Torkelson, widely in demand to bless the sick, records that two sisters went to his Salt Lake home "to wash and anoint my wife before her confinement. Since it happened that I was at home, the sisters called upon me to bless her. After I had blessed her and then sealed the holy ordinance which the sisters had performed, . . . I could see the power of God come upon [Sister Phelps]" and she prophesied in tongues upon Brother Torkelson himself, his household, and the unborn child.[72]

By the end of the nineteenth century, questions had arisen about the propriety of women's participation in and use of spiritual gifts. However, the "leading sisters" of the church had successfully maintained their right to these gifts and had been supported by the church hierarchy in their positions. A defense, however, indicates an attack, and the Mormon church entered the twentieth century at the price of some elements of its nineteenth-century identity. Mormonism's "peculiar institution," plural marriage, had officially been abandoned. The church had also exchanged its dream of a theocracy for statehood. And perhaps some Mormons—high and low—

began to wonder whether the practice of spiritual gifts might be inappropriate—not "respectable." In any case, the twentieth century saw a definite shift in the status of the practice of these gifts among Mormons.

As late as 1910, the traditional definition of tongues was current. Apostle Heber J. Grant in October conference told his oft-repeated story of playing on the floor as a child in the presence of his mother, Elizabeth Ann Whitney, Eliza R. Snow, and Zina D. Young among others. Sister Whitney sang in tongues. Also in tongues, Sister Snow blessed those who were present. Sister Young translated. Then Sister Snow "turned and blest the boy playing on the floor, and Sister Young gave the interpretation. I did not understand it, but my mother made a record of it, and twenty years after it was given it was fulfilled. What was it? It was that the boy should grow to manhood, that he should become one of the leaders of the Church, and that God would bless him in proclaiming the gospel in foreign lands." He then testified that "the gift of tongues is in this Church." Furthermore, in the same talk, Apostle Grant told how his wife "pronounced a blessing upon my head by the spirit of tongues, all of which has been fulfilled."[73] In another general conference nine years later, he reported again on these incidents and others, giving even more details.[74]

However, warnings against misuse of this gift were again evident, giving preference to the association of tongues and missionary work. In 1900 Joseph F. Smith as president of the Quorum of the Twelve had warned: "There is perhaps no gift of the spirit of God more easily imitated by the devil than the gift of tongues. Where two men or women exercise the gift of tongues by the inspiration of the spirit of God, there are a dozen perhaps that do it by the inspiration of the devil." Then he gave an example of being a missionary in a foreign land and seeking "earnestly for the gift of tongues, and by this gift and by study, in a hundred days after landing upon those islands I could talk to the people in their language as I now talk to you in my native tongue. This was a gift that was worthy of the Gospel. There was a purpose in it. There was something in it to strengthen my faith, to encourage me and to help me in my ministry. If you have need of this gift of tongues, seek for it and God will help you in it. But I do not ask you to be very hungry for the gift of tongues, for if you are not careful the devil will deceive you in it."[75]

In 1901 Apostle Abraham O. Woodruff echoed this kind of warning, saying that bishops should exercise discernment about this practice and recommend, if appropriate, that members "restrain this gift." In his cautions about the use of the gift of tongues, he also voiced a theme that was to gather power and momentum during the next two decades: the supremacy of the priesthood and the importance of hierarchy. "No man or woman has a right to find fault with the Bishop for restraining him or her in any of these matters. The Bishop is the responsible party. . . . We ought to be obedient to our Bishops."[76] Regarding the gift of tongues, Apostle Matthew Cowley in 1949 told of learning Maori in twelve weeks. "They do speak with new tongues," he said, giving a solid new interpretation to that scripture—"those who accept the call to the ministry of our Lord and Saviour Jesus Christ."[77] This interpretation—assistance in learning languages—is used almost exclusively in the modern church. In October 1980 conference, Elder Gene R. Cook of the First Quorum of the Seventy, reported that "missionaries learn through the gift of tongues to speak Spanish, Aymara, Quechua, and many other Indian dialects."[78]

Other less frequently cited examples occur when church members are able to understand another language or at least the spirit of what is being said. Marvelee Soon Tahauri wrote in the March 1982 *Ensign*:

> One day, after I had presented a lesson on turning our weaknesses into strengths, a sister stood, weeping while bearing testimony in her native tongue. Suddenly she reached over to where I sat and embraced me, kissing me time and time again.
>
> "Thank you, thank you!" she sobbed.
>
> The revelation hit me with unexpected force. We were truly sisters in God's kingdom! She was not just a Samoan sister; she was *my* sister, and I really loved her. With so many previous dawnings of knowledge, I should have been prepared to experience this realm of the Spirit; yet I was trembling, and the tears flowed unrestrained.[79]

As the offical interpretation of the gift of tongues slowly shifted, so uneasiness increased about the women's continued exercise of the gift of healing. Ruth May Fox wrote in her diary in 1901: "And if the brethren decided that women could not seal the anointing then we should do as they say." But she failed to see any reason why women could not, for "Aunt Zina did." When this same Zina Young was asked by Ruth Fox if women held the priesthood in connection with their husbands, she answered "that we should be thankful for the many blessings we enjoyed and say nothing about it. If you plant a grain of wheat and keep poking and looking at it to see if it was growing you would spoil the root." This circumspect metaphor, Ruth Fox, future YLMIA general president, added, "was very satisfying to me."[80]

But always someone was eager to poke, and each time the spiritual roots of the women were imperiled. Some, like Louisa Lula Greene Richards, former editor of the *Woman's Exponent*, responded indignantly. She wrote a somewhat terse letter on 9 April 1901 to President Lorenzo Snow concerning an article she had read in the *Deseret News* the previous day. It had stated: "Priest, Teacher or Deacon may administer to the sick, and so may a member, male or female, but neither of them can seal the anointing and blessing, because the authority to do that is vested in the Priesthood after the order of Melchizedek." The question of sealing was thus added to the long list of ambiguities. Richards says, "If the information given in the answer is absolutely correct, then myself and thousands of other members of the Church have been misinstructed and are laboring under a very serious mistake, which certainly should be authoritatively corrected." She gives a hint of the kind of authority that would be necessary by stating firmly, "Sister Eliza R. Snow Smith [her correspondent's sister], from the Prophet Joseph Smith, her husband, taught the sisters in her day, that a very important part of the sacred ordinance of administration to the sick was the sealing of the anointing and blessings, and should never be omitted. And we follow the pattern she gave us continually. We do not seal in the authority of the Priesthood, but in the name of our Lord and Savior, Jesus Christ."[81] There is no available record of Lorenzo Snow's reply.

This short newspaper item, however, was a straw in a rising wind. Over the next few years, an emerging definition of priesthood authority and an increased emphasis on its importance would remove more and more spiritual responsibilities from women and link them with the priesthood alone. The statements authorizing the continuance of women's blessings only signaled their dependence on that permission. One month after Lula Richards's inquiry, the general presidency of the Relief Society sent President Lorenzo Snow a copy of President Wilford Woodruff's 1888 letter to Emmeline B. Wells. This letter, discussed earlier, made the distinction between washings and blessings as ordinances (confined to the temple under priesthood authority) and washings and blessings as sisterly acts (performed outside the temple). As president of the church, Lorenzo Snow reaffirmed the position explained there, with the exception that blessings should be "confirmed" rather than "sealed."[82]

Sometime during that first decade of the new century, the Relief Society circulated a letter called simply "Answers to Questions," written on Relief Society letterhead. Undated, it ended with the notation: "Approved by the First Presidency of the Church." This two-page letter was the most complete document to date on the subject of healing the sick and may have been a response to an unsigned 1903 *Young Woman's Journal* lesson that asserted: "Only the higher or Melchisedek Priesthood has the right to lay on hands for the healing of the sick, or to direct the administration, . . . though to pray for the sick is the right that necessarily belongs to every member of the Church."[83] This may be the earliest published claim that only the Melchizedek Priesthood had authority to heal. But the Relief Society's approved letter directly countered that position.

The first question concerned washing and anointing: "Is it necessary for one or more sisters to be set apart for that purpose? . . . or should it be done under the direction of the Presidency of the Relief Society, or could any good sister officiate?" The answers to this three-part question were that, first, any endowed sisters in "good standing" might wash and anoint a sister "previous to confinement," if requested. Second, sisters "gifted in ministering and comforting in faith" would attend to confined sisters within their own ward but would not necessarily be called by the presidency of the Relief Society. Third, without waiting to consult the Relief Society presidency, sisters could attend to sick children "both in administering and in the washing with pure water and anointing with consecrated oil." The letter allowed, further, that there were often sisters "specially adapted to minister to children, and who have in a large degree the gift of healing under the influence of the Holy Spirit."

The second question asked: "Should the washing be sealed?" And the answer: "It is usual to do this in a few simple words, avoiding the terms used in the Temple, and instead of using the word 'Seal' we would use the word 'Confirm' in the spirit of invocation."

The third question asked: "Have the sisters a right to seal the washing and anointing, using no authority, but doing it in the name of Jesus Christ, or should men holding the Priesthood be called in?" The answer: "The sisters have the privilege of laying their hands on the head of the one officiated for and confirming the anointing in the spirit of invocation, and in the name of Jesus Christ, not mentioning authority. Therefore it is not necessary to call in the Brethren. The Lord has heard and answered the prayers of the sisters in these ministrations many times." [84]

This letter clarified some issues that had previously been ambiguous or contradictory. Women's administrations to the sick were not necessarily Relief Society functions, nor did women need priesthood permission or participation to do them. Any endowed woman had authority to perform such services, and these blessings were not confined to her own family. The letter also cautioned the women to avoid resemblances in language to the temple forms, and although the blessings should be sealed, the sisters did not need a priesthood holder to do it.

In 1908 Nephi Pratt, the mission president in Portland, Oregon, wrote President Joseph F. Smith, inquiring whether Relief Society sisters, when set apart, should be given the authority to wash and anoint sisters before childbirth and also whether there were any forms they should follow in carrying out these services. President Smith answered that the washing and anointing in question was a practice that "some of our Relief Society sisters appear to have confounded . . . with one of the temple ordinances. . . . We desire you therefore to impress upon the sisters of your Relief Society that this practise is in no sense whatever an ordinance, and must not be regarded as such, unless it be attended to under the direction of proper authority [meaning the priesthood] in connection with the ordinance of laying on hands for the healing of the sick." He emphasized, however, that even women who had not received their endowments could participate in the washing and anointing "as there is no impropriety whatever in their doing so, inasmuch as they do it in a proper way, that is, in the spirit of faith and prayer, and without assumption of special authority, no more in fact than members of the church generally might do in behalf of members of their own families. . . . No member of the church therefore need be barred from receiving a blessing at the hands of faithful women. . . . As to the particular form of words to be used, there is none, not any more than there is for an elder to use in administering to the sick." [85]

On 17 December 1909 the First Presidency, still headed by Joseph F. Smith, again endorsed President Woodruff's 1888 letter to Emmeline B. Wells, making one correction, "namely in the clause pertaining to women administering to children, President [Anthon H.] Lund had said those sisters need not necessarily be only those who had received their endowments for it was not always possible for women to have that privilege and women of faith might do so [give blessings]." [86] Apparently for the first time, directly and decisively, a president of the church had enunciated a policy about who could give and receive such blessings, separating such actions clearly from the temple ceremony and making these rites accessible to any member of the household of faith, male or female.

Also, sometime during that first decade in the twentieth century, a rare document—perhaps the only known example of its kind—emerged: the written-out form of the blessing to be pronounced in a washing, an anointing, and a sealing before childbirth. The text of the blessing, undated, is contained in the 1901-9 minutes of the Oakley (Idaho) Second Ward Relief Society. Even though Joseph F. Smith had said that there was no special form for such occasions, the sisters were apparently more comfortable following a prescribed form. We do not know whether they followed the text exactly or deviated from it, but its very existence bespeaks an insistence that the words be used in a certain way and that the process be linked to the Relief Society. They did follow earlier counsel to avoid the wording used in the temple ordinances, and, of course, the blessing and sealing are different in concept from the temple washing and anointing.

The words of the blessings for washing and anointing follow each other very closely with only occasional and minor changes. The blessings were specific and comprehensive: "We anoint your back, your spinal column that you might be strong and healthy no disease fasten upon it no accident belaff [befall] you, Your kidneys that they might be active and healthy and preform their proper functions, your bladder that it might be strong and protected from accident, your Hips that your system might relax and give way for the birth of your child, your sides that your liver, your lungs, and spleen that they might be strong and preform their proper functions, . . . your breasts that your milk may come freely and you need not be afflicted with sore nipples as many are, your heart that it might be comforted." They continue by requesting blessings from the Lord on the unborn child that it might be "perfect in every joint and limb and muscle, that it might be beautiful to look upon . . . [and] happy," and that "when [its] full time shall have come that the child shall present right for birth and that the afterbirth shall come at its proper time . . . you need not flow to excess. . . . We anoint . . . your thighs that they might be healthy and strong that you might be exempt from cramps and from the bursting of veins. . . . That you might stand upon the earth [and] go in and out of the Temples of God." [87] The document combines the practical physiological considerations of neighborly concern shared over the back fence with the reassuring solace and compassion of being anointed with the "balm of sisterhood." [88] The women sealed the blessing:

> We unitedly lay our hands upon you to seal this washing and anointing where with you have been washed and anointed for your safe delivery, for the salvation of you and your child and we ask God to let his special blessings to rest upon you, that you might sleep well at night that your dreams might be pleasant and that the good spirit might guard and protect you from every evil influence spirit and power that you may go your full time and that every blessing that we have asked God to confer upon you and your offspring may be litterly fulfiled that all fear and dread may be taken from you and that you might trust in God. All these blessings we unitedly seal upon you in the name of Jesus Christ Amen. [89]

Evidence shows that this practice continued in similar form for several decades. In Cache Valley, a 1910 Relief Society meeting was devoted to the topic of healing. President Lucy S. Cardon "read some instructions to the sisters on the washing and anointing this [*sic*] sick, and how it should be done properly," adding a testimony of the importance of having the Spirit of the Lord. One sister asked a question on "the sub[ject] of washing and anointing," and Sister Martha Meedham, with a brisk earthiness that comes off the page, answered that she had done "as much washing and anointing as anyone in this Stake. . . Said she had written to Pres. J. F. Smith on the sub. and he told her to keep on & bless & comfort as she had done in the past. It was a gift that was only given to a few, but all sisters who desired and are requested can perform this." One sentence in the minutes speaks volumes about the independence of the Relief Society, but in a mingling of pride and trepidation: "The sisters felt that the Bishop should be acquainted with the work we do." Relief Society president Margaret Ballard added "how she had been impressed to bless and administer to her father who was sick and suffering and he had been healed. Had also been impressed to bless her husband and he was healed." The meeting closed, appropriately, with singing, "Count Your Many Blessings." [90]

Another source records the practice "from the early 1930s" of Relief Society women in the Calgary Ward in Canada requesting that they be washed and anointed by other sisters before going to the hospital for surgery or for childbearing.[91] The procedure described is similar to that recorded in the Oakley Second Ward minutes given above.

These rare glimpses of Mormon women discussing anointings and blessings are revealing. They show women who were faithful, concerned about their personal worthiness and the companionship of the Holy Ghost, and anxious to teach and bless one another. These women had personal testimonies born of experience; and they provided role models, validation, and encouragement to their community. As we read the accounts of these earlier Mormon women practicing these spiritual gifts, we are brought to ask: How do these experiences relate to the priesthood? That, after all, was and still is a crucial question.

An 1896 article in the *Young Woman's Journal* had reiterated a belief common among many church members that a missionary's wife "bears the priesthood of the Seventy, in connection with her husband, and shares in its responsibilities more closely and effectively than any other office of the priesthood entails upon womankind"—largely because she "bears the burdens of her husband's absence, when all alone the cares of the family and home rest upon her."[92] But with the coming of the twentieth century, the early generation that had taught that women held the priesthood in connection with their husbands was passing. In 1907 the *Improvement Era* published the query: "Does a wife hold the priesthood with her husband? and may she lay hands on the sick with him, with authority?" Speaking for a new generation, President Joseph F. Smith answered: "A wife does not hold the priesthood in connection with her husband, but she enjoys the benefits thereof with him; and if she is requested to lay hands on the sick with him, or with any other officer holding the Melchizedek priesthood, she may do so with perfect propriety. It is no uncommon thing for a man and wife unitedly to administer to their children, and the husband being mouth, he may properly say out of courtesy, 'By authority of the holy priesthood in us vested.'"[93]

As a clearer definition of priesthood emerged, it redefined the role of women. In 1901 B. H. Roberts, a member of the third presiding quorum, the Seventies, lamented how "common" the priesthood seemed to be held and insisted that "respect for the Priesthood" went far beyond respecting the General Authorities to include "all those who hold the Priesthood . . . presidents of stakes; . . . Bishops . . . the Priests, who teach the Gospel at the firesides of the people . . . and the humblest that holds that power."[94] Thus, the priesthood was defined not only as a power from God but also as the man on whom it is conferred. Statements such as this initiated the practice in the church of referring to its leaders and eventually to all male members as "the priesthood." Joseph Fielding Smith, a young apostle in 1910, put the case even stronger in a conference talk on respecting the presiding brethren, particularly the First Presidency: "It is a serious thing for any member of this Church to raise his voice against the priesthood, or to hold the priesthood in disrespect; for the Lord will not hold such guiltless."[95] His father was church president, and he would eventually succeed to that position.

It is evident in 1913 that the priesthood—meaning, by this time, the authoritative structure of the church—had authority also over those gifts that had once been the right of every member of the household of faith. The Relief Society minutes for a meeting held on 7 October 1913 record a growing concern of Emmeline B. Wells, then president: "In the early days in Nauvoo women administered to the sick and many were healed through their administration, and while some of the brethren do not approve of this, it is to be hoped the blessing will not be taken from us."[96] This is the earliest acknowledgment extant that some members of the church hierarchy disapproved of the general exercise of the gift of healing by women.

Already that spring in April conference, President Joseph F. Smith had expressed his concern over the divisive tendency of the various church organizations to act independently of the priesthood. He then placed the Relief Society among the auxiliaries—Sunday School, Primary, and young people's Mutual Improvement Associations—rather than in its traditional position as a companion or parallel to the priesthood. The auxiliaries "are not independent," he insisted: "Not one of them is independent of the Priesthood of the Son of God, not one of them can exist a moment in the acceptance of the Lord when they withdraw from the voice and from the counsel of those who hold the Priesthood and preside over them. They are subject to the powers and authority of the Church, and they are not independent of them: nor can they exercise any rights in their organizations independently of the Priesthood and of the Church; and I want you to take it home to you now—every one of you. You may hear something stronger than that from me if you don't."[97]

The Relief Society would loyally respond with an article in the second number of its 1914 *Bulletin,* the successor to the *Woman's Exponent* and the predecessor of the *Relief Society Magazine.* Explaining that new officers and teachers needed orientation to the general rules of the organization, it commented that each group had "great liberty" in local arrangements but that "one rule . . . should be written deep in the heart of every women in this kingdom—and conned frequently by those who hold office in this great organization, namely, respect for the priesthood." All systems have their law. The church has "the law of God" and defines priesthood as "the power to administer in the ordinances of the Gospel. . . . Associated with this Priesthood is the right of presidency. Out of this grows the functions and offices of the presiding authority; of the Church, and of every quorum in the Church. Those who preside over the auxiliary organizations receive their authority from the presiding Priesthood."

"Women do not hold the Priesthood," it continues, without making the traditional qualification about their holding it in connection with their husbands or benefiting from its blessings if married to a worthy priesthood holder. "This fact must be faced calmly by mothers and explained clearly to young women, for the spirit that is now abroad in the world makes for women's demand for every place and office enjoyed by men, and a few more that men can't enter. Women in this Church must not forget that they have rights which men do not possess." The writer does not specify these rights. The address further assures women that even the superior woman will marry "the right one," identifiable because "he will be just one or more degrees superior in intelligence and power to the superior woman." In any case if he holds the priesthood, "women everywhere, as men who may be under his jurisdiction, should render that reverence and obedience that belongs of right to the Priesthood which he holds."

After assuring readers that this article was "only repeating the same things that have been told in this organization" by Eliza R. Snow, Zina D. Young, and Bathsheba W. Smith, the writer reversed the policy of solving women's problems strictly within the Relief Society, as enunciated by Eliza Snow in 1884, and told the women that the general office of the Relief Society would gladly answer questions from the field, including those on "washing and anointing the sick, . . . yet any and all of these questions might be referred to the ward or stake Priesthood and their answers should be taken as final. We should always be glad to hear of such decisions, but would respect the authority in any given instance. This may be taken as the general rule or law of this Society."[98] The message could not be clearer. The Relief Society was firmly subordinated to the priesthood as an auxiliary.

In October 1914, eight months later, President Joseph F. Smith and his counselors sent a letter to bishops and stake presidents, establishing official policy on "washing and anointing our sisters preparatory to their confinement." Though little of the information was new, for the first time it did not come from the Relief Society. It formalized policy that had taken shape over the years: Lorenzo Snow's stipulation that the blessing must be confirmed rather than sealed and Wilford Woodruff's that it was not a Relief Society function and neither was it an ordinance. However, there were two significant additions. After affirming that sisters may seal their anointings and that the Lord has answered such prayers, the First Presidency letter continues: "It should, however, always be remembered that the command of the Lord is to call in the elders to administer to the sick, and when they can be called in, they should be asked to anoint the sick or seal the anointing."[99] This may not be an attempt to curb the women's practice of spiritual gifts as much as it may represent an attempt to distinguish between the "woman's work" of giving birth and the more general human problem of illness. However, *command* must have given many women pause and turned them toward the elders when they might have asked for ministration from women. This First

Presidency letter further stated that women who had received their endowments are generally stronger in the faith and especially qualified to wash and anoint other women prior to confinement. But the directive made clear that this act could be performed by any "good faithful sisters" who were requested.[100]

This clarified the questions left unanswered since the days of Eliza R. Snow. And the concluding paragraph also resolved the question of who is empowered to decide policy on these issues: "In all sacred functions performed by our sisters there should be perfect harmony between them and the Bishop, who has the direction of all matters pertaining to the Church in his ward."[101] Thus, no longer a Relief Society function, blessings remained a woman's function only under priesthood direction. A link which had existed from Eliza R. Snow's day between the women in the ward and the presiding women of the church had been severed.

This new orderliness was in harmony with the pattern being established throughout the church, perhaps partially in response to the challenge of factions which continued the practice of plural marriage. In 1918 Joseph Fielding Smith reaffirmed in general conference the importance of the gift of revelation but stressed that the Lord would send revelations "for the guidance of this people . . . to the presidents of stakes and the bishops of the wards over the signatures of the presiding authorities, or it will be published in some of the regular papers or magazines under the control and direction of the Church or it will be presented before such a gathering as this, at a general conference." He also made two blanket exclusions: "The Lord is not going to give unto any woman in this Church a revelation for the Church. He is not going to give unto any man in this Church, other than the one who is properly appointed, a revelation for the guidance of the Church."[102] Three years later in general conference Rudger Clawson of the Quorum of the Twelve said: "The Priesthood is not received, or held, or exercised in any degree, by the women of the Church; but, nevertheless, the women of the Church enjoy the blessings of the Priesthood through their husbands. This emphasizes very strongly the importance of marriage."[103]

Later in the same conference, President Penrose of the First Presidency referred to Elder Clawson's remarks and added his own commentary: "There seems to be a revival of the idea among some of our sisters that they hold the priesthood. . . . When a woman is sealed to a man holding the Priesthood, she becomes one with him. . . . She receives blessings in association with him. . . . Sisters have said to me sometimes, 'But, I hold the Priesthood with my husband.' 'Well,' I asked, 'what office do you hold in the Priesthood?' Then they could not say much more. The sisters are not ordained to any office in the Priesthood and there is authority in the Church which they cannot exercise: it does not belong to them; they cannot do that properly any more than they can change themselves into a man."[104] This more detailed explanation did not clarify a great deal because even if a woman were "one" with her priesthood-holding husband, she still could not *do* anything as a result of that union. Furthermore, President Penrose conveyed the impression that priesthood does not exist apart from priesthood offices.

Penrose then reported women asking him "if they did not have the right to administer to the sick," and he, quoting Jesus' promise to his apostles of the signs that will follow the believers, conceded that there might be

> occasions when perhaps it would be wise for a woman to lay her hands upon a child, or upon one another sometimes, and there have been appointments made for our sisters, some good women, to anoint and bless others of their sex who expect to go through times of great personal trial, travail and 'labor;' so that is all right, so far as it goes. But when women go around and declare that they have been set apart to administer to the sick and take the place that is given to the elders of the Church by revelation as declared through James of old, and through the Prophet Joseph in modern times, that is an assumption of authority and contrary to scripture, which is that when people are sick they shall call for the elders of the Church and they shall pray over them and officially lay hands on them.[105]

Even though he here cited the authority of Joseph Smith, and even though Joseph Smith certainly taught the propriety and authority of elders to heal the sick, President Penrose contradicted the extension of healing privileges to women by Joseph Smith. In fact, Joseph Smith had cited that same scripture in the 12 April 1842 Relief Society meeting but, ironically, had made a far different commentary: "These signs . . . should follow all that believe whether male or female."[106]

President Penrose continued: "These sisters, too, claim the right to go around and hold meetings of their own and speak in tongues and interpret the same and to prophesy." He conceded that both men and women may have the gift of tongues but attacked the idea of independent, unsupervised action: "Sisters, it is not your right to organize meetings either for the sisters or for the brethren in your respective wards without the regulation and permission of the presiding authorities of the ward." He cited the case of a group of sisters who "used to meet together, relate visions, speak in tongues, and [have] a glorious time" but who, when the stake president informed them that they must have the bishop's permission, "have never asked permission of the bishop nor held such meetings since that time."[107] The point was clear: all ward activity must be authorized. Even though President Penrose used the example of a sisters' meeting such as was common during the nineteenth century, he was not particularly singling women out. An unauthorized meeting of men would fall under the same condemnation. But to many women, it must have chafed.

Another clarification of women's position came in 1922 when the First Presidency issued a circular letter setting up separate presidencies for the

Sunday School and the YMMIA (positions usually held by the president of the church in addition to his other duties) and defining the purposes of each auxiliary. The Relief Society was first: "Women, not being heirs to the priesthood except as they enjoy and participate in its blessings through their husbands, are not identified with the priesthood quorums." Some of the purposes for the Relief Society were listed: enabling women to study "Church doctrine and government," doing charitable work "under the direction of the Bishopric, nursing the sick, preparing the dead for burial, . . . comforting the afflicted," developing faith, and progressing "in literary, social and domestic activities." [108]

By 1928 Apostle Heber J. Grant had told of tongues and prophecy exercised on his behalf by women and as president of the church defended the priesthood against "complaint about . . . the domination of the people by those who preside over them." He quoted Doctrine and Covenants 121, then asked rhetorically, "Is it a terrible thing to exercise the priesthood of the living God in the way that the Lord prescribes: 'By kindness and gentleness' "? [109] The pattern had now been established, clarified, and validated.

The strength of that pattern can be seen through a letter from Martha A. Hickman of Logan, who in 1935 wrote to the Relief Society general president, Louise Yates Robison, asking if it was "orthodox and sanctioned" for the women to perform washings and anointings of women about to give birth. Reporting that church women in Logan had performed these duties for years through "committees," she concluded: "Is it orthodox and sanctioned by the Church[?] We have officiated in this capacity some ten years, have enjoyed our calling, and have been appreciated. However, since . . . questions have arisen we do not feel quite at ease. We would like to be in harmony, as well as being able to inform correctly those seeking information. Our Stake Relief Society President, nor our Stake President seem to have nothing definite on this matter." [110]

Significantly, Martha Hickman had first addressed her query to a priesthood holder, one of the Salt Lake Temple Presidency. Sister Robison, dutifully following channels, sent the letter to the stake Relief Society president in Logan and explained:

> In reference to the question raised [by Martha Hickman], may we say that this beautiful ordinance has always been with the Relief Society, and it is our earnest hope that we may continue to have that privilege, and up to the present time the Presidents of the Church have always allowed it to us. There are some places, however, where a definite stand against it has been taken by the Priesthood Authorities, and where such is the case we cannot do anything but accept their will in the matter. However, where the sisters are permitted to do this for expectant mothers we wish it done very quietly, and without any infringement upon the Temple Service. It is in reality a mother's blessing, and we do not advocate the appointment of any committees to have this in charge, but any

worthy good sister is eligible to perform this service if she has faith, and is in good standing in the Church. It is something that should be treated very carefully, and as we have suggested, with no show or discussion made of it.

We have written to Sister Hickman and told her to consult you in this matter, as it is always our custom to discuss matters of this kind with our Stake [Relief Society] Presidents, and have them advise the sisters in their Wards.[111]

There is an air of wistful timidity in Sister Robison's letter that bespeaks near-resignation toward the change that was happening, not because the policy against blessings had changed *per se,* but because the policy about priesthood had changed the environment in which these blessings occurred. Nonpriesthood blessings were now suspect.

One of the last documents on the subject is a little notebook containing a record of "Washing[s] and Anointing[s] done by sisters in 31st Ward" in Salt Lake City. It begins in 1921: "Sister Dallie Watson for confinement, Dec. 1, 1921—by Emma Goddard and Mary E. Creer. 1033 Lake Street." Every few weeks there is another entry, usually for childbirth, but sometimes for illness. The last entry is 2 July 1945 to Jane Coulam Moore by three sisters, one of them the same Sister Goddard who had officiated twenty-four years earlier at the first anointing in the book.[112] She had, incidentally, been one of the members of the YLMIA general board under Elmina S. Taylor, its first general president.

The next year brought the official death knell of this particular spiritual gift. On 29 July 1946 Joseph Fielding Smith, soon to become president of the Quorum of the Twelve, wrote to Belle S. Spafford, Relief Society general president, and her counselors, Marianne C. Sharp and Gertrude R. Garff: "While the authorities of the Church have ruled that it is permissible, under certain conditions and with the approval of the priesthood, for sisters to wash and anoint other sisters, yet they feel that it is far better for us to follow the plan the Lord has given us and send for the Elders of the Church to come and administer to the sick and afflicted."[113] It would certainly be difficult for a woman to say that she did *not* wish to follow "the plan the Lord has given us" by asking for administration from her sisters rather than from the elders. One Relief Society worker in Canada recalled: "This ordinance was a comfort and strength to many. But it was discontinued and the sisters were asked to call for administration by the Priesthood instead when necessary or desirable."[114]

Joseph Fielding Smith's pronouncement officially, for all practical purposes, ended administration by women where it had not already stopped. Further evidence of such blessings being given in conjunction with the Relief Society is rare, although some modern cases—none of them Relief Society related—have recently been reported.[115] Current official recommendations follow the line found in the January 1981 *Priesthood Bulletin,* suggesting that the advances of medical practice in this century preclude a wholehearted reliance on spiritual blessings. Expectant mothers, said the handbook, are to be encouraged "to get the best prenatal and delivery care available from medically and legally qualified practitioners."[116] The instruction is for members to receive healing blessings in concert with qualified medical treatment.

From the 1940s through the 1960s other pronouncements affecting women and spiritual gifts were given in the broadest terms, and the role of priesthood was repeatedly stressed. J. Rueben Clark, Jr., a member of the First Presidency, defined the priesthood in 1940 as "the authority of God bestowed upon men to represent Him in certain relationships between and among men and between men and God." But in the remainder of his talk President Clark referred to himself and other male members as "the Priesthood" rather than men with priesthood authority, power, or callings. Women, he continued, were "the 'first aid' to the Priesthood" and the moral superiors of men, who were marred by grumblings, failings, and short-comings. "We Priesthood need your courage, your steadfastness, your faith, your knowledge, your testimony, to cheer us on, to keep us in the way." And he charged them with the duty of teaching chastity to the children, for unless women do, "the whole world will sink into a welter of sin and corruption."[117]

Increasingly the women were associated with the home and family and not with the affairs of the church or the practice of spiritual gifts. David O. McKay, first counselor in the First Presidency, in the priesthood session of April conference in 1944, thanked the women "who have remained at home to take care of household duties, and to carry on other responsibilities of farms and businesses while we have been here receiving instruction regarding our spiritual work."[118]

Apostle John A. Widtsoe in 1947 agreed with previous presidents of the church that mothers were more responsible than fathers for the spiritual training of the children and that women were "spiritually, morally, religiously, and in faith" stronger than men. Having grown up in a home headed by a devout mother in the absence of a father, Elder Widtsoe concluded: "The Lord helped her. The Lord does not limit his blessings according to sex, but according to our faith and devotion in him."[119]

In 1952 Stephen L Richards, first counselor in the First Presidency, reaffirmed that "a women does not hold the priesthood, but she shares it with her husband, and she is the immediate beneficiary of many of its great blessings. When she unites in marriage with a man of the priesthood in one of the temples of the kingdom, the blessings pronounced upon her are of equal import to those given her husband, and these blessings are to be realized only through the enduring compact of the marriage."[120] But in 1956 when Marion G. Romney, a member of the Quorum of the Twelve, spoke in general conference on the topic of spiritual gifts, he made no mention of women receiving or exercising spiritual gifts: "Righteous men, bearing the holy priesthood of the living God and endowed with the gift of the Holy Ghost, who are magnifying their callings . . . are the only men upon the earth with the right to receive and exercise the gifts of the spirit."[121]

John A. Widtsoe's influential 1954 revision of his *Priesthood and Church Government* discusses the powers of priesthood. The chapter on spiritual gifts examines each in turn after an introduction announcing that "spiritual gifts are properly enjoyed by the Saints of God under the direction of 'such as God shall appoint and ordain over the Church'—that is, the Priesthood and its officers."[122] And priesthood, as we have seen, by then meant the ordained male members of the church. The discussion of revelation, discernment, healing, translation, and power over evil is studded with phrases like "a man must have the discerning of spirits," "through the medium of the Priesthood," "Priesthood must be in touch with the source of truth," "the first great gift of the Priesthood is revelation," "it is to the Priesthood that heavenly beings reveal themselves." There is no acknowledgment that these gifts may exist outside the ordained priesthood.

When it comes to women, Elder Widtsoe writes the oft-quoted passage: "The man who arrogantly feels that he is better than his wife because he holds the Priesthood has failed utterly to comprehend the meaning and purpose of Priesthood." Why? Because "the Lord loves His daughters quite as well as His sons," and "men can never rise superior to the women who bear and nurture them," and "woman has her gift of equal magnitude— motherhood."[123]

From the 1950s to the early 1980s, at least in official pronouncements, equal citizenship for women in the kingdom seems to have been replaced with the glorification of motherhood. Equating motherhood with priesthood requires one to ignore fatherhood in the equation. Thus, anything traditionally considered "male" in the church came to be attached exclusively to the priesthood, and this emphasis stressed—even magnified—the differences between the sexes. Restricting the definition of priesthood to chiefly ecclesiastical and administrative functions tended to limit rather than expand the roles of both sexes. While it can be argued that the female role in pregnancy, birth, and nursing is balanced by the father's role in giving a priesthood blessing and name, baptizing, confirming, and ordaining his children, these acts do not remove the father from the responsibility of day-to-day nurturing. And even though the father is often permitted in the delivery room to witness the birth of his children and be part of the birthing and bonding processes, the mother is still not invited into the blessing circles. If women do, indeed, hold the priesthood with their husbands, this should be no problem, particularly since non-priesthood-holding fathers are sometimes allowed in the blessing circle. All this aside, the role of fathering is being stressed more and more by church leaders, moving us closer to the model that Grethe Peterson describes in her essay in this volume:

brotherhood-sisterhood, motherhood-fatherhood, all functioning in the larger realm of ungendered priesthood.

The motherhood-priesthood stance also ignores the fact that from the beginnings of church history women did not sacrifice their important role as mothers while participating fully in the spiritual gifts of the gospel. Nor is there evidence to suggest that women's spiritual activities or their independence within the Relief Society organization in any way diminished men's priesthood powers or their exercise of them.

In the extreme, this more recent attitude toward women has led to views such as those set forth in Rodney Turner's compilation of folk doctrine in "Woman and the Priesthood," an address delivered at a BYU Six-Stake Fireside in 1966. Turner asserted, usually without citation or explanation of his reasoning, such contradictions to readily observed fact as "It is axiomatic that a woman cannot lead" and "The stewardship of a woman is encircled in the stewardship of the man. His stewardship comprehends her stewardship. Hers does not comprehend or embrace his." Through his interpretation of the temple covenants, Turner found that "woman therefore finds her fulfillment in man as man finds his in God." "Where there is not priesthood there cannot be true motherhood and wifehood." "A woman, in the highest sense, [is] not a woman if she is not a mother." The ultimate degradation in his work, however, came via four lines of doggerel, purportedly written by a woman:

> Women are doormats and have been
> The years those mats applaud. —
> They keep their men from going in
> With muddy feet to God.

Turner commented, "I am afraid that that is only too true. A man needs that kind of support so that he can go back home without muddy feet." [124]

Although Turner diffused much of this rhetoric when he expanded his "Woman and the Priesthood" into a full-length book by the same title, the underlying sentiments remain in the published book. That his commentary on LDS women became a standard resource for some was as much the fault of sounder minds as of Turner's eagerness. Although he claims his work "does not purport to be an authoritative statement on any of the doctrines of The Church," [125] the church's semi-official publisher produced it in 1972 and reprinted it in 1978; and no doctrinally more defensible books have appeared to balance his view. However, the same year the Turner book was reprinted, Elder Bruce R. McConkie gave a more enlightened view of women and their relationship with God. He told those gathered at the March 1978 dedication of the Nauvoo Women's Monument that in "all the gifts of the Spirit . . . the receipt of revelation, the gaining of testimonies, the seeing of visions, . . . men and women stand in a position of absolute equality before the Lord." He explained that Rebekah of the Old Testament was an initiator of faith in her family. When she inquired of the Lord, the Lord spoke to her.[126]

Many other statements designed to explain the place of Mormon women have recently appeared, but they have generally been historically shallow and defensive. The most ambitious, Oscar W. McConkie's 1979 publication *She Shall be Called Woman*, asserts that the eternal nature of women is essentially different from that of men, that women's primary role in life (and chief contribution to the church) is motherhood, that women have "great[er] sensitivity to spiritual truths," and that righteous husbands are "the saviors of their wives." Withal, he acknowledges the equal responsibility of fathers in rearing children and admits, "Many of the brethren, who are otherwise disciplined Christians, exercise unrighteous dominion over women."[127]

Perhaps Mormon women past and present have gained some measure of comfort from Apostle James E. Talmage, writing early in this century: "When the frailties and imperfections of mortality are left behind, in the glorified state of the blessed hereafter, husband and wife will administer in their respective stations, seeing and understanding alike, cooperating to the full in the government of their family kingdom. Then shall women be re-compensed in rich measure for all the injustice that womanhood has endured in mortality. Then shall woman reign by Divine right, a queen. . . . Mortal eye cannot see nor mind comprehend the beauty, glory, and majesty of a righteous woman made perfect in the celestial kingdom of God."[128]

Other more recent pronouncements by church leaders are a signal that that vision has not been lost. Daniel H. Ludlow in December of 1980 answered a query in the *Ensign* relating to the gift of prophecy. "The gift of prophecy is a special spiritual endowment that is available to every worthy member of the church," he said, then he quoted Elder George Q. Cannon's statement that "the genius of the kingdom [is] . . . to make every man a prophet and every woman a prophetess, that they may understand the plans and purposes of God." Elder Ludlow also recalled an earlier statement by President Joseph Fielding Smith wherein he said that women of the church were "entitled . . . to the gift of prophecy concerning matters that would be essential for them to know."[129] As recently as January 1981 James E. Faust of the Quorum of the Twelve echoed this theme however faintly when he told a group of Mormon psychotherapists: "The priesthood is not just male or husband centered, but reaches its potential only in the eternal relationship of the husband and the wife sharing and administering these great blessings to the family."[130] And the 1980–81 Melchizedek Priesthood study guide quotes President Joseph Fielding Smith: "There is nothing in the . . . gospel which declares that men are superior to women. . . . Women do not hold the priesthood, but if they are faithful and true, they will become priestesses and queens in the kingdom of God, and that implies that they will be given authority."[131]

For contemporary Latter-day Saint women, the pendulum has made its arc from Joseph Smith's prophetic vision of women as queens and priestesses, holders of keys of blessings and spiritual gifts, to Rodney Turner's metaphor of women as doormats. The statements of Elder Faust, Elder McConkie, President Smith, and others, however, may signal a theologic reevaluation of woman's roles. A rediscovery of the history of Mormon women's spiritual gifts may also awaken interest in the idea of mothers and fathers jointly anointing and blessing their own children; of husbands like Wilford Woodruff and Heber J. Grant receiving blessings *from* their wives as well as giving them; and of women jointly exercising these gifts on behalf of each other. But until then Susa Young Gates's statement still rings clear: "The privileges and powers outlined by the Prophet [Joseph Smith] . . . have never been granted to women in full even yet."

NOTES

1. Mark 16:17–18.

2. *Woman's Exponent* 41 (March 1913): 46.

3. Patty Sessions, Diary, 17 March 1847, Historical Department, Archives of the Church of Jesus Christ of Latter-day Saints, Salt Lake City, Utah, hereafter cited as LDS Church Archives.

4. Relief Society Minutes, Cache Stake, Utah, 1881–1914, 5 March 1910, pp. 438–39, LDS Church Archives.

5. Two important works that preceded this study of women's spiritual gifts are Carol Lynn Pearson's *Daughters of Light* (Salt Lake City: Bookcraft, 1973), and Claudia L. Bushman's essay "Mystics and Healers" in *Mormon Sisters*, ed. Claudia L. Bushman (Cambridge, Mass.: Emmeline Press, 1976).

6. 1 Corinthians 12:8–10. Paul's list included "the word of wisdom, . . . the word of knowledge, . . . faith, . . . the gifts of healing, . . . the working of miracles, . . . prophecy, . . . discerning of spirits, . . . divers kinds of tongues, . . . [and] the interpretation of tongues."

7. Doctrine and Covenants 46:13–26.

8. Joseph Smith, quoted in *History of the Church of Jesus Christ of Latter-day Saints*, ed. B. H. Roberts, 2nd ed. rev. 7 vols. (Salt Lake City: Deseret Book Co., 1974) 1:297–98.

9. Ibid., 105:33.

10. George A. Smith, 18 March 1855, *Journal of Discourses* 26 vols. (Liverpool: Franklin D. Richards et al., 1855–86) 2:215, hereafter cited as *JD*, with speaker and date.

11. Presendia Huntington, quoted in Edward W. Tullidge, *The Women of Mormondom* (New York: Tullidge and Crandall, 1877; reprint ed., Salt Lake City: n.p., 1965), pp. 208–9.

12. Mary Fielding Smith to Mercy Fielding Thompson, 18 July 1837, LDS Church Archives.

13. Wilford Woodruff, Journal, 3 February 1854, LDS Church Archives.

14. Caroline Barnes Crosby, Journal, n.d., n.p., holograph in the Utah State Historical Society, microfilm of original and typescript in LDS Church Archives.

15. *History of Sarah Studevant Leavitt,* copied from her history by Juanita Leavitt, 1919 (n.p., n.d.), pp. 9-10.

16. Joseph Smith, Sr., quoted in Pearson, *Daughters of Light,* p. 65.

17. "The Book of John Whitmer," carbon copy of typescript, p. 13, LDS Church Archives, and *Book of Commandments,* 53:20.

18. Frederick G. Williams to Dear Brethren [in Missouri], 10 Oct. 1833, in *History of the Church* 1:419.

19. Joseph Fielding Smith, ed., *Teachings of the Prophet Joseph Smith* (1938; 14th printing, Salt Lake City: Deseret Book Co., 1964), p. 25.

20. Ibid., pp. 229, 247.

21. *History of the Church* 4:607.

22. Susa Young Gates, "The Open Door for Women," *Young Woman's Journal* 16 (1905): 117

23. Willard Richards took minutes until Eliza R. Snow was appointed secretary halfway through the meeting. "A Record of the Organization, and Proceedings of the Female Relief Society of Nauvoo," 17 March 1842, pp. 7-8, LDS Church Archives, microfilm of original, Joseph Smith collection, hereafter cited as "Relief Society Minutes of Nauvoo." Also see Susa Young Gates typescript of those minutes, Susa Young Gates Collection, LDS Church Archives. Although this copy contains some errors, they are not substantial. The Reorganized Church of Jesus Christ of Latter Day Saints Library-Archives in Independence, Missouri, has a microfilm copy and typescript of the original minutes.

24. Doctrine and Covenants 25.

25. Gates, "The Open Door for Women": 117.

26. Elizabeth Ann Whitney, "A Leaf from an Autobiography," *Woman's Exponent* 7 (1 November 1878): 91.

27. Relief Society Minutes of Nauvoo, 30 March 1842, p. 22.

28. Ibid., 28 April 1842, pp. 24, 40.

29. *History of the Church* 4:607. The changed wording appears in the book's earliest manuscript.

30. Dean C. Jessee, "The Writing of Joseph Smith's History," *BYU Studies* 11, no. 4 (Summer 1971): 458.

31. Relief Society Minutes of Nauvoo, 27 May 1842, p. 58.

32. For a more complete discussion of the temple and women's place in it, see Carol Cornwall Madsen's essay in this volume.

33. John Smith Patriarchal Blessing Book, vol. 11, Book F, Blessing number 351, p. 162, dated 1850; copy provided to the author by Mary Brown Firmage. There is an ambiguity implied here; the phrase "fulness of priesthood" refers also to the "second anointing," an ordinance in which husband and wife participate together.

34. "First General Conference of the Relief Society," *Woman's Exponent* 17 (15 April 1889): 172.

35. "Duty of Officers of F. R. Society. Written by S. M. Kimball, revised by E. R. Snow," Fifteenth Ward Relief Society Minutes, 1868-1873, LDS Archives.

36. John Taylor, 8 August 1880, *JD* 21:367-68.

37. Relief Society Minutes of Nauvoo, 19 April 1842, pp. 31, 33.

38. Ibid., 28 April 1842, p. 36

39. Ibid., 19 April 1842, p. 32.

40. Ibid., 28 April 1842, pp. 40, 41.

41. Seventies Record, 9 March 1845, typescript, Church Archives.

42. "A Venerable Woman: Presendia Lathrop Young," *Woman's Exponent* 12 (1 June 1883): 2.

43. Eliza R. Snow, Journal, 2 February 1846-4 April 1847, 1 January, 2 February, 14 March 1847, autograph, Huntington Libraries, San Marino, Calif.

44. "A Venerable Woman": 11.

45. Meanwhile, spiritual gifts were manifest overseas. Sarah Brown in England wrote in 1849, "The gift of tongues and of interpretation of tongues are [*sic*] also common amongst us, as well as that of seeing visions, dreaming dreams, and of prophesy" (*Millennial Star* 11 [1 January 1849]: 6). The context, unfortunately, does not make it clear whether *us* means her family or the Saints. An elder in England wrote the same year of blessing a sick sister: "Everyone present could feel the renovating influence of the Holy Spirit of God; and, in less than 2 minutes, sister Petty began to sing in tongues and prophesy" (Ibid. 11 [15 June 1849]: 190). Eliza Jane Merrick also reported healing her younger sister: "I anointed her chest with the oil you consecrated, and also gave her some inwardly. That was about four o'clock in the afternoon. She continued very ill all the evening: her breath very short, and the fever very high. I again anointed her chest in the name of the Lord, and asked his blessing; he was graciously pleased to hear me, and in the course of twenty-four hours, she was as well as if nothing had been the matter" (Ibid. 11 [1 July 1849]: 205).

46. Mary Ellen Kimball, Journal, 2 March 1857, LDS Church Archives.

47. Wilford Woodruff, Journal, 3 February 1854, LDS Church Archives.

48. George Goddard, Diary 1875-76, 8 September 1875, LDS Church Archives.

49. Brigham Young, 14 November 1869, *JD* 13:155.

50. Cache Valley Stake Relief Society Minutes 1868-81, 18 June 1868, LDS Church Archives.

51. Ruth M. Fox, "Emmeline B. Wells: A Tribute," *Young Woman's Journal* 32 (June 1921): 346.

52. Orson Pratt, 26 March 1876, *JD* 18:171.

53. Guy Messiah Keysor, Reminiscences and Journal, 2 January 1857, pp. 40-41, photocopy, LDS Church Archives. For other examples of Eliza R. Snow's role as "prophetess" see Maureen Ursenbach Beecher, "The Eliza Enigma: The Life and Legend of Eliza R. Snow," in *Essays on the American West, 1974-75*, ed. Thomas G. Alexander, Charles Redd Monographs in Western History, no. 6 (Provo: Brigham Young University, 1974-75), pp. 34-39.

54. Ella Dallas, "Annual Meeting of YLMIA Seventeenth Ward," *Woman's Exponent* 15 (15 February 1887): 144.

55. Santa Clara Ward Relief Society Minutes, 1873-93, 27 November 1880, pp. 47-48, LDS Church Archives.

56. Thomas Chamberlain, Diary, 1854-1882, 18 February 1881, LDS Church Archives.

57. Frederick Kesler, Diary, 4 May 1875, University of Utah Marriott Library, Special Collections.

58. Jens Christian Anderson Weibye, Journals, 1 January 1877-81, 12 May 1878, 9 December 1879, LDS Church Archives.

59. Emily Dow Partridge Young, Diary, carbon of typescript, 23 June 1874, p. 2, LDS Church Archives.

60. Zina Diantha Huntington Young, Diaries, August–December 1881, 23 December 1881, Zina Card Brown Family Collection, LDS Church Archives.

61. Helen Mar Whitney, in the *Woman's Exponent* 5 (15 March 1877): 158.

62. Amy Brown Lyman, "In Retrospect," *Relief Society Magazine* 29 (May 1942): 312–13.

63. As reported in *Woman's Exponent* 7 (1 November 1878): 86.

64. John Taylor, 8 August 1880, *JD* 21:368.

65. First Presidency circular letter, Salt Lake City, Utah, 6 October 1880, LDS Church Archives.

66. Eliza R. Snow, in the *Woman's Exponent* 13 (15 September 1884): 61.

67. Cache Valley Stake Relief Society Minute Book B, 11 September 1886, pp. 46–48, LDS Church Archives.

68. "Sketch of the Labors of Sister Lucy B. Young in the Temples," *Young Woman's Journal* 4 (April 1893): 299.

69. Clifford J. and Marsha Romney Stratton, "Catherine Jane Cottam Romney: Life Sketch," unpublished manuscript in possession of author.

70. Wilford Woodruff to Emmeline B. Wells, 27 April 1888, Correspondence of the First Presidency, LDS Church Archives.

71. *Woman's Exponent* 17 (15 April 1889): 172.

72. Torkel Torkelson, Diary, 7 November 1895, LDS Church Archives, trans. Richard Jensen.

73. Official Report of the General Conference of the Church of Jesus Christ of Latter-day Saints (Salt Lake City: Church of Jesus Christ of Latter-day Saints, 1898–1986), 9 October 1910, pp. 119–20, hereafter cited as *Conference Report,* with date and page.

74. *Conference Report,* 3 October 1919, p. 32.

75. *Conference Report,* "second day," 1900, p. 41.

76. *Conference Report,* "first day," April 1901, p. 12.

77. *Conference Report,* 3 October 1949, p. 156.

78. Gene R. Cook, "Miracles Among the Lamanites," *Ensign,* November 1980, p. 68, reports his Conference speech.

79. Marvelee Soon Tahauri, "Dissolving Language Barriers in Hauula," *Ensign* 12 (March 1982): 55. Thanks to Janath Cannon for bringing this to my attention.

80. Ruth May Fox, Diary, 16 September 1901.

81. Louisa L. G. Richards to Lorenzo Snow, 9 April 1901, LDS Church Archives.

82. Relief Society Minutes, special meeting of officers of the General Board, 2 May 1901, vol. 1, p. 352, LDS Church Archives.

83. *Young Woman's Journal* 14 (8 August 1903): 384.

84. "Answers to Questions," undated form letter from Relief Society General Presidency, LDS Church Archives.

85. Joseph F. Smith to Nephi Pratt, December 18–21, 1908, Correspondence of the First Presidency, LDS Church Archives.

86. Relief Society Minutes, 21 January 1910, vol. 3:187, LDS Church Archives.

87. Oakley [Idaho] 2nd Ward Relief Society Minutes, vol. 1, 1901-09, pp. 195-97, LDS Church Archives.

88. Maureen Ursenbach Beecher, untitled commentary on the Oakley blessing, n.d., typescript, pp. 1-2.

89. Oakley Minutes, pp. 197-98.

90. Cache Valley Stake Relief Society Minutes 1881-1914, 5 March 1910, pp. 438-40. Other testimonies borne that day included:

> Sister Moench felt that we had had so much good said today. Said while she was very young she went out to wash and anoint the sick. Said Sister Richards had given them a foundation to go by and had said to get the spirit of the Lord then they would do right. Related an experience in blessing a child who had been given up by the doc and it got well. Know that if we get the faith and the spirit of God with us we can bless as well as the Brethren. . . .
>
> Pres. Hattie Hyde spoke of her experiences in Wyo. where the brethern had helped the sisters to bless and anoint the sick.
>
> Sister R. Moench said that Pres. Young had said that the sisters need not be set apart for this calling but if they can call in any good brethren to seal the anointing so much the better.
>
> Pres. Lucy S. Cardan said they use to in the Temple have the brethern seal the anointing but now they do not. Knows that one sister can bless another. We have that privilege but when we can get the brethern we should have them seal the blessing.

91. Lucile H. Ursenbach, statement, 14 August 1980, in possession of Maureen Ursenbach Beecher, used with permission.

92. A. J., "The Seventy's Wife," *Young Woman's Journal* 7 (June 1986): 398.

93. *Improvement Era* 10 (February 1907): 308.

94. *Conference Report*, 5 October 1901, p. 58.

95. Ibid., 7 October 1910, p. 39.

96. Relief Society Minutes, 7 October 1913, vol. 4, p. 124, LDS Church Archives.

97. *Conference Report*, 4 April 1913, p. 7.

98. *Relief Society Bulletin* 1 (February 1914): 1-3.

99. Joseph F. Smith, Anthon H. Lund, Charles W. Penrose, "To the Presidents of Stakes and Bishops of Wards," *Messages of the First Presidency,* ed. James R. Clark, 6 vols., (Salt Lake City: Bookcraft, 1935-51) 4:314-15. It reads in full as follows:

> Questions are frequently asked in regard to washing and anointing our sisters preparatory to their confinement. . . . We quote some of these questions and give our answers:
>
> 1. Is it necessary for one or more sisters to be set apart to wash and anoint the sick?
>
> 2. Should it be done under the direction of the Relief Society?
>
> Answer: Any good sister full of faith in God and in the efficacy of prayer may officiate. It is therefore not necessary for anyone to be set apart for this purpose, or that it should be done exclusively under the direction of the Relief Society.

3. Must the sister officiating be a member of the Relief Society?

Answer: It is conceded that most of our sisters, qualified to perform this service and gifted with the spirit of healing and the power to inspire faith in the sick, belong to the Relief Society, but if the sick should desire to have some good sister who is not a member of the Relief Society administer to her, that sister has the right to so administer.

4. Have the sisters the right to administer to sick children?

Answer: Yes; they have the same right to administer to sick children as to adults, and may anoint and lay hands upon them in faith.

5. Should the administering and anointing be sealed?

Answer: It is proper for sisters to lay on hands, using a few simple words, avoiding the terms employed in the temple, and instead of using the word "seal" use the word "confirm."

6. Have the sisters a right to seal the washing and anointing, using the authority, but doing it in the name of Jesus Christ, or should men holding the priesthood be called in?

Answer: The sisters have the privilege of laying their hands on the head of the person for whom they are officiating, and confirming and anointing in the spirit of invocation. The Lord has heard and answered the prayers of sisters in these administrations many times. It should, however, always be remembered that the command of the Lord is to call in the elders to administer to the sick, and when they can be called in, they should be asked to anoint the sick or seal the anointing.

7. Are sisters who have not received their endowments competent to wash and anoint sisters previous to confinement?

Answer: It must always be borne in mind that this administering to the sick by the sisters is in no sense a temple ordinance, and no one is allowed to use the words learned in the temple in washing and anointing the sick. Sisters who have had their endowments have received instructions and blessings which tend to give them stronger faith and especially qualify them to officiate in this sacred work; but there are good faithful sisters, who through circumstances have not received their endowments, and yet are full of faith and have had much success in ministering to the sick, who should not be forbidden to act, if desired to do so by our sisters.

In conclusion we have to say that in all sacred functions performed by our sisters there should be perfect harmony between them and the Bishop, who has the direction of all matters pertaining to the Church in his ward.

The letter was signed "Your brethren, Joseph F. Smith, Anthon H. Lund, Charles W. Penrose, First Presidency."

100. Ibid.

101. Ibid.

102. *Conference Report,* 5 October 1918, p. 55. Three years later, Anthony W. Ivins of the Quorum of the Twelve virtually repeated these same instructions, asserting that revelation "belongs to every member" but that "revelations for the benefit of the Church . . . will never come through emotional women; they will never come through men whose right it is not, and never has been, to receive them."

103. *Conference Report,* 3 April 1921, pp. 24-25.

104. Ibid., p. 198.

105. Ibid.

106. Relief Society Minutes of Nauvoo, 12 April 1842.

107. *Conference Report,* 3 April 1921, pp. 199-200.

108. Clark, *Messages* 5:216.

109. *Conference Report,* 5 October 1928, pp. 8-9.

110. Martha A. Hickman to Louise Y. Robison, 28 November 1935, Church Archives.

111. Louise Y. Robison and Julia A. F. Lund to Mrs. Ada E. Morrell, 5 December 1935, copy in possession of the author.

112. Record of washing and anointing, 1921-1945, Salt Lake City 31st Ward, LDS Church Archives.

113. Clark, *Messages* 4:314.

114. Ursenbach, statement.

115. Since the publication of part of this essay as "A Gift Given, A Gift Taken: Washing, Anointing, and Blessing the Sick among Mormon Women," *Sunstone* 6 (September/October 1981): 16-25, about ten women have told the author of their experiences in exercising spiritual gifts. One woman gathered her sister's frail, cancer-ridden body in her arms and blessed her with one pain-free day. Two other women, in separate instances, each blessed and healed a child in her care. Neither of these women had ever discussed the blessing with anyone before for fear it would be considered "inappropriate." And several women together blessed a close friend just prior to her having a hysterectomy. Others asked that their experience not be mentioned—again fearing that what had been personal and sacred to them would be misunderstood and viewed as inappropriate by others. Of course, the same kinds of blessings, when performed by priesthood holders, are commonly told in church meetings as faith-promoting experiences and are accepted by members of the church in that spirit.

116. *The Bulletin,* ([Salt Lake City]: Church of Jesus Christ of Latter-day Saints, January 1981), [p. 3].

117. *Conference Report,* 5 April 1940, pp. 20-21.

118. *Conference Report,* 9 April 1944, p. 154.

119. *Conference Report,* 5 October 1947, pp. 152-54.

120. *Conference Report,* 5 October 1952, pp. 99-100.

121. *Conference Report,* 7 April 1956, p. 72.

122. John A. Widtsoe, *Priesthood and Church Government* (1939; Salt Lake City: Deseret Book Co., rev., 1954), pp. 38-39.

123. Ibid., pp. 89-90.

124. Rodney Turner, *Woman and the Priesthood* (Provo: Brigham Young University Press, 1966); also *Woman and the Priesthood* (Salt Lake City: Deseret Book Co., 1972).

125. Turner, *Woman and the Priesthood,* preface, both editions.

126. Bruce R. McConkie, "Our Sisters from the Beginning," *Ensign* 9 (January 1979): 61-63; Gen. 25:22-3.

127. Oscar W. McConkie, *She Shall Be Called Woman* (Salt Lake City: Bookcraft, 1979), pp. 117, 4, 124.

128. James E. Talmage, "The Eternity of Sex," *Young Woman's Journal* 25 (October 1914): 602–3.

129. Daniel H. Ludlow, "I Have a Question," *Ensign* 10 (December 1980): 31.

130. James E. Faust, "Psychotherapists, Love Your Wives," *AMCAP Journal,* January 1981, p. 5.

131. *Doctrines of Salvation* 3:178, as quoted in *Choose You This Day,* Melchizedek Priesthood Personal Study Guide, 1980–81 (Salt Lake City: Church of Jesus Christ of Latter-day Saints, 1979), p. 200, italics omitted.

MARYANN MACMURRAY

Full Circle

I understand Stonehenge now
The need for a circle
In relation to the sun.
I understand Sisterhood now
The need for a circle
In relation to the Son.

We have long since
Lifted the hands
That weighed congenially
Upon each other.

I can still see
The two concentric circles
We made and how they
Closed and opened to
Our embracing there.

I can still hear our voices
Praying:
Mother, Father, conjoin
To join our voice
With the songs and
Prayers we hear
And would be singing,

Saying:
In His name, may
Our Endowment confirm
And no fraility impede this

Blessing from distilling
Upon her,
    upon us,
        upon all women

Reprinted by permission from *Dialogue: A Journal of Mormon Thought* 16 (Spring 1983): 89.

"Strength in Our Union": The Making of Mormon Sisterhood

A cluster of white these leading Mormon women would have been, the high collars and cuffs of their long white dresses set off with lace perhaps. But as women officiators in the Salt Lake Temple, they had eschewed outward adorning for the hidden ornament of spirit, a commitment that linked these "holy women" to the temple where they were meeting and bound them to one another. Zina Diantha Huntington Jacobs Young, priestess and presidentess, had begun calling them together shortly after the temple was dedicated in April 1893, "to cultivate a greater feeling of love and sisterly kindness by a better acquaintance with each other."[1] Many of them already knew each other well, for the ties in this group epitomize the complicated relationships and patterns that have bound Mormon women together through the church's history.

Central to the group were women from Zina Young's extended family. Lucy Walker Smith Kimball, like Zina, had been a plural wife of the Prophet Joseph Smith, making the two women "sister wives." When, after Joseph's death, Zina became a plural wife of Brigham Young, she acquired more sister wives, including Lucy Bigelow Young. Margaret Whitehead Young was the daughter-in-law of another sister wife. And there were two daughters of yet another sister wife, Maria Young Dougall and Phebe Young Beatie. An even larger number of women in the group were connected through official positions in the hierarchy of LDS women's organizations. Zina presided simultaneously over women's temple work in Salt Lake City and the Mormon women's Relief Society. Among the women temple officiators was her friend, counselor in both presidencies, and successor, Bathsheba W. Smith. Bathsheba's sister wife, niece, and grandniece were in the circle. Six of the female temple workers would eventually serve with Zina and Bathsheba on the Relief Society's governing or general board. Maria Young Dougall was second counselor in the general presidency of the church's organization for young women, the Young Ladies Mutual Improvement Association (YLMIA); three women from that general board were temple workers. One, Minnie J. Snow, was Zina's second counselor in the women's temple presidency. Zina's grandniece in-law, Louisa Lula Greene Richards, was a member of the general board of the Primary Association, the church organization for children. The circle thus encompassed familial, administrative, and ecclesiastical ties—plus a political one, woman suffrage. Lula had been first editor of the Mormon *Woman's Exponent* (1872–77), which had urgently advocated suffrage. Zina, Maria, and Phebe actively supported the Utah movement for woman suffrage as did others in this group of temple workers, including Margaret A. Caine, first president of the Utah Territorial Woman Suffrage Association. Some of the women served as leaders in local suffrage associations and others attended meetings of the National American Woman Suffrage Association or later supported its affiliates, the National and International Councils of Women.

These temple officiators, united in their spiritual commitment to Mormonism and designated to administer the church's highest ordinances to their sisters, were linked to one another and to women outside their circle by various female networks and support systems. If their faith as Latter-day Saints was monolithic, clearly their sisterhood was not. The bonds among them were intricate and complex, forged as a result of family ties, friendships emerging from shared feelings and experiences, common goals and tasks within the organization, and their commitment to work publicly for the good of women. That such a variety of bonds existed within one small group of women makes them exceptional among Mormon women but also exemplary of the diverse nature of Mormon sisterhood.

"Sisterhood" is a term popularly applied by Latter-day Saints to the official organizations for Mormon women. The YWMIA's 1969 centennial history was entitled *A Century of Sisterhood,* and in recent years the Relief Society has discussed its membership as "a worldwide sisterhood." In these instances, "sisterhood" seems to mean both the collectivity of sisters, i.e., female church members, and the "sisterly" quality of their interactions in the women's organizations of the church. Because this popular Mormon understanding of sisterhood may differ from the definitions of scholars and feminists, it will clarify our discussion to understand sisterhood as the bonding among women on both personal and public levels, from simple friendships to massive organizations. In this sense Mormon women have a complex and vital heritage of sisterhood.

Within the Church of Jesus Christ of Latter-day Saints, women have been a crucial part of one another's lives—spiritually, emotionally, intellectually, socially, and politically. And the question we wish to explore is the extent to which their being Mormon has enhanced this bonding.

I

In the nineteenth century, Mormon women, like their American counterparts described by Carroll Smith-Rosenberg, played a "central emotional role in each other's lives."[2] Smith-Rosenberg's pioneer study of relations among nineteenth-century American women suggests that the society in which Mormonism developed was "characterized in large part by rigid gender-role differentiation within the family and within society as a whole, leading to the emotional segregation of women and men." Biological realities (pregnancy, childbirth, nursing, menopause) emphasized the separateness of a female world where women were in close, if not exclusive, contact with other women and children for days or even weeks at a time. It was "a world bounded by home, church, and the institution of visiting" where female support networks, clustered around an "inner core of kin," carried forth the rituals that accompanied marriage and pregnancy, childbirth and weaning, sickness and death.[3]

Women who answered the call to "go out from Babylon" and join with the Latter-day Saints often abandoned old social and emotional attachments. The successive westward moves of the Latter-day Saints, like the general geographic mobility of mid-nineteenth-century Americans, eroded many female networks. Fourteen-year-old Emmeline Blanche Woodward (later Wells), for example, joined the church in midterm at her "select school for girls" in New Salem, Massachusetts. Such schools, according to Smith-Rosenberg, were settings where adolescent girls "incorporated each other into their own kinship systems" and established networks of their own.[4] Young Emmeline's conversion separated her emotionally from her peers. Her marriage at age fifteen and subsequent move to Nauvoo, almost certainly an effort to establish other bonds, marked an abrupt end to the friendship networks of her girlhood.

In contrast, when extended families and clusters of friends joined the church, other networks seemed to remain intact, even though distance separated the parties. In the spring of 1838, twenty-seven-year-old Elizabeth Haven, a convert, left her home in Holliston, Massachusetts, to migrate with her brother and niece to the Mormon settlement of Far West, Missouri. A year later, she began a letter to a cousin, Elizabeth Howe Bullard, still in Holliston, describing the expulsion from Far West and their refuge in Quincy, Illinois. "If I could sleep with you one night," Elizabeth wrote, "[I] think we should not be very sleepy, at least I could converse all night and have nothing but a comma between the sentences, now and then." The next day she continued: "After a day of sober reflection I resume my pen to converse with one [with] whom I have spent many happy hours in days past and gone, and hope to spend many, yes many more, but with far different objects in view. The understanding and knowledge we have of the Scriptures, make *friends* and every thing appear in a very different light to me."[5] Elizabeth included her "testimony as to the truth of this work" and then in a series of fourteen postscripts asked about Holliston news—"Marriages, births and deaths," as well as family and friends—concluding: "Tell Maria and Eliza Ann to bring me a handful of Chesnuts. Write soon, E. M. must write a few lines too. Where is Adelia? Love to her if in H[olliston]. Does she love the Truth?"[6] Clearly in the case of these cousin Elizabeths and their circle of friends and family, faith became critically interwoven with friendship and confidence.

Some aspects of early Mormonism worked against the continuance or development of distinct female networks. Many converted couples, rather than maintaining separate spheres, worked together in assimilating themselves into the new community. Furthermore, though American religion was becoming the domain of women and clerics, Mormonism's lay priesthood usually made men at least as active as their women in the new religion.[7]

Drusilla Dorris, for example, was twenty-six years old and had been married nine years to James Hendricks when both were baptized in Tennessee in 1836. Drusilla recalled how at the time the two of them "had the same feelings." Male and female Saints "met together often and had good meetings" where "we all praised God for we had all drank of that same Spirit."[8] James and Drusilla moved to Missouri to join the Saints clustering first in Clay County, later in Caldwell County. They apparently worked side by side, cultivating the land, harvesting its bounty, and preserving food for the family. Drusilla said that she, like Book of Mormon women, became "strong like unto the men." When James was severely wounded in the skirmish at Crooked River, Missouri, she was at his side almost immediately, defending him and the children as best she might when mobs harassed them. Together they made a painful escape to Illinois, where they struggled to build a new life.

Women were not spared the difficulties of the Mormon experience, but not all of them shared them with their men. Unlike Drusilla, Sarah De-Armon Pea Rich was "left alone in the midst of the mob after my husband had to leave." Just before Charles C. Rich's departure from Missouri with Hosea Stout (the mob had sworn to kill both men), "him and Hosey Stout made a covenent to stay together untill we should meet again and Hoseys wife and I made a coven[an]t that her and I would remain together as true friends untill we should meet our husbands again."[9] For Sarah, this was to be the first of many long separations from Charles, an active Mormon apostle and colonizer. Similarly, Bathsheba W. Smith would spend most of her married life apart from her husband, George A. Smith, missionary, apostle, church historian, and counselor to Mormonism's second president, Brigham Young. He left her in Nauvoo when he "took a mission" to Great Britain and from there she wrote him about the coming together of missionaries' wives: "When I get a letter first all the rest come to heare it. The breatherns wives have all been to see me this week."[10]

The forces within the church, in other words, simultaneously promoted and impeded an identity of men's and women's interests, efforts, and understanding. Unity was a theological requirement and a practical necessity. An early revelation commanded that the Saints must "be one, and if ye are not one ye are not mine."[11] This theological ideal became socially imperative as ostracism, hostility, and violence escalated, first in New York, again in Ohio and Missouri, and still again in Nauvoo. Union was seen as essential to salvation. Fifty years before she gathered the women temple workers together, Zina Jacobs (Young) had recorded that Nauvoo church leaders were teaching that "union in Families is [the] first recquisite before any great exaltation can take place." On 10 March 1845 she wrote: "The Church is in prosperous circumstances for there appears to be the most union that has ever ben. The faithful are determined to keep the law of God. O Father binde us as a People to gether in the bonds of love that we neve[r] shall sepperate."[12] The Church of Jesus Christ of Latter-day Saints was to be a collective soul—the "members many but one body" as described by the ancient apostle Paul. In this sense Zina's sister wife, friend, and co-worker Eliza R. Snow declared that the interests of Mormon men and women could not be separated.[13]

Despite this commonality of male and female interests, philosophically, organizationally, and doctrinally Mormonism nurtured separate roles for men and women. Through the 1830s as the church grew in size, the number of priesthood-bearing males active in administration and proselyting increased, and official obligations took more and more husbands and fathers away from wives and children who had no comparable organizational assignments. Caroline Crosby recollected "the sensations with which my mind was actuated when I learned the fact that my husband had been called and ordained to the Melchisedek priesthood and would undoubtedly be required to travel and preach the gospel to the nations of the earth." But even before Jonathan Crosby left Kirtland, where he and Caroline were boarding with the Pratt family, he was involved in meetings with other males "almost every evening," leaving Caroline with Thankful Pratt, who "would look about her and say, 'well it is you and I again, Sister Crosby.'"[14]

Politically, socially, and economically, Nauvoo, a church-dominated city-state, represented a seven-year oasis in Mormonism's first turbulent fifteen years. Between 1839 and 1846, there was time for the organization to consolidate itself, set up administrative procedures, and concentrate on proselyting and theological development. These activities were, overwhelmingly, male. A significant fraction of Mormon men in Nauvoo served short- or long-term missions. Even when they were in the city, their days might typically be spent in public works construction or other city maintenance while their evenings were given over to the educational and administrative meetings of emerging priesthood quorums.

As Mormon men built the kingdom, Mormon women were constructing new networks, some of them formal and organizational, but most informal and personal. Visits to and from other women, often overnight, occupy a prominent place in Zina Jacobs (Young)'s 1844–45 Nauvoo diary. Those involving both men and women relatives and friends appear only about half as often as records of visits with women.[15] Significantly, however, Nauvoo also saw three efforts which served to formalize female relationships: the organization of the Relief Society, the introduction of temple ordinances, and the commencement of the practice of plural marriage.

Women's own yearnings to be organized led to the establishment of the Female Relief Society of Nauvoo. Originally a seamstress, a Miss Cook, hoped to combine her own skill with the financial resources of her employer, Sarah M. Kimball, in providing shirts for workmen on the Nauvoo Temple. As the two women discussed this charitable partnership, they envisioned and brought together a larger "ladies society" of neighborhood women. This group came under the still larger ecclesiastical umbrella when Joseph Smith organized them "under the priesthood after the pattern of the priesthood," that is, with a three-member presidency who would "serve as a constitution—all their decisions be considered law; and acted upon as such."[16]

When twenty women assembled above Joseph Smith's store on 17 March 1842, they elected his wife Emma Smith (previously designated in a revelation to him an "elect lady") as the society's president. She chose as her counselors Elizabeth Ann Whitney and Sarah Cleveland; and after some discussion, the group unanimously proclaimed itself the Female Relief Society of Nauvoo, Emma Smith articulating the collective understanding of the society's purposes: "its duties to others also its relative duties to each other Viz. to seek out and relieve the distressed—that each member should be ambitious to do good—that the members should deal frankly with each other—to watch over the morals—and be very careful of the character and reputation of the members of the Institution &c."[17] Some 1,341 women (between 10 and 15 percent of the city's Mormon population) became society members between the founding of the Relief Society in March 1842 and its disbanding in spring or summer 1844.

Some women may have felt a need for formal meetings of their own to parallel those of the men, or perhaps they longed for an organization comparable to the numerous contemporary women's auxiliaries and benevolent and reform societies. Benevolent societies had begun appearing in America before 1800. By 1840 the organizations numbered well into the thousands.[18]

Certainly Mormons, male and female, who had lived east of the Mississippi for any period of time would have been familiar with these institutions. In fact, those gathered together in the first meeting of the Female Relief Society of Nauvoo referred negatively to existing benevolent societies; and Eliza R. Snow, the new society's secretary, proclaimed, "As daughters of Zion, we should set an example for all the world, rather than confine ourselves to the course which had been heretofore pursued."[19]

Yet like these early female collectives, the Nauvoo Relief Society formed a bridge between women's private and public lives, with sub-groups emerging out of existing family and friendship networks. Central to the Nauvoo Relief Society, for example, was that early Cook-Kimball neighborhood group along with church leaders' wives and daughters. The rapid expansion of the organization may account for an early request that "Auxiliary Societies [be] form'd in other parts of the City." Three months and 661 members after the founding of the society, it was agreed that members would not be admitted "but by presenting a regular petition signed by two or three members in good standing in the Society."[20] Clearly it had grown beyond a collection of friends.

Furthermore, the Relief Society provided Mormon women with a common task and goal that inched them into the public sphere. Nauvoo's *Times and Seasons,* in heralding the new organization, praised the benevolence that flowed from the sisters' "humane and philanthropic bosoms" and observed that Mormon women had not hitherto extended "the hand of charity in a conspicuous manner."[21] A few weeks later the same semiweekly carried Eliza R. Snow's six-stanza poem describing the institution's aim to bless

The poor, the widow, and the fatherless —
To clothe the naked and the hungry feed,
And in the holy paths of virtue, lead.[22]

The group's official minutes account for the carrying out of that work, including the donation of money, food, materials, and services; attempts to house the homeless and provide work for widows; and countless decisions on how to help individual "objects of charity."[23] By the end of its first year the society had disbursed $306.48 with another $200.52 still on hand to relieve the distressed.[24] There had been one discordant note: a sister "thought we were taking the Bishop's place in looking after the poor & soliciting donations," but she was assured by an elder present that the women "were not acting in the Bishops place nor intruding upon them in their calling."[25] He enunciated the prevailing view: charity was not a power issue but a task. It gave the women an organization, visibility, and legitimacy; their work was appropriate and appreciated as integral to the church's work. Nearly a hundred years would pass before the central role of women in the church's charitable efforts would change.

The Relief Society, however, was more multifaceted than its name would indicate. It was perhaps Lucy Mack Smith, Mormonism's revered matriarch, who first suggested that the organization could provide an opportunity for women to refresh one another spiritually. "This Institution is a good one," she said at the society's second meeting. "We must cherish one another, watch over one another, comfort one another and gain instruction, that we may all sit down in heaven together."[26] She was present at the society's fifth meeting when "nearly all present arose & spoke, and the spirit of the Lord like a purifying stream, refreshed every heart." Counselor Sarah Cleveland had exercised the gift of tongues, blessing many in the room, and Patty Sessions had interpreted her blessings and prophecies for those present.[27]

At the following meeting of the society, Joseph Smith laid to rest some apparent misgivings about the appropriateness of such spiritual sharing. Still, the exercise of spiritual gifts was never a prominent part of the meetings of the Nauvoo society, perhaps in part because of its size. Testimony bearing and gospel instruction were then, as in today's Relief Society, the most common forms of spiritual nurturance. Joseph had told the sisters that their minutes would be "precedents for you to act upon—your Constitution and law,"[28] and his instructions regarding spiritual gifts were heartily absorbed by some and held in reserve. Immediately following the Nauvoo period, at Winter Quarters and later in Utah until after the turn of the century, clusters of women freely exercised a variety of spiritual gifts when they gathered informally as friends or officially in meetings of Relief Society, Young Ladies Mutual Improvement Associations, and Primary Associations deriving their authorization from Joseph's statement in Nauvoo. (See Linda King Newell, "Spiritual Gifts: Women's Share" in this volume.)

Part of the doctrinal definition occurring in Nauvoo concerned the nature of priesthood. Since women did not hold priesthood offices, what authority did they bring to their organizational relationships with one another or to their collective relationship with the priesthood-directed church? This issue extended far beyond permission to speak in tongues and to heal. Joseph Smith's instructions to the Relief Society (he addressed nine of their thirty-three meetings) indicated that their group was to be "a select Society . . . a kingdom of priests as in Enoch's day," to whom "the keys of the kingdom are about to be given."[29] This allusion to *keys* would later cause considerable concern since the term was generally used in connection with priesthood offices. In this statement, however, it would seem the term was used in reference to the temple endowment, a church ordinance bestowing "power from on high" upon both men and women, an ordinance in which women administer with divine authority to other women. The temple endowment was introduced in Nauvoo to men 4 May 1842 and to women a year later, when Emma Smith received the ordinances at the hands of her prophet-husband and thus became the first of many "priestesses" who would officiate for women in the sacred ritual. (See Carol Cornwall Madsen, "Mormon Women and the Temple: Toward a New Understanding," in this volume.)

The ordinances and ceremonies that Joseph Smith introduced in connection with the Nauvoo Temple were profoundly significant and unique in the experience of women. For most of them, however, these temple "blessings," including celestial or eternal marriage, were interwoven with the Prophet's reinstatement of the ancient practice of plural marriage. Introduced by Joseph Smith to an intimate group of male church officials in 1841, plural marriage developed along with the fledgling Relief Society and likely contributed to its disbandment in 1844. The practice united and divided Mormon women almost simultaneously.

Rumors that Mormon leaders were practicing polygamy were rampant at the time the Relief Society was organized in 1842. Both Emma and Joseph Smith expressed hopes that Relief Society members would assist in "correcting the morals and strengthening the virtues of the female community,"[30] which in part meant quieting the potentially explosive rumors of "immorality" connected with the theologically approved but socially unconventional and secretly contracted marriages. Fanning the sparks of rumor into flame were the open accusations of then-apostate John C. Bennett, who had begun publishing a series of exposés in local newspapers during the summer of 1842. Bennett, enraged when he was unceremoniously displaced from Joseph Smith's favor, church positions, and community standing for his unsavory conduct, indicted the Relief Society itself, then only a few months old, as a "Mormon Seraglio."[31]

Indignantly, the society assembled outdoors in the Nauvoo Grove on 23 June 1842. "Mrs. Pres. propos'd that a Circular go forth from this Society, expressive of our feeling in reference to Dr. Bennett's character—requested all who could wield the pen, to write and send in their productions out of which, a selection should be made . . . [that] the true situation of matters might be represented." Accordingly, in the *Times and Seasons* of 1 October 1842 such a circular appeared, signed by nineteen Relief Society members.[32]

The situation was not quite as simple as their moral indignation would indicate. Several society members were, in fact, plural wives of church officials including Joseph Smith himself. However, their understanding of the term "spiritual wifery" with its connotations of licentiousness was far different from the "holy" system of plural marriage that they had embraced as part of the new and everlasting gospel and their signatures appear on the refutation of Bennett's system along with those of other women.

At the same time, many other women were less than whole-hearted in endorsing plural marriage. Emma Smith, notably, saw the new system as perpetuating rather than eliminating a double standard of moral conduct for men and women. While her husband and other church officials openly alluded to celestial marriage by use of coded references in public speeches, Emma Smith, in many of her addresses to the Relief Society, openly attacked sexual sin. On one occasion she read an epistle from the First Presidency and the Quorum of the Twelve to the Relief Society warning the women of "unprincipled men" who would try to lead them into practices "contrary to the old established morals & virtues & scriptural laws, regulating the habits, customs, & conduct of society."[33] Emma Smith said "her determination was to do her Duty effectually—in putting down transgression" and exhorting the sisters "to follow the teachings of Preside[nt] J Smith—from the Stand. . . . Said she wanted to see a reformation in Both Men & Women."[34]

Emma Smith's remarks reflected her own concerns and very probably those of other Nauvoo women. Certainly they reflected a broader concern among American women for moral reform, a blanket term under which they "organized to eliminate prostitution and inaugurate a single moral standard governing sexual relations."[35] One scholar has observed that the movement among women for moral reform tended to be anti-male.[36] Some male-female conflict over plural marriage was probably inevitable. That the greatest division should take place within the Prophet's own household throws the issues into starker relief. Joseph Smith's support for and Emma Smith's opposition to plural marriage were veiled in public addresses but privately both advocated their own positions with directness, vigor, and persuasiveness.

Although Emma Smith on two known occasions gave permission for Joseph Smith to take plural wives, she later rescinded it and was never reconciled to the new doctrinal practice. A collision was inevitable. At the last recorded meeting of the Female Relief Society of Nauvoo on 16 March 1844, she declared "if their ever was any Authority on the Earth she had it—and had [it] yet."[37] The note of stridency is probably not exaggerated, yet its urgency is that of despair.

Nascent feminists in America were at the time beginning to voice their own conviction that only women had the right to speak for women, but Emma Smith's peculiar circumstances made her own claim to female authority reach beyond that right. She was the "elect lady," the high priestess of a new dispensation. She had been promised: "You shall be crown'd with honor in heav'n and shall sit upon thrones, judging those over whom you are plac'd in authority, and shall be judg'd of God for all the responsibilities that we confer'd upon you."[38] Within ten years it would be widely understood by endowed women that the priestess-presidentess combination gave a woman unique authority over other women. Emma Smith was claiming that authority but undercutting it at the same time. Her husband, the Prophet, had earlier told the society that they should "move according to the ancient Priesthood" but "all must act in concert or nothing can be done."[39] Disharmony with the larger priesthood structure of the church brought the women's work to a halt. Whether the termination of Relief Society minutes 16 March 1844 signals an abrupt end to Relief Society meetings at that time or whether they continued longer is not clear (Zina

D. H. Jacobs [Young] records going "to the Masonic Hall with the sisters," 18 June 1844).[40] Meetings may have been discontinued after the assassination of Joseph Smith on 27 June 1844, in the wake of Emma Smith's other disagreements with the Council of the Twelve. Nearly forty years later, in 1880, John Taylor of the Council would explain that the Nauvoo society had been disbanded because Emma "made use of the position she held to try to pervert the minds of the sisters in relation to [plural marriage]."[41]

By dissolving the Relief Society, by allowing ten years to elapse before its reorganization, and by literally choosing which women would be allowed to enter the temples to be built later in Utah, the men gave to women a clear organizational message about ultimate authority and power in the church. In 1845 Brigham Young declared that women "never can hold the keys of the Priesthood apart from their husbands. When I want Sisters or the Wives of the members of the church to get up Relief Society I will summon them to my aid but until that time let them stay at home & if you see Females huddling together veto the concern and if they say Joseph started it tell them it is a damned lie for I know he never encouraged it."[42]

The idea of a unique sisterhood, presided over by a woman who had been given divine authority through the proper channels was a potent one, though clearly such a sisterhood could not operate if its female leadership was in conflict with the male leadership of the church. Within such boundaries, however, the claim to female authority was real and recognized, although, ironically, it was Eliza R. Snow, not Emma Smith, who later publicly claimed and carried the titles of priestess and presidentess.

II

Ten years later a more confident Brigham Young would reclaim the Relief Society organization; but in the meantime, Mormon sisterhood survived, in part through the same institution that had caused the society's disbandment — plural marriage. The new marriage system, in connection with the Mormon practice of "adoption" (wherein grown men and women were spiritually adopted or "sealed" as children to prominent church leaders), reconstituted Mormon families out of people who had been separated geographically or emotionally from their families of origin and from each other.[43] By forging new kinship relations, the Saints found relief from the sense of isolation and achieved new social solidarity.

The Saints' westward movement toward the Great Basin, which recommenced in 1846 as they left Nauvoo, transported their unique family relationships as well. The trail journal of Patty Bartlett Sessions reveals the intense joy and sorrow she experienced with the new marriage system. Her husband David had been sealed to Rosilla Cowans 3 October 1845, four months before he and Patty left Nauvoo. Rosilla joined them in Iowa in

June 1846, demanding (according to Patty's account) an undue share of David's attention, affection, and loyalty. A painful estrangement between Patty and David resulted. Rosilla returned to Nauvoo in December; and in the months that followed, Patty turned her attentions to a happier aspect of her life in plural marriage. In the Nauvoo Temple, she had been sealed to Joseph Smith as one of his plural wives in eternity (an arrangement that left her own marriage to David intact during mortality) and had thereby acquired another and more agreeable set of "sister wives," who became her new kin.[44]

The plural wives of Joseph Smith formed the nucleus of women gathering at Winter Quarters, Nebraska, to nurture one another spiritually. These sisters were joined in their blessing meetings by "Brigham's girls" or "Heber's girls," as Patty termed them, and others—wives of members of the Quorum of Twelve Apostles, the group most deeply involved in practicing plural marriage at this time. Underlying this emerging network was the individual and collective conviction that plural marriage was a "holy principle," a conviction that plural wives renewed and celebrated as they met together at Winter Quarters and later in Utah, administering to one another in echoes of the sacred rites they had given and received in the Nauvoo Temple.

Out of this early sisterhood of plural wives the female elite of the church would emerge.[45] The secretiveness of plural marriage gradually subsided after its public acknowledgement in 1852; over the decades, the circle of initiates grew, but the plural wives of high church officials stayed at its center. Though the exact composition of this inner circle seems to have varied (Patty Sessions, for one, faded from prominence), it remained the hub of the Great Basin sisterhood. As these wives traveled throughout the territory with their husband-officials, they connected with the plural wives of local church officials and a network of "faithful women" grew. Certainly the women who officiated with Zina D. H. Young in the Salt Lake Temple in 1893 were part of this critical mass, as were most female temple officiators and Relief Society officers.

From their sororal beginnings at Winter Quarters, this cluster of women were also the key proponents of plural marriage. Gathering together to testify to the rightness of plural marriage became an important part of the Mormon female support system throughout the nineteenth century. The testimony of Margaret A. Smoot to a meeting of Mormon women in 1870 is typical: "I have had a voice in my husband taking more wives; for this I am thankful. I have taken pleasure in practicing this pure principle, although I have been tried in it. Yet since the birth of our first child by the second wife, I have never felt to dissolve ties thus formed."[46]

During the antipolygamy campaign of the 1880s, female crusaders would accuse prominent Mormon women such as Eliza R. Snow and Zina D. H.

Young of brainwashing or coercing sisters into accepting plural marriage as the will of God; but for Aunt Eliza and Aunt Zina (as sisters affectionately called them), bearing witness of the truth of the "holy principle" and the purifying power of the sacrifice it involved had been part of their relationships with other Mormon women for nearly forty years. The role of the plural wife as collectively understood by Mormon women required both spiritual commitment and emotional suffering, and those who took on the role entered a sisterhood that assumed common aspiration and commiseration.[47]

Over the years, public testimonials to the truth of the principle of plural marriage became so conventional and ritualized that one wonders to what extent women shared personal and not merely institutionalized feelings about the practice. Jane Charters Robinson Hindley is one who seems to have felt ideological commitment but almost no positive feelings personally. An immensely private person, Jane felt compelled to hide her pain when her husband's new wives entered the home. Entries in her diary for December 1862 express her feelings:

> Monday 22 he has returned and brought two I cannot call them wives yet   it seems so strange. Oh what my feelings are this moment, life to me is not so joyous, it seems dark. My God help me in my weakness and forgive me if I falter in my duty and affection to him I love....
> December 29th. The house is full of company music and dancing but there is a void in my Heart and my eyes are full of tears   Oh, I am very unhappy, and my pride will not suffer me to appear so. I do hope the knew year will bring happiness to me.[48]

A Mormon Mother, Annie Clark Tanner's poignant account of her life in polygyny, suggests that she, too, struggled to reconcile her personal frustrations in plural marriage with her commitment to the church and its teachings. There is no indication that female companionship assuaged the pain of the "obscure and lonely life" Annie often lived as the second wife of Joseph Marion Tanner.[49]

Like other plural wives who were literally exiled during intense anti-polygamy prosecution in the late 1880s, Annie was for a time a fugitive for whom frequent and secret moves made connecting difficult. In six years on the "underground," she moved every few months and sometimes every few weeks to avoid detection as a plural wife. She did not live in her own home until she was pregnant with her second child in her eighth year of marriage. During those years, she lived in fourteen different homes that she names. Of only six of them does she mention by name the woman in the house and of only five does she give information about that woman to suggest any kind of relationship — and those five were all related to her or to her husband.

Annie took an active part in some church, social, and political groups, and attended women's mass meetings opposing the prosecution's treatment of polygamists. Yet she was fiercely independent (took pride that she "had never imposed my work and responsibility on my mother and had never expected her to be present at the birth of my children"),[50] and one suspects that her personal battle with polygyny was largely self-contained until later years when she wrote her autobiography.

The question of bonding in Mormon sisterhood becomes more complex if we look at women who were not plural wives. Statistics regarding the number of church members who practiced plural marriage suggest that a significant percentage of Mormon women were never involved in the system. Recent estimates indicate that between 25 and 50 percent of the Mormon population practiced plural marriage; and since more women than men were involved, the percentage of women might be as high as 80 percent.[51] Unquestionably, those who unitedly supported the practice were able to forge a sisterhood unique in its complexity and achievement, but where did nonparticipants and nonadvocates find support? Women who actively opposed the practice, such as Ann Eliza Young and Fanny Stenhouse (who both published exposés and presented lectures refuting the Mormon marriage system) were branded apostates and pushed outside the sisterhood of faithful women. More passive resisters and malcontents may have felt connected only loosely—if at all—to that sisterhood.[52]

Martha Cragun Cox recalled that a large number of young women in St. George in the early 1870s rejected plural marriage as a personally relevant principle and scorned her decision to enter into it: "It had always seemed to me that plural marriage was the leading principle among the L.D.S. and when I came to know how generally my action in going into it was denounced, especially the fact I had married into poverty, I was saddened [as] well as surprised. . . . One who had been my admiring friend said: 'It is all very well for those girls who cannot very well get good young men for husbands to take married men, but *she* (me) had no need to lower herself for there were young men she could have gotten.' And she and other friends 'cold shouldered' me and made uncomplimentary remarks." However, Martha also found that social displeasure, even within the church, had united the family and "the good kind women whom I had chosen to share the burdens of life with gave me strength and comfort with their sympathy and love."[53]

In some plural families the wives were blood sisters or even mothers and daughters; thus, the relationship in their family of origin was transferred almost intact into the reconstituted plural family, virtually determining the dynamics of those particular units. In other families, nonrelated plural wives became lifelong friends and companions, who, as Martha Cox described, "loved each other more than sisters children of one mother love."[54] According to Susa Young Gates, sister wives Mary and Lillie Freeze had a "perfect friendship . . . which neither death nor misfortune can lessen or cut asunder."[55] Persis Young, the niece of Louisa Lula Greene Richards, was also her sister wife. Her child died shortly after birth, and her life thereafter centered around caring for Louisa's children and the household while Louisa pursued her writing and church activities. Their husband died in 1914, but the women lived together in the family home till Louisa's death in 1944, followed within a few weeks by the death of Persis.[56]

In some marriages, common tasks, temporal and spiritual, became the basis for unity among wives. In 1851 Lucy Meserve Smith wrote her husband that she and two sister wives, Hannah and Bathsheba, had administered by the laying on of hands to another sister wife, Sarah, who was dying. Zina D. H. Young joined them in the circle. Wrote Lucy to George: "Bathsheba said when she and Zina and Hannah and I layed our hands on her [Sarah] she felt as though she was praying over an infant we prayed with our right hand uplifted to the most high and we all felt the blessing of the holy spirit Zina said there was a union of faith."[57] Although letters of these wives indicate occasional squabbles and jealousies, for the most part their interchanges attest Bathsheba's reflection that "we have worked and toiled togather, have had joy in our labors have had our recreations, and have taken comfort in each others society."[58] The Smith wives, though often geographically scattered, cooperated economically, those in outlying settlements sometimes sending handwoven fabric to wives in Salt Lake City who sent back dyed cloth or sewn clothing. Many plural wives were economically independent or interdependent because of their husbands' intensive involvement in missionary and colonization efforts.

A second commonality that marked the world of women, separating them from men and bonding them with other women, was their children. "Our children are considered as stars in a mother's crown," wrote Helen Mar Kimball Whitney, articulating Mormon emphasis on women's child-bearing/child-rearing role.[59] Far from being unique, this position echoed popular American sentiments about motherhood. However, according to at least one critic, Fanny Stenhouse, Latter-day Saints emphasized children at the expense of other aspects of marriage such as "the companionship of soul; the indissoluble union of two existences."[60] Certainly many plural wives reveal in their personal writings a primary emotional involvement with their children rather than with their husbands. Female kin including plural wives frequently shared childbirth and child care experiences. Sister wives sometimes served as midwives, even without specific training. Jane Snyder Richards recalled that she was unsure she would ever be able to tolerate "any other child than hers that should call him [her husband] papa," but when the first child, a daughter, was born to a plural wife, she cared for both daughter and mother, later remarking that "for these children she has always felt an interest, though it was not at all the same feeling she had for her own flesh and blood."[61] In an 1848 letter to her mother-in-law, Clarissa Smith, Lucy Meserve Smith conveyed her grief at "the painful seen [scene] of burying my sweet boy" and described the infant's last days with emphasis on the concerned involvement of sister wives Bathsheba, Sarah, and Zilpha in obtaining and giving medicine, and finally washing, anointing, and praying over the dying child.[62]

These shared experiences centered in children had the potential of bonding together the children as well as their mothers. Non-Mormon Elizabeth Wood Kane, describing to her father her 1872 Utah visit, noted more than once that she could not determine which children were the biological offspring of which wife because of the affection that existed between children and their "aunts," as the sister wives were called.[63]

The practice of plural marriage legitimized the commitment of one woman to another in a complex social, emotional, spiritual, and theological relationship. The form of the ceremony itself, as described by Martha Spence Haywood, often included the first wife in a significant way: "Brother Haywood stood on the floor, his wife taking hold of his left arm with her right and taking first Sister Vary [about to become the second wife] by the right hand and placing it in that of Bro. Haywood's right hand and in that way she was sealed to him for time and eternity by a form of words most sublime. When done she fell back by taking Sister Haywood's arm. I then went forward going through the same ceremony."[64] The structure of the ceremony suggests that the wives were to have some eternal relationship with one another as well as with their husband. Martha Cragun Cox, for one, expressed delight at the prospect of an eternal union with her sister wives, a bond that would continue beyond death. Other plural wives would not have rejoiced at the prospect of sisterly paradise.

All of the means of female bonding normally available to women in the broader American culture were open to Mormon women: intense attachment to their sisters, mothers, and cousins; acceptance of the distinctiveness of the woman's world; concentration on nurturing of children; and expertise in tasks acknowledged as exclusively the province of women. The religious dimension afforded by Mormonism—and particularly the institution of plural marriage—had the potential of intensifying all of these common "womanly" elements. As the American culture generally supported women's social relationships with other women, the Mormon practice of plural marriage ideologically sanctified them.

III

During the early Utah period, Young and other church leaders continued to espouse a hierarchically laddered society in which women and children were the lowest rungs. In 1859, when Horace Greeley visited with Brigham

Young in Utah, he reported that he had "not observed a sign in the streets, an advertisement in the journals, of this Mormon metropolis, whereby a woman proposes to do anything whatever."[65] Such male perspectives minimize women and their world and imply that their culture (sphere) was a subservient one. Yet during this period Mormon women seemed to feel no need to change their status. Political activism and social change did not bring them together. Instead, they united to confirm the separateness, not the subservience, of woman's sphere. Eliza R. Snow versified the sentiment in 1856 for a weekly gathering of the male-female Polysophical Society in Salt Lake City, observing that "there are rights and privileges too,/To Woman's sphere," disclaiming any need to plead for greater rights, and even offering "apologies/For ladies who demand a wider sphere."[66]

The roles to which women were bound by biological realities and popular convention provided a common experience that was distinctively female. Discussion of that experience was itself a means of mutual support and bonding. For example, one plural wife, writing to a friend who was a plural wife in another family, observed that she longed "to write one good sentimental letter (one of my favorite amusements in past years) But since I've become a wife & mother all sentiment has died away in the realities of life, such as, cooking, washing, waiting on babies, &c, also the continual trafic of borrowing & lending." She told her friend that though the letter might not be interesting, it would serve its purpose "if it wiles away a few moments of the dull tedium of domestic affairs." This "love letter," as the writer described it, is largely autobiographical with frequent quips about her housekeeping inabilities. The writer speaks of her appreciation of "the rich blessing of children to give tone & exercise to the long treasured up woman's feelings" and of her realization over the years "that I had a good *mother,* whose teachings & precepts comes in play every day of my present life."[67] Here a commonality of feelings toward the female experience link writer and reader in a friendly confirmation of woman's sphere.

Women's journals extant recount the continual house-to-house visiting that connected women community-wide and lasted, particularly in rural areas, into the twentieth century. Visiting was so frequent it was often noted only in passing and conversations were not recorded, though sometimes hinted at as in Eliza Partridge Lyman's diary notation for August 20, 1849: "Platte DeAlton Lyman one year old to day. Made a dinner in honor of the event. Sisters Billings, Warner, Burk, Walker, Paulina and Priscilla Lyman, Emily Young and Sarah Clark took dinner with us. Not a man there but one who will be a man if he lives a few years."[68] With a sense of celebration Lucy Meserve Smith reminisced about the days in Provo's early history when she and other women "took our spinning Wheels and went to a large room in the Seminary and tride our best to see who could reel of[f] the greatest No. of knots from sunrise to sunset. Sister Terril 100,11. knots. Sister Holden not quite so many but better twist on hers. Sister H. M. Smith and I made the best yarn. It was equal for twist but I had a few knots the most but she spun and reeled 80. knots. On the whole we concluded we all beat. We had refreshments four times during the day, indeed, we took solid comfort in our days labour, and our association together."[69]

With women's work and women's world self-contained it was possible to take all or part of a day off. Mary Jane Mount Tanner described such a day spent in February 1878 when she and four other women started off at 8:00 A.M. in the buggy "to make Sister Hannah Smith a supprise visit": "With light hearts and merry jests we made our way to sister Smith's, who was as much supprised as we could wish. We sent for Frances Clark, Sister Holden came and we spread the table with the ample good cheer we had brought, and enjoyed our dinner and visit with the best of good feelings. About 4 p.m. Sister Beebe's team came for her, and Sister Carter. I loaded my buggy, going around by Sister Holden's to take her home. I took sister Pratt and Sister Clark home, and we all felt better for our little visit."[70]

Mormon women did not remain politically isolated from the larger world of American social concerns for long. Although the gatherings which followed the 1848 Seneca Falls convention would likely have seemed "radical" to Mormon women who had organized along much more conventional lines during the same period, they did share in some of the national concerns. Women's health and health care, which motivated the forming of ladies' physiological societies and the publication of Mary Grove's *Lectures to Ladies on Anatomy and Physiology* (Boston, 1842) concerned Mormon women as well. Their own Female Council of Health was begun in Salt Lake City in 1851, an outgrowth of weekly meetings of midwives from the local Council of Health, founded in 1849 and open to both men and women. It was considered indelicate for women to discuss their physiology and health with men, and the female council provided an opportunity for women to keep such matters to themselves. In addition, they "heard lectures by local physicians, discussed the use of faith and herbs in healing, attempted to design more healthful female fashions, spoke and sang in tongues and enjoyed a social and spiritual interchange."[71] The female council served to complement rather than oppose the larger male-directed council.

Similarly, the Relief Societies Mormon women organized in the early 1850s complemented the larger church organization. By late 1853, the Walker War, a series of skirmishes with the Ute Indians, was coming to an end, and church president Brigham Young instructed the Saints first "to civilize [the Indians] teach them to work, and improve their condition by your utmost faith and diligence."[72] Responding to this and other exhortations to "feed and clothe the Indians," Matilda Dudley, Mary Hawkins, Amanda Smith, and Mary Bird met 24 January 1854 and decided to organize "a society of females for the purpose of making clothing for Indian women and children."[73] The formal organization, instituted two weeks later, included some seventeen women, who elected their own officers and determined their procedures. Young suggested in June that the LDS women "form themselves into societies," meeting "in their own wards" to make clothing for the Lamanites. As with the Nauvoo Relief Society, official male sanction for an organization created by women encouraged expansion but lessened autonomy. The women who had organized their own society for Indian relief disbanded to join the new organizations being formed in their various wards.

Some twenty-two Indian Relief Societies, as they were commonly called, were organized in Salt Lake City and outlying settlements in 1854, and most of the Indian relief was concentrated in that year, sisters eventually contributing clothing and bedding valued at $1,540, more than enough to meet the demand for such goods, plus some $44 in cash. Many of the societies remained organized for the long-range goal of assisting the poor within their wards, as well as for short-range projects such as meetinghouse carpets or clothing and bedding for destitute handcart pioneers.

"I never took more satisfaction and I might say pleasure in any labour I ever performed in life, such unimity [unanimity] of feeling prevailed," wrote Lucy Meserve Smith with obvious relish of her Provo Relief Society's efforts in collecting goods for the handcart pioneers in 1856. "My councilors and I wallowed through the snow until our clothes were wet a foot high to get things together give out noticeses &c." Under Lucy's direction the "willing hands" in Provo's Third Ward found one task after another from making mittens for the Mormon army protecting Salt Lake City against approaching federal troops to making a silk flag for the Provo Brass Band.[74] Such organized tasks brought women together in pursuits which both they and the community recognized as good.

Another ten-year hiatus in Relief Society operations, 1857–67, followed the widespread disorganization of wards when Saints moved south to avoid federal troops and the ensuing bloodless Utah War. But despite this interruption, early Utah Relief Societies established the task-orientated pattern which would be the basis of Mormon sisterhood until the turn of the century.

From Mormon beginnings through the 1850s and 1860s, extensive family ties as well as friendships emerging from shared feelings and experiences in the woman's sphere were the main components of Mormon sisterhood. Overlaid onto this network through the 1870s, 1880s, and 1890s was the churchwide organization of Mormon women into local Relief Society units that not only provided women with common goals and tasks but aroused their commitment to work publicly for the good of women.

IV

Brigham Young's 1867 reestablishment of the Relief Society ushered the organization into 120 years of continuous operation to the present. The women were to organize themselves, he said, and "get women of good understanding" to be their leaders, though they were to seek the counsel of their bishops, "men of understanding." Sisters would be the "mainspring of the movement," Young predicted,[75] and he assured his prophecy's fulfillment by appointing Eliza R. Snow to assist women and bishops in organizing local societies. A plural wife of Brigham Young, though she never took his name or bore him children, Eliza Snow came to function as a special consultant to President Young in most, if not all, matters related to Mormon women. Her loyalty and obedience gained her trust and influence among the governing priesthood counsels unprecedented for a woman.

Eliza Snow became a central figure in moving nineteenth-century Mormon women into the public sphere and clarifying the importance of women in Mormon theology and church organization. She traveled indefatigably, instructing Mormon women of all ages on both spiritual and temporal topics. She was instrumental in organizing Relief and Retrenchment Societies for women, Retrenchment or Mutual Improvement Associations for teenage girls and young married women, and Primary Associations for children. She helped choose and ordain or "set apart" female presidencies for these associations on ward (local) and stake (regional) levels. These activities paralleled those of Brigham Young and the Quorum of Twelve with local priesthood leaders, and she was accorded parallel authority in spiritual and administrative matters.

In a Mormon world still largely divided into male and female spheres, Eliza R. Snow presided over the female sphere, filling the priestess-presidentess gap left by Emma Smith's estrangement from the church. Susa Young Gates suggested that early Utah Relief Societies had not remained intact because of the absence of a strong, central female figure, Eliza Snow being in poor health during this period.[76] It is perhaps significant that Eliza was not officially set apart as general president of the Relief Society until 1880, a few months after the death of Emma Smith in Nauvoo. Yet long before this time Mormon sisters were calling her "the president of the entire Female Relief Societies," or the "head of the women's organizations of the church." One group she visited greeted her as "the president of the female portion of the human race," and several years after her death Mormon sisters were offically teaching their children "a reverence for the Prophet Joseph Smith, Sister Eliza R. Snow and the Holy Priesthood."[77] These last two accolades are more understandable if we consider the place afforded those who first officiated for women in the temple.

Eliza Snow had been a recorder in the Nauvoo Temple. In Salt Lake City she was the president or matron of women in the Endowment House until her death, and she worked for long periods in the temples at St. George and Logan as they were completed. Her position as head of women in the holy sanctuary made her a presiding priestess in addition to being Relief Society "presidentess." The connection between the Relief Society and the temple ordinances, begun in Nauvoo, was realized in Eliza R. Snow in the Endowment House and in her successors, Zina D. H. Young and Bathsheba W. Smith, in the temple. Each presided simultaneously over the Relief Society and women's temple work in Salt Lake City. Women who presided over female officiators in the temple, as well as the more numerous female officiators themselves, received authority to administer the church's highest ordinances to women in the house of the Lord. Relief Society leaders and YLMIA leaders (such as those in Zina Young's circle of female temple officiators) carried some of the temple's ideas and phrases into public and spoke directly to their sisters regarding women's spiritual potential. In a widely published 1873 address, Eliza R. Snow told women: "Inasmuch as we continue faithful, we shall be those that will be crowned in the presence of God and the lamb. You, my sisters, if you are faithful, will become Queens of Queens, and Priestesses unto the Most High God. These are your callings. We have only to discharge our duties. By and by our labors will be past, and our names will be crowned with everlasting honor, and be had in everlasting remembrance among the Saints of the Most High God."[78]

The fact that Eliza Snow spoke to her sisters not only with inspiration but with what they considered to be divine authority to preside over women made the Relief Society much more than a charitable organization, a social club, or a women's auxiliary to more important men's activities. It was a holy sisterhood, wholly necessary to the church—God's kingdom on the earth. "Neither is the man without the woman, neither the woman without the man, in the Lord"; neither the brotherhood without the sisterhood.[79]

The labors and duties of which Eliza R. Snow spoke to her contemporaries were significantly, though not exclusively, temporal. The partnership of Mormon women and men, rooted in temple theology, had its flowering in community tasks during the cooperative movement of the 1860s and 1870s. "It is the duty of every man and of every woman to do all that is possible to promote the kingdom of God on the earth," said Brigham Young in 1875, when the economics of the kingdom were receiving particular emphasis.[80] To strengthen the kingdom against Utah's growing gentile population, Mormons were to become self-sufficient through home industry and manufacture and the formation and support of local Latter-day Saint cooperatives.

The Relief Society staunchly advocated the individual and collective involvement of women in home industry and cooperatives. Eliza Snow told women that if they assisted in home industries, including silk culture, straw weaving, tailoring, and home canning, they would be "doing just as much as an Elder who went forth to preach the Gospel."[81] Women's collective work began simply with the gathering of means to relieve the poor. Ruth Page Rogers of the Second Ward in Parowan, Utah, recorded that in one year she donated eight eggs, five pounds of carpet rags, twenty cents worth of straw, and two pairs of stockings to the local society of which she was president.[82] Most groups through donations acquired the surplus to build their own halls. The first Relief Society hall was dedicated in Salt Lake City's Fifteenth Ward in April 1869. The upper story provided a hall for spiritual meetings and sewing sessions; the lower story was a cooperative store where Relief Society sisters and other ward members could sell homemade goods on consignment. Over the next five decades, similar Relief Society halls were built throughout Utah and later in Idaho, Arizona, Canada, and Mexico.

During Sarah M. Kimball's forty-year presidency of Salt Lake City's Fifteenth Ward Relief Society, the sisters not only built their hall but constructed a granary and filled it as part of a Relief Society grain-storage program initiated by Brigham Young and directed by Emmeline B. Wells beginning in 1876. The society also contributed funds for Perpetual Emigration, the Salt Lake and Logan temples, and Deseret Hospital; purchased shares for a ward organ; and provided carpet for the ward meetinghouse — activities typical of Relief Societies throughout the church during this period. Beyond these substantial undertakings, however, the Fifteenth Ward society also sent assistance to those who suffered in the Chicago fire, mailed the *Woman's Exponent* to English sisters too poor to subscribe, began a ward kindergarten and financed the teacher's professional training as well as paid tuition for poor children, founded a ward library, and sponsored quarterly parties for the ward's widowed and aged.

On one occasion when she was asked what had made the society so successful, Presidentess Kimball replied, "It was because we had acted in unison and had kept in motion that which we received." Her 1868 report to Brigham Young and Eliza R. Snow made it clear that progress on the society's hall had "not been accomplished by the labor of our hands and our offerings alone. We have received aid and encouragement from B[isho]p Burton and the other brethren of the Ward." Eight years later she told her sisters there "had not been the least jar" between Bishop Burton and her. Indeed, minutes recount a member of the bishopric visiting a society meeting in 1878 to assure the sisters that he had no fear of them "transcending the bounds of the Priesthood. Felt to render them support and faith. Hoped we [the sisters] would sustain each other in the office chores as faithfully as they would be sustained by the Bishop and counsel."[83]

Most Mormon women had never held formal positions of church leadership until after the Relief Society was reestablished in 1867, followed by the Young Ladies Retrenchment (Mutual Improvement) Associations in 1869, and the Primary Associations (for children) in 1878. While some, like Sarah Kimball, were eager and ready to shoulder the new responsibilities, others were far more hesitant and needed encouragement. At one meeting in the Fifteenth Ward two sisters "wished to be excused from speaking as they had had no experience in that line," whereupon a third sister indicated "she had no sympathy with those who would not try to speak . . . felt there was a barrier between them when they would not express their feelings." Sister Jones, a counselor to Sarah Kimball, tried to bridge these differences and keep the sisterly relationship intact, explaining that "women would yet be better known" and that she, too, "used to feel that it was dreadful for women to attempt to speak in public." [84] This scene, undoubtedly acted out in dozens of wards as women assumed new roles and duties, suggests the emotional support women gave each other in those unfamiliar roles.

In 1888, after the Relief Society had been in full swing for some twenty years, Apostle Franklin D. Richards commented on sisters' continued "reluctance to assume public positions, or public duties. . . . Some of the sisters feel intimidated in their meetings when the brethren are present; while others believe that if the brethren would attend and give them counsel and encouragement, they would be stronger and more able to launch out in the liberty of the spirit and discharge the duties incumbent upon them with a consciousness and heavenly assurance. . . . It has been so from the beginning of this work that has been laid upon the sisters; it has been looked upon by some of them as being something out of their life and place." [85]

Some brethren likewise viewed women as out of place in public life. "The brethren do not understand us, they feel that we want to usurp power," Relief Society president Rachel Ivins Grant confided to her quorum of visiting teachers in the Salt Lake City Thirteenth Ward. Emily Dow Partridge Young remembered when her bishop attended a Relief Society meeting in 1878, informing the sisters that he and the other trustees of the ward schoolhouse "wanted to manage the affairs of the house and would be glad if the sisters would please not interfere. He repeated it the same several times in the course of his remarks and wound up by saying he was too mad to talk and sat down." [86]

In his 1888 address Franklin D. Richards acknowledged that the disapproval of men could hinder women in fulfilling church callings, to the detriment of the church as a whole.

> Every now and again we hear men speak tauntingly of the sisters and lightly of their public duties, instead of supporting and encouraging them. There are also some who look with jealousy upon the moves of the sisters as though they might come to possess some of the gifts, and are afraid they will get away with some of the blessings of the Gospel, which only men ought to possess. That is the way some look upon woman and her work. They don't like to accord them anything that will raise them up and make their talents to shine forth as the

daughters of Eve and of Sarah. But have feelings of envy and jealousy; and instead of dealing open handedly with them, tell them to go forward and do all the good they can, it seems as though they would like to keep them back and not let them do anything — more than is really necessary.[87]

Like Eliza R. Snow, Richards traced women's "blessings, powers and rights" to the temple. The sisters were not to be passive partners; they were to be "cooperators with us," as one bishop said. "We never go in opposition to the Priesthood," Eliza R. Snow wrote Willmirth East, Relief Society president in an Arizona ward where the bishop was questioning some aspects of the society's program. For Eliza Snow unity and cooperation seemed entirely compatible with creativity and even a degree of autonomy. Concerned that in Ogden "the Relief Society here has no house of its own — no house that it can control," she advised them to get the brethren's sanction, then undertake to build it. They were to initiate, she said, reminding them: "It is said that God helps those who help themselves, and the brethren are so godlike that they will help you." Two weeks later she told sisters assembled in Salt Lake City: "As sure as the sisters arise and take hold of the work, the brethren will wake up, because they must be at the head."[88]

Ideally, the women's organizations and their leaders were an important organizational counterpart to priesthood quorums and priesthood leaders. They were not to be simply a "sisterhood of the brotherhood," as Marilyn Warenski has indicated.[89] Yet even in the nineteenth century, women questioned how a male-female partnership could work when only males held priesthood offices.

Mary Elizabeth Rollins Lightner, ward Relief Society president in Minerville, Utah, was eager to have her presidency ordain the teachers or visiting committee. "The time will probably be when the Society will set apart its different officers," wrote Eliza R. Snow with optimism, "but, as yet, we have to work with much crude material, and it seems wisdom to merely appoint by vote." Eliza's conclusion to the letter was a personal statement rather than a policy statement, and one wonders how extensively she, the church's most powerful woman, had pondered the concept. "Tell the sisters to go forth and discharge their duties, in humility and faithfulness and the Spirit of God will rest upon them and they will be blest in their labors. Let them seek for wisdom instead of power and they will have all the power they have wisdom to exercise."[90]

It is important to know that women asked such questions and discussed them with one another in the midst of making an impressive place for themselves within the church organization. As Relief Society delegate to the first meeting of the International Council of Women in Washington, D.C., in 1888, Emily S. Richards indicated that 22,000 of the church's 160,000 membership were Relief Society members owning halls and other property valued at $95,000, in addition to some 32,000 bushels of grain. She also mentioned their semi-monthly paper, the *Woman's Exponent,* with "a woman editor, women writers, women business agents and women compositors," as well as the Relief Society's Deseret Hospital "with a lady M.D. as Principal."[91] In addition local Relief Societies had been active in providing relief to the poor in their wards as well as in raising silk, contributing to temple and emigration funds, funding obstetrical training for midwives and some M.D.s, and defending the practice of plural marriage through mass meetings and petitions.

Widespread participation in these activities gave Mormon women a sense of accomplishment. Their work affected the community as a whole, and because the community was holy, the women's work took on colossal significance. Augusta Joyce Crocheron wrote rather grandiosely about women's grain saving:

> Then loyal daughters, who obeyed
> A noble leader's word,
> Ye shall come forth, in power arrayed,
> Named, with the earth's accord,
> With blessings, from the lips of those
> Saved by thy deeds of worth,
> And reverence from thy fallen foes —
> The grain queens of the earth.[92]

Besides their public achievements (enthusiastically lauded by priesthood officials, too), women also rejoiced in the spiritual bonds that emerged from their association. On 31 August 1878 at an interward gathering known as General Retrenchment, Elizabeth Ann Whitney rose and blessed the sisters present, probably through the gift of tongues. Afterward, Sarah M. Kimball suggested that the elderly Sister Whitney, whose days were "almost numbered," had given so much of herself in the blessing that she ought to receive a reciprocal blessing from the group. "'I feel to say God bless Sister Whitney, comfort and cheer her heart; may her pathway be smooth, and may honor and blessing be multiplied on her head forever.' By request of Pres. Horne, all sisters present then rose to their feet, Sister Kimball repeated the blessings, and the whole congregation confirmed it by a hearty Amen."[93] Similarly, at one of the gatherings of female temple workers Zina D. H. Young "felt there was some one in the room who was in trouble & in need of help & if she would make it know[n] we would all join in prayer & unite our faith for her; whereupon Sister C. C. Wells said she felt she was the one who needed the comfort; prayer was then offered by her and repeated by the sisters."[94]

Through the letters, poems, essays, and reports in the *Woman's Exponent,* women could connect themselves to sisters all over the church. One subscriber praised the semimonthly as "a white winged messenger of peace and joy." Another, located hundreds of miles from Salt Lake City called it "our valuable little paper, which is ever welcome, bringing with it so much encouragement to the sad and weary mothers, sisters and daughters in Israel."[95]

Through reports of Relief Society, YLMIA, and Primary Association activities, women were kept abreast of what other wards and stakes were doing. Elizabeth D. (Libbie) Noal regularly reported on the work of Mormon women, mostly the wives of missionary elders, on the Sandwich Islands (Hawaii). "Eight months ago we formed ourselves in a school of the missionary sisters, eight in number and have since that time held regular weekly meetings, studying the principles of the Gospel, and other subjects pertaining to the advancement of woman," she wrote in 1892. Without men, these sisters visited adjacent islands, where they were greeted with much excitement as "reverends" since for many natives it was "the first time they had seen a Missionary Sister of our Church." During that year the sisters collectively traveled 580 miles by water, 100 miles by horseback, 25 miles by train, and 64 miles by cart.[96] An 1893 report from Snowflake, Arizona, indicated sisters there had just gathered for stake Relief Society conference in their new society hall, "a neat brick building," complete with a room "set apart for the sisters to pray in."[97]

One article, submitted from a YLMIA newspaper in Orangeville, Emery County, Utah, portrayed the desires of its author, S. A. Fullmer, to develop strong bonds of sisterhood within the local organization for young women: "Then, my dear sisters, let us strive to be one, for the Lord says unless we are one we are not His. Let us try to build each other up; put away all evil from our hearts, and seek to do good. Let us pray for our young sisters of the presidency, that the Lord will inspire their hearts, that wisdom and understanding may be given them, and that the power of speech and language may be theirs, so that they may be able to impart the instruction necessary for the advancement of our society."[98]

Poets of varying ability commemorated birthdays and deaths, celebrated nature, and considered life's perplexities in the *Exponent*'s pages. Problems and questions raised by one poet often elicited a poetical response from another. The dozens of obituaries, filled with gratitude and solemn resolutions of respect, memorialize not only the deceased but women who cherished one another.

As Mormon women assumed public responsibilities, they pulled together to advance themselves, others, and the kingdom of God, preserving and expanding sisterly networks within the Mormon circle. In affiliating with the nineteenth-century woman's rights movement, they looked beyond that circle and celebrated their connectedness to a larger group of American sisters.

In 1869 Elizabeth Cady Stanton and Susan B. Anthony had organized the National Woman Suffrage Association, and a few months later, Lucy Stone and her husband Henry Blackwell organized the more conservative

American Woman Suffrage Association. The *Woman's Exponent* followed the progress of both groups and reprinted articles from the AWSA *Woman's Journal*, its contemporary.

Utah's territorial legislature had granted the vote to women on 12 February 1870, just two months after Wyoming had passed a bill enfranchising women, the first U.S. state or territory to do so. The month previous, January 1870, Latter-day Saint women in virtually every community in the territory had been gathering in mass "indignation meetings" to protest antipolygamy legislation proposed by Congressman Shelby M. Cullom. Most eastern papers editorialized positively about the knowledge, logic, and rhetoric of the "so-called degraded ladies of Mormondom," even comparing them with powerful suffrage advocates.[99] William H. Hooper, Utah's delegate to Congress, suggested the suffrage bill may have been an effort to extend the positive effects of Mormon women's public involvement, "to convince the country how utterly without foundation the popular assertions were concerning the women of the territory."[100]

In any case, the enfranchisement of Mormon women and their enthusiastic endorsement of the suffrage cause gained them the support of the National Woman Suffrage Association. NWSA leaders Elizabeth Cady Stanton and Susan B. Anthony visited Utah a few months after the vote was granted, and beginning in 1878 some Mormon delegates traveled east to attend NWSA conventions. Mormon women and men spoke in support of female suffrage (Utah's non-Mormons generally opposed it), and Anthony and the National Woman Suffrage Association lobbied against proposed federal antipolygamy legislation disfranchising women.

The involvement of Mormon women in the national suffrage battle was more intense after 1887, when the Edmunds-Tucker Act disfranchised Mormon women as part of the final legislative blow to plural marriage. The women promptly formed a territorial suffrage association with local chapters that corresponded closely, if not absolutely, to local Relief Societies. At the first meeting of the Utah County Woman Suffrage Association, held in Provo 23 October 1889, newly elected president Mary Jane Mount Tanner indicated that "we desire to give the weight of our labors toward strengthening the hands of those, who have so long and valiantly fought the good fight in behalf of the women of this nation."[101]

In their suffrage meetings Mormon women used popular songs and their church hymns as settings for suffrage verses they wrote themselves. Lucinda Lee Dalton, poet and ardent suffragist from Beaver, Utah, penned these lines in 1874; the *Exponent* reprinted them in 1893.

> O, Woman, arise! this glow in the skies
> Betokens the advent of morning;
> Thy spirit should smile, exulting the while,
> In the day which has published its warning.

. . . .

Thy desolate cry through ages gone by
To the ear of thy God has ascended;
He bids thee prepare thy armor to bear
For soon shall thy penance be ended.
Full soon shalt thou stand co-equal with man,
Untrammeled, yet faithful and lowly,
Triumphantly meek, resistless though weak,
A conqueror, guileless and holy.[102]

Many women, Mormon and non-Mormon, found spiritual significance in the movement for women's rights. Sister A. L. Cox from the Sanpete County Woman Suffrage Association expressed her concern that "we who have accepted the new gospel of Equal Rights, must labor with untiring zeal for the redemption of the masses."[103] Mormon women saw substantial improvements in the sphere and status of women as a direct result of the restoration of the gospel, and especially Joseph Smith's turning of the key to women.[104] In 1895 Mormon women on local and state levels fought their final battle for local suffrage with real religious fervor, succeeding in including woman suffrage in the proposed state constitution. Idaho's Mormon women also organized and successfully won the vote in 1896.

These victories would not have been possible without official Mormon sanction for the expansion of women's responsibilities beyond the traditional private sphere. During the last three decades of the nineteenth century large numbers of Mormon women assumed new leadership positions within the women's organizations of the church, emerging more visibly as partners who shared with priesthood officials responsibility for building the kingdom of God. Eliza R. Snow, Zina D. H. Young, and other Mormon leaders saw these new public roles for women as an extension of the divine partnership of woman and man emphasized in Mormon temple theology. Mormon women joined their American sisters in the movement for woman's rights with a conviction of the practical advantage and cosmic importance of woman standing "co-equal with man."

V

The battle for suffrage entwined several strands of sisterhood including family ties, long-term friendships, formal female church organization, and a widespread, unified commitment to work publicly for the good of women. That all of these elements of sisterhood should be concurrently present led to a culmination of strength and union unique in the history of Mormon women. By 1920 when the Nineteenth Amendment received final national ratification, this collective strength was partially dispersed. By contrast, the second American movement for women's rights, in the 1970s, found Mormon women with diverse, even divisive, ideas of women's best interests. Ironically, these divisions could trace their roots to the 1890s, when ties with groups outside the circle of LDS women began modifying the monolithic Mormon sisterhood.

By 4 January 1896, when Utah was formally admitted to statehood by signature of U.S. president Grover Cleveland, substantial changes had occurred in the lives of Mormon women. The year 1887 marked not only passage of the stringent Edmunds-Tucker Act, which spelled polygamy's eventual end, but also the deaths of Eliza R. Snow and church president John Taylor. In 1890 Taylor's successor, Wilford Woodruff, issued his Manifesto announcing that Latter-day Saints should "refrain from contracting any marriage forbidden by the law of the land." For nearly half a century, defending plural marriage had united large numbers of Mormon women and provided them an opportunity to make their presence felt in the public sphere. While their advocacy of plural marriage resulted in their negative image nationwide, the women perceived themselves and were perceived by the Mormon community as integral defenders of the faith during this time. After 1890 involvement in the battle for suffrage seems to have supplanted Mormon women's public defense of plural marriage, but as suffragists they were less unique, less tied to their past, and, as they reached out to women nationwide, less exclusively bound to one another.

Plural marriage had separated Mormon women from the majority of church-going American middle-class women, but abandonment of "the principle" beginning in 1890 reduced the tension between Mormon women and their American counterparts. "Now that the extraneous doctrine of polygamy is swept away, the world will judge more fairly of the Mormon citizens of Utah," declared the non-Mormon *Woman's Tribune*, cited in the *Woman's Exponent*.[105] Latter-day Saint women first had reached beyond their own circle to the suffrage movement, gaining initial acceptance from its radical wing, the National Woman Suffrage Association, but not from its respectable wing, the American Woman Suffrage Association, whose members condemned polygamy. In 1888, when negotiations for the merger of the two suffrage associations were underway, the NWSA sponsored a meeting in Washington, D.C., with the intention of forming an international alliance for woman suffrage. Latter-day Saint women were delegates at this organizational convention of the International Council of Women. When ICW's United States affiliate, the National Council of Women, was organized in 1891, the Relief Society and YLMIA became charter members and are still members.

In part the National Council's purpose was to foster "better understanding among organized women of varying interests and beliefs"—a purpose in complete harmony with the need of LDS women to be better understood and accepted among American women. Apostle Franklin D. Richards in

1894 applauded the sisters' affiliation with the two councils: "In the great world there are many Societies of worldwide importance, ours is one with them now, and is of like importance in a national and international sense ... the sisters when they go down to Washington to these great Councils will have influence and power there, and they have had."[106] In connection with council affiliation both the Relief Society and the YLMIA incorporated and prefixed their names with the word "national." The Young Ladies National Mutual Improvement Association dropped the prefix in 1913, but the National Woman's Relief Society retained it until 1945. Aside from the National Woman Suffrage Association these councils were the first of several extra-organizational affiliations of LDS women's organizations, and ultimately they were the most enduring. Relief Society president Belle S. Spafford was president of the National Council of Women from 1968 to 1970, and other Mormon women have been officers.

This affiliation left the greater body of Mormon women untouched, however. They moved beyond the Mormon circle through the club movement. Starting with the founding of Sorosis in New York (1868) and the New England Woman's Club in Boston (1870), American women rapidly organized cultural clubs throughout the United States. The 1890 organization of the General Federation of Woman Clubs signaled the beginning of a proliferation of nationwide ties for women. "Association is the watchword of the age — associations for labor, for trade, for instruction, for entertainment, for advance of all kinds," declared one women's club founder. "Women naturally feel the impulse and are banding together for work."[107]

Mormon women felt the impulse belatedly. Club women had been among the most vocal opponents of plural marriage, and Utah's early culture clubs (begun as early as 1874) excluded Mormon women. The *Woman's Exponent* occasionally reported on happenings in national women's clubs during the 1870s and 1880s, but the first Mormon culture clubs were organized after 1890. In October 1891 *Woman's Exponent* editor Emmeline B. Wells, her predecessor, Louisa Lula Greene Richards, and her successor, Susa Young Gates, organized the Utah Woman's Press Club, patterned after the Woman's Press Club of New York founded in November 1889. Established "for the benefit of women engaged in active journalistic or newspaper work in Utah Territory," the club was limited to women whose writings had been published.[108] Monthly Press Club meetings consisted of the reading of original compositions as well as discussion of current topics. The Reapers Club, founded in 1892, featured discussions of literature, political science, and current events at its biweekly meetings. The Authors Club (1893) focused on great authors and their works, and often included history and art.

All three of these clubs followed parliamentary rules, chose colors or symbols to represent their purposes, and affiliated with the Utah Federation of Women's Clubs shortly after its founding in 1892 and later with the General Federation of Women's Clubs. Similar groups were established in other Utah towns. A woman's social and literary club called Sorosis was formed in Pleasant Grove in 1894, for example. The American History and Literary Club was organized in South Bountiful in 1895.

Another Mormon response to the "age of association" was the Daughters of Utah Pioneers, organized by fifty-four Mormon women in Salt Lake City in April 1901 "to perpetuate the names and achievements of the men, women and children who were the pioneers in the founding of this commonwealth." Since membership was limited to women whose ancestors had arrived in Utah before the 1869 completion of the railroad, members were primarily, but not exclusively, LDS. The group itself was nonpolitical and nonsectarian, modeled after the Sons or Daughters of the American Revolution and similar patriotic groups, with a central company leading local camps in marking and preserving historic sites and landmarks, collecting relics and documents, and writing life histories of their ancestors.

Over time, the fifty-four charter members of the DUP were individually affiliated with such other groups as the Ladies Literary Club, Women's Democratic Club of Utah, Daughters of the American Revolution, Daughters of the Revolution, League of Women Voters, Women's Legislative Council of Utah, Authors Club, Friendship Circle, Cleofan, Red Cross, Daughters of the Utah Handcart Pioneers, Neighborhood House Association, Country Club, and Kindergarten Club.[109] Many women joined two, three, or half a dozen or more clubs, societies, and associations. "They fill a need for older people," explained a retired teacher in 1981 — a member of some eleven different groups.[110]

If the institution of house-to-house visiting so prevalent in the nineteenth century was fading, these women's groups replaced it for large numbers of American women, including Mormon women. In an 1894 *Exponent* editorial Emmeline B. Wells explained that local clubs helped cultivate home talent, serving as "married women's colleges" and filling "a place left vacant as woman grows away from the friends of her girlhood."[111] The younger or older woman could meet her need for female society through regularly scheduled two-hour meetings one to four times per month, keeping herself socially and intellectually active, where a house-bound woman might feel isolated in the increasingly urbanized and industrialized American society. This shift had peculiar importance within the Mormon culture. Political diversity had replaced a single Mormon party. Economic diversity replaced cooperative self-sufficiency. For Mormon women, their clubs, associations, and societies signaled, allowed, and even accelerated social diversity.

The groups themselves were diverse, though all were secular in that they centered on something other than Mormonism. Most culture clubs studied literature, music, art, or history, along with current topics. The stated object of the Reapers Club, for example, was "social and intellectual development."[112] Some still exist: Cleofan and Authors Club both are nearly a century old. The Music Circle in Salt Lake City spans at least three generations, featuring monthly lessons on music and composers with performances by some of the club's twenty-five to thirty members. Mormon women have continued to establish clubs for cultural enrichment. A recent and demanding music club for fourteen LDS women in Salt Lake City is the Piano Club, composed of musicians who perform for one another regularly.[113]

Although from the outset use of the word "club" distinguished these women's groups from charitable societies, many culture clubs, particularly those with national affiliations, have had a service or social welfare component. In the early years of the twentieth century, the Authors Club worked to create a traveling library, contributed money to sufferers of the Scofield mine disaster, raised money for a free kindergarten, and protested public entertainments that "in any way have a tendency towards immorality and coarseness."[114] These tasks not only bound women together but greatly benefited their communities.

Less formal Mormon women's clubs have centered around traditional female concerns. One group of expectant mothers in Calgary, Canada, jokingly calling themselves the A.A., "Abdomens Anonymous," organized in the 1950s around the women's shared concern about child-bearing. During the 1930s in Granger, Utah, nineteen Cyprus High School graduates formed the Nimble Fingers. They sewed their own trousseaus, then baby clothes, Halloween costumes, doll clothes, prom formals, and trousseaus again, this time for their daughters. In 1981, after forty-five years, the Nimble Fingers group still met regularly.[115]

For more than thirty years, the Sew'n Sews of Pasadena, California, have provided needed fellowship and sociability. When they asked a new young mother to join their group, she responded: "Why would I ever want to leave my house and my baby on an evening when my husband could be home?" The Sew'n Sews gave the young mother two years and invited her back— whereupon she accepted with feverish gratitude. In Salt Lake City a group of college friends decided at the outset to leave husbands at home as they renewed friendship ties through monthly dinner meetings of "Club," where ideas, interests, and experiences were exchanged along with recipes.[116] These women, like their nineteenth-century counterparts, gathered in homes rather than halls or clubhouses. They played an important emotional role in one another's lives long before the widespread emphasis on "self-disclosure" during the psychologized 1960s and 1970s.

"I went to Club as religiously as I went to church," said Suzanna Mae Grua, who, in 1932, had joined the Business and Professional Women's Club in Provo. Almost all of its members were Latter-day Saints active in church and community. About half were married. She had been part of the club only a few months when her physician husband died, leaving her with four children. The support of club members was subsequently invaluable. A teacher, Mrs. Grua found BPW's tasks significant, particularly its legislative program in support of women's rights, its scholarships, and charitable fund-raising. For her, the club was a complement to the Mormon religion, and she daily repeated Mary Stewart's "Collect for Club Women," concluding:

> And may we strive to touch and know the great common
> woman's heart of us all.
> And, O Lord, let us not forget to be kind.[117]

This comfortable harmony between club affiliation and church member-ship has not been the rule among Mormon women. Nor has the church encouraged such attachments for women or men. Through the 1920s, the Relief Society General Board was repeatedly queried about the propriety of club membership for LDS women. Secret societies were readily condemned, but other groups were harder to write off, especially since most members of the general board itself had some outside affiliation. General president Clarissa S. Williams told members assembled at the Relief Society annual conference in April 1927 that she "did not object to the women having literary or sewing or social clubs." She said she belonged to a "circle" which met monthly and was both "restful" and "entertaining." "But," she observed, "I make it a point always that this pleasure afternoon shall not interfere in any way with my Relief Society or my other Church activities."[118]

In April 1936 Relief Society general board member Lotta Paul Baxter asked a meeting of Relief Society officers if "clubs and other interests" might be "encroaching" upon the society's field of activity. "With no thought of depreciating the worth of these other organizations which women are in-terested in, and rightly so," said Baxter, "we still maintain that we have a program of such varied interests that the needs and desires of all women can find expression herein." By 1936 the Relief Society was sponsoring a work-day which focused on welfare sewing, a chorus for "singing mothers," and what Baxter termed "better and more profound reading and research than is found in other courses of study."[119]

Twenty-two years earlier, in 1914, the Relief Society had introduced its first standardized monthly program which incorporated some elements of study similar to those in a variety of clubs. One meeting each month was to be given to "Work and Business," (mostly charity), another to "Home Gardening and Ethics," a third to literature, art, and architecture, and the fourth meeting to "Genealogy and Testimony." A ten-minute talk or discus-sion on current events (three minutes each for local, national, and inter-national news) was to be part of each weekly meeting.

Earlier, the YLMIA had published its first suggested program for weekly meetings in 1890. The Primary Association General Board began publishing lessons in the first issue of the new *Children's Friend* in 1902. Relief Society general president Emmeline B. Wells had resisted the trend—"We are getting too far away from the spiritual side of our work"—but she was fighting an irresistible standardization.[120] Susa Young Gates, editor of the successor to the *Woman's Exponent,* the *Relief Society Magazine,* took pleasure in noting in 1915 the connection between club offerings and the new Relief Society courses:

> There are no limitations to our possible growth and development. We find admirable truth germs in the literary studies carried on in some clubs; we discover elements of rare joy in the art lessons given by some other club; while the patriotic societies, both at home and abroad, certainly are doing a good work in fostering a love for history and genealogy among their members.
>
> Then why not open up in the Relief Society all of these avenues of culture and education, by establishing departments for the study of all these truths and beauties of life and nature?[121]

This change in curriculum further emphasized increasing similarity between the Relief Society and other American women's clubs, societies, and associations. During the early decades of the twentieth century, all three LDS women's organizations were influenced by national trends and events. Domestic science or home economics, prominent in the popular press, was featured in Mormon women's magazines and curriculum. Each of the three organizations became involved in Red Cross work during World War I and was subsequently active in progressive reforms. The Primary Association supported the national Children's Year in 1918–19, and in 1922 established a day nursery and convalescent home for children in Salt Lake City. The YLMIA campaigned for prohibition and "the non-use and non-sale of tobacco." In 1919 the Relief Society set up a professional social service department for the church, and from 1921 through 1929 its general board and local units led out in improving maternity and infant health care through extensive support and implementation of the national Sheppard-Towner Act. Further, in 1929 Relief Society women joined other Utahns in successfully petitioning the legislature for a state training school for the feeble-minded. Such efforts connected Mormon women to their American sisters and obscured differences.

"You have more or less taken on the attributes that are attached in the world to cultural clubs," J. Reuben Clark, a member of the First Presidency, scolded the Relief Society conference assembled 3 April 1936.[122] He was challenging LDS women to separate themselves from the world more definitely by taking up the church's new Security Plan or welfare program, itself an effort to separate the church from the world by eschewing federal relief programs in favor of "taking care of our own." Traditionally local bishops and Relief Society presidents had been responsible for the welfare of ward members. Both had collected and disbursed charity funds, bishops receiving direction from the Presiding Bishopric, and ward and stake Relief Society presidents from the Relief Society general presidency and board. The Presiding Bishopric and Relief Society general presidency met regularly to coordinate their efforts and encouraged local leaders to do likewise. The new plan introduced in 1936 set up a Church Security Committee, later Welfare Committee, which assumed the primary leadership role for church-wide welfare, essentially replacing the Presiding Bishopric and Relief Society general presidency and board in that capacity.

Whatever reservations Relief Society general president Louise Y. Robison had about the plan she expressed in private to the general board. In Relief Society conference she advocated wholehearted support of the new program and encouraged women to be involved in the assignments given the Relief Society, including sewing, quilting, and canning. Belle S. Spafford recalled how personally significant it was to be a counselor in the Belvedere Ward Relief Society presidency as they became involved in a local canning project during the depression. "I would go out with my car, a little Ford, and my Relief Society sisters and I would pick up the windfall peaches and the windfall apples. Then we would go back to the meetinghouse where the sisters would bring their pressure cookers, and we'd gather up the bottles and put them in great big tubs with boiling water and sterilize the bottles. We'd work all day long. And when the canning was done, before the bottles were cool, people would be standing in line, our fine families in the ward, waiting to receive the commodities that we'd prepared. Those were trying days. . . . But to me that was Relief Society."[123]

LDS women were praised for giving "whole-souled" service to the Security Plan, renamed in 1938 the Welfare Plan. In addition, they continued to manage their own limited local service programs. In 1936 many ward societies still raised and collected their own general fund, used to purchase for the ward such items as a carpet, piano, or sacrament set, and their own charity funds, used to provide commodities and expenses for families in need. Relief Societies carrying out such programs "should not be hampered or restricted by Stake Presidents or Ward Bishoprics," said Presiding Bishop Sylvester Q. Cannon in 1937, adding that "their funds for specific purposes should not be diverted."[124]

Even so, introduction of a new churchwide welfare program eventually lessened Relief Society involvement in the work for which it had been named. The Relief Society general presidency served on the Church Welfare Committee, sometimes as members but sometimes only as consultants, and for months at a time were not included in committee decision-making.[125] After the establishment of Deseret Industries in 1938, where handicapped and unskilled laborers were employed to refurbish donated goods, Relief Society sisters no longer made over clothing for needy families. As part of streamlining welfare procedures, in October 1944 visiting teachers discontinued their monthly collection of charity donations and local Relief Societies ceased to disburse their own relief funds and commodities. The ward Relief Society president continued to work under the direction of her bishop in administering to families in need, but she worked confidentially and alone, using ward funds, not Relief Society stores. Relieving the poor was no longer a collective task initiated by sisters. In response to ecclesiastically determined schedules and quotas, they periodically sewed quilts and clothing, and worked in efficiently mechanized regional canneries.

Erosion of the Relief Society's participation in welfare work was hastened by the professionalization and governmentalization of services which had once been the responsibility of volunteer organizations. In 1940, for example, Relief Society general secretary-treasurer Vera Pohlman gave the annual statistical report, explaining that the decline in home visits to the sick and in the number of bodies prepared for burial was due to the increased availability of home nurses and morticians.[126] The emergence of state and county welfare systems through the 1930s likewise made private relief less urgent. The Social Security Act, passed in 1935 and amended in 1939, provided work relief, unemployment and survivors insurance, old age assistance and insurance, and aid to widows and dependent children. It also gave support to public services for health care during pregnancy and infancy—superseding the local programs in which the Relief Society had been extensively involved.

Charitable work remained central to Relief Society's ideological identity, but the real time spent on it shrank steadily from the 1940s through the 1960s as women spent a greater proportion of Relief Society time in lesson work, fund-raising, and socials, all typical of non-Mormon groups as well. Whether Relief Society membership and attendance were affected significantly by this changing organizational emphasis will be ascertained only through much-needed quantitative analysis. Percentages of women involved in the Relief Society may not vary appreciably over time or differ substantially from other voluntary organizations. But by the late 1930s the Relief Society itself was concerned about slow growth—an increase of 2,000 during 1937. In the spring of 1938 the general board decided "to launch a big membership building program." The goal was to reach 100,000 members by the society's one hundredth anniversary, 17 March 1942.

During 1938, five thousand new sisters paid the annual dues and affiliated, a step toward the 100,000 goal. "Will we keep them with us?" asked Rae B. Barker, chair of the drive. "Perhaps we could stress a little more in our organizations bonding (cementing) through friendliness."[127] The number of dropouts was substantial. While 13,990 women became new Relief Society members during 1939 (bringing the total membership to 86,142), the net increase was slightly over one-third that number since 992 members died during the year and 7,096 were listed as "removed or resigned." Between 1937 and 1940 the drive added some 16,000 new members to the Relief Society, bringing the total membership to 91,064, representing 51 percent of the approximate total of 177,000 women in the church.[128]

The 100,000-member goal was reached and exceeded by an additional 15,000. But this did not allay concern over the lack of active participation in Relief Society. In the September 1942 issue of the *Relief Society Magazine* church president Heber J. Grant and his counselors told members of the women's organization that enrollment itself was not enough. Again, the issue was "competitive interests." Members of the Relief Society, the First Presidency message said, "should permit no other affiliation either to interrupt or to interfere with the work of this Society. They should give to Relief Society service precedence over all social and other clubs and societies of similar kinds." The message noted the unique intellectual, cultural, and spiritual values of the organization, which it called "sufficient for all general needs of its members."[129]

Though President Grant had expressed repeated concern to the Relief Society General Board about LDS women's non-church affiliations, this 1942 statement was the strongest and certainly the most widely publicized. "I felt so guilty when I went to club instead of Relief Society," commented one woman, who nonetheless kept attending her club.[130] Many twentieth-century Latter-day Saint women did not see involvement in Relief Society as an integral part of living the gospel or being committed to the church. Dues and membership cards, luncheons, bazaars, handicrafts, and lessons in culture and civics were neither uniquely Mormon nor infused with church ordinances and doctrine.

Like the culture clubs, the Relief Society continued to serve some sisters as a "middle-aged women's university," still featuring lessons on great books, art, and social science along with domestic and theological topics. For other women these lessons could not compete with the more in-depth study of literature clubs or gospel study groups, for example, or with widely available college and extension courses. A young mother from Salt Lake City who had attended college to become a teacher and then worked with other professionals did not enjoy Relief Society lessons because she felt "the standards were not sufficiently high."[131] For members of the general presidency and board, many of whom held college and graduate degrees, improving the quality of Relief Society lessons was a perennial concern, complicated by the growing diversity of members that accompanied the church's international expansion.

The weekly Relief Society meeting, centered around a standardized lesson, assembled women but did not necessarily bind them to one another in friendship. Less structured situations seemed to work better for that. One woman said she cherished the association at Relief Society, not during lessons when sisters were primarily passive, but in the mingling afterward when she could chat with people one to one. A Swedish sister concurred, saying she felt unwilling to share her own views and feelings during Relief Society lessons but liked the association available in socials and luncheons. "We just don't open our mouths and let ourselves be known at Relief Society," observed a Massachusetts woman. "Often, we don't trust other Mormon women not to criticize us, not to judge us as lacking if we actually say what we think or expose our lives as they really are." A sister from a rural Utah ward said that the women in her local Relief Society were *sisters*, but not *friends* like those in her club with whom she felt she could be herself.[132]

Relief Society's educational program had taken on increasing importance as its older collective tasks became outdated in the twentieth-century church. Women's defense of plural marriage and their battle for suffrage ended before 1900. Shortly after the turn of the century Utah's silk industry failed, ending Relief Society sericulture. The society's other cooperative economic ventures had not lasted that long, except for grain storage, which continued until 1918 when the federal government purchased all 205,518 bushels of Relief Society wheat. In 1921 the Presiding Bishopric asked for an end to construction of separate Relief Society halls. Nurses' training ended in 1921, and nurse's aides' training in 1924. Maternity and child health care faded in the mid-thirties at the same time the church's new welfare plan limited Relief Society responsibility to administer care for the needy. Though the general board continued to operate a small social services department offering professional direct services to church members, the last of dozens of Relief Society social service institutes which had trained thousands of volunteer social workers was held in 1939. Relief Society's major effort in 1945 to provide postwar relief to European Saints in connection with the Church Welfare Program was widespread but short-term. All of these tasks had taken women beyond their homes to make a contribution to the larger community, strengthening their sense of collective identity and efficacy and building bonds of sisterhood.

After World War II the Relief Society was unable to involve large numbers of women in new responsibilities of commensurate community importance. Sisters' programs were centered largely in their own wards and stakes and less oriented to the larger community. Women disappointed in the Relief Society's diminished public role channeled their community service energies into other groups.

The most significant collective enterprise of the 1950s was construction of the Relief Society Building in Salt Lake City, dedicated in 1956, a project which required sisters to raise some $500,000 within a one-year period. In meeting this goal, as in publishing the monthly *Relief Society Magazine* and managing finances at both local and general levels, the organization had

considerable autonomy, which strengthened its *esprit de corps*. But this independence, unlike that which accompanied earlier Relief Society tasks, tended
to separate the society from the work of the church as a whole since these
newer projects had little importance to the general membership.

Unlike an earlier Woman's Building, planned between 1900 and 1907
but never constructed, the Relief Society Building included no space for the
Primary Association and YWMIA, a reflection of the lack of unified programs and purposes among the general presidencies and boards of the three
women's organizations. Each was financially independent, wrote and published its own lesson materials, and sponsored general conferences and local
meetings apart from the other two. The social activism which had marked
the work of the YWMIA and Primary Association after World War I had
largely disappeared by the end of World War II, though the Primary Children's Hospital (which acquired a new building in 1952, expanded in 1966)
and the Primary's involvement in the Boy Scouts of America allowed it a
uniquely high community profile. While Relief Society's tasks had fluctuated
significantly, the YWMIA and Primary Association maintained their responsibility for teaching the youth of Zion, a work of singular importance to the
church as a whole. At the local level, Primary and YWMIA officers and
teachers were often younger women, camaraderie among whom was encouraged by their common organizational tasks and life stage experiences.
Primary and YWMIA workers in a ward or stake sponsored their own separate socials and meetings for teacher training and preparation. Frequently
women with demanding positions in these organizations did not attend
weekly meetings with Relief Society sisters, who were generally, though not
always, older. At both the general and local level, therefore, women were
more fragmented than unified in their church responsibilities.

The nature of Mormon sisterhood changed significantly during the first
half of the twentieth century, an extended period of transition that altered
women's networks of kinship and friendship as well as their organizational
tasks and goals. The immediate impact of plural marriage both as a forging
tie and as a shared experience faded after the Manifesto. Nationwide emphasis on the nuclear family, not the extended family, gave new importance to
husband-wife and mother-child relationships with little attention to female
kinship ties. There was also new emphasis on economic and emotional self-
sufficiency for individual households in lieu of cooperation.

Efforts to establish new extra-familial ties swept the United States as an
"age of association" that had a delayed but forceful impact on Latter-day
Saints. Not only did Mormon women organize their own clubs, societies,
and associations, but second-generation leaders incorporated into the programs and activities of the women's organizations of the church elements
from these outside groups. Such changes promoted LDS women's affilia-

tion with and acceptance by their American sisters but obscured the collective sense of uniqueness so pronounced among first-generation Mormon women.

In the midst of these shifting networks, Mormon women's organizational tasks changed, particularly within the Relief Society. Sisters moved from the unique economic and political responsibilities of the nineteenth century into a period of activity in social welfare. Then as the nation and the LDS church dramatically altered welfare practices, Relief Society continued some welfare work but primarily focused on educational work in wards and stakes.

While the number of officers, teachers, and members of the Relief Society, YWMIA, and Primary Association steadily increased during the first half of the twentieth century, as did the membership and workload of their central governing boards, the three women's organizations decreased their connection with one another. Their separateness reflected diversification among Mormon women generally. Nineteenth-century Mormon women had pulled together through family ties, shared experiences, and common organizational goals, forming relationship patterns that might be mapped as several large concentric or intersecting circles. In contrast, as their options for female association multiplied, twentieth-century Mormon women pulled apart into separate circles of varied size which touched or overlapped at random. This polynuclear sisterhood lacked a clear and single focus, though church leaders continued to insist that the Relief Society play a central, unifying role.

VI

Historically, Relief Society had been the channel through which leading sisters and brethren articulated the place of women within Mormon theology, the theological significance of women's lives. It was to members of the Relief Society that Joseph Smith first affirmed that women were responsible for saving themselves. Nineteenth-century Relief Society presidentesses and temple priestesses were also prophetesses who gave LDS women a vision of their place in the eternal plan. Women who shared this vision with one another, in Relief Society and as leaders of young women and children, were empowered with an understanding of their ecclesiastical authority (in the women's organizations) and liturgical authority (in temple ordinances), as well as their connectedness to female deity, their Mother in Heaven. The commitment of Relief Society leaders to articulate women's priestly function faded with the death in 1910 of Bathesheba W. Smith, last Relief Society general president to preside over women's work at the central temple in Salt Lake City. A department for temple and burial clothing was established at Relief Society headquarters in 1912, but society leaders were no longer intensely involved as officiators in temple ceremonies. Occasionally, a general authority affirmed the importance of temple ordinances for women. Joseph Fielding Smith, president of the Quorum of the Twelve, did so in an October 1958 Relief Society conference address, declaring that "it is within the privilege of the sisters of this Church to receive exaltation in the kingdom of God and receive authority and power as queens and priestesses."[133] But twentieth-century women leaders rarely if ever expounded this doctrine, and it was not connected with their organization. Belle Spafford said she received insights about the "divine" mission of the Relief Society not from women but from President Joseph Fielding Smith.[134] The sense of sacred female collectivity so apparent to the Nauvoo generation did not live beyond them and the title of priestess passed from the public vocabulary of Latter-day Saint women.

Instead, the concept of priestess and queen was replaced by exalting the concept of mother. Nineteenth-century church leaders, male and female, had stressed motherhood and the private sphere along with important responsibilities for women in the public sphere. But as Relief Society tasks in the public sphere shrank, leaders inflated their rhetoric about women's role in the home. By the end of the Great Depression, women's chief role within the church was in the private sphere: being a good wife and mother. As the church focused on preventative social work among its own members, the economic, physical, social, and emotional well-being of families received unprecedented emphasis. Although the crisis was primarily economic and women had little opportunity or encouragement to earn money, they were assigned responsibility for managing family resources. The homemaker played a key role. Harold B. Lee, managing director of the Church Welfare Program, asked sisters at the April 1940 Relief Society conference if they were aware that "ninety percent of those now being assisted are from homes where the mother does not know how to bake bread?"[135] Teaching women to be good mothers and homemakers increasingly became the major work of Relief Society, women's contribution to strengthening the church. Relief Society president Amy Brown Lyman, who had been active in social work and social reform for three decades, told women that the Relief Society's October 1940 conference would focus on "the home and the desirability of building up and strengthening family life," emphasizing that the home should come first with every Relief Society woman, and work outside the home should come second.[136]

This rhetoric, which continued for three decades, fit comfortably into postwar America, where popular periodicals such as *Ladies Home Journal, Woman's Home Companion,* and *Good Housekeeping* glorified the role of wife, mother, and homemaker in a barrage of words and images that Betty Friedan came to call the "feminine mystique." Her 1963 best-seller by the same title called upon women to "break out of the housewife trap and truly find fulfillment as wives and mothers—by fulfilling their own unique possibilities as human beings."[137] The book helped to launch a twentieth-century movement of women's rights or "liberation" to which LDS church leaders responded quickly and negatively. "We hear so much about emancipation, independence, sexual liberation, birth control, abortion, and other insidious propaganda belittling the role of motherhood," observed N. Eldon Tanner, a counselor in the First Presidency, "all of which is Satan's way of destroying woman, *the home, and the family—the basic unit of society.*"[138]

Many Mormon women found that certain questions raised by the new movement merited consideration. Relief Society general president Belle S. Spafford disapproved of militant feminist tactics and the Equal Rights Amendment, but she spoke in favor of equal pay for equal work, nondiscrimination in hiring practices, and the need for women to develop their full potential. Still, for her being a wife, mother, and homemaker was the most demanding and rewarding role and took "precedence over all others for women."[139]

It was this pervasive, monolithic model of womanhood which created difficulties for many women. Like their American counterparts, Mormon women began to seek the diversity discernible in women's lives, past and present. Copies of the Relief Society's official history published in 1966 were perused with new interest. Leonard Arrington's 1955 work on the "Economic Role of Pioneer Mormon Women" was amplified. Old copies of the *Woman's Exponent* rediscovered by Boston women in the stacks of Harvard's Weidner Library led, in the summer of 1971, to the publication of the "pink" *Dialogue,* which argued for "acceptance of the diversity that already exists in the life styles of Mormon women." In assembling the issue these Boston women had looked for "examples of widely varying life styles possible within an orthodox gospel framework" and decided to include personal essays on mothering, stepmothering, families and careers, birth control, and priesthood authority, in addition to journal entries and letters of single women, poetry, short stories, two photographic essays, and a survey of Relief Society general board members.[140]

This growing commitment to diversity was not entirely welcome. To some extent it was tainted by association with the women's movement; but more significantly, grass roots interest in diversity came at a time when LDS officials were stressing unity and uniformity. A movement for correlation, begun in the 1960s to streamline procedures for the explosive growth of the worldwide church, was in full control by the 1970s. Under this new system, all publications and programs were produced, approved, and distributed through priesthood committees and officers. The general boards of the three women's organizations no longer prepared curriculum. The *Relief Society Magazine* and the Primary *Children's Friend* ended in 1970. Finances, too, were to be handled by priesthood officers at general, stake, and ward levels, ending women's long tradition of financial autonomy. Relief Society membership lists swelled as all women eighteen years of age and older—active or inactive, willing or unwilling—were automatically enrolled and instructed to support the organization which would in turn support them in their homemaking role. The department of social services in operation at the Relief Society Building was incorporated into a churchwide system of social services directed by priesthood officers, and the Primary Children's Hospital was merged into the church's hospital system, later sold to a private corporation. These changes, intended to smooth the way for international expansion and management and give full institutional support to LDS families, had unintended consequences for women—further diminishing any sense of female leadership and collective identity, and focusing even more narrowly on woman's role in the home.

The contrasting messages—expansive from the larger society, constrictive from the church—caused considerable tension for many Mormon women. Some disenchanted women separated themselves from the church but most tried to deal with the dissonance. Following the nationwide trend toward "consciousness-raising" groups, some met in clusters where they could openly share their feelings and frustrations. One such group of a dozen women in Salt Lake City named itself "Retrenchment," after a nineteenth-century group composed of Eliza R. Snow and her associates who met together for many years outside their local ward Relief Societies. In the Boston area—a hotbed of the new feminism—the same LDS women who had put together the 1971 women's issue of *Dialogue* provided a new sounding board for LDS women—*Exponent II*, a quarterly newspaper whose publication began in July 1974 with a masthead entreating, "Am I not a woman and a sister?" This unofficial spiritual descendant of the *Woman's Exponent* shared excerpts from the old tabloid and carried forward its tradition of encouraging news and views from widely scattered sisters. Aiming both "to strengthen the Church of Jesus Christ of Latter-day Saints and to encourage and develop the talents of Mormon women," *Exponent II* editors and staff provided a forum for considering the full gamut of women's concerns and interests from careers and cottage industries to family planning, child rearing, and adoption; from physical fitness and sex to church service and curriculum, biographical sketches, poetry, fiction, and book reviews. In articles, letters to the editor, and a "Sisters Speak" section, readers expressed different and sometimes opposing points of view. One responded negatively to the paper's emphasis on achieving women, for example, questioning "the outcome of the offspring of Super Women," while another felt that such features stirred readers' imaginations and gave "a glimpse of the potential of Mormon women, and more importantly, of themselves as individuals." "An open and frank forum," according to an Oregon sister, it was, to an Arizona reader "an indication that Sisterhood may yet save itself."[141]

The unofficial and uninhibited nature of *Exponent II* was one manifestation of a growing revival of sisterhood and closeness reminiscent of the nineteenth century. LDS women gathered outside structured church meetings in luncheons, firesides, small groups, and even conferences. Unlike earlier clubs whose commonalities had usually been interests other than Mormonism, these sisters, influenced by the women's movement, met to discuss ideas and feelings about the place of Mormon women in church doctrine, history, and organization. Sisterly intimacy bonded them as they shared the tensions of emotional and cultural cross currents.

These currents also served to pull Mormon women apart. A national climate charged with tension over women's issues accentuated differences in the educational, social, and political experience of Latter-day Saint women, some of them recent converts from diverse backgrounds. Some sisters had been part of professional and civic groups which supported legislation for women's economic, political, and social equality, particularly the Equal Rights Amendment. Politically conservative women were reluctant to involve the federal government in changing women's political and economic status and worked against the ERA. For others, their lives had been satisfactorily and exclusively centered in home, family, and church and these issues were of little concern. Many Mormon women had difficulty understanding or respecting this diversity, although it had been developing for at least half a century. Within the Relief Society, little tradition or opportunity existed for discussing differences of opinion or experience.

The December 1974 announcement by newly sustained Relief Society general president Barbara B. Smith that she opposed the Equal Rights Amendment, and a similar official pronouncement by the church's First Presidency in October 1976, ended any possibility of discussion for many sisters who subsequently questioned the faithfulness of Latter-day Saints supporting the ERA. Some sisters changed their position on the proposed amendment, but many Latter-day Saint women who viewed themselves as both feminists and devoted Mormons—among them proponents of the ERA—firmly believed that their support of women's rights had precedents in Mormon doctrine and history.

Divisiveness over issues connected to the women's movement peaked during 1977, the International Women's Year. Mormon women participating in IWY state conventions and later at the national convention in Houston made national headlines when they voted with seeming uniformity against the IWY national platform, particularly resolutions supporting the ERA, abortion, and rights for homosexuals.

In Utah an invitation from the Relief Society general presidency to the state IWY convention transmitted through ecclesiastical channels resulted in acute polarization. Many conscientious Mormon women, encouraged toward long-neglected community involvement, came under the influence of

highly organized radical conservatives who channeled them into preconfer-
ence "informational" sessions which, while affirming traditional Mormon
values, engendered suspicion and hostility toward IWY purposes. When
15,000 women assembled in Salt Lake City's Salt Palace—one of the nation's largest IWY meetings—an overwhelming majority of delegates, most
of them Latter-day Saint women, voted against the national resolutions,
leading to charges that church leaders had packed the convention with
women voting blindly as instructed.

One frustrated LDS woman expressed the grief of many at this situation.
"Women who are informed and have awareness of the historical inequities
find their voices muffled by a cacophony of assumptive, negative reaction to
almost any mention of the rights of women as persons rather than as role
players. I have heard from women who work, who are happily married, who
are divorced, who are widowed, who have never married. There is no forum
for them here presently. Because they see themselves as individuals, as independent thinkers, because they feel that a general recognition, even a Con-
stitutional recognition, that women and men are equal would strengthen
society, families and individuals, they risk being considered heretical—even
subversive."[142] One woman who voted with the majority of LDS women
and later attended the national meeting in Houston felt shunned and dis-
missed by feminists and similarly expressed her hurt at being labeled "ultra-
conservative," "right-wing," "subversive."[143] The pain of divisiveness could
be excruciating. "I find my belief in the sisterhood we profess to have been
deeply shaken," lamented one sister as the International Women's Year came
to a close.[144]

From 1978 through 1980 the First Presidency continued to issue statements opposing the Equal Rights Amendment, but male and female church
leaders also made a concerted effort to focus on less divisive concerns for
women. In September 1979, at the second in a series of annual worldwide
women's firesides, Camilla Kimball read to assembled women the address of
her ailing husband, church president Spencer W. Kimball, affirming the
critical importance of righteous women.[145] Motherhood and wifehood were
praised, but now within the broader context of parenthood, Christian service, personal development, and sisterhood. A few weeks later Sonia Johnson
was excommunicated for her continued public support of the ERA, an un-
timely severance when a new regard for the importance of encouraging
women to build and sustain bonds with one another was emerging.

As the time for ratifying the ERA ran out, so did some of the tension—
partly out of exhaustion, partly as Betty Friedan documented, because feminism was moving to a "second stage" that rued polarities and gave new
honor to family bonds, and partly as concern about the threat of nuclear war
gave women a new purpose on which to unite. Mormon women, while
feeling the effects of these larger trends, also found healing common ground

in learning more about the richness of their unritualized past. Official Relief Society activities—including conferences, lessons, and restoration of the Sarah M. Kimball home in Nauvoo—looked to women of the past with an urgency unknown a decade earlier.

VII

"It may be that in a time of widening uncertainty and chronic stress the historian's voice is most needed. . . . The story and study of the past, both recent and distant, will not reveal the future," wrote historian Barbara Tuchman, "but it flashes beacon lights along the way and it is a useful nostrum against despair."[146] In this sense precisely, contemporary Mormon women have found in their history precedents, possibilities, and hope for the future. The study of women's life experiences and women's institutions apart from those of men, while preliminary to a truly integrated history, has affirmed the identity and importance of a female culture centered in women's relationships with one another. Historically, it would seem that being Mormon has often enhanced the bonding process for women.

In the nineteenth century the kinship and friendship networks common among American women were replicated and expanded for Mormon women in families forged by church practices of adoption and plural marriage. Bonds thus established in the private sphere strengthened networks that emerged in the public sphere when women assumed new responsibilities in the Relief Society, YLMIA, and Primary Association. Via these organizations women united in a variety of social, economic, and political endeavors through which they drew closer together and gained a new sense of collective competence. As women became part of the organizational structure of the church, leaders emphasized the theological importance of the partnership of man and woman in and beyond the home. Mormonism's most sacred ordinances sanctified the roles of wife and mother and projected the marital relationship into eternity, where both women and men would exercise priesthood, reigning together as parents and gods.[147] Practically and ideologically, nineteenth-century Mormon women felt a strong commitment to work for women's rights, a cause in which they joined other suffragists and became part of a larger network of women.

As American women sought privileges and responsibilities once reserved for men, the old boundaries which had defined and separated male and female worlds were obscured. Traditional kinship and friendship networks centered in women's private lives were replaced by more public and formal support systems. During the twentieth century, after Latter-day Saints had abandoned plural marriage and had begun to place ever-increasing emphasis on the nuclear family, Mormon female kinship networks became less extensive and less essential. New women's clubs and associations emerged, pulling

Mormon women into hundreds of private and public women's circles and drawing energy away from the three LDS women's organizations, which were themselves less and less united over time. Thus, while nineteenth-century Mormon women's networks were centered in Mormon organiza-tion, theology, and family life, the affiliations of twentieth-century Mormon women were far more diversified, and the sense of collective closeness and identity waned.

Concurrently, twentieth-century changes in LDS church organization and administration had the unintended consequence of lessening Mormon women's sense of collective competence. In meeting the challenges of mem-bership growth, leaders sought to make the church organization more effi-cient and effective by strengthening the hierarchical chain of command and encouraging standardization and specialization. Leaders deemphasized the partnership of women and men outside the home and defined LDS women's organizations as auxiliary to the ecclesiastical priesthood structure. Profes-sional specialists relieved women of the health and charity work that had served at once to rally sisters and benefit the community, and these tradi-tional collective female tasks were gradually replaced by standardized educa-tional programs.

While many Mormon women in and outside the United States continued to derive a sense of relatedness and responsibility from their association with sisters in the Young Women, Primary, and Relief Society organiza-tions, others did not and looked elsewhere to fill needs for emotional sup-port, personal development, and community service. During the 1970s the twentieth-century feminist movement exacerbated ideological and experien-tial differences among American Mormon women, and dividedness reached painful extremes. If, as psychologist Carol Gilligan observed,[148] women need both to affiliate and to achieve, Mormon women have recently expe-rienced a collective crisis of closeness and competence, a crisis they have begun to address both individually and institutionally.

"Can we cease to contend one with another because of the circumstances we find ourselves in by choice or by chance, and focus instead on our com-mon goals?" asked one Chicago sister, writing in the pages of *Exponent II* in the early 1980s, one of many voices pleading with women to "grasp and hold on to the spirit of sisterhood."[149] The vitality of recent informal friend-ship networks is an indication that Mormon women seek closeness in set-tings where relationships take clear precedence over roles and rules, where women can, in the words of Emma Smith to the Relief Society, "deal frankly with each other."[150] Potentially, as with the kinship and friendship networks of the past, official LDS women's organizations can draw strength from these informal support systems. Cooperation among the general leaders of the Primary, Young Women, and Relief Society and their 1984 decision to geographically unite their offices in the Relief Society Building are harbingers of a rediscovered commitment to organizational unity, legitimizing and celebrating the importance of relationships between women.

Long encouraged to be full and active partners in marriage, Mormon women also have a heritage of partnership within the church organization. "Relief Society women have never been satisfied with mere self-improvement," said Relief Society general president Amy Brown Lyman in October 1941. Historically Mormon women have united to respond to the needs of the world about them, changing their tasks as needs changed. Indeed, as Sister Lyman observed, women "have had a feeling that life was incomplete unless through their work and themselves they were able to make a contribution toward the welfare of others."[151] Creatively, voluntarily, women united through the Relief Society and its sister organizations in tasks that promote the welfare of others will renew their sense of collective competence and identity, honoring diversity because their common goal is not to conform but to contribute. "Our strength is in our union," Zina D. H. Young told female temple officiators meeting in 1894,[152] affirming for all generations of Mormon women that sisterly bonds strengthen holy women and the sacred community to which they are bound.

NOTES

1. Salt Lake Temple, Minutes of a Special Meeting of Sister Workers, 6 July 1893; manuscript, Archives of the Historical Department of the Church of Jesus Christ of Latter-day Saints, Salt Lake City, Utah, hereinafter cited as LDS Church Archives.

2. Carroll Smith-Rosenberg, "The Female World of Love and Ritual: Relations between Women in Nineteenth Century America," *Signs: Journal of Women in Culture and Society* 1 (Autumn 1975): 4.

3. Ibid.: 9–11.

4. Ibid.: 19. Brief facts about Emmeline's early life are presented in *Representative Women of Deseret: A Book of Biographical Sketches*, comp. Augusta Joyce Crocheron (Salt Lake City: J. C. Graham & Co., 1884), p. 64.

5. Elizabeth Haven to Elizabeth Bullard, 24 February 1839, as quoted in *The Israel Barlow Story and Mormon Mores* (Salt Lake City: Ora H. Barlow and the Israel Barlow Family Association, 1968), pp. 144, 146.

6. Ibid., pp. 149, 152.

7. Ann Douglas, *The Feminization of American Culture* (New York: Alfred A. Knopf, 1977), pp. 97–103. According to Douglas, "The nineteenth century minister moved in a world of women. He preached constantly to women; he administered what sacraments he performed largely for women; he worked not only for them but with them, in mission and charity work of all kinds" (p. 97).

8. Drusilla Dorris Hendricks, "Historical Sketch of James and Drusilla Dorris Hendricks," in *Henry Hendricks Genealogy*, comp. Marguerite H. Allen (Salt Lake City: Hendricks Family Organization, 1963), p. 14.

9. Sarah DeArmon Pea Rich autobiography, 2 vols., holograph, 1:41–42, LDS Church Archives.

10. Bathsheba W. Smith to Mr. George A. Smith, 2 September 1843, holograph, George A. Smith Papers, LDS Church Archives.

11. Doctrine and Covenants 38:27.

12. "'All Things Move in Order in the City': The Nauvoo Diary of Zina Diantha Huntington Jacobs," ed. Maureen Ursenbach Beecher, *BYU Studies* 19 (Spring 1979): 302, 305.

13. I Cor. 12:20: "many members, yet but one body"; Romans 12:4: "many members in one body"; remarks of Eliza R. Snow, "Twenty-fourth of July, Ogden," *Deseret News Weekly,* 26 July 1871.

14. Caroline Barnes Crosby, Reminiscence and Journal, microfilm of holograph, LDS Church Archives.

15. Between 1 September 1844 and 1 September 1845, Zina noted a total of 111 visits, 56 of which were to women, 29 to church and prayer meetings, and 26 with male and female family members. "The Nauvoo Diary of Zina Diantha Huntington Jacobs," ed. Beecher, pp. 291–320.

16. "Sarah M. Kimball, Secretary of the LDS Women's Organizations," in *Representative Women of Deseret: A Book of Biographical Sketches,* comp. Augusta Joyce Crocheron (Salt Lake City: J. C. Graham & Co., 1884), p. 27; "A Record of the Organization and Proceedings of the Female Relief Society of Nauvoo," 17 March 1842, microfilm of holograph, LDS Church Archives, hereafter cited as Relief Society Minutes of Nauvoo.

17. Relief Society Minutes of Nauvoo, 17 March 1842.

18. Keith E. Melder, *Beginnings of Sisterhood: The American Woman's Rights Movement, 1800–1850* (New York: Schocken Books, 1977), p. 42.

19. Relief Society Minutes of Nauvoo, 17 March 1842.

20. Ibid., 24 March 1842, 9 June 1842.

21. "Ladies' Relief Society," *Times and Seasons* 3 (1 April 1842): 743.

22. E. R. Snow, "The Female Relief Society of Nauvoo. What Is it?" *Times and Seasons* 3 (1 July 1842): 846.

23. Relief Society Minutes of Nauvoo, 16 June 1843, for example.

24. Eliza R. Snow, "The Female Relief Society," *Times and Seasons* 4 (1 August 1843): 287.

25. Relief Society Minutes of Nauvoo, 13 August 1843.

26. Ibid., 24 March 1842.

27. Ibid., 19 April 1842.

28. Ibid., 17 March 1842.

29. Ibid., 30 March 1842, 28 April 1842.

30. Ibid., 17 March 1842.

31. See John C. Bennett, *The History of the Saints; or, An Exposé of Joe Smith and Mormonism* (Boston: Leland and Whiting, 1842), pp. 217–25, which includes Bennett's article for the *Louisville Journal* and his promised "full account" of the "lodge of the Mormon ladies."

32. "On Marriage," *Times and Seasons* 3 (1 October 1842): 939–40. Society members whose signatures appeared were Emma Smith, Elizabeth Ann Whitney,

Sarah M. Cleveland, Eliza R. Snow, Mary C. Miller, Lois Cutler, Thirza Cahoon, Ann Hunter, Jane Law, Sophia R. Marks, Polly Z. Johnson, Abigail Works, Catharine Pettey, Sarah Higbee, Phebe Woodruff, Leonora Taylor, Sarah Hillman, Rosannah Marks, and Angeline Robinson.

33. Relief Society Minutes of Nauvoo, 28 September 1842.

34. Ibid., 16 March 1844.

35. Melder, *Beginnings of Sisterhood*, p. 51. See also, Mary P. Ryan, "The Power of Women's Networks: A Case Study of Female Moral Reform in Antebellum America," *Feminist Studies* 5, no. 1 (Spring 1979): 67-85.

36. Melder, *Beginnings of Sisterhood*, pp. 52-53.

37. Relief Society Minutes of Nauvoo, 16 March 1844.

38. Ibid., 28 September 1842.

39. Ibid., 30 March 1842.

40. "The Nauvoo Diary of Zina Diantha Huntington Jacobs," ed. Beecher, p. 291.

41. John Taylor, address to women's conference, 17 July 1880, *Woman's Exponent* 9 (1 September 1880): 54-55.

42. Seventies Record, 9 March 1845, manuscript, LDS Church Archives.

43. Gordon I. Irving, "The Law of Adoption: One Phase of the Development of the Mormon Concept of Salvation, 1830-1900," *BYU Studies* 14 (Spring 1974): 291-314.

44. Diaries of Patty Bartlett Sessions, 1846-1880, 8 September and 2 November 1847, 16 June 1860. For a discussion of this conflict within the context of Patty's marriage, see Susan Sessions Rugh, "Patty B. Sessions," in *Sister Saints*, ed. Vicky Burgess-Olson (Provo: Brigham Young University Press, 1978), pp. 310-11.

45. Maureen Ursenbach Beecher, "'The Leading Sisters': A Female Hierarchy in Nineteenth Century Mormon Society," *Journal of Mormon History* 9 (1982): 26-39.

46. Fifteenth Ward, Riverside Stake Relief Society Minutes, 1868-1873, 6 January 1870, manuscript, LDS Church Archives.

47. Jennie Anderson Froiseth, *The Women of Mormonism; or, The Story of Polygamy as Told by the Victims Themselves* (Detroit, Mich.: C. G. G. Paine, 1882), pp. 45-46, 150-63.

48. Jane Charters Robinson Hindley, Journal, 22 and 29 December 1862, holograph, LDS Church Archives.

49. Annie Clark Tanner, *A Mormon Mother* (1969; rpt., Salt Lake City: Tanner Trust Fund, University of Utah Library, 1976), pp. 136, 150-54.

50. Ibid., p. 158.

51. See, for example, Lowell "Ben" Bennion, "The Incidence of Mormon Polygamy in 1880: 'Dixie' versus Davis Stake," *Journal of Mormon History* 11 (1984): 27-42.

52. Ann Eliza Young, *Wife No. 19; or, The Story of a Life in Bondage, Being a Complete Exposé of Mormonism* . . . (Hartford, Conn.: Dustin, Gilman Co., 1876; reprint ed., New York: Arno Press, 1972); Mrs. T. B. H. [Fanny] Stenhouse, *Tell It All: The Story of a Life's Experience in Mormonism* (Cincinnati: Queen City Publishing, 1874).

53. Martha Cragun Cox, Biographical Record, holograph, LDS Church Archives, from typescript by Kathy Stephens, pp. 125-26.

54. Ibid., p. 133.

55. Susa Young Gates, *History of the Young Ladies' Mutual Improvement Association* (Salt Lake City: General Board of the YLMIA, 1911), p. 151.

56. Carol Cornwall Madsen, "Louisa G. Richards," in Burgess-Olson, *Sister Saints*, pp. 446-47.

57. Lucy Meserve Smith to George A. Smith, 19 April 1851, holograph, George A. Smith Papers, LDS Church Archives.

58. Autobiography of Bathsheba W. Smith, typescript, LDS Church Archives, p. 38.

59. Helen Mar Whitney, *Why We Practice Plural Marriage By a "Mormon" Wife and Mother* (Salt Lake City: Juvenile Instructor Office, 1884), p. 11.

60. Stenhouse, *Tell It All*, pp. 343-44.

61. Hubert Howe Bancroft, *Inner Facts of Social Life in Utah* (Berkeley: Bancroft Library, 1888), p. 3.

62. Lucy Meserve Smith to Clarissa Smith, 10 May 1848, holograph, George A. Smith Papers, LDS Church Archives.

63. Elizabeth Wood Kane, *Twelve Mormon Homes Visited in Succession on a Journey through Utah to Arizona*, ed. Everett L. Cooley (Salt Lake City: Tanner Trust Fund, University of Utah Library, 1974), pp. 47, 85.

64. Juanita Brooks, ed., *Not By Bread Alone: The Journal of Martha Spence Heywood, 1850-1856* (Salt Lake City: Utah State Historical Society, 1978), p. 47.

65. Horace Greeley, "Two Hours with Brigham Young," *Daily Tribune* (New York), 20 August 1859, as quoted in *Among the Mormons: Historical Accounts by Contemporary Observers*, ed. William Mulder and A. Russell Mortensen (New York: Alfred A. Knopf, 1967), p. 327.

66. Eliza R. Snow, "Woman," *Poems: Religious, Historical and Political*, 2 vols. (Salt Lake City: LDS Printing and Publishing Establishment, 1877) 2:174, 176.

67. Martha Spence Heywood to Emmeline Free Young, 9 December 1855, in Brooks, ed., *Not By Bread Alone*, pp. 133-34.

68. Journal of Eliza Marie Partridge Lyman, 1846-1863, 20 August 1849, holograph, LDS Church Archives.

69. Lucy Meserve Smith, "Historical Narrative," holograph, Special Collections, Marriott Library, University of Utah, Salt Lake City, Utah.

70. Mary Jane Mount Tanner, Journal, 1 February 1878, holograph, Special Collections, Marriott Library, University of Utah, Salt Lake City, Utah.

71. Richard L. Jensen, "Forgotten Relief Societies," *Dialogue: A Journal of Mormon Thought* 16 (Spring 1983): 107. This article provides the most comprehensive discussion of Mormon women's formal meetings between the last meeting of the Female Relief Society of Nauvoo in 1844 and the permanent reorganization of ward societies in Utah in 1867.

72. *Deseret News*, 24 November 1853, as quoted in ibid.: 108.

73. "Record of the Female Relief Society organized on the 9th of February in the City of Great Salt Lake 1854," Louisa R. Taylor Papers, Special Collections, Harold B. Lee Library, Brigham Young University, as cited in Jensen, "Forgotten Relief Societies": 109.

74. Smith, "Historical Narrative."

75. Brigham Young, 8 December 1867, *JD* 12:115.

76. Susa Young Gates, "Relief Society Beginnings in Utah," *Relief Society Magazine* 9 (Spring 1922): 191-92.

77. *Woman's Exponent* 9 (1 April 1881): 165; "Review of Primary Associations and Instructions," *Juvenile Instructor* 25 (15 November 1890): 685. An excellent analysis of the life and legend of Eliza R. Snow is Maureen Ursenbach Beecher, "The Eliza Enigma," *Dialogue: A Journal of Mormon Thought* 11 (Spring 1978): 31-43.

78. Eliza R. Snow, "An Address," *Woman's Exponent* 2 (15 September 1873): 62.

79. I Cor. 11:11.

80. Brigham Young, 31 August 1875, *JD* 18:77.

81. E. R. Snow to Mrs. L. G. Richards, *Woman's Exponent* 3 (15 April 1875): 173; First Ward Relief Society Minutes, 7 June 1877, in *Woman's Exponent* 6 (15 November 1877): 94.

82. "Sketches and Incidents in the Life of Ruth P. Rogers," manuscript, LDS Church Archives, as quoted in Audrey M. Godfrey, "Starting from Scraps: The Mormon Village Relief Society," paper presented at 1980 Sperry Symposium, Brigham Young University, Provo, Utah.

83. Fifteenth Ward, Riverside Stake Relief Society Minutes, 1868-1873, vol. 1, 25 February 1869; 1873-1883, vol. 4, 6 January 1876; 1874-1894, vol. 5, 8 January 1878, all in LDS Church Archives.

84. Ibid. 1868-1873, vol. 1, 24 May 1872.

85. "Memorial Anniversary," *Woman's Exponent* 17 (1 September 1888): 153.

86. Relief Society Minute Book 1875 (Teachers' meetings), manuscript, LDS Church Archives, 1 April 1875, as quoted in Leonard J. Arrington, *From Quaker to Latter-day Saint: Bishop Edwin D. Woolley* (Salt Lake City: Deseret Book Co., 1976), p. 458; Emily Dow Partridge Young, Diary, 3 January 1878, typescript, LDS Church Archives.

87. "Memorial Anniversary."

88. Eliza R. Snow Smith to "My Dear Sister Willmirth East," 23 April 1883, photocopy of holograph, LDS Church Archives; "An Address by Miss Eliza R. Snow, August 14, 1873," *Woman's Exponent* 2 (15 September 1873); Salt Lake Stake, [General or Cooperative] Retrenchment Association Minutes, 1871-1875, 30 August 1873.

89. Marilyn Warenski, *Patriarchs and Politics: The Plight of the Mormon Woman* (New York: McGraw-Hill Book Co., 1978), see chapter 5.

90. Eliza R. Snow to Mary Elizabeth Rollins Lightner, 25 May 1869, photocopy of holograph, LDS Church Archives.

91. "The Women of Utah Represented at the International Council of Women ...," *Woman's Exponent* 16 (1 April 1888): 164-65.

92. "The Grain Queens of Zion," *Wild Flowers of Deseret: A Collection of Efforts in Verse by Augusta Joyce Crocheron* (Salt Lake City: Juvenile Instructor Office, 1881), pp. 49-50.

93. "R. S. Reports," *Woman's Exponent* 7 (15 September 1878): 58.

94. Salt Lake Temple, Minutes of a Special Meeting of Sister Workers, 28 December 1893, manuscript, LDS Church Archives.

95. "The Woman's Paper," *Woman's Exponent* 16 (15 May 1888): 188; "Woman's Voice," *Woman's Exponent* 15 (15 March 1887): 157.

96. Elizabeth D. (Libbie) Noal, "Woman's Work on the Sandwich Islands," *Woman's Exponent* 21 (1 October 1892): 53 and (1 January 1893): 98.

97. *Woman's Exponent* 21 (1 February 1893): 119.

98. *Woman's Exponent* 17 (15 July 1888): 27.

99. For a discussion of events surrounding the 1870 granting of suffrage to Utah women see Beverly Beeton, "Woman Suffrage in the American West, 1869-1896" (Ph.D. diss., University of Utah, 1976), pp. 35-58. Beeton quotes *New York Herald* on p. 49.

100. William H. Cooper, speech in House of Representatives, 29 January 1873, as reported in *Deseret News,* 14 February 1873, in ibid., p. 49.

101. "A Mass Meeting," *Woman's Exponent* 18 (1 December 1889): 103-4.

102. "Woman, Arise!" *Woman's Exponent* 3 (15 June 1874): 10; 21 (1 March 1893): 131. The 1893 version is somewhat revised.

103. "Equal Suffrage," *Woman's Exponent* 22 (15 October and 1 November 1893): 49.

104. This interpretation of Joseph Smith's turning the key was widely promulgated. In 1945 church president George Albert Smith told women assembled at Relief Society Conference that "when the Prophet Joseph Smith turned the key for the emancipation of womankind, it was turned for all the world, and from generation to generation the number of women who can enjoy the blessings of religious liberty and civil liberty has been increasing." George Albert Smith, "Address to Members of the Relief Society," *Relief Society Magazine* 32 (December 1945): 717.

105. "The Third Star," *Woman's Exponent* 24 (1 February 1896): 107.

106. Minutes for Relief Society Conference, 5 April 1894, in Emmeline B. Wells, "National Woman's Relief Society Board Record," 3 vols., vol. 1, 5 April 1894, holograph, LDS Church Archives.

107. Maria Owen, founder of Springfield, Massachusetts, Woman's Club, as quoted in Karen J. Blair, *The Clubwoman as Feminist: True Womanhood Redefined, 1868-1914* (New York, London: Holmes and Meier Publishers, 1980), p. 61. Blair's study is the finest available on American women's clubs.

108. Mary F. Kelly Pye, "Utah Women's Press Club History," manuscript or typescript, LDS Church Archives.

109. "The Daughters of Utah Pioneers," *Heart Throbs of the West,* 11 vols. (Salt Lake City: Daughters of Utah Pioneers, 1957), 10:329-428.

110. Interviews of Jill Mulvay Derr with ten Mormon women in Salt Lake and Utah counties, Utah, February 1981, notes in author's files.

111. Emmeline B. Wells, "A Few Thoughts: . . . Talent . . . in Woman's Clubs," *Woman's Exponent* 22 (15 May 1894): 132-33.

112. Reapers Club Report at Third Annual Meeting of the Utah Federation of Women's Clubs, *Woman's Exponent* 25 (June 1896): 1.

113. Lavina Fielding Anderson to Jill Mulvay Derr, 22 December 1980, in the author's possession.

114. Authors Club Papers, Special Collections, Marriott Library, University of Utah, as cited in Donna T. Smart, "Sage Green and Paintbrush Red: Symbols for

Authors Club, Established in 1893," copy in the author's possession.

115. Maureen Ursenbach Beecher to Jill Mulvay Derr, ca. December 1980, in the author's possession; Ann Kilbourne, "Staying in Stitches for over 45 years," *Salt Lake Tribune*, 15 November 1981.

116. Lavina Fielding Anderson to Jill Mulvay Derr, 22 December 1980; Winnifred Jardine, "Dining with Friends," *Deseret News*, 26 August 1984.

117. Interview with Suzanna Mae Grua by Jill Mulvay Derr, 2 September 1983, notes in author's possession. Mary Stewart, "Collect for Club Women" as quoted in "Elks Ladies Club Yearbook, 1980-1981," Special Collections, Marriott Library, University of Utah, Salt Lake City, Utah.

118. "Relief Society Conference," *Relief Society Magazine* 14 (June 1927): 265.

119. Lotta Paul Baxter, "Our Heritage," *Relief Society Magazine* 23 (May 1936): 323.

120. Minutes of the Relief Society General Board, 10 December 1913, typescript, LDS Church Archives.

121. Susa Young Gates, "The Scope of the Relief Society," *Relief Society Magazine* 2 (April 1915): 199.

122. J. Reuben Clark, Jr., "The Present Duty of the Relief Society," *Relief Society Magazine* 23 (May 1936): 274.

123. Belle S. Spafford, oral history, interviews by Jill Mulvay [Derr], 1975-76, typescript, p. 14, the James Moyle Oral History Program, LDS Church Archives.

124. Sylvester Q. Cannon, "[Relief Society] Conference Address," *Relief Society Magazine* 24 (June 1937): 350.

125. Spafford oral history, p. 73.

126. Vera White Pohlman, "Annual Report [to Relief Society Conference]," *Relief Society Magazine* 27 (May 1940): 301.

127. Rae B. Barker, "From Corner Stone to Keystone," *Relief Society Magazine* 25 (May 1938): 328-29; Rae B. Barker, "Progress of the 1938 Membership Drive," *Relief Society Magazine* 26 (May 1939): 325.

128. Vera White Pohlman, "Relief Society of the Church of Jesus Christ of Latterday Saints: Selected Data from the Annual Financial and Statistical Report, Calendar Year, 1939 . . ." *Relief Society Magazine* 27 (June 1940): 426-28; "Membership Pictographs," *Relief Society Magazine* 28 (May 1941): 314.

129. "Message of First Presidency to the Presidency, Officers, and Members of the Relief Society," *Relief Society Magazine* 29 (September 1942): 1.

130. Interviews of Jill Mulvay Derr with ten Mormon women in Salt Lake and Utah counties, Utah, February 1981.

131. Spafford oral history, p. 13.

132. Interviews of Jill Mulvay Derr with ten Mormon women in Salt Lake and Utah Counties, Utah, February 1981; comments of Carrel Sheldon in "Sisters Speak," *Exponent II* (Summer 1981): 18.

133. Joseph Fielding Smith, "Relief Society—An Aid to the Priesthood," *Relief Society Magazine* 46 (January 1959): 5; see also Bruce R. McConkie, "The Relief Society and the Keys of the Kingdom," *Relief Society Magazine* 37 (March 1950): 148-51.

134. Spafford oral history, p. 118.

135. "The Church Welfare Program," *Relief Society Magazine* 27 (July 1940): 462.

136. "President's Report and Official Instructions," *Relief Society Magazine* 27 (November 1940): 753-54.

137. Betty Friedan, *The Feminine Mystique* (New York: Dell, 1974), p. 325.

138. N. Eldon Tanner, "No Greater Honor: The Woman's Role," *Ensign* 4 (January 1974): 7, italics in the original.

139. Belle S. Spafford, address to Lochinvar Group, 12 July 1974, in "Most Rewarding Role: Being Wife and Mother," *Church News,* 13 July 1974.

140. Claudia Lauper Bushman, "Women in Dialogue: An Introduction," *Dialogue: A Journal of Mormon Thought* 6 (Summer 1971): 5-8.

141. Comments by Diane L. Bottger and Connie Cannon in "Sisters Speak" and Jerry W. Hurd, "Long Live Exponent II!" in *Exponent II* 4 (Winter 1978): 8, 18, 19; Lou Ann Dickson to Dear Sisters, in *Exponent II* 1 (December 1974): 8.

142. Aileen H. Clyde, "Other Voices," *Exponent II* 4 (Fall 1977): 5.

143. Georgia Peterson, "After Houston, What?" *Exponent II* 4 (Winter 1978): 9.

144. Reba L. Keele, "Houston: A Personal Journey," *Exponent II* 4 (Winter 1978): 8.

145. Spencer W. Kimball, "The Role of Righteous Women," *Ensign* 9 (November 1979): 102.

146. Barbara W. Tuchman, "The Historian's Opportunity," in *Practicing History: Selected Essays* (New York: Ballantine Books, 1982), pp. 51, 55.

147. Historian Barbara Welter has suggested that Mormons' projecting of the marital relationship into eternity with parenthood as the highest mutual goal gave Mormon women greater status in that role here and hereafter. Barbara Welter, "The Feminization of American Religion," in *Clio's Consciousness Raised: New Perspectives on the History of Women,* ed. Mary S. Hartman and Lois W. Banner (New York: Harper & Row, 1974), pp. 149-50.

148. Carol Gilligan, *In a Different Voice: Psychological Theory and Women's Development* (Cambridge, Mass.; Harvard University Press, 1982).

149. Holly O'Neil Andrus, "The Challenges of and to Sisterhood," *Exponent II* 7 (Fall 1980): 7.

150. Relief Society Minutes of Nauvoo, 17 March 1842.

151. Amy Brown Lyman, "Remarks, Welfare Session of General Conference . . . October 4, 1941," *Relief Society Magazine* 28 (November 1941): 727.

152. Salt Lake Temple, Minutes of a Special Meeting of Sister Workers, 9 March 1894, manuscript, LDS Church Archives.

LINDA P. WILCOX

Mormon Motherhood:
Official Images

Motherhood is more than the biological process of reproduction. Much more. As an institution it consists of customs, traditions, conventions, beliefs, attitudes, mores, rules, laws, precepts, and the host of other rational and non-rational norms which deal with the care and rearing of children. It has also, like other institutions, a powerful symbolic component as well.

Jessie Shirley Bernard[1]

Mother, goddess of love, to whom we all can go for protection and unconditional love, perfect human being we have all been taught to believe in, whom poets have compared to the earth itself, who kneels down, arms outstretched, to enclose us and fend off the rains, whom none of us has ever met, but who continues to haunt us mercilessly; Mother, I can't find you, let alone be you.

Jane Lazarre[2]

As more women, both Mormon and non-Mormon, try to find or rediscover a divine Heavenly Mother, they also confront their need for a mother as both a nurturer and a role model and—perhaps even more difficult—their own feelings of uncertainty or inadequacy as mothers. Emphasis by former Mormon church president Spencer W. Kimball and others on the importance of the family has increased both the status and the stresses of motherhood for Mormon women in the 1980s, but the close identification of motherhood with Mormon culture, values, and theology is nothing new. "Our people, the 'Mormon' people, believe in motherhood," one Mother's Day speaker said more than seventy years ago. "If we have any distinctive contribution to this world it is right along these lines."[3] Clearly, the concept of motherhood is a powerful one in Mormon society, surrounded by many vaguely defined but strongly felt beliefs, attitudes, conventions, and expectations. Being a mother is considered the pinnacle of female achievement, the most significant work and the most exalted role a Mormon woman can have—more primary (though perhaps just barely) than that of a wife.

How did motherhood become so important in Mormonism, and what are the sources of Mormon ideas about motherhood? A logical place to start looking for a theological basis is in scriptures, beginning with the fundamental directive to the first woman and man to "be fruitful and multiply."[4] But references to women are sparse in the scriptures acknowledged by Mormons, and those relating specifically to mothers or motherhood are almost nonexistent except in the Bible.[5] Consequently the Bible provides most of the scriptural role-modeling Mormon leaders use to indicate what women ought to be doing, and particularly what they ought to be doing as mothers. Eve, Sarah, Hagar, Hannah, Rebekah, Leah, Rachel, Naomi, and in the New Testament Mary and Elisabeth are women whose main significance lies in their role as mothers. Eve is important because she is mother of all, Mary because she is the mother of Jesus. Sarah and Hannah exemplify the barren woman, denied motherhood until rescued by divine intervention.

All of these biblical examples emphasize biological motherhood—the physical bearing of children—rather than what might be called "social motherhood." The Bible says little about nurturing, teaching, styles of mothering, or the importance of the role. We must look, then, to elements in the larger American culture for the source of most of Mormon society's concepts of motherhood.

In the early years of the Mormon church—in fact, even later in the nineteenth century—sermons and rhetoric about motherhood as an institution are relatively uncommon. Motherhood seems to have been taken for granted, requiring little comment. Leaders then did not dwell on the popular twentieth-century themes of numerous children and the evils of birth control, except occasionally in the context of defense of plural marriage. Of course, considering the state of contraceptive knowledge and technology at the time, women had fewer options than are available now.

Nor was there much idealization of motherhood or romanticizing of the mother's role. The frontier societies of Missouri, Nauvoo, and the Great Basin had little room for the Victorian image of the pure, gentle, ever-patient mother. Because of geographical distance and cultural lag, this image would not reach Utah until the turn of the century, although it would then flourish well into the 1930s. We do see in the late nineteenth century, however, some expression of the idea that mothers influence not only their children but the larger course of history and the fate of nations—a theme strengthened when Victorian idealization took hold a few years later. In early Utah much of the focus of the mother's influence was directed toward her power to "build up the kingdom" through her children. This excerpt from an 1867 sermon by George Q. Cannon, then an apostle, is typical: "A great glory is bestowed on woman, for she is permitted to bring forth the souls of men. You have the opportunity of training children who shall bear the holy priesthood, and go forth and magnify it in the midst of the earth. It is a glorious mission which God has assigned to his daughters, and they should be correspondingly proud of it, . . . Great interests are in the hands of mothers. God has reposed in them great power; if they wield that power for good it will be productive of peace and happiness and exaltation to them."[6]

Wilford Woodruff, also an apostle, spoke of the important position women held by virtue of their "responsibility of correctly developing the mental and moral powers of the rising generation, whether in infancy, childhood, or still riper years. Your husbands—the fathers of your children, are messengers to the nations of the earth, or they are engaged in business, and can not be at home to attend to the children."[7]

Brigham Young's model included a division of responsibilities: mothers were "to direct the child until it is of a proper age, and then hand it over to the husband and father"—a model which suited agrarian Utah more than it does today's urban society.[8] However, he emphasized that it would be difficult for the father to control the children at this point if the mother had failed to teach them "to revere and follow the counsel of their fathers."[9] Thus, any failure on the fathers' part would still be the mothers' responsibility.

Nineteenth-century Mormon church leaders gave practical, rather than theoretical, advice. Brigham Young told mothers to dress their children simply and appropriately, keep dangerous items out of their hands, supervise them adequately, and not let them run about "wild and contentious."[10] Such practical advice was mirrored and augmented in the pages of the *Woman's Exponent,* which carried numerous articles about diet, health, hygiene, clothing, discipline, and training of children. This equivalent of a nineteenth-century Dr. Spock compendium, largely drawn from outside sources, was very much in the cultural mainstream of the time. Little in these articles was specifically Mormon. Similarly, most sermons of Brigham Young and his associates were not scripturally or theologically Mormon but were rather part of the common wisdom of the time about how to raise clean, competent, well-behaved boys and girls. Mormon motherhood, in this sense, would have been virtually indistinguishable from motherhood in the larger society.

The nineteenth-century Mormon concept of motherhood also acknowledged that mothers often worked outside the home. Out of economic necessity Annie Clark Tanner would leave her home for two weeks to nurse a patient but frequently expressed concern for her nine-year-old son: "I could not bear to leave the little fellow depending on the care of our home with no mother there," she wrote.[11] Yet she and many other mothers did just that with little or no criticism. In their support, a General Epistle from the First

Presidency in 1856 emphasized the importance of mothers' economic self-sufficiency: "Mothers in Israel, you are also called upon to bring up your daughters to pursue some useful avocation for a sustenance, that when they shall becomes [*sic*] the wives of the Elders of Israel, who are frequently called upon missions, or to devote their time and attention to the things of the kingdom, they may be able to sustain themselves and their offspring."[12] In fact, a case could be made that in nineteenth-century Mormon culture, "mothering" was not considered woman's primary task, elevated above her other responsibilities. Rather it was one of many responsibilities, all of them necessary and important. With so much other work to do, devoting most of one's time, energy, or thought to mother work was an unrealistic luxury.

In the first half of the twentieth century, Mormon views about motherhood became more defined and visible. The Victorian image, which reached Utah about the turn of the century, provided a detailed model for motherhood which was adopted practically wholesale by the Mormon culture and remained the primary image of motherhood during the next thirty or forty years. Except for some limited theological underpinnings, most of Mormon rhetoric about mothers emerged from the larger American society, with some culture lag, and mirrored it faithfully.

Two major elements of the Victorian model were a strong emphasis on the power and influence of mothers and a romantic idealization of mother's self-sacrifice, love, and divine purity and gentleness. In 1944 David O. McKay, second counselor in the First Presidency of the church, called motherhood "the noblest office or calling in the world," "the greatest of all professions," and "the greatest potential influence either for good or ill in human life."[13] He was echoing a sentiment expressed thirty-six years earlier when a general conference speaker asked the women present, "Could you have any greater honor, could you possibly have any greater ambition in the world, than to be the medium through which a child of God shall come to earth? ... Do you realize that ... the future of this Church, this community, this state, or this nation as a commonwealth, depends very largely upon you as mothers in Israel?"—thus widening the nineteenth-century sphere of a mother's influence from the Church to the world.[14] A 1923 speaker asserted in a radio address that "the standards of motherhood during any given period of history are absolutely the controlling moral factors in the world at the time. The standards of civilization are fixed by woman. The quality of the manhood of every period is created by woman. No great moral or intellectual progress can be made without her and no great decline ever comes to a nation without she, by her conduct and influence, points the downward course. ... An unwomanly mother is a misfortune in society. She may be a dreadful calamity."[15] Even in 1923, there was concern that women might reject the traditional obligations and attitudes of the feminine role.

Another important theme in the early twentieth-century image of Mormon motherhood was its holiness. David O. McKay spoke about "the sublime, we might say the Divine attributes of Motherhood, for the true Mother, in her high and holy office, comes closer to the Creator than any other sentient being" and urged that we "teach girls that motherhood is divine, for when we touch the creative part of life, we enter into the realm of divinity."[16] A First Presidency message in 1942 called motherhood "the highest, holiest service to be assumed by mankind. It places her who honors its holy calling and service next to the angels."[17] "Since God is love," said a *Deseret News* Mother's Day editorial, "this tireless, eternal mother-love is most like God."[18] Motherhood, then, was seen as both divine and eternal, the feminine equivalent of godhood.

A logical consequence of such rhetoric is the tendency to separate mothers from the rest of humanity. J. Reuben Clark, later a counselor in the First Presidency, for example, advocated that we "place woman upon the pinnacle. Let us place motherhood above and beyond everything else that any women [*sic*] can do, her highest mission, her richest blessing. Let us put her upon the mountain peak of our respect, of our love, and of our honor; and having put her there let us keep her there, honored, trusted, revered."[19]

Other church leaders of this period stressed the beauty and romance of motherhood to help women see their role in the best light possible. Joseph J. Cannon, a local YMMIA leader and later a counselor in its general presidency, commented: "The spirituality of motherhood, the romance of motherhood, these are the things which should touch our emotions today and every day. The life of mother, the ordinary mother would seem to be somewhat drab, somewhat monotonous, a struggle with petty details, against disorder, disobedience, bad temper, sickness, a struggle with the details of preparing food and preparing the house after the food has been consumed, a worry over the financial conditions of the family. . . . It is not difficult, should not be difficult, to make romantic and beautiful, the common things of life." However, this same speaker, perhaps unconsciously, provided a realistic corrective to an overly romanticized view of motherhood. The husband of a neighboring family with several children was on a mission with the wife supporting them all. The speaker's father sent over a son to offer a sack of flour if she needed it. "She sent back this word: 'Tell Brother Cannon if I ever ask for help, don't send flour, send me bread. I will be too far gone to bake.' "[20]

Sacrifice became motherhood's supreme virtue. One historian points out: "Mothers have been honored from time immemorial, assessed above rubies in value, as the Proverbial woman was, or as the Roman matron was, or the chatelaine of a medieval castle might be. But the mother adored for her self-abnegation, her 'altruistic surrender,' even for her self-immolation, was a nineteenth-century Victorian creation."[21] Melvin J. Ballard, an apostle, said, "Those who sacrifice most and serve best love most. That is why a mother's love is the greatest love in the world." He saw suffering as the only source of a mother's love: "If her suffering and pain were not the price she pays—that marvelous thing, a mother's love, would die."[22] In so saying, he followed in David O. McKay's eloquent footsteps: "Motherhood is just another name for sacrifice. From the moment the wee, helpless babe is laid on the pillow beside her, mother daily, hourly, gives of her life to her loved one. . . . All through the years of babyhood, childhood, and youth, . . . she tenderly, lovingly sacrifices for them her time, her comfort, her pleasures, her needed rest and recreation, and if necessary, health and life itself!"[23]

Why might this rhetoric of sacrifice seem appropriate and satisfying to the Mormon men who, perhaps unconsciously, took it in from the American culture and disseminated it to their Mormon audiences? For one thing, there was probably some truth to the image. Many, perhaps most, mothers *did* "sacrifice" to provide their children with the comforts—often even the necessities—of life. In idealizing the situation, Mormon leaders may have wished to give some comfort to mothers, as well as to assure the continuation of such self-sacrificing behavior. The men, of course, also may have benefited personally from the continuation of such patterns.

If the rhetoric was romantic, the results expected had a strikingly realistic outcome—large families. During the first three decades of the twentieth century, Mormon leaders took disapproving notice of birth control. The years around the turn of the century saw the development of leagues for promoting birth control and the mass availability of contraceptive information. Margaret Sanger had begun her work in 1913 with birth control clinics established in several states by the 1920s. New forms of old contraceptive methods were developed, and medical approval of contraception led to corresponding changes of opinion in science, law, sociology, and economics. Birth rates began to fall, reaching a low point in Europe and North America in the 1930s.

Mormon leaders, in response, urged women to follow Mother Eve's example—to "multiply and replenish" the earth and to provide homes for waiting spirits. President Joseph F. Smith in 1915 asked, "Can [a woman] be saved without child-bearing? She indeed takes an awful risk if she wilfully disregards what is a pronounced requirement of God. How shall she plead her innocence when she is not innocent? How shall she excuse her guilt when it is fastened upon her?"[24] J. Reuben Clark in the 1920s called motherhood "a duty, a mission. It is a destiny." He viewed with alarm the ebbing spirit of motherhood in the world: "On all sides we see the apprehension, the failure, the unwillingness of your young daughters to become mothers. My brothers and sisters, I repeat to you that motherhood is a duty. That is why we are here."[25] Woman's main purpose, Clark asserted on a later occasion, was "to build, to organize, through the power of the Father, the bodies of mortal men, . . . This was [Eve's] calling; this was her blessing, bestowed by the Priesthood. This is the place of our wives and of our mothers in the Eternal Plan."[26]

Encouragement or even pressure to bear children is not unique to Mormon society, of course, but is common to Western society, which mobilizes powerful instruments to convince girls and women that this is their primary role and obligation.[27] Mormon leaders used an interesting variety of appeals. "The women who prefer society, entertainment, luxury, even a career, to motherhood, are not really intelligent," one leader noted and further warned, "Divorce is a very much more frequent thing in families where a woman has economic independence and no children than under older fashioned conditions."[28] A third argument to Mormons—and apparently very potent from its popularity—was the accusation that a woman reluctant to bear children was preventing the progress of unborn spirits. J. Reuben Clark called the "countless myriads" of spirits waiting to come to earth an "incentive behind every mother in Israel."[29] Melvin J. Ballard presented a graphic picture of the many anxious spirits awaiting mortal bodies and said that women's reluctance to bear children "violates a promise and an agreement which undoubtedly we made to our Father . . . to multiply and replenish the earth." In impassioned tones he warned: "Oh we who slight that obligation, who wilfully, maliciously and premeditatedly debauch these glorious bodies endowed with their wonderful creative powers, and make of them mere harps of pleasure, shall come to reap distress and sorrow in this life, and condemnation when we meet the accusing finger of those who we might have given the glorious opportunity of coming into this life."[30]

The LDS church, in line with a nationwide movement for "educated motherhood," instigated not only mother's classes in Relief Society but "parenting" classes which by 1914 were reaching an estimated 30,000 fathers and mothers. Yet the general assumption continued that mothers were primarily responsible for training children. Some General Authorities asserted that this was because of the inadequacy of fathers. J. Reuben Clark, for example, said: "Now, brethren, at best we are somewhat clumsy at leading and directing our children. We are away from home, of necessity, a great part of the time, our thoughts are along other lines, we have to battle for our existence, for the livelihood of our families. Those of us who hold Church positions are absent in the evenings, in addition to the days that we spend getting our livelihood. I repeat, we are a little bit clumsy."[31]

Paralleling the idealization of motherhood came disapproval of wage-earning mothers in the early part of the twentieth century. In the nineteenth, as we have seen, there was no question that women, including mothers, would work for gain. Increasingly, however, as the Industrial Revolution moved most productive work from the home to the outer world, woman's role as worker in the home suffered attrition. A growing number of women, including many mothers, began moving into the work force outside of the home. This trend would accelerate through World War II, creating increasing uneasiness in the minds of those concerned about maintaining the "traditional" home.

Some Mormon church leaders were aware of the changing world economic situation and accepted the new patterns which were emerging in women's work choices. One speaker in 1929 noted without disapproval, indeed as part of "the growth of civilization," that "motherhood may be deferred for a number of years" and that "women will take part in modern industrial life at least until some revolutionary change comes in our social and economic state."[32] Lacking any such revolution, Mormon women, many of them mothers, have continued to follow approximately the same patterns as their sisters nationwide in employment out of the home.

Still, this trend has usually been resisted forcefully by most Mormon leaders, who seem to assume that the children of mothers who work for wages will be neglected and/or delinquent. The First Presidency said in 1942, in the face of national appeals to women to work as a patriotic service during wartime, "The mother who entrusts her child to the care of others, that she may do non-motherly work, whether for gold, for fame, or for civic service, should remember that 'a child left to himself bringeth his mother to shame.'"[33] Aside from the inconsistency of considering a child in the care of others as being "left to himself," this blanket statement did not deal with the issue of women who leave their children to do church work, surely more demanding for most Mormon women than the denounced "civic service."

In 1956 the *Church News* called earning mothers "one of the greatest threats we have to stable home life in America" and editorialized: "The Lord has said that he will hold parents responsible if they neglect their children, and working mothers and wives might well consider what he has said on the subject. There is no economic necessity today which will justify neglect of children."[34] This editorial assumes that an earning mother leaves a neglected child; the equation is considered an obvious one. Another assumption seems to be that an earning mother is fully to blame if her child should "fail" in any sense. The presence of problems in children of earning mothers seems to be based on the premise that no one can properly care for a child except its biological mother and that care by anyone else (presumably including the father) implies neglect. To date, research has not supported either of these assumptions.

After World War II Mormons participated with the rest of America in the rush to domesticity. The 1950s were the era of "togetherness," and it was probably during this period that motherhood became the central factor in the identity ascribed to the Mormon woman. One indication of this primacy is the virtual equation of the words *mother* and *woman*. All women were tacitly assumed to be mothers, as in Relief Society's "Singing Mothers." And being a mother, over a period of time, came to connote not only bearing, teaching, nurturing, and caring for children but any activity deemed suitable for a woman. For example, a *Deseret News* Mother's Day editorial listed the multitudinous roles of mothers: the Cook, the Clothes Washer, Ironer, Interior Decorator, Do-It-Yourself Expert, and Gardener.[35] What is missing from this list? Only the relationship of the mother with her child. There is in the entire editorial no mention of a child at all, no reference to a mother as a *mother*. Instead, the mother role here is identified totally with housework—work that could as well be done by a childless woman, a man, or even a child.

In the last twenty years, much of the Mormon rhetoric about mothers has remained virtually indistinguishable from that of the previous thirty or forty years. However, other views about mothers have developed, in part because of the influence of the women's movement.

The glorification of motherhood has continued with little or no change. For example, in a 1974 general conference, N. Eldon Tanner, then first counselor in the First Presidency, said that "no greater honor could be given" to a woman than to be "a co-partner with God in bringing his spirit children into the world." He warned, "A mother has far greater influence on her children than anyone else, and she must realize that every word she speaks, every act, every response, her attitude, even her appearance and manner of dress affect the lives of her children and the whole family."[36] A mother's power to influence her children thus becomes a two-edged sword. Not only can she mold her children to be good and admirable adults, she also can create neuroses, poor character, and delinquent tendencies. Harold B. Lee, an apostle in 1970, also repeated the earlier theme of the power of mothers to remake the world. "If you would reform the world from error and vices begin by enlisting the mothers," he said. "The future of society is in the hands of mothers. If the world [is] in danger, and [it] is in danger, only the mothers can save it."[37] He thus gave mothers exclusive responsibility for the future state of the world.

But this power which mothers exert through their influence on their children is less sweeping than the foregoing rhetoric would sometimes suggest. As Jessie Bernard has pointed out:

> Actually, the hand that rocks the cradle has not ruled the world. In fact, rocking the cradle has been precisely what has prevented the hand from ruling the world. However much truth there might have been in the old saying, such private, fragmented, interpersonal power did not add up to genuine, public political power. . . . The power of a million . . . mothers with great power at home does not amount to much if they are not organized. . . . Unorganized, they cannot sway policy. They cannot have an input in public decisions. They cannot exert pressure. They cannot protect the outside environment of children. That calls for genuine political power, and the will to use it humanely.[38]

The official position of the LDS church has not followed the national trend on a crucial aspect of motherhood, the issue of birth control and abortion. As general attitudes have eased, the church's rhetoric has intensi-fied against the widespread use of contraceptives. In 1967, for example, Apostle Marion G. Romney said: "The charge to bear children, which the Lord gave to Eve, and to women, generally, is, by many, flouted today. The sordidness of our society, which on the one hand tolerates, encourages, and even condones such abominations as unchastity and other types of licen-tious debauchery, and, on the other hand, legalizes abortions, encourages, and in some cases attempts to enforce birth control, is a prostitution of the functions of life."[39] N. Eldon Tanner called birth control, abortion, "eman-cipation, independence, [and] sexual liberation" "Satan's way" of "belittling the role of motherhood" and "destroying woman, *the home, and the family—the basic unit of society.*"[40] Shortly thereafter, in the church's official organ, the *Ensign*, there appeared an article expressing acceptance of family plan-ning as a matter of individual choice, to be worked out prayerfully between the couple involved and the Lord.[41]

Even though rhetoric about a mother's responsibility and the seriousness of birth-control has remained the same or intensified, some aspects of the image of a mother have changed. Today's ideal Mormon mother is still un-selfish, patient, kind but firm, and always loving, but she is also capable, educated, informed about the world, and involved in the community. The ecstasy of self-abnegation of the early twentieth century has been replaced by such qualities as those Marion D. Hanks of the Presidency of the First Quorum of the Seventy outlined in a 1978 Mother's Day pamphlet: they "make homes happy," are "resourceful," "courageous and fun"; they impart wisdom, teach valuable lessons, and (still) "have special capacity for sacri-fice." He illustrates this last quality with an eighty-five-year-old woman who, with her husband, made and sold peanut brittle for a stake building fund. Again, this example identified her as a mother even though her motherhood was irrelevant.[42]

In recent years the women's movement has been one influence on Mor-mon rhetoric about motherhood, the father's responsibilities, and earning mothers. Mormon fathers have always been admonished to preside over, direct, and teach their children but have not usually been encouraged to involve themselves in the day-to-day physical and emotional care of those same children or of the home. In fact, as late as 1956 a *Church News* editorial scolded, "No one can take the place of mothers, not even dads wearing their wives' aprons and doing their wives' cooking and scrubbing." It suggests not a participating partner but a mousy, henpecked husband doing unmanly housework.[43]

In the last few years, however, fathers are not only directed to provide priesthood leadership by conducting family home evenings and teaching their children the gospel, they are also encouraged to help and to cuddle their children and even to change diapers. President Tanner said recently, "While they are at home fathers should assume with mothers the duties attendant upon the young children, the discipline and training of the older ones, and be a listening ear for those who need to discuss their problems or want guidance and counseling."[44]

Sometimes these directives suggest a father who "helps out" because he is a good fellow; but there are some hints that Mormon society, lagging slightly behind American society, is encouraging fathers to actively parent and nurture, not as a duty or as an aid to their wives, but as a rewarding and valuable activity in itself—an experience that will bind them closer to their children and provide joy and growth for both fathers and children. To the extent that this trend continues, Mormon views about motherhood are bound to shift slightly as well. The prescribed omnipotence of mothers' influence will no doubt be modified to a more realistic view, for instance.

The issue of earning mothers has become increasingly controversial in the past twenty years as greater numbers of Mormon mothers have entered the labor force.[45] Women have been encouraged to be *prepared* to earn before and after child-raising and in cases of death or divorce, but women who *actually* earn have usually faced disapproval. In 1961 Hugh B. Brown, then an apostle, suggested that such a woman works for selfish reasons—"to increase the income, to improve her wardrobe, or to satisfy social status and urges." He warned that those "who do leave the home weaken its foundation, . . . and, thereby, they weaken the Church."[46] Two years later, Spencer W. Kimball, then an apostle, pointed out some social and political reasons for keeping mothers at home: "If a few million of the working mothers who need not work were to go home to their families," he said, "there might be employment for men now unemployed and part and full-time work for youth who ought to help in family finances and who need occupation for their abundant energy."[47]

A decade later H. Burke Peterson, first counselor in the Presiding Bishopric, asserted again that most women do not really need to work for financial reasons and should instead manage their husbands' incomes more effectively and "read stories . . . to a little girl in a faded blue hand-me-down dress [rather] than have her entertained by a color TV because you are away working to make the payments."[48] In 1979 Ezra Taft Benson, then president of the Quorum of the Twelve, told his Brigham Young University audience, "Women, when you are married, it is the husband's role to provide, not yours," and to the men, "You are the provider, and it takes the edge off your manliness when you have the mother of your children also be a provider."[49] On three recent occasions he has repeated his earlier themes of the importance of mothers being in the home rather than at work and suggested that earning mothers are the causes of emotional disturbances in children, divorce, depression, suicide, sexual promiscuity, homosexuality, drug abuse, alcoholism, vandalism, pornography, and violence.[50]

Even though this discouraging of employment has been firm and con-

sistent, recent years have simultaneously seen a growing acknowledgment
—however slight or reluctant—that some mothers must work. H. Burke
Peterson, in the same talk as above, acknowledged, though with only one
sentence, that "there are some mothers with school-age children who are
the breadwinners of their family and they must work; they are the exception."[51] A. Theodore Tuttle of the First Council of the Seventy made exceptions in his 1967 talk for "widows or women who because of *necessity*
must become a bread winner" and also "women who have no children in the
home at this particular time."[52]

These changes no doubt reflect a shift in the last few decades in American
society at large—a revised opinion about women's major value. Previously
women were valued primarily as mothers, and society was willing to pay
them to perform only that function. The Mothers' Pension laws and Aid to
Families with Dependent Children programs express that value. In Mormon
society, a single mother with small children was—and is—eligible for "the
ample arm of the Welfare Program in which she can work some at home,
where she can stay with her children, and yet contribute to her own support," as a *Church News* editorial of 1956 says.[53] (It assumed, incidentally,
that she would be "widowed," not divorced or unmarried.) It is not known,
furthermore, how many single mothers are so supported and whether this
aid is temporary or long-term—as long as they have preschool children.

Now, society seems to place higher value on another role for women.
Sociologist Jessie Bernard queries:

> What do we *really* want women to do? If we have to choose between having
> them perform the child-care role or having them perform the worker role,
> which do we opt for? The answer slowly emerging is: the worker role. And
> once this decision is accepted it cannot be limited to welfare women.... If the
> tender loving care of the welfare mother is expendable vis-a-vis her children, so
> is it for other women....
>
> We may hem and haw and say that labor-force participation is only the lesser
> of two evils. But the principle remains: a woman must take a job to support her
> children.[54]

Mormon leaders seem to follow this trend. H. Burke Peterson does not
tell "mothers who are the breadwinners in your family" that they should go
on church welfare. Instead he prays, "May you be blessed with an abundance
of the spirit of heaven to strengthen and sustain you as you direct the lives of
these beautiful little ones."[55] Ezra Taft Benson offers earning mothers his
"love and sympathy for your present, and I hope, temporary situation[s]."[56]
Implicit in these statements is an admission that twenty-four-hour-a-day
mothering is expendable for the children of divorced and widowed mothers.
The inescapable next step is that it may also be expendable for the children
of married mothers.

This historical overview has, of necessity, ignored childless women, but their position has received some official attention. One strain of Mormon thought implies that a childless woman is somehow not complete. "The woman who is not blessed with motherhood or with the care of children, has not reached the sweetest and finest development of her nature," said a *Deseret News* editorial.[57] And President McKay expanded *mother* to include those who *do* mothering, praising adoptive mothers for their "ability characteristic of and inherent in true womanhood," to "fill the lives of their darlings with a love that only the yearning soul of such a mother can know. Such are true mothers, indeed, though part of the experience of motherhood be denied them." Melvin J. Ballard of the Quorum of the Twelve offered childless women the prospect in the eternities of mothering those children who die in infancy whose mothers are not worthy to go with them at the time of resurrection.[58] Brigham Young went further than surrogate motherhood in the eternities by promising childless women "millions of children. . . . You will become Eves to earths like this; and when you have assisted in peopling one earth, there are millions of earths still in the course of creation."[59] Biological motherhood thus becomes part of the promise for women in the eternities.

The Mormon view that conscious existence extends before and after earth life carries special implications for how motherhood is viewed. J. Reuben Clark pointed out that because pre-existing spirits must receive mortal bodies through mortal mothers, "motherhood to the Latter-day Saints is and must be something more, I take it, than it is to those who have not received the light and intelligence which God has given to us."[60] On the other end of the continuum is motherhood as an eternal reality which exists beyond the present life. One speaker noted the "peculiar feeling" Mormons have about motherhood because it "carries over into the life to come, into the hereafter."[61] This belief includes not only mothering one's mortal children but having "millions" more. Motherhood, as many church leaders have noted, is as eternal and endless as is godhood.

Although there are some theological underpinnings for Mormon views about motherhood, Western society has had by far the greatest impact, and at least one critic has observed problems with that model: "The way we institutionalize motherhood in our society—assigning sole responsibility for child care to the mother, cutting her off from the easy help of others in an isolated household, requiring round-the-clock tender, loving care, and making such care her exclusive activity—is not only new and unique, but not even a good way for either women or—if we accept as a criterion the amount of maternal warmth shown—for children. It may, in fact, be the worst. It is as though we had selected the worst features of all the ways motherhood is structured around the world and combined them to produce our current design."[62] Researchers in cross-cultural studies found that women with the heaviest load of child care were more inconsistent in expressing affection, more hostile, more unstable in their emotional reactions, and more likely to control expressiveness to avoid further drain on their emotional resources. Young American mothers who spend a large proportion of time caring for children corroborate: "They find joy in their children, but they do not like motherhood."[63]

Most Mormon women are mothers. Most love and enjoy their children. Most of them, too, feel the weight of cultural *and* ecclesiastical expectations about how they are to perform their roles as mothers. For in addition to all of the expectations of our larger society, there are special pressures on Mormon mothers—some from church leaders, some from other mothers, and some from themselves. A 1980 documentary, *The Plan,* shows the day-to-day life of Utah's 1979 Young Mother of the Year, Michele Meservy, Mormon mother of five children under the age of six. She is efficient and well organized despite distractions and obvious fatigue. She is generally patient, manages to take care of her children's physical needs and mental development, and even teaches them religious faith. In many ways, Michele epitomizes what some think a good Mormon mother "ought" to be doing. But there are also few smiles on her taut face, little cuddling, and little one-to-one attention in the finished documentary.[64]

Mormon mothers are expected to do all the things our culture expects from mothers and to do them with a larger family. They also have the additional responsibilities of teaching children the gospel, providing a good role model of Mormon ideals, and promoting conformity to such church requirements as tithing, Word of Wisdom, chastity, genealogy, missions, and temple marriage. Mormon mothers also feel a special charge to, as one mother put it, help their children "put off the natural man and become spiritual,"[65] even though this goal sometimes stops at quelling and repressing such so-called negative parts of themselves as their sexuality, anger, and sloth and does not move on to develop inner spiritual resources. With all of these responsibilities, motherhood for Mormon women thus takes on cosmic significance. It is a full-time job not only for this life but for the eternities as well.

How have Mormon women responded to these expectations? Many have found ways to match expectations with resources, enjoy their children, and ignore the parts of the image that seem unrealistic. Some express ambivalence—loving their children but disliking the constrictions and guilt connected with the image. Some have experienced depression, as an influential 1979 documentary by KSL-TV's Louise Degn has illustrated.[66] Some desperately redouble their efforts to live up to what they see as the ideal—trying new child-rearing techniques, fasting, praying, reading the scriptures more diligently, exercising self-control. Others in frustration turn away from the church and sometimes even from their children.

Not all responses to this image are negative, of course; but one of the commonest and potentially most treacherous traps for Mormon mothers is judging themselves, their worth, and the value of their lives by the success of their children. For Mormon mothers, "success" means not only economic and social achievement, but faithfulness to the church and status within its structure. Mormon mothers are under even more stress than mothers in Western society at large, who, as Elizabeth Janeway observes, must

> bring off something of an emotional *tour de force*. First, they are asked to regard the bearing and raising of children as at least a very large and significant concern of their lives and, perhaps, as the crown and center of their existence, although, in the nature of things, this undertaking will demand their full efforts for something less than two decades out of a life that will run to seventy years. Second, they must fit their children for a society whose needs and aims are at best uncertain, and which may in fact seem to the mothers as well as the children morally unjustified and emotionally unsatisfying. At the same time, the most admired goals of society are pretty well closed to these women themselves. Third, they are expected to do all this *only* by means of an emotional relationship, instead of (as in the past) with the help of economic activities and social processes that relate to the larger world. The sanctions of the community seldom join directly with parental injunctions inside the home circle, but instead are conveyed to the children through their parents. Fourth, having called forth this relationship, mothers are aware that they should maintain it in such a delicate balance that the child can grow out of it without harm to his own psychic strength. This program they are supposed to carry through with little training and little support from society itself, in the belief that any failure will justly be laid at their door.[67]

Despite the mitigating factors of Mormon theology, Mormon mothers for over a hundred years have sometimes suffered keenly by feeling that they, totally responsible for their children's development and future, have failed. Children have sometimes assumed primarily symbolic value for their mothers. Over a century ago, Mary Jane Mount Tanner said, "I would rather bear children to die than not bear them, for . . . some day they will be stars in my crown of glory."[68] And though she yearned to write, she consoled herself: "If I did no other work the honor of having such a son is more pride and pleasure than a dozen books."[69]

This vicarious satisfaction is problematic. Mary Jane's daughter-in-law, Annie Clark Tanner, plural wife of the illustrious son described above, wrote: "I wondered if I would be a failure. I remember of earnestly telling one of my boys after another of his escapades that my hope for success depended on him. 'If you should go wrong,' I felt compelled to say, 'my whole life would be a failure.'"[70] Mary Jane wrote painfully of spending "the twenty best years of my life . . . in the drudgery strain and wory [*sic*] of raising a family. . . . If they fill places of honor we are proud and content. If places of care and worry, poverty or disgrace, then the heart mourns and there is no rest."[71]

Contemporary Mormon mothers are also likely to experience intermittent feelings of inadequancy, depression, anxiety, and/or failure in their roles as mothers—along with the joy and delight of nurturing and loving their children. Relief Society's mother education lessons, while providing valuable training, can also be perceived as another burdensome expectation, as they were by a woman who confided to her friend, "Today I'm going to attend the social relations class. I just can't take Mother Education today. I already feel terribly inadequate."[72]

Yet the picture is not all bleak. The realities of motherhood have a way of revising unrealistic ideals, and most mothers develop ways of mothering which suit them—sometimes in spite of external expectations. The process of mothering itself teaches women that motherhood transcends any one image, assignment, or ideal: "A mother can be any sort of person, great or ordinary, given to moderation or intensity, inclined toward amazonian aggression or receptivity. But whatever type you are, being a mother forces you to accept your limitations. And when you acccept your limitations as a mother, you begin to accept your limitations in other areas of life as well. The daily grinding friction of motherhood will give you the chance, at least, of relinquishing some of your egotism. You will finally cease to be a child."[73]

NOTES

1. Jessie Shirley Bernard, *The Future of Motherhood* (New York: Dial Press, 1974), p. vii.

2. Jane Lazarre, *The Mother Knot* (New York: Dell, 1976), p. 224.

3. Howard R. Driggs, "Responsibilities and Honors of Motherhood," address, 10 May 1914, *Deseret Evening News*, 6 June 1914.

4. Genesis 1:28.

5. A look at concordances to the Book of Mormon, Doctrine and Covenants, and Pearl of Great Price reveals that the Book of Mormon contains these references to mothers: Sariah, the Ammonite mothers, such symbols as mother earth, a mother tree, the mother of harlots, and the mother of abominations; Mary as the mother of Jesus; and the Isaiah imagery of queens as nursing mothers to the house of Israel. The Doctrine and Covenants contains only four references: two dealing generally with fathers and mothers, one mother of abominations, and one reference to John in his mother's womb. The Pearl of Great Price contains four references by Joseph Smith to his mother and five from Moses and Abraham which closely parallel Genesis. Prescriptive exhortations in these scriptures are generally directed at parents— "Inasmuch as parents have children in Zion. . ." (D&C 68:25)—but there are no directives given specifically to mothers.

6. Sermon by George Q. Cannon, 3 March 1867, *Journal of Discourses*, 26 vols. (Liverpool: Franklin D. Richard, et al., 1855–86, reprint ed. 1967), 11:338–39, hereafter cited as *JD* with speaker, date, volume, and page.

7. Wilford Woodruff, 6 April 1872, *JD* 15:11-12.

8. Brigham Young, 7 April 1861, *JD* 9:38.

9. Brigham Young, 8 April 1852, *JD* 1:68.

10. See, for example, ibid., pp. 66-68; 7 April 1861, *JD* 9:38-39; and 19 July 1872, *JD* 19:69-77.

11. Annie Clark Tanner, *A Mormon Mother* (Salt Lake City: Tanner Trust Fund, University of Utah Library, 1969), p. 245.

12. "Fourteenth General Epistle of the Presidency of the Church of Jesus Christ of Latter-day Saints," 10 December 1856, in James R. Clark, comp., *Messages of the First Presidency,* 6 vols. (Salt Lake City: Bookcraft, 1965-1975) 2:208-9.

13. David O. McKay, "Motherhood," address to the Sunday School of the Twenty-sixth Ward, Pioneer Stake, 14 May 1944, *Deseret News,* 20 May 1944.

14. Heber C. Iverson, 5 April 1908, *Seventy-eighth Annual Conference of the Church of Jesus Christ of Latter-day Saints* (Salt Lake City: Deseret News, 1908), pp. 70-71, hereafter cited as *Conference Report* with year and page.

15. Nephi L. Morris, radio address, 13 May 1923, in *Deseret News,* 19 May 1923.

16. McKay, "Motherhood."

17. Message of the First Presidency, read by J. Reuben Clark, Jr., 3 October 1942, *Conference Report,* 1942, pp. 12-13.

18. "Mother's Day," editorial, *Deseret News,* 10 May 1924.

19. J. Reuben Clark, Jr., "The Mission of Motherhood: What it Means in the Light of Tenets Held Sacred by Latter-day Saints," address, 13 May 1928, *Deseret News,* 19 May 1928.

20. Joseph J. Cannon, "The Glory of Motherhood: Its Spiritual, Physical, and Social Necessity as Conceived by Latter-day Saints," address, 12 May 1929, *Deseret News,* 18 May 1929.

21. Bernard, *Future of Motherhood,* p. 12.

22. Melvin J. Ballard, "A Tribute to Mothers," *Deseret News,* 13 May 1933.

23. David O. McKay, "Mother," *Millennial Star* 86 (8 May 1924): 296-97.

24. Joseph F. Smith, "Motherhood," *Juvenile Instructor* 50 (May 1915): 290.

25. Clark, "Mission of Motherhood."

26. J. Reuben Clark, Jr., "Our Wives and Our Mothers in the Eternal Plan," Relief Society general conference address, 3 October 1946, *Relief Society Magazine* 33 (December 1946): 800-801.

27. For an excellent discussion of this subject, see Bernard, *Future of Motherhood,* ch. 2, "The First Imperative and the Future."

28. Cannon, "Glory of Motherhood."

29. Clark, "Mission of Motherhood."

30. Melvin J. Ballard, "Tribute to Motherhood: Its Rewards and Responsibilities," address, 8 May 1921, *Deseret News,* 9 May 1921.

31. J. Reuben Clark, Jr., general conference address, 6 October 1951, in *Conference Report,* October 1951, p. 58.

32. Cannon, "Glory of Motherhood."

33. Message of the First Presidency, 3 October 1942, p. 12. The scripture cited is Proverbs 25:15.

34. "Should Mothers Go Out to Work?" editorial, *Church News,* 25 August 1956, p. 16.

35. "She Knows No Competition," editorial, *Deseret News*, 11 May 1957.

36. N. Eldon Tanner, "No Greater Honor: The Woman's Role," general conference address, 7 October 1973, *Ensign*, January 1974, p. 8.

37. Harold B. Lee paraphrasing DeWitt Talmage, "The Three Phases of Motherhood," Primary general conference, April 1970, typescript, Church Archives, p. 3.

38. Bernard, *Future of Motherhood*, pp. 350-51.

39. Marion G. Romney, "Mother Eve, A Worthy Exemplar," address delivered at the stake board session, Relief Society general conference, 28 September 1967, *Relief Society Magazine* 55 (February 1968): 86.

40. Tanner, "No Greater Honor," p. 7.

41. Dr. Homer Ellsworth, "I Have a Question," *Ensign*, August 1979, p. 23.

42. Marion D. Hanks, *Gifts from a Mother* (Salt Lake City: Deseret Book Co., 1978), pp. 4, 6, 9-11.

43. "Should Mothers Go Out to Work?" p. 16.

44. Tanner, "No Greater Honor," p. 10.

45. See Francine Bennion, "LDS Working Mothers," *Sunstone* 2, no. 1 (Spring 1977): 7-15.

46. Hugh B. Brown, "Relief Society—An Extension of the Home," address delivered at the general session of Relief Society general conference, 27 September 1961, *Relief Society Magazine* 48 (December 1963): 814.

47. Spencer W. Kimball, "Keep Mothers in the Home," general conference address, 4 October 1963, *Improvement Era* 66 (December 1963): 1071-73.

48. H. Burke Peterson, "Mother, Catch the Vision of Your Call," general conference address, 5 April 1974, *Ensign*, May 1974, p. 32.

49. Ezra Taft Benson, "In His Steps," address at Fourteen Stake fireside, Brigham Young University, 4 March 1979, typescript, Church Archives.

50. Ezra Taft Benson, "The Honored Place of Woman," Relief Society general meeting, 26 September 1981, in *Ensign*, November 1981, pp. 104-5; general conference address, 3 October 1982, in *Ensign*, November 1982, p. 59. He returned to this theme in similar terms at a "family fireside" broadcast churchwide 22 February 1987. The *Church News*, 1 March 1987, report of his speech did not include his statements on employed mothers.

51. Peterson, "Mother, Catch the Vision of Your Call," p. 32.

52. A. Theodore Tuttle, "On Being A Father," general conference address, 8 April 1967, *Improvement Era* 70 (June 1967): 87.

53. "Should Mothers Go Out to Work?" p. 16.

54. Bernard, *Future of Motherhood*, p. 280.

55. Peterson, "Mother, Catch the Vision of Your Call," p. 33.

56. Benson, "The Honored Place of Women," pp. 104-5.

57. "Mother's Day," *Deseret News*, May 10, 1924.

58. McKay, "Motherhood"; also Ballard, "Tribute to Motherhood."

59. Brigham Young, 14 October 1860, *JD* 8:208.

60. Clark, "Mission of Motherhood."

61. Cannon, "Glory of Motherhood."

62. Bernard, *Future of Motherhood*, p. 9.

63. Ibid., p. 10.

64. Diane Orr and C. Larry Roberts, *The Plan* (Salt Lake City: Beecher Films,

1980). In an interview, Michele Meservy protested its "incomplete" portrayal and noted the omission of a flowershop business, leisure, practicing the violin with a daughter, reading to the children, or holding them. "A Conversation with Michele Meservy," *Exponent II* 8 (Fall 1980): 9-10.

65. Claudia T. Goates, "When You Feel Inadequate as a Mother," *Ensign,* March 1976, p. 25.

66. Louise Degn, "Mormon Women and Depression," KSL-TV, 17 February 1979, transcript printed in *Sunstone* 4 (March-April 1979): 16-26.

67. Elizabeth Janeway, *Man's World, Woman's Place: A Study in Social Mythology* (New York: Dell, 1971), p. 162.

68. Mary Jane Mount Tanner to Mary Bessac Hunt, 6 August 1879, in *A Fragment: The Autobiography of Mary Jane Mount Tanner,* ed. Margery W. Ward in cooperation with George S. Tanner (Salt Lake City: Tanner Trust Fund/University of Utah Library, 1980), p. 176.

69. M. J. M. Tanner, Diary, 5 May 1878, in *A Fragment,* p. 214.

70. Annie Clark Tanner, *A Mormon Mother,* pp. 239, 251.

71. M. J. M. Tanner, Diary, 12 October 1879, in *A Fragment,* p. 217.

72. As cited in Goates, "When You Feel Inadequate as a Mother," p. 24.

73. Lazarre, *Mother Knot,* p. 216.

MARYBETH RAYNES

Mormon Marriages in an American Context

Awash in rhetoric of "disintegrating" families, contemporary Americans are inclined to accept a Laura Ingalls Wilder view of nineteenth-century marriages: large, happy families that worked hard, surmounted adversity, and abounded in love. Father-headed and mother-hearted, the family represented solidarity, identity, and acceptance of its members. The idealization is accepted eagerly by Mormons, who, like their fellow Americans, imagine the families of their nineteenth-century past in the same sturdy mold. As Davis Bitton observed, it is "our view of the traditional American dream: strong, faithful families growing stronger in a new and fruitful land."[1] The reality of such monolithic families in both the American and Mormon pasts is questionable;[2] evidence shows variation from norms to have been frequent then and, despite a tenacious clinging to the ideal, even more frequent in the present century. What of the last century's practice has remained in contemporary Mormon marriages? What has altered? Since issues of decision-making (or power) and sexual expression are inseparable from marriages in any time or context, it will be helpful to focus on both in this survey.

Although personal writings from the nineteenth century indicate that many women were widowed or abandoned, often with large families, the majority of American families were probably father-headed. The husband usually held the balance of power because he held the resources, a dominance reinforced by laws, social climate, religious teachings, and parental power patterns. The wife had her own areas of competence and real decision making, although they were usually of lesser status. Such divisions of labor were usually clear, despite significant variations from era to era and family to family. Milking cows may have been women's work in one family at one time, but men's work in another or at another period. Less certain than who headed a family is how family decisions were made and what styles of agreement and support were seen as options.

However, nineteenth-century America saw several social experiments which challenged the traditional patriarchal/authoritarian pattern on the basis of ideas about "perfect" relations. They include the Shakers, who implemented celibacy, the Oneida Community, which implemented group marriage under experimental regulations, and the Mormons, who reinstituted the biblical practice of polygyny.[3] The impact of alterations in the marriage patterns in the attempt to establish "perfect" ways of human interrelationship was varied; one constant was the stress each attempt incurred in the group's membership.

At the same time, the women's movement was budding. In reaction to abuses of male power, some of which were carried out in the name of God and the church, women were beginning to advocate equality of women with men, especially in the home. The Industrial Revolution was transferring such survival functions as production of food and clothing from the home to the marketplace, hence out of women's hands. The work left for women in the home was motherhood, a glorified and exclusive function for women. The tightly restrictive "cult of true womanhood" emerged in prescriptions for women.[4] However, neither new religions nor feminist movements had much impact on American family life generally.

Family patterns were, however, affected by generally held sexual beliefs and practices. From the Puritan view that sexuality was a natural and healthy but restricted part of a person's being to the Victorian attitude that sexual expression, particularly in women, was impure and base is a long evolution; by the time of the beginnings of Mormonism, both strains were represented in the general attitude. Given the variety of people converted to Mormonism, it is probably safer to assume a multiplicity of attitudes and behavior than any degree of unanimity.[5]

It was a heterogeneous group, then, which came under the influence of Joseph Smith in the first decade of Mormonism's shaping. A product of his time, he taught that the man was the "head" of the family and that his wife was subject to him in his "holy purposes." An attitude is discernible of woman as holy object to the man, to be well treated, but object nonetheless. Joseph Smith also shared his culture's assessment of female virtues: women were naturally "charitable" and "kind"; they were to "do good continually"; they should not direct their husbands but were to "honor and obey" them and not "jangle, tease or contradict" them. In return, husbands had a "great duty" to "fulfill" their wives.[6]

In these respects, Joseph Smith's teachings seem in the mainstream of American domestic patterns. Even his emphasis on kindness, charity, and patience rather than authority as the basis of power in a patriarchal home was not unusual. It is, however, remarkable that the ideal of kindness and love as the source for male (priesthood) power was institutionalized through scripture and example with a gradual transfer of the value into family governance. One of Joseph Smith's contributions was to emphasize these qualities until they acquired a trademark status.

One aspect of Joseph Smith's later thought, however, came into conflict with his teachings on domestic accord. As the church developed organizationally and women became more involved in the religious life than was usual among other Christian churches, they gained power beyond their homes. Joseph Smith's teaching—that women should be responsible for their own salvation rather than relying on their husbands to guarantee their place in heaven and that they should govern their own organizations—placed them in a position to move toward equality in their homes as well. The doctrine that a man cannot be exalted without his wife any more than a woman can without her husband created a conflict with prevailing attitudes in the intimacy of the family as well as in the group at large.[7] The implications of the equal participation of men and women in temple ordinances are discussed in other essays of this collection; for this present purpose it should be noted that tensions in family dynamics could have resulted from breaching old thought patterns.

With his introduction of plural marriage, of course, Joseph Smith impacted family behavior patterns markedly. Even though the majority of Mormon marriages continued to be monogamous, the doctrinal implications of the principle affected attitudes toward patriarchal marriage patterns. Among the polygynous marriages themselves, as Eugene Campbell observed, "many of the normal problems of marriage, such as finance, personality adjustment, sexual relationships, jealousies, child-rearing and discipline were all magnified."[8] Among such marriages, variety was the norm; diversity of marital patterns existed throughout the fifty-odd years during which the practice was encouraged. No one pattern emerged.[9] The dynamics of decision-making and sexual relations, on which this paper will focus in its second part, varied from family to family, but so did they among monogamous marriages. The husband who was accustomed to making unilateral decisions and announcing them to one wife in a monogamous marriage would very likely do the same with two or more wives.

Joseph Smith may, however, have made his most distinctive change in family dynamics with his introduction of the concept of eternal marriage.[10] Apparently a genuine departure from popular contemporary thought, the concept that marriages contracted with proper authority extended into the afterlife became institutionalized and took a place at the core of salvation. While plural marriage has left Mormon practice, the accompanying doctrine that "families can be together forever" has become central in its doctrine.

Bumper stickers attached to Mormon stationwagons, affirming values such as "Happiness is Family Home Evening" or "Families are Forever," suggest the continuation of a Mormon sense of distinctiveness in their familial solidarity. Whether they are demonstrably different now, or whether they ever really were, Mormons early became convinced of the peculiarity of their marriage and family patterns. Polygyny was an obvious departure; that gone, the Mormons shifted toward, instead of away from, the norms of nineteenth-century American family life, as they understood it. Into the present century, lag in time has replaced a departure in practice, as Mormons continued to cling to their sense of being peculiar. Being the same, yet feeling different, has become a part of growing up Mormon.

How similar or how different are Mormon families in the context of American families? Many of the statistics available unfortunately measure only external, relatively accessible behavior in Mormon families, leaving the internal dynamics of the marriages studied largely untouched. Furthermore, they tend to measure only elements in common with American family patterns in general, such as the exercise of power in the home and premarital sexual activity rates. Until very recently, little attention has been given to the Mormon context of Mormon marriages.

Although comparing Utah to the United States is not the same as comparing Mormon patterns to the United States' patterns, about 70 percent of Utah's population is Mormon, allowing some rough comparisons. Generally, Mormon families have higher marriage and birth rates, (the highest birth rates in the nation) and lower divorce, illegitimacy, and abortion rates.[11] These rates give the impression of more children, which certainly coincides with the doctrinal emphasis on families.

As we would expect, being a devout or "active" Mormon usually creates even greater differences. For example, Utah's divorce rate is equal to the national average (though lowest in the western states),[12] but Mormon temple marriages end in divorce only one-fifth as often as the national average.[13] Also, Utah brides marry at an average age of nineteen years, while those married in the temple average twenty-one. Since higher ages at marriage and marriages performed religiously generally result in a lower divorce rate, temple marriages have two factors in their favor.

Demographic statistics, however, do not measure happiness, security, or patterns of interaction. In a comprehensive essay on the Mormon family, Campbell and Campbell list six distinctive characteristics of Mormon families that their overview of family dynamics research had identified:

1. Mormons, much more commonly than other groups, believe in strong, nuclear families.

2. People with temple marriages have higher levels of marital satisfaction: the wives are more secure, and the couples have greater empathy for each other.

3. Mormon families tend to be more child centered from the start than other American families.

4. Mormons have markedly lower rates of premarital sexual intercourse. (Though not technically a statistic about Mormon marriages, this characteristic is extremely important to Mormon families as a whole.)

5. Although extended family networks are important in the country as a whole, LDS families seem to give them slightly more emphasis.

6. Mormons give elderly family members higher status and include them in more activities.[14]

Despite these differences, Campbell and Campbell still conclude that "in many, perhaps most, ways the Mormon family of today resembles the stereotyped 'white, middle-class American family.' "[15] In short, they are more similar than different.

This is not surprising. Latter-day Saints largely grow up in the same culture, speak the same language, read the same news, see the same TV shows, and go to the same schools as most other Americans. All these factors foster common values and concerns. All ethnic family types, whether religiously or nationally based, find that their distinctiveness erodes to the extent they are assimilated into American culture.

Some external indicators of that assimilation are:

1. The Mormon birth rate, as extrapolated from Utah statistics, rises and falls to the same degree as the national birthrate, although it is consistently higher. That trend, true since comparison began in 1900, has changed in only the last decade.[16]

2. Variables that affect other family subcultures (i.e., Irish, Italian, Catholic, Jewish) affect Mormons also. They include urbanization (which increases the rate of mixed religious marriages), region, and degree of education. The greater the degree of urbanization, the more a Mormon family resembles the American families surrounding it.[17]

3. Mormons, like others, report a decline in marital satisfaction after the birth of the first child.[18]

4. Parenting lifestyles of Mormons and non-Mormons do not differ. Mormon parents desire different goals (i.e., temple marriage and missions) but employ means similar to those used by other American families in reaching them. Also, Mormon fathers do not spend more time with their children or see fathering as more important than do non-Mormon men.[19]

5. Temple divorce rates are increasing; national divorce rates are increasing.[20]

6. Mormon women work out of the home at rates similar to those of the rest of the nation. However, during childbearing years Mormon women are more likely to work part-time than their national counterparts. A higher percentage of Mormon women with older children or whose children have

left the home work than do non-Mormon women. (It is probable that women work to help finance their children's missions or college education.)[21]

7. Mormons practice birth control about as much as Americans in general.[22]

8. The diversity of power arrangements in Mormon marriages is similar to the rest of the nation. Patriarchal, matriarchal, equalitarian, and mixed styles all exist.[23]

Other strong religious subcultures, such as Catholic or conservative Protestant families, show similarities to Mormon families. They also have lower divorce rates, higher birth rates, and lower abortion rates than those of the rest of the nation, but all are influenced by nationwide trends. The Amish and Hutterites likely have even higher birth rates and lower alcoholism and sexual- and child-abuse rates than Mormon families. Hutterite women still average birth rates similar to those of the nineteenth century, when women bore nine to eleven children.[24]

Statistical comparisons reveal a pattern of both similarities and differences. My conclusion is that the feeling of uniqueness Mormons experience about their marriages derives from a blend of cultural and historical factors, a distinctive melding of both religious and secular streams of influence. That blending can be seen in an examination of Mormon patterns of decision making and sexual relations.

Decision-making roles and patterns in Mormon homes have been entwined with theological issues since the beginning of the church. In traditional patriarchal families, the male head controls most of the family resource and occupies the position of highest status. This does not mean that the woman is powerless, but usually her power is derivative: she is assigned certain tasks, assumed for cultural reasons to be "naturally" suited for her or, by her husband's tacit or explicit permission, adopts still others. Since the balance of power is tilted toward the husband, a woman's influence is almost inevitably smaller. If she is recognized as "in charge" of any area within the family, it is generally a responsibility with less status and fewer measurable rewards, such as child care or housekeeping. Her supportive role means that much of her power comes from influencing her husband's decisions. Some have suggested that the necessity for indirect influence has given rise to a view of women as manipulative or "sneaky." Some women have these characteristics, just as some men do. The idea that they result from a subordinate position in the power structure and not from inherent personality deserves to be explored.

One view of the Mormon patriarchal family also follows this general model. Rodney Turner, in *Woman and the Priesthood*, views the family patriarch as both priest and king—ruling wife and children and mediating between them and God.[25] J. Joel Moss of Brigham Young University's Department of Family Sciences, however, asserts that the "stewardship" process revealed by Joseph Smith (when implemented) resulted in a different family structure.[26] The Mormon patriarchal family, when it follows the injunctions in the Doctrine and Covenants,[27] is powered by love, with the husband and father acquiring the right to rule (or "preside," in the words of former church president Spencer W. Kimball)[28] from the respect freely given to him by those in the household. This structure would require the father to equate others' needs with his own. Tradition, status, and breadwinning abilities alone would not be decisive in influencing other family members. Also, supporting a decision would be as crucial as making it.

Additionally, other teachings expanded the concept of family to possibly create a distinct family type: the doctrine that deity has both male and female components (that is, Mother in Heaven) and that a complete unity is necessary to return to God—in fact, that "God" may comprise a glorified couple—and the view that priesthood power is shared by both marriage partners. Such ideas, of varying degree of officialness, modify a solely "patriarchal" model.[29] These additional concepts also broaden the possibilities for decision making, particularly toward joint, not unilateral, decisions. This creative and human process, however, still assumes a male-headed home. Neither Joseph Smith nor any of his successors have proposed any major variation of that dictum. In the first decades of church history, Mormons echoed Christian themes held since Paul—that women were to be submissive to their husbands.[30] Thus, there is no ideological ambiguity although several forces have influenced how power is actually wielded in Mormon homes. From the 1850s to the 1900s, polygamy, missions, building the kingdom, and woman suffrage influenced how Mormon men and women related to each other in marriage.

Polygamy has been assumed to be the most restrictive form of patriarchal power possible. The actuality was probably very different for many women. Each person or couple has only so much time to engage in cooperative decision making; when that time is divided with other pairings within the family, often each person gains more autonomy. Many women supported households entirely by themselves. Additionally, maintaining separate households when husbands were hiding from polygamy persecution on "the underground" meant wives of necessity made more decisions. Of course, this pattern could simply mean that women made decisions by default in the absence of their husbands. Present husbands, if only occasionally, could still make arbitrary decisions.

Missionary work during these same decades took many men away for two or three years—sometimes longer—leaving wives to support themselves and their husbands in addition to their usual roles of managing the household, childrearing, and partial economic sustenance. Current research on families separated from each other by war, prison sentences, or illness for long periods of time suggests that the power structure changes when the family is reunited.[31] We can assume transitions in the homes of returning missionaries.

Another factor that influenced change was the frontier: requirements of survival and community building in a new and arid land required men and women to work side by side, with sex roles often overlapping.[32] Women later took the initiative in community building by erecting schools, stores, and hospitals. The women's movement in the late nineteenth century, gaining momentum in the eastern United States, influenced Mormon women at home and at church. Suffrage, which Utah women were granted in 1870 and then regranted in 1896 after nine years without the vote as a result of the 1887 Edmunds-Tucker Act, gave them their voice in political affairs. Professional status in medicine, law, journalism, and education achieved by some of their number opened possibilities for more. In many facets of their lives, intellectually active women in Utah found support for a growing challenge to both the concepts and the practice of male rule in domestic and commercial spheres.[33] Unfortunately, no comprehensive research is available.

In the twentieth century, the family-life education movement of the 1930–40s and new psychological ideas brought fresh interest to the subject of power in marriage. By the middle of the century, democratic marriage became a fashionable topic for discussion in family sociology research, popular women's magazines, newspapers, and college classes. The structure of American marriage has continued to change in ensuing decades.

Mormons heard the same democratic messages as the rest of America. The *Relief Society Magazine* published articles on marriage and family life (including democratic marriages) as early as 1939.[34] When family-life and business-management professionals returned to Utah after education elsewhere, some received assignments to write church manuals. The ideas of the scholarly world were thus translated into gospel language and presented to the members of the church as Mormon principles.[35]

During this same time, research about decision-making patterns in LDS marriages began. In 1949, Moss found that Mormon couples generally espoused patriarchal ideals but their actual practice was democratic.[36] In a 1956 study, Victor A. Christopherson, an LDS professor of child development and family relations at the University of Connecticut, confirmed that most Mormon couples accepted a patriarchal form but only in certain areas of marriage. These areas varied from couple to couple, but most felt that the husband legitimately ruled over religious functions. In short, "Mormons exercise democracy to a high degree, but with patriarchal flavorings."[37] A 1963 study showed high-school-age Mormon girls wanted egalitarian relationships.[38]

The desire for egalitarian relationships was often paradoxically matched by a longing for more traditional modes. This ambivalence is documented in two studies. Looking at mothers and daughters in 1965, Genevieve M. Wise of the Department of Family Life at Weber State College in Ogden and Don C. Carter of the Department of Family and Child Development at Utah State University concluded that "even though nearly as many of [the daughters] were employed as their mothers, they reported a more conservative role-ideal expectation for themselves. Women in this particular culture are participating as 'providers' in the move to factory and office, but are evidently not ready to define their roles accordingly."[39] Similarly, in a 1961 study of the wife's role in the family, prepared as a thesis for the Department of Human Development and Family Relationships at Brigham Young University, Herbert Irvin Mote concluded that women were more willing to accept the companionate (equal-dominant rather than husband-dominant) role for other wives than they were for themselves.[40]

Robert A. Christensen and I, in separate studies for the Department of Child Development and Family Relationships at Brigham Young University, found that Mormon husbands have more power in their marriages than do their wives.[41] My research showed that if husbands saw their wives as less powerful, they were more satisfied with the marriage than if they saw their wives as more powerful than themselves. Paradoxically, husbands perceived themselves as generally egalitarian with limited dominance in some specific areas.[42] Harold T. Christensen, then professor of sociology at Purdue University and one of the most persistent sociological chroniclers of Mormon family patterns, maintained in 1972 that patriarchal authority has not declined among Mormons as much as in the rest of American culture.[43] In a comparison of religion and family roles among Catholic, Mormon, and Protestant families, Stephen J. Bahr and Howard M. Bahr concluded, "We might have expected that the patriarchal nature of the Mormon family would mean that Mormon husbands would exercise more control in their families than did husbands in the other religious groups, but this was not consistently so."[44]

Another source of information on Mormon power relationships in families, though indirect, is the numerous talks, articles, and lessons in manuals. My observation is that within the last three decades, General Authorities of the church have echoed recommendations by marriage counselors, family-life educators, and interested lay persons concerning ideal power patterns. Slowly the preferred marriage model has moved from a patriarchy tempered with love to a patriarchal-egalitarian (egalitarian—both share equally, either identically or in complementary fashion) combination. One example is former church president Spencer W. Kimball's reinterpretation of the biblical phrase "he shall rule over thee": "I have a question about the word *rule*. It gives the wrong impression. I would prefer to use the word *preside* because that's what he does. A righteous husband presides over his wife and family."[45] In a 1967 essay, Garth Mangum, a professor of business at the University of Utah, commented: "[It] may be that the male dominance and patriarchal priesthood were always separate but coincidental phenomena, the one a creation of temporary technological and economic circumstances, the other eternal. The essence of priesthood may be only specialization of labor . . . the male specializing in the external and the female in the internal affairs of family life, but neither with exclusive jurisdiction. A household only needs a head when the alternative candidates cannot agree. When a 'boss' is necessary, it should be the wisest—but wisdom is not an exclusive characteristic of either sex."[46] In a discussion of "Free Agency and Conformity in Family Life," Veon G. Smith, then professor of social work at the University of Utah, said, "For husband/wife relationships to enhance free agency, spouses should be allowed/encouraged to express their feelings, those ideas and feelings must be given credence and both spouses must participate in decision making."[47]

One area of frequent interpretation derives from the temple injunction that the wife should follow her husband "in righteousness." That phrase is interpreted at one end of the continuum to mean that a wife should follow her husband in everything except blatant sinfulness (a judgment which varies from person to person), and at the opposite end to mean that a woman is free to follow her own conscience in accordance with (in parallel manner) her husband's righteousness. This latter view was delightfully illustrated by Carlfred Broderick, a former LDS stake president and marriage counselor, who recalled once, during the first part of their marriage, telling his wife to do something. She replied, "Let me understand. Is that just a suggestion or is that an order?" He explains, "Well, I decided very quickly it was just a suggestion."[48]

Mormons are clearly in an era of transitional patriarchy, living daily with the paradox—one person should head the family but both partners should jointly steer the marriage. Church instructional materials, such as Family Home Evening manuals and *Ensign* articles, use the terminology of traditional patriarchy but describe a mixed model. Theory aside, however, I conclude that the term "patriarchal family" has been so diluted that each individual and each couple now decide what it means for them.

Early statements and sermons from the church's beginning years include positive views of marriage and sex simultaneously with denunciations of the unclean or lascivious side of human nature, a reflection of the duality within Christianity itself. For example, Parley P. Pratt reports Joseph Smith teaching in Philadelphia in 1840 regarding the "idea of eternal family organization, and the eternal union of the sexes." And Parley P. Pratt himself in 1855 said, "There is scarcely a more damning sin on earth than the prostitution of female virtue or chastity at the shrine of pleasure, or brutal lust or that promiscuous and lawless intercourse which chills and corrodes the heart, perverts and destroys the pure affections, conquers and destroys, as it were, the well-springs, the fountains or essence of life."

Joseph Smith's personality was a factor in the emerging Mormon definition of sexuality. Lawrence Foster, professor of American history at the
Georgia Institute of Technology, comments, "Many of Joseph Smith's statements reveal basically a positive attitude towards sexual expression, as well
as the difficulty he sometimes had in keeping his impulses in check."[49]
Joseph Smith's positive view of sexuality may be deduced from his affirma-
tion of marriage. Although he assumed a patriarchal structure, he advocated
close, loving ties in marriage and a positive view of women. Also, he declared sex to be eternal in the form of eternal marriage, eternal procreation,
and "eternal lives."[50] Finally, as polygamy was instituted, he emphasized its
positive features. At times he reportedly acknowledged the practical difficulties of living with new marriage patterns and confronted them at home
with his first wife, Emma, but there is no evidence that he apologized for
what he considered a revelation from God. And according to several of his
polygamous wives, they were not married in spirit only.[51]

However, this positive view of sexuality did not eliminate the problem of
appropriate sexual expression. At times, most people experience impulses
that would not be congruent with their own moral code were they to put
them into action. Foster notes, "Smith's detractors have not adequately understood the extent to which he was aware of his motives, and how close he
may have come to realizing that the doctrine of plural marriage might partly
reflect a need [to rationalize and sanction] his own impulses and behavior."
In a public speech in April 1840, he reportedly declared: "I have my failings
and passions to contend with the same as has the greatest stranger to God. I
am tempted the same as you are, my brethren. I am not infallible. All men
are subject to their passions and sinful natures. There is a constant warfare
between the two natures of man." This statement eloquently describes the
universal effort to make feelings and actions match. Another indication of
Joseph's attempts to find appropriate expression for his sexual feelings is
a journal entry by Joseph Lee Robinson, a contemporary, reporting that
Smith "felt anxious with regard to himself that he enquired of the Lord,
that the Lord told him that he Joseph had never committed Adultery."[52]

Certainly other church members experienced positive and negative feelings about sexuality as they learned of plural marriage. Morality was commonly equated with monogamy. Immorality was anything else. Some were
able to carry their old concepts of sexual purity into the new marriage
practice, but others experienced doubt and confusion. And although the
whole community did not practice plural marriage, probably no couple's
sexual relationship remained unaffected. Polygamy multiplied the number
of possible relationships for many. Moreover, no one could rely on the
certainty of marital exclusivity. Some women were married to men both in
this life and in the next, the ordinary form of a temple marriage today. But
other women were sealed to a man for the next life only, with no legal

connection in this life, while still other women were married legally for mortality to one man while they were sealed spiritually to another.[53] We would expect these situations to cause tensions which not all marriages nor all commitments to the new religion would survive.

Despite the documentation available on nineteenth-century polygamy, personal feelings about sexuality are not clear. According to Klaus Hansen, "A perusal of diaries, journals and letters for this period is most unrewarding. When it comes to sex, the Saints left little record."[54] For example, a 1975 review by Vicky Burgess-Olson of 120 diaries revealed only one reference to sexual material.[55] Some General Authorities occasionally addressed the subject with euphemistic language and in a context of duty. Parley P. Pratt, an apostle, gave voice to other dimensions of sexual interaction: "The object of the union of the sexes is the propagation of their species, or procreation; also for mutual affection and cultivation of those eternal principles of never-ending charity and benevolence which are inspired by the Eternal Spirit; also for mutual comfort and assistance in this world of toil and sorrow and for mutual duties toward their offspring."[56] Defenses of polygamy between the 1850s and 1890s provide some indirect evidence about sexual feelings. Strict premarital chastity and postmarital fidelity echo Christian precepts. The sincerity of these statements is borne out by discipline for sexual transgression, but at least a partial motivation was to defend to the world the elevated moral status of polygamy contrasted with the world's morally "loose" monogamy.

Victoria Grover-Swank argues that the move West insulated church members from the negative effects of Victorianism until after the polygamous system was disbanded.[57] If this is true, the timing was fortunate. It is possible that the Mormon effort to gain respectability after the Manifesto ended polygamy encouraged an adoption of Victorian sexual attitudes (i.e., sex is base; all nonprocreative acts are unnatural) while retaining its own distinctive doctrines (sex is for an eternal and wonderful purpose within marriage but illicit sex is one of the gravest of sins). My impression is that the duality has continued to the present, adapted to contemporary values.

During the sexual revolution of the 1960s, a gap began to reappear between Mormon and American attitudes. Research, though basically limited to premarital sexual intercourse, birth control, and birthrates, suggests a great deal about Mormon views of sexuality. Harold T. Christensen has conducted the most impressive research about Mormon sexual patterns; his longitudinal studies cover twenty years and three cultures (Intermountain Mormon and non-Mormon, Midwestern, and Danish). He found that over the last twenty-year period, Mormon college students have remained remarkably similar in their adherence to the church's norm of chastity, reporting only a 5 percent drop from 78 percent adherence in 1958 to 73 percent adherence in 1978. In contrast, the Midwestern non-Mormon sample dropped 20 percent and the intermountain non-Mormon group dropped 35 percent. He concludes that: (1) Mormon premarital sexual norms are strikingly more conservative than those of the rest of the country, particularly compared to the non-Mormon population in the same areas; (2) Mormon offenders, although fewer in number, are apt to pay a heavier price in guilt, anxiety, and loss of self-esteem and often become inactive or leave the church; (3) Mormon conservatism in sexual matters tends to be remarkably resistant to change.[58] Wilford Smith, professor of sociology at BYU, in two similar studies (1968, 1976) reports essentially the same results: unmarried church-going Mormon college students, in contrast to inactive Mormon students, held firmly to the ideal of chastity. They generally disapproved of and did not engage in petting, masturbation, and homosexuality, although intercourse was considered more serious than any other behavior. In the three decades covered by his research, sexual conservatism actually increased; and he concluded that Mormons are becoming more restrictive in their sexual norms as the outside world becomes more liberal. An interesting note is that one-third of his 1968 respondents felt guilty about their sexual involvement, no matter how serious or trivial.[59]

Two similar studies yield identical results. Armand Mauss, professor of sociology at Washington State University, in a 1969 study found in all age groups studied (below 25 to above 55) that a common norm of chastity prevailed (averages for all groups: 87 percent against premarital sex, 94 percent against extramarital sex). However, he measured attitude only, not actual behavior.[60] Harold Christensen and Kenneth Cannon combined results from 1935 and 1973 surveys and found that 88 percent of the 1935 respondents disapproved of premarital sexual intimacy. This high level had, by 1973, gone even higher—to 98 percent; percentages against necking in 1935 and 1973 were 16 and 35. Again, Mormons had grown more conservative, not less.[61]

Church activity is a consistently important variable. Active members have more conservative attitudes and report more conservative behavior than those who are inactive. Christensen found that young people whose parents have a stable marriage are more likely to be chaste. General conformity to church-imposed rules seems to increase the likelihood of chastity. Furthermore, the church has increasingly emphasized rules and externally governed behavior. The Word of Wisdom and sexual restrictions have become hallmark items in the past few decades—more often preached and more closely watched.[62] All of these studies deal with young, premarital people except for one attitudinal survey by Armand Mauss which considered divorced or widowed Mormons. As a group nationally, these older single people are more sexually active than the young and never married. It would be important to know if the experience of older church members is similar to the national pattern, particularly since an estimated 30 percent of adult Mormons over eighteen are single according to a 1983 *Church News* article.[63]

The second research area, birth control, has been the most variously studied phenomenon of Mormon sexual behavior in marriage. In an exhaustive survey of birth control studies among married Mormons from 1935 to 1972, Lester Bush found that all of the studies essentially conclude that married Mormons not only overwhelmingly use birth control (the percentage ranged conservatively from 70 to 90 percent through the decades), but they consistently differ with LDS church authorities about the reasons for using contraceptive methods. Despite admonitions to the contrary, members accept economic and educational reasons as adequate justification for contraception. Also, the injunction that "the mother's health and strength should be conserved" has become an elastic clause, covering whatever a couple feels is necessary for their marriage. Bush quotes a "subhierarchical" Mormon leader who said, "It's interesting . . . that while the body of the Church rarely has a chance to vote on Church doctrine anymore, they have effectively voted on this subject."[64]

However, most Mormons disagree with church recommendations at the price of private guilt and confusion. Active Mormons generally conform to church rules, and church leaders have persistently and explicitly discouraged the use of birth control. But for most couples, the availability of effective methods, a normal pattern of sexual activity, freedom from unwanted pregnancy, and active planning for children are persuasive. One woman confided that she and her husband use birth control after years of discussion and prayer. She said, "When I realized we were using it to space our children, not limit them, I felt relieved."

The Mormon birthrate is an indirect indicator of Mormon sexual attitudes and behavior. The Utah birthrate, as well as birth rates among LDS church leaders, paralleled the nation's from 1900 to 1970, remaining consistently higher, but exhibiting the same rises and dips; after 1970, the Utah birthrate climbed to 27 births per 1000 population while the national birthrate dropped to 14 per 1000 population. By 1980, the Mormon birthrate again paralleled the U.S. decline, although at a higher level.[65]

In articles and speeches on sexuality, General Authorities, other church leaders, and lay members stress that sex is God-ordained and positive in marriage but sinful outside of marriage. The section on "Teaching about Procreation and Chastity" in the 1983 Family Home Evening Resource Book is a representative example of this dual emphasis.[66] Marvin and Ann Rytting have shown how the theme has received increased emphasis since the 1960s, typically by cataloguing the ills of a sexually permissive society and linking personal and social disasters to sexual permissiveness. A typical claim is that America's faulty sexual norms are undermining the family.[67]

It is true that the rates of both divorce and sexual activity are rising in America, but how they are linked is unclear. (Frequency of intercourse within marriage is also rising.) Also, the American marriage rate has not dropped; it has risen in the last ten years. Although the percentage rate of people ever marrying has dropped in the last three decades, it is still around 90 percent, (97 percent in late 1950s); and the overwhelming majority want long-term, committed relationships within marriage. The family is not disappearing; more types of families are developing.[68]

More and more Mormon family-life educators and marriage and family counselors are writing and teaching sexual materials geared toward members of the church. Their message is strikingly different from official statements. Val D. MacMurray, Harold Christensen, Corydon Hammond, Carlfred Broderick, Kenneth Cannon, Wilford Smith, Marvin Rytting, Klaus Hansen, Armand Mauss, and Brent Miller, for example, all convey a positive attitude typical of other professionals in their field:

1. Sex is not only a good but a great part of our nature.

2. Satisfactory sexual functioning and activity promote not only a good self-image but positive growth in other areas of our lives.

3. Church members have at least as many sexual problems as other Americans, but not necessarily more.

4. The church has tried to teach a positive principle using negative means.

5. The church and church members should be actively involved in sex education for members of all ages. One area of crucial concern is for preteens and teens, as many are sexually active early and give Utah one of the highest teen birthrates in the nation.[69]

6. The church system for dealing with sexual transgression should be revised to include more emphatic, supportive methods for helping people change their lives in addition to the disciplinary process.

Any summary of sexual beliefs and behavior among the Mormons would reflect several paradoxes, as would a summary of sexuality in any culture. Sexuality is a paradoxical experience, with the tension between feelings and behavior always present. Among Mormons the first is that sex is God-given and therefore good, yet sexual drives are instinctual and carnal and therefore bad. The debate about whether sex has lawful functions beyond procreation has been intense. One of the most thoughtful discussions published in church literature is by Homer Ellsworth, M.D., who argued in the August 1979 *Ensign* that decisions about family size are basically the prerogative of the couple and the Lord alone. How much secrecy surrounding sexuality should be because of its "sacred" nature? Is it possible to feel spiritual and erotic feelings at the same time? Is that good or bad?

Confusion, guilt, and anxiety come when a person tries to operate on two conflicting assumptions simultaneously. For example, many people believe that open sexual expression with one's spouse is healthy and good, yet feel embarrassed or guilty when "talking about sex." Parents clearly express the conflict when they say, "I want to teach my children openly about sex because my parents never told me anything but whenever the opportunity comes I get embarrassed and clam up." Girls and boys are taught very different things about procreation: young women learn their menstrual cycles are a part of their preparation for co-partnership with God; young men learn they have "little factories" in their bodies that will naturally discharge excess when appropriate.

A second general paradox lies in the dissonance between what is taught and how it is taught. Mormon doctrine has an extraordinary potential for a more expansive view of sexuality than is usually found in Christian religions, but that potential is not translated into the feelings and actions of the general membership because the focus remains primarily on what one should *not* do or feel. That focus becomes a message in itself. Positive principles cannot be learned from negative methods. Even though Mormons want to *be* good as well as *feel* good about sex, my experience as a marriage therapist indicates that some simply have not been able to harmonize lofty principles, experience, and ideal behavior.

The need for such harmony is urgent. Church members who are able to resolve or accept the paradoxes of both decision-making and sexual interaction in the home find that the church remains a cohesive force in their lives. Members who cannot may pay an excessive price. Christensen's research documents a consistent backlash in the sexual area: unchaste Mormons become even more permissive than people in the surrounding American culture, suffer guilt and confusion, and often become ecclesiastically inactive. Thus a substantial minority of Mormons must live with a great deal of pain.[70] It is crucial to face the task of resolving seemingly opposing beliefs or ways of action. Success in resolving paradoxes comes from shifting perspectives and approaches, stepping out of the old framework, and seeking new ways of integrating experience and values.

NOTES

1. Davis Bitton, "Great-Grandfather's Family," *Ensign* 7 (February 1977): 50.

2. An excellent recent article is Carri P. Jenkins, "The Myth of the Traditional Family," *BYU Today* 39 (October 1985): 40–41, 45–47. For a more in-depth overview of trends in American families from the 1860s to the present, see Arland Thornton and Deborah Friedman, "Changing American Families," *Population Bulletin* 38 (October 1983): 3–37.

3. For the impact on groups of such radical change in marriage pattern, see Lawrence Foster, *Religion and Sexuality: The Shakers, the Mormons, and the Oneida Community* (1981; rpt. Urbana: University of Illinois Press, 1984), and Louis J. Kern, *An Ordered Love: Sex Roles and Sexuality in Victorian Utopias, the Shakers, the*

Mormons, and the Oneida Community (Chapel Hill: University of North Carolina Press, 1981).

4. In 1837, for instance, Sarah Grimke challenged the Congregational clergy's refusal to sanction women's antislavery activities, a position based on the view that it was against "God's will" for women to be active outside of the home. Barbara Welter, "The Cult of True Womanhood: 1820-60," in *Woman's Experience in America*, ed. Esther Katz and Anita Rapone (New Brunswick, N.J.: Transaction Books, 1980), pp. 193-218; also Lawrence Foster, "From Frontier Activism to Neo-Victorian Domesticity: Mormon Women in the Nineteenth Century," *Journal of Mormon History* 6 (1979): 3-21.

5. Victoria Grover-Swank, "How the LDS Church Internalized Victorian Morality in the Twentieth Century," paper delivered at "A Mosaic of Mormon Culture," 2 October 1980, Brigham Young University, Provo, Utah. Copy in possession of the author. Klaus J. Hansen deals with the issues in *Mormonism and the American Experience* (Chicago: University of Chicago Press, 1981).

6. Donna Hill, *Joseph Smith, The First Mormon* (Garden City, N.Y.: Doubleday and Co., 1977), pp. 356-57; and Joseph Fielding Smith, ed., *Teachings of the Prophet Joseph Smith* (Salt Lake City: Deseret Book, 1977), pp. 212, 223-29.

7. For a description of Joseph Smith's influence on woman's place, see Maureen Ursenbach Beecher, "Women in Winter Quarters," *Sunstone* 8 (July-August 1983): 11-19.

8. Eugene Campbell, as quoted in Bitton, "Great-Grandfather's Family," p. 51.

9. Vicky Burgess-Olson, "Family Structure and Dynamics in Early Utah Mormon Families, 1847-85," Ph.D. Diss., Northwestern University, 1974, pp. 130-33, 135-36, 120. See also Phillip R. Kunz, "One Wife or Several? A Comparative Study of Late Nineteenth-century Marriage in Utah," in Thomas G. Alexander, ed., *The Mormon People: Their Character and Traditions* (Provo: Brigham Young University Press, 1980), pp. 53-73.

10. Leonard J. Arrington and Davis Bitton, *The Mormon Experience: A History of the Latter-day Saints* (New York: Knopf, Inc., 1979), p. 193.

11. "LDS Influence Shown," Church News section of *Deseret News*, 13 September 1980, p. 19; Kenneth L. Cannon, "Utah's Divorce Situation," *Family Perspective* 1 (Spring 1966): 10-17; and Phillip R. Kunz, "Mormon and Non-Mormon Divorce Patterns," *Journal of Marriage and the Family* 26 (May 1964): 211-22; Arland Thornton, "Religion and Fertility: The Case of Mormonism," *Journal of Marriage and the Family* 41 (February 1979): 131-42. A good source of statistics from Utah and the nation on alcohol consumption, bankruptcy, crime, divorce, venereal disease, teenage pregnancy, abortion, infant mortality, teenage suicide, leading causes of death, welfare, and education is *Utah in Demographic Perspective: Regional and National Contrasts*, published in typescript form by the Family and Demographic Research Institute at Brigham Young University in 1981. Death rates in Utah from non-disease causes, specifically accidents, suicide and conditions originating in the prenatal period, are as high as or higher than in the rest of the nation, p. 77. Also Darwin Thomas "Family in Mormon Experience" in William V. D'Antonio and Ivan Aldores (eds.), *Families and Religion* (Beverly Hills, Calif.: Sage, 1983).

12. Howard M. Bahr and Kristen L. Goodman, "Divorce," in *Utah in Demo-*

graphic Perspective, pp. 31–45. Also, Stephen J. Bahr, "Mormon Divorce," Brigham Young University, Provo, Utah, typescript 1983, p. 19. Copy in possession of the author.

13. Kenneth L. Cannon and Seymour Steed, "Religious Commitment and Family Stability for LDS Marriage," *Family Perspective* 4 (Fall 1966): 43–48.

14. L. Campbell and Eugene E. Campbell, "The Mormon Family," in Charles H. Mindel and Robert W. Habenstein, *Ethnic Families in America: Patterns and Variations*, 2nd. ed. (New York: Elsevier North-Holland, Inc., 1981), p. 399. Burgess-Olson, "Family Structures," p. 135, clearly shows that both monogamous and polygamous families were very concerned about their children.

15. Campbell and Campbell, "Mormon Family," p. 393.

16. Church News section of *Deseret News*, 13 September 1980, p. 19. Judith C. Spicer and Susan O. Gustavus, "Mormon Fertility Through Half a Century: Another Test of the Americanization Hypothesis," typescript. Copy in possession of the author. Arland Thornton, "Religion and Fertility: The Case of Mormonism," *Journal of Marriage and the Family* 41 (February 1979): 131–42.

17. Brent Barlow, "Notes on Interfaith Marriages," *Family Coordinator* 26 (April 1977): 143–50. Campbell and Campbell, "Mormon Family," in 1st ed., 1976, pp. 407–8; (all other information is the same as in the second edition).

18. Boyd C. Rollins and Harold Feldman, "Marital Satisfaction Over the Family Life Cycle," *Journal of Marriage and the Family* 36 (May 1974): 271–82.

19. Phillip R. Kunz, "Religious Influence on Parental Discipline and Achievement Demands," *Marriage and Family Living* (now *Journal of Marriage and the Family*) 25 (May 1963): 224–25. Additionally, from a fairly comprehensive review of time-use studies in and out of the LDS Church, LDS men do not spend more time in the home and with their families than do their non-LDS counterparts. There is not much evidence of role-sharing or of egalitarian attitudes. In discussing issues related to the mental health of women, . . . these factors have to contribute considerably to the loads women are carrying. This seems particularly critical given the amounts of time men and women spend on a weekly basis in Church related activities (over 20 hours for most men and women under 55 years of age). Donald A. Herrin, private conversations, 1981, 1983. Also see Donald A. Herrin, "Use of Time by Married Couples in Multiple Roles," (Ph.D. diss., Brigham Young University, 1983), pp. 138–50, 296–99, 306–07.

20. Bahr, "Mormon Divorce," pp. 25–26.

21. Francine Bennion, "LDS Working Mothers," *Sunstone* 2 (no. 1, 1977): 7–15; Perry Cunningham, Marie Cornwall, Donald A. Herrin, Joseph Folkman, "Labor Force Participation of LDS Married Women," paper presented at the Ninth Annual Brigham Young University Family Research Conference, 16–17 October 1980, pp. 4–6.

22. Lester Bush, "Birth Control among the Mormons: Introduction to an Insistent Question," *Dialogue* 10 (Autumn 1976): 78–84.

23. Victor A. Christopherson, "An Investigation of Patriarchal Authority in the Mormon Family," *Marriage and Family Living* 18 (November 1956): 328–33; Stephen J. Bahr and Howard M. Bahr, "Religion and Family Roles: A Comparison of Catholic, Mormon and Protestant Families," in Phillip R. Kunz, ed., *The Mormon*

Family [Proceedings of] Research Conference (Provo, Utah: Brigham Young University, 1975), pp. 45-60. Arland Thornton, "Family and Religion in a Changing World," paper presented at Conference on Religion and Family, Brigham Young University, Provo, Utah, March 7-8, 1984, p. 18.

24. Thornton, "Family and Religion," p. 18.

25. Rodney Turner, *Woman and the Priesthood* (Salt Lake City: Deseret Book, 1972), p. 52.

26. J. Joel Moss, "Family Organization," *Supplementary Readings for Family Relationships,* rev. ed., ed. Wesley R. Burr, Richard W. Cantrell, Everett Pollard (Provo, Utah: Brigham Young University Press, 1970), pp. 346-47.

27. Doctrine and Covenants, Section 121, verses 35-37, 41-43:

> 35:   ... they do not learn this one lesson—
>
> 36:   That the rights of the priesthood are inseparably connected with the powers of heaven, and that the powers of heaven cannot be controlled nor handled only upon the principles of righteousness.
>
> 37:   That they may be conferred upon us, it is true; but when we undertake to cover our sins, or to gratify our pride, our vain ambition, or to exercise control or dominion or compulsion upon the souls of the children of men, in any degree of unrighteousness, behold, the heavens withdraw themselves; the Spirit of the Lord is grieved; and when it is withdrawn, Amen to the priesthood or authority of that man.
>
> 41:   No power of influence can or ought to be maintained by virtue of the priesthood, only by persuasion, by longsuffering, by gentleness and meekness, and by love unfeigned;
>
> 42:   By kindness, and pure knowledge, which shall greatly enlarge the soul without hypocrisy, and without guile—
>
> 43:   Reproving betimes with sharpness, when moved upon by the Holy Ghost; and then showing forth afterwards an increase of love toward him whom thou has reproved, lest he esteem thee to be his enemy;

28. Spencer W. Kimball, "The Blessings and Responsibilities of Womanhood," *Ensign* 6 (March 1976): 72.

29. Joseph F. Smith, *Millennial Star* 60 (4 August 1898): 476-86. Bruce R. McConkie, "The Eternal Family Concept," Devotional Address, Brigham Young Univeristy, June 23, 1967, pp. 90-91. Private correspondence, Donald A. Herrin, 28 November 1984, used by permission.

30. Arrington and Bitton, *Mormon Experience*, p. 225.

31. Hamilton I. McCubin, Barbara B. Dahl, Gary R. Lester, and Beverly A. Ross, "The Returned Prisoner of War: Factors in Family Reintegration," *Journal of Marriage and the Family* 37 (August 1975): 471. This article is just one example of a body of literature that has investigated effects of separation on families since the end of World War II.

32. Arrington and Bitton, *Mormon Experience*, p. 224.

33. Ibid., pp. 22-240. Claudia Bushman, ed., *Mormon Sisters: Women in Early Utah* (Cambridge, Mass.: Emmeline Press Limited, 1976). See Jill C. Mulvay, "Zion's Schoolmarms," ibid., pp. 67-88.

34. Paul Popenoe, "Family Relationships: Can the Family Have Two Heads?" *Relief Society Magazine* 26 (April 1939): 278-80, and Caroline M. Hendricks, "Problems of Modern Family Life," *Relief Society Magazine* 26 (June 1939): 390-95, are two excellent examples.

35. Donald A. Herrin, private conversations, 1981, 1983. Notes in possession of the author. Even today there is a tendency to present ideas from contemporary family life education and research in Church periodicals and popular books aimed at Church audiences without crediting the original sources of thought. This creates the illusion that the ideas are generated in isolation from the mainstream of family life education thought and come from inspiration concerning gospel principles.

36. J. Joel Moss, "A Comparison of the Attitudes and Practices of Two University Housing Groups of Married Veterans Concerning Family Size and Family Limitations," (M.S. thesis, Brigham Young University, 1949).

37. Victor A. Christopherson, "An Investigation of Patriarchal Authority in the Mormon Family," *Marriage and Family Living* 18 (November 1956): 328-33, and his "Is the Mormon Family Becoming More Democratic?" in *The Latter-day Saint Family,* ed. Blaine Porter (Salt Lake City: Deseret Book Co., 1963), pp. 317-28.

38. Gary P. McBride, "Marriage Role Expectations of Latter-day Saint Adolescents in Utah County," (M.A. thesis, Brigham Young University, 1963), pp. 48-52.

39. Genevieve M. Wise and Don C. Carter, "A Definition of the Role of Homemaker by Two Generations of Women," *Journal of Marriage and the Family* 27 (1965): 531-32.

40. Herbert I. Mote, "The Wife's Role in the Family: A Comparative Study of Three Educational Levels with a Male and Female Group at Each Level" (M.A. thesis, Brigham Young University, 1961), pp. 62-69.

41. Robert A. Christensen, "The Effect of Reward and Expert Power in the Distribution of Influence in Mormon Couples" (Ph.D.. diss., Brigham Young University, 1970).

42. Marybeth Raynes Black, "The Relationship Between Wives' SIMFAM Relative Effective Power Scores and Husbands Marital Satisfaction," (M.A. thesis, Brigham Young University, 1969), pp. 68-69.

43. Harold T. Christensen, "Stress Points in Mormon Family Culture," *Dialogue* 7 (Winter 1972): 32.

44. Bahr and Bahr, "Religion and Family Roles," p. 60.

45. Genesis 3:16; Kimball, "Blessings and Responsibilities," p. 72.

46. Garth Mangum, "Technological Change and Erosion of the Patriarchal Family," *Dialogue* 2 (Autumn 1967): 45-52.

47. Veon Smith, "Free Agency and Conformity in Family Life," *Dialogue* 2 (Autumn 1967): 64-68.

48. Carlfred Broderick, "Gospel-Centered Therapy: An Interview with Carlfred Broderick," *Dialogue* 8 (Spring 1980): 68.

49. Foster, *Religion and Sexuality*, p. 126. Also Hill, *First Mormon*, pp. 343-44.

50. Hill, *First Mormon*, p. 343, addresses possible reasons for polygamy. See also

the excellent discussion in Linda King Newell and Valeen Tippets Avery, *Mormon Enigma: Emma Hale Smith* (New York: Doubleday, 1985).

51. Foster, *Religion and Sexuality*, p. 156.

52. Foster, *Religion and Sexuality*, p. 148; ibid., n. 76 for the journal entry reprint. Hansen, *Mormonism and the American Experience*, pp. 165–66, and Hill, *First Mormon*, pp. 343–44 also discuss the same material.

53. Foster, *Religion and Sexuality*, pp. 163–66. These pages include a fascinating discussion of the dynamics of these and other unusual marital arrangements, including proxy husbands. Also Hill, *First Mormon*, p. 351.

54. Hansen, *Mormonism and the American Experience*, p. 151.

55. Burgess-Olson, "Family Structure and Dynamics," p. 117. Also personal interview, December 1980, notes in possession of the author.

56. Parley P. Pratt, *Key to the Science of Theology: A Voice of Warning*, rev. ed. (Salt Lake City: Deseret Book Company, 1979), p. 105. This wording is identical to that of the original edition published in 1855.

57. Grover-Swank, "Victorian Morality," p. 8.

58. Harold T. Christensen, "The Persistence of Chastity: A Built-in Resistance within Mormon Culture to Secular Trends," *Sunstone* 7 (March–April 1982): 7–14. Originally presented at the Mormon History Association annual meeting, Rexburg, Idaho, May 1981.

59. Wilford Smith, "Morality on the Campus," *Dialogue* 3 (Summer 1968): 161–65, and his "Mormon Sexual Standards on College Campuses, or Deal Us Out of the Sexual Revolution!" *Dialogue* 10 (Autumn 1976): 62–75.

60. Armand Mauss, "Shall the Youth of Zion Falter? Mormon Youth and Sex: A Two-City Comparison," *Dialogue* 10 (Autumn 1976): 82–88.

61. Harold T. Christensen and Kenneth L. Cannon, "The Fundamentalist Emphasis at B.Y.U., 1935–73," *Journal for the Scientific Study of Religion* 17: 53–57.

62. Christensen, "The Persistence of Chastity," p. 66. Marvin and Ann Rytting, "Exhortations for Chastity: A Content Analysis of Church Literature," *Sunstone* 7 (March–April 1982): 15–21.

63. Twila Van Leer, "Singleness Becoming More Common," *Church News*, 6 November 1983, pp. 4, 14.

64. Bush, "Birth Control," pp. 12–44.

65. *Church News*, 13 September 1980.

66. "Teaching about Procreation and Chastity," *Family Home Evening Resource Manual* (Salt Lake City: Church of Jesus Christ of Latter-day Saints, 1983), pp. 253–59.

67. Rytting and Rytting, "Exhortations to Chastity."

68. Rate of divorce: *Statistical Abstracts*, 1982–83, p. 84; Rate of sexual activity: Melvin Zelnik and John F. Kanter, "Sexual Activity, Contraceptive Use and Pregnancy Among Metropolitan Area Teenagers: 1971–79," *Family Planning Perspectives* 12 (September–October 1980): 230–37; frequency of intercourse: Reiss, *Family Systems in America*, p. 270–75; rate of marriage: *Statistical Abstracts 1982–83*, p. 83; Hugh Carter and Paul C. Glick, *Marriage and Divorce: A Social and Economic Study*, rev. ed. (Boston: Harvard Press, 1976); by percentage of marriages: Peter J. Stein, *Single Life: Unmarried Adults in Social Context* (New York: St. Martin's Press, 1981), pp. 15, 358; majority want long-term relationships: "Most Are Still Singleminded

about Marriage," *Deseret News*, 21 December 1983, Section A, p. 11, which quotes a study by Edward Kain of New York State College of Human Ecology at Cornell University. The *BYU Today* article from footnote 2 is an excellent summary.

69. Brent C. Miller, "Beginning Too Young: Teen Childbearing and Parenthood," revised version of a paper given at Brigham Young University, Provo, Utah, First Annual BYU Academy of Medicine, July 7, 1983, pp. 2, 18.

70. D. Jeff Burton, "The Phenomenon of the Closet Doubter, *Sunstone* 7 (September–October 1982): 34–38. Janet L. Dolgin, "Latter-day Sense and Substance," in Irving I. Zaretsky and Mark P. Leone, eds., *Religious Movements in Contemporary America* (Princeton: Princeton University Press, 1974), pp. 519–46.

GRETHE BALLIF PETERSON

Priesthood and Latter-day Saint Women: Eight Contemporary Definitions

Ecclesiastical authority is a sensitive yet inescapable issue among religious women today. It is intimately enmeshed not only with a woman's relationship to her church but also with her God. Mormon women share in that concern as they contemplate their roles in their church and their access to ecclesiastical power and responsibility.

Latter-day Saints usually phrase that concern in terms of "priesthood," a term that is not easy to define or describe. Because the Church of Jesus Christ of Latter-day Saints is a thoroughly lay church, most Mormons participate in priesthood functions on all levels and in all the manifestations of priesthood power. Limiting the administrative function of priesthood to males raises obvious questions of equality in practice even while the church affirms it in principle. In sorting out these apparent contradictions, Mormon women are forging living definitions, based on their own experience, understanding of the scriptures, and perceptions about their access to God.

This essay reports interviews with eight contemporary Mormon women about their understanding of and experience with priesthood. They were interviewed separately, and each spoke for herself. They share commitment to their church and extensive experience in its organizations. They are all Utah residents, all college graduates, all well read in scriptures and informed in church history. Six are married and five have raised five or more children each while carrying out major church callings on local and general levels. Four of them would say that the term "feminist" applies to them in some way. A generational difference may be important here. The four feminists— Jane, Karen, Mary, and Nora—are all in their late thirties or early forties. The four more traditional women—Ann, Betty, Susan, and Sarah—are all in their late fifties or early sixties. To divide them into traditionalist or feminist is to make very fine distinctions. It is fair to say that all eight are a great deal more alike than they are different in their basic religious and personal values. Two are single, both involved in higher education in the state. Two served a proselytizing mission. Six have served on general church committees. None of them has been divorced. They have been assigned fictitious names to preserve confidentiality, but care has been taken to maintain their individual voices.

These women were not, of course, chosen at random. They were selected because their approach to the sometimes problematic issue of priesthood and women is insightful, thoughtful, and personally productive for them. But although they speak only for themselves, the same issues, the same questions, and the same gropings toward answers have been reflected in literally hundreds of conversations and discussions among LDS women, in and out of church contexts, whose probings for meanings have ranged from amusement to agony. And despite the current relevance of this topic, the question of women's relationship to the priesthood has been discussed ever since there has been Mormon priesthood and Mormon women, and certainly throughout the span of my own life. Although many questions could have been discussed, the three I used were:

1. Do women have direct access to the powers of the priesthood even though they do not "hold the priesthood," i.e., have not been ordained?

2. Is a woman's relationship to deity any different than that of a priesthood bearer?

3. How, and on what levels, does priesthood function?

No aspect of Mormon doctrine is more central to its beliefs and practices than the doctrine of the priesthood. Yet there is no subject more complex, subtle, and open to misunderstanding than the exercise of the priesthood. Mormon apostle Joseph Fielding Smith defined the priesthood as "nothing more nor less than the power of God delegated to man by which man can act in the earth for the salvation of the human family."[1] Church president Harold B. Lee said, "The priesthood is the center, the core, the power by which all the activities of the Church are to be directed."[2] These statements are concise and confirm the centrality of the doctrine, but the application of the priesthood in the government of the church or in the individual lives of its members is less clear, even, at times, confusing.

Mormon boys and girls are baptized at age eight. At twelve, ordination to priesthood takes place for boys. There is no comparable ordinance for girls. It is a rite of passage with both cultural and religious significance. Without yet knowing exactly why, the boy probably senses that ordination into the priesthood is the most significant institutional event of his religious life. From that time on, his religious education focuses on the "rights and responsibilities" of the priesthood.

For Mormon women, the relationship to "the priesthood" is far more complex and often vicarious. To little girls, the priesthood is something that happens to the boys when they turn twelve. As girls grow older, they may perceive "priesthood" as the bishop leading the ward, the deacons at the sacrament table, or the missionary elder baptizing a new member. A young woman may experience the priesthood more directly through a blessing from a father or a grandfather or a patriarchal blessing, usually given during the teens, both of which boys may also experience. She may, in other words, experience priesthood only as an onlooker and recipient but not as a participating "holder." Her perceptions will necessarily be different from those of a young man who is both agent and recipient.

Because Mormon women are not ordained, the hierarchical order of church government is male. Thus, nearly all public statements made about the interpretations of the priesthood are made by men. The subject is discussed frequently in priesthood quorums and by General Authorities — again usually in terms of rights and responsibilities rather than theological meaning — but there are few expressions from women about their relationship to priesthood. Rather, the woman's relationship is discussed and defined by men; and depending upon the individual man's background and experience, male to female descriptions may or may not be helpful to women in quest of understanding.

John A. Widtsoe, a theologian and member of the church's second ruling body, the Quorum of the Twelve, in his *Priesthood and Church Government* spoke expansively in the 1930s on the relationship of women to the priesthood: "Priesthood is to be used for the benefit of the entire human family, for the upbuilding of men, women and children alike. There is indeed no privileged class or sex within the true Church of Christ; and in reality there can be no discrimination between the sexes only as human beings make it or permit it. Men have their work to do and their power to exercise for the benefit of all the members of the Church regardless of sex or age."[3]

By contrast to this expansive view, a 1979 church manual, *The Latter-day Saint Woman,* defines that relationship in an exclusionary way, though doubtless this was not the writers' intent: "The chief responsibility for governing and controlling the affairs of the Church belongs to men. The priesthood is power and authority from God to help accomplish these things. Women do not hold the priesthood because there is no *need* for them to. Neither the Church nor the family needs two heads."[4] These two statements present conflicting assumptions. John A. Widtsoe speaks of the priesthood as an inclusive function that benefits "men, women, and children alike." He rejects the suggestions that the priesthood is a male "privileged class," saying that there is no place for that notion in the true church of Christ. He states his vision of the priesthood as a unifying principle. In contrast, attitudes underlying the first version in *The Latter-day Saint Woman* sound political: The priesthood "govern[s] and control[s] the affairs of the

Church" and "belong[s]" to the men, suggesting that priesthood is an exclusive male possession. For a family just learning about the priesthood and the nature of eternal relationships, this somewhat restrictive description might have made women feel less valued. The 1981 edition of the same manual replaced that section of its text with a broader description, one based on and quoting from Widtsoe's view, suggesting that reviewers recognized the limitations of their earlier definition. The later discussion clarified further, in the words of Apostle Bruce R. McConkie: "In the true Patriarchal Order man holds the priesthood and is the head of the household . . . but he cannot attain a fulness of joy here or an eternal reward hereafter alone. Woman stands at his side a joint-inheritor with him in the fulness of all things."[5]

Another interesting view which may reflect only a passing historical interpretation occurred in a 1931 editorial published "under the direction of the Council of the Twelve." Under the heading, "Why Priesthood At All?" it lists such spiritual gifts as prayer, answers to prayer, revelations, visions, the Holy Ghost and its gifts, noting that they are available "without holding any Priesthood." Why then priesthood? "Chiefly Priesthood functions in connection with organization, comparing its function to the legal phenomenon of power of attorney."[6]

The eight women interviewed for this paper all perceived priesthood as functioning on more than one level in their lives: (1) as an organizational function of the church; (2) as a personality-mediated function of the individual men who hold it; and ultimately (3) as a universal principle that seems to transcend organization or person. All of them indicated that how they felt about the priesthood as a working vehicle or as an eternal principle depended upon the quality of their relationships with the men in their lives.

Betty, an older woman with many years of experience at the general level, defined priesthood this way: "The definition of priesthood is really very simple. It is the delegated power of God. It is the power which underlies God's organization here and everywhere, and he happens to delegate it to men to have his work performed. Part of the work is organization and part of it is developmental toward the individuals who are holders. It isn't removed from the way we run things in the world ourselves. It is just upon a much higher level and it deals with powers that we don't fully understand. It operates whether we understand it or not. It is through this endowment from God that the rest of us function within that structure."

Betty defined priesthood on both organizational and personal levels, then placed those functions within a universal power, the implications of which she felt few understand. Later she affirmed that all people—men, women, and children—can connect with God's power through the light of Christ and the Holy Ghost. She spoke of "the endowment" of priesthood as a special gift from God to the men of the church, suggesting that women have the power to act under God's inspiration even though they do not have the ecclesiastical authority to do so within the organizational offices of the church. She implied that men perform public functions by designation from God while women function in the private sphere of spiritual ministrations, suggesting that the forms of ministration are different for men and women but that the power involved is the same.

Making similar distinctions about priesthood and spiritually guided functions, Sarah, a single woman in her fifties, said: "I separate the power of the priesthood, which to me is synonymous with the power of God, from the priesthood administrative power given to the men of the Church. I feel that that particular position of the priesthood power given to them upon their ordination into the 'so-called' priesthood (which I feel is a misnomer) is for administrative purposes and very exactly identified."

Karen, also a single woman, spoke of the priesthood as a subset of leadership: "By that, I mean leadership is the overriding principle, and I see the performing of ordinances as separate from leadership. Except for the performing of these ordinances, I don't think there is anything that a man can do who holds the priesthood that a faithful woman can't do. She can heal and give blessings, but perhaps not using the same procedures. We do it through prayer, petitioning the Lord in our own way."

Karen also suggested that women have not been taught how to work with priesthood leaders, asserted that the difference between men and women in leadership is that the men understand their stewardship and the women do not, and recommended: "We need models—a great variety of models. The men can look at all those General Authorities, see their different styles and approaches, and find their own identity. The women have only about three —even though things are getting somewhat better. But we still need more visible women leaders."

Mary, a woman in her forties and a returned missionary, raises questions about the responsibilities men and women have in their church calling because of the assumptions made about "priesthood callings."

> The missionary definition we used was, "Priesthood is the authority to act in God's name." That's fine as far as it goes, but it doesn't say what you're doing when you're acting in God's name, what the authority is for. There are usually three functions: performing necessary ordinances (like baptism), administering the Church (running meetings, issuing callings), and "blessing the lives of people." The problems with all of those definitions is that they are not mutually exclusive; these functions overlap most of the time. An ordinance is a blessing in someone's life. So is a good lesson.
>
> When a man is ordained to the priesthood, he gets something, namely priesthood, but as nearly as I can tell within my reading and observations, the ordination to priesthood per se does not occur separately from also being designated to a specific office which comes with specific duties, duties related to the second or administrative function of running the Church. In other words, ordination looks very much like being set apart to specific tasks. Women are set

apart but not ordained. Since both men and women are set apart to do specific tasks, why is it necessary for men to hold the priesthood to do them but not women? Right now women are excluded from doing many of the same things men do administratively and the reason given is because those are "priesthood callings." Well, which came first? Do they require priesthood so that only men can do them, or do only men do them, hence the assumption that priesthood is necessary? There's no control group. We don't know why women can't do them or what would happen if women did do them.

In a perspective which sees priesthood as a task-related function, Nora recalls thinking as a child of priesthood as simply being another name for men: "The priesthood will set up the chairs for the ward dinner." Now, she says, "I see it as the power of God without reference to offices, functions and designees. One of the things I've been impressed with as I read scriptures and history is that God has always used it selectively in terms of specific keys or functions. God has specifically dispensed specific priesthood keys for specific jobs. But the power to create souls and affect their lives—the task of godhood itself—is not circumscribed by any talk of keys."

Looking more closely at the organizational responsibility of the priesthood, Ann talked about her experience of being given "keys" (authority) by a General Authority in his blessing that "set her apart" for a calling on the general level. Citing the statement by John A. Widtsoe that the authority and the function of the church is delegated to men and women, she suggested that since the prophet of the church holds all the "keys" of authority, then he may determine, under inspiration, how they are delegated. She affirmed: "When I was set apart . . . it was said that I was given all the keys that would be required to carry out that administrative responsibility. . . . Perhaps the Church is not ready to receive the magnification that comes with the understanding of this concept of priesthood. I think that it will come, I know that it will come, and I see it coming now through different windows." Her statement implies that women may not be fully used within a priesthood-run organization because of a limited understanding of the concept of priesthood. Nevertheless, it is clear that she is comfortable with the delegation of priesthood "keys" as she has experienced the process.

Nora, continuing her differentiation of task-related keys and priesthood power suggested that the personal blessing received with and through a priesthood-bearing husband is one of the means of tapping into the power of God at an entirely different level.

> If priesthood just means "authority to govern the institution," then women have no access to it. None whatsoever. Every function they perform in the Church is directly or at best indirectly under male supervision. Even in the temple they relate to God only through the marriage covenants and through their husbands' priesthood keys.
>
> If the power of God is more pervasive—and I believe it is—then everyone has potential access to it.

It's more than simple acts of faith. It actually has to do with the ability to call upon God with some degree of entitlement, with the right to exercise his power in this life. I know women who do that. We have seen them exercise healing powers, powers of discernment, and revelation in their own lives and even in ways that have impact on the Church, even though it is not acknowledged.

All eight women made a distinction between the function of the priesthood and the man holding the priesthood. Looking more closely at the impact of individual male personality on perceptions of the priesthood, Susan, an older woman, remarked: "I do see the priesthood as male, simply because that is the way it has always been. But I don't see some of the spiritual powers as male. On the contrary, one of the reasons the Church can't function without women is the sensitivity that women bring to the organization. Holding the priesthood does not make the man better unless he really works at it. A woman can work at it, too, but I can't see priesthood as female, or even gender-neutral, when all the General Authorities are male. The organization of the Church is male."

Karen acknowledges such a view but dismisses it: "Priesthood is really considered by some a secondary sex characteristic, like whiskers. Whether they like it or not, they get it." Since day-to-day involvement with "the priesthood" always involves interaction with a male, the origin of that view is obvious.

Sarah agreed that "referring to priesthood as male is really limiting," then argued:

Priesthood as described in the scriptures speaks of man as the agent, but it also makes it clear that priesthood is the power of God in *my* life. The men in my life have the commission from God to serve and learn to serve the Lord. I honestly believe that priesthood is the power to bless all humankind. Priesthood is not male. It is God. It is a gift to men and other gifts are given to women. The women who live close to the Lord and do not have the endowed [ordained] priesthood still function in the power of the priesthood. It is the power to direct our lives—response to prayer is an emanation of that power.

I almost see the priesthood as a compensatory gift to help them seek out some opportunities that come inherently to women, especially if they marry and have children. I think that priesthood is an encouragement to nurturing and I think it is a necessary encouragement because I don't see that as standard equipment for men. I think that through the endowment of the priesthood the Lord is saying "feed my sheep," and I think that is [already] an instinct in many women, [both] married and single.

Mary and Nora both acknowledged this view but took strong exception to it. Mary observed:

I agree that all human beings need nurture and that all human beings need to learn how to nurture. I do not see "exercising priesthood" as necessarily teaching men how to nurture. Many men do not, I believe, serve their parents, their wives, or their children except vicariously. They're out serving human-kind. That service is usually limited in time, place, and scope. It is also limited in intensity, duration, and ultimately responsibility. Hence, it falls short of the most direct and consequential lessons in service. In other words, all that "priest-hood service" is a complicated and backwards way of learning service. Many men are badly taught about service (and so are many women, granted); but they see service as restricted to a very few limited functions and expect a payoff of status, gratitude, or power when they perform those functions. The kind of selfless invisible service that most women render day in and day out is simply not seen or acknowledged—let alone replicated—by men.

Nora's perspective was similar:

> On the basis of personal observation, my impression is that the exercise of priesthood administrative authority does very little to enhance the moral vision of most men. What makes a stake president a model in the eyes of his superiors is not his ability to relate to people and change their lives in a spiritual sense. It's his ability to keep his budget in shape, his buildings up to snuff, and his quotas in order. Bishops are caught in that tension between the demands for nurture coming from their congregations and the demands for administrative accountability coming from the institution. My husband's been a bishop. I know how tough it is. My impression is that men with nurturing skills and a commitment to nurture take those abilities into their priesthood assignments; those who don't have them don't.

Priesthood is seen by Latter-day Saints as organizationally significant not only in the church but also in the home. While some of the women inter-viewed felt comfortable with the patriarchal familial order and acknowl-edged the strength of the concept in the home, they expressed strong con-victions that they were personally accountable for their own lives and their relationship to the Lord. Priesthood was to them no substitute for individual initiative. One typical statement was: "I, personally, cannot live comfortably with the fact that I have to go through any individual to reach the Lord or to reach my Savior. I feel I have direct access to the Godhead and their love, and blessings, to even invoke and cry out for blessings, which I do." Karen, single, agreed: "I refuse to believe that my link with God is through a priest-hood holder. I don't believe that. My link is direct."

Speaking about priesthood in marriage, Betty simply saw the issue as broader:

> One of the great messages that the gospel has for the world is the com-panionship of men and women. It really does not trouble me to have a man preside in our home. I do not perceive him as telling everyone what to do. I feel that our responsibility as women is to find as many ways we can to relieve men of the pressures in their lives so they can do the same for us. That is what we should be striving for.
>
> Remember from Paul: Woman is not to be without man nor man without

woman. It seems to me that that's not only for creative purposes, but I feel that we are so created with the power of the priesthood emanating from both men and women, that every situation needs the complementary pattern of our strength. Regarding differences, I am just not sure what they are. I know that they exist but it is hard to pin them down. Different attributes exist but that they are uniquely masculine or uniquely feminine, I am not sure.

Betty's view of the complementary nature of men and women and the necessity of both enables her to find value in the male and female qualities which she acknowledges, without stereotyping the roles. She seems to feel valued within this context.

Sarah, unmarried, concurs: "The priesthood is only activated when people live the commandments—that's the only way. The Doctrine and Covenants makes that very clear, and priesthood power cannot be activated under any other conditions other than those set up by the Lord. Priesthood cannot function unrighteously. It cannot function in the lives of men and women if they are trying to 'lord' over someone, or take unrighteous dominion, or deprive someone of their agency. There *are* power struggles—I'm aware of that—but for me the power of the priesthood in my life is the power to feel the strength of eternal things." She sees priesthood as "an encouragement to nurturing," a "necessary" supplement for men who lack the "sensitivity" which she sees as "an instinct for many women, single as well as married."

As a matter of group process, she concedes, there has to be a "head" of the household, a central leadership line. Certainly it can be challenged, but ultimately someone has to take the final responsibility for a family or institution. However, responsibility is not the same thing as domination: "Manipulation or oppression is an abrogation of priesthood power. It is inadequate performance of priesthood."

Jane, married with two children, remarked: "Being head of the house doesn't have anything to do with priesthood. Kids should have input from both parents, and someone has to make the decision. Sometimes I override my husband's decisions, but it is done sensitively and respectfully. It is good for the kids to see that we can disagree and still love each other. We can change our minds, but there is always a place where the buck stops. My husband does not think that being the head means that he can do anything he wants."

On both the organizational and personal level, these women spoke of the abuses of authority, or the limited views of some priesthood leaders. These women all expressed appreciation for the blessings that they received by a priesthood leader in being set apart for a specific church calling as well as a more general sense of being the recipients of inspiration. Being female did not limit the outpouring of the Spirit, but some women commented on specific occasions when not being male sometimes interfered with their interaction with priesthood leaders. The problems always seemed to be related to the priesthood leader's perception of what it meant to "hold the priest-hood." If he saw priesthood as an extension of self or maleness, it seriously interfered with efficient work. One woman cited the example of a bishop who, because he only trusted the judgment of male priesthood holders, appointed the counselors to the Relief Society president himself without consulting her.

Acknowledging similar problems, Susan said: "We know that there are times when the priesthood is not being exercised righteously and that it is withdrawn from the individual. . . . There are men who use their priesthood role as one of power, and there are women in the Relief Society who do it, too. Our weaknesses as human beings are overwhelming, and maybe the organizational structure encourages this misuse, but I doubt that the Lord approves of it." Or, more succinctly, "I think there is hardly a man holding the priesthood who does not, at some time or another, worm his way out of a situation by invoking his priesthood authority. But that does not invalidate priesthood [as a principle]. It is just another sign of personal inadequacy. Women tend to feel inferior; maybe that isn't a good word, but there is a feeling that the priesthood bearer is superior and then we have to work with the priesthood in that way. When you have an experience—when you dis-agree with something that a priesthood leader is doing—you are often told that it is your fault and you are not responding properly." The position in which women find themselves, after such an exchange, is debilitating. "In the future, you are pretty cautious about being open and forthright—really being the kind of person you want to be."

A 1980 panel discussion at Brigham Young University on the topic of "Unrighteous Dominion" reflected the conflicts with such questions as: "How do you improve a working relationship with priesthood leaders when, despite an approach on a feeling level or as a 'daughter of God,' you still feel that your opinion and/or experience is less valued simply because you are a woman and do not hold the priesthood?" or "I get uncomfortable when leaders of the church insist that the women are 'equal.' I feel patronized when I am told I am just as good as any man. Help me understand my feelings of being dominated by leaders who are telling me they are not dominating me."

The church long ago decided officially that the personal "unworthiness" or "abuses" of an individual priesthood holder did not invalidate the ordi-nances he performed. This decision, which maintains order and continuity in the simplest and most practical way for the organization, still leaves open the personal question: what does it mean for the individual who *is* "un-worthy"? That question falls outside the scope of this examination, but the fact that the women being interviewed perceived a real difference between valid ordinances and "unrighteous" priesthood holders demonstrates their belief that priesthood as a universal power exists apart from—and above—

the individuals who exercise and use it. Karen, who saw priesthood as a subset of leadership, referred to hierarchical problems in the application of priesthood functions: "Often when there are problems in peoples' lives, there seems to be a feeling that the word of a priesthood holder on a higher administrative level is more valid than that of a husband or bishop. I had an experience with this. I had a problem and my parents insisted that I should go to a General Authority. I followed their wishes, but it was clear that the General Authority I saw did not know me well enough to be helpful. I should never have done it—it was the wrong route."

Abuse or mistaken application of priesthood does not always originate with the priesthood holders themselves. Sarah talked about the women she knew who were "wearing out their husbands" by their own refusal to participate in the decision-making process in the family. Instead, they would say, "You hold the priesthood, so you decide." The woman added, "This is their excuse for not taking responsibility for their marriages, for the decisions they make, for everything. . . . I tend to see too many women walking behind their husbands, little children hanging on them, and all looking very burdened."

Betty added the perspective of how their husbands and leaders perceive their own relationship to priesthood:

> Some men of the Church find priesthood authority very strengthening in personal ways, righteously or unrighteously. Others feel *so* much responsibility in the welfare of their families, which is right and necessary, but it seems to me it has to be shared. The sensitive men carry an enormous load trying to fulfill their priesthood magnification. If you carefully scrutinize the words of the prophets, especially President Kimball, I cannot imagine how priesthood leaders get the impression they carry the full load.
>
> I think some of the arrogance we see in some priesthood leaders drives other men away. If there is some way to establish a kind of partnership in service, in the home, in every priesthood-oriented activity that involves men and women, then men wouldn't feel so burdened. I think some men have left their homes and families because they felt they could not measure up, or that they didn't want to pay the price to measure up to what they perceived as demands of priesthood. . . . The pressure is so great in some homes that they finally just throw the whole thing over.

Nora was one of the few women interviewed who was willing to probe the dark side of priesthood authority:

> Sure, they've got the responsibility to govern, and those responsibilities are heavy. But along with the burden, they also get to be in charge of everything. You're a responsible public citizen. So am I. We know the rewards of that kind of power. They make the burden of responsibility worth it. That's why we are attracted to public service. But many men are made so uncomfortable by their own attraction to power that they hypothesize women without any of those

needs. All my adult life, I've been astonished to meet so many men in the church who are unable to relate to me as a person *like them*.

I remember a very discouraging experience with a professor who was a personal mentor—even a kind of father figure—before I was married. We were talking about problems of women's inequality in our larger society and in church government. It was obvious that he was having trouble understanding what I was saying. I said, "You've had an active, public career. You've done important work. You care about ideas and your work. Try to imagine what it would have been like for you as a twenty-year-old with your talents, training, and inclinations if someone had told you, 'You can teach elementary school or be a nurse, but what you should really do is stay home and raise children. You have no place in public life.'"

He was baffled. "No one would say that to me."

"Pretend," I insisted. "*Pretend* someone did."

"That's irrelevant," he said. "A woman doesn't feel the same way about those things that I would have felt when I was twenty."

I could barely get the words out. "They do," I said. "*I* do."

To do him credit, he's changed a great deal in the last twenty years, but I still remember that pain. He had dealt with brilliant, capable women in his own family all his life. What I was hearing, I think, was the voice of men who need to believe *in their very bones* that women are different. Because if they once accept that women have similar aspirations and needs—that there isn't a fundamental psychic difference between them—then they've lost every foothold they had.

Mary also challenged Betty's assumption of underlying, eternal differences between men and women that validate differential treatment:

> I first heard that statement about "eternal differences"—perhaps it had been made before—by Bruce R. McConkie when he was dedicating the women's monument at Nauvoo. It raised the hair on the back of my neck, and I've responded to its increasing repetition since that point with consistent dismay. It's one of those nonreasons that is somehow being twisted into the reason for everything. It is, first, a sexist assumption that men are by nature brutal and selfish and need something special to compensate while women are naturally spiritual and compassionate. I know both spiritual men and spiritual women. I refuse to believe that spiritual stereotyping is any more accurate than any other kind of stereotyping.
>
> In the second place, why are only men—not women—making that observation? Is that not in itself suspicious? In the third place, if it is true that women are more spiritual and that men have somehow perceived that fact faster than women, then women should be the role models and should be in positions where they could be more easily emulated. There should be active efforts on the parts of men to emulate women. If any man thinks he is "comforting" a woman by telling her that he needs the priesthood and she doesn't because he's a spiritual cripple, he is indulging in a kind of triple-think, not just double-think.

As the women interviewed talked about how they relate to the priesthood, issues of equality were continually mentioned. Some talked about feeling valued; others shared feelings of not being taken seriously; some did not know how to deal with differences of opinion with their priesthood leaders; but all of them acknowledged the need to be valued as equal, contributing partners. "You can't separate it from the equality issue," said one woman. She described "good experiences with the priesthood leaders [that] have come when I have been treated with respect, as an equal, and have been valued for my abilities. . . . It is all dependent upon the sensitivity of the priesthood holders."

On the other hand, Sarah rejected the notion of equality between the sexes as a valid concern: "I am baffled at the unilateral cry for equality because I don't see equality anywhere. Why we ask for equality in any aspect of our lives is inscrutable to me. What we should be asking for is individuality. We should be asking for the opportunity and the support to fulfill our individuality." This appreciation of individuality she ascribed to her own experience:

> When my mother died and I encountered some depression because the pattern of my life had been broken, and I experienced the feelings for the first time of not being needed, I had to go through a period of struggle to realize that I really was created not only as a member of my family unit or only as a partner in another family unit but also as a single spirit and a single individual and that my fulfillment, regardless of my experience, would have to come as an individual. And I think, in some ways, that this emerging awareness of women who are single, widowed, divorced is all part of our maturing in society and in the church. It may strengthen women in poor marriages if they can realize that they are still individuals and [that] there are still opportunities for fulfillment. These opportunities are available because we were created solo and singular and totally unequal.

Regardless of the word used, whether it is *equality* or *individuality,* these women are talking about the same thing—about being valued as persons. They are concerned about having equal access to the institution that is central to their lives. They want to be positive contributing members.

A standard question in Mormon settings is: Why don't women hold the priesthood? A standard response is "because they have children." It was interesting in the present study that of the eight women interviewed only one reflected this notion. The other seven found it inadequate. Sarah sees the real parallel as "motherhood and fatherhood, and priesthood and leadership. Leadership for a woman is equivalent to leadership for a man, but it does so happen that the men have the priesthood." Nora said crisply,

> A parallel between motherhood and priesthood makes no logical sense, it makes no historic sense, it makes no biological sense. It's so patently illogical

on its face that I wonder people can continue to make it. What's so interesting is that the men who promulgate that parallel as a pacifier for us never seem to see the absolutely terrible implications of what they are saying for their own parental responsibilities. They never seem to see that by equating their priesthood/adminstrative functions with the functions of motherhood they must entirely take out of the equation any value to be assigned to the value of fatherhood. I can't count the number of times I've heard prominent leaders of the Church, including members of the First Presidency, credit their wives with raising their children. They seem to feel no shame in making that admission. How can a woman feel honored in her motherhood when she is praised for it by a man who, in praising her, is making a clear but unspoken statement about the degree of his regard for the parenting function?

After talking about the first two levels of priesthood—organizational and personal—the women interviewed talked about an awareness of the role of the priesthood that went beyond person or function. Betty defined priesthood as "the power to act for God, a power that has been restored by the ministrations of angels to make it possible to establish the kingdom of God on the earth. The function [of priesthood] is to teach the gospel to all the world and to administer ordinances of salvation to men and women. It enhances my relationship with the Lord and facilitates the acquisition of knowledge. Priesthood came to bless all mankind. It administers the ordinances and teaches the gospel to all. The great power that connects God and man, heaven and earth, is the power from which all understanding grows."

Ann agreed and gave specific personal examples:

I have had experiences when I have had to call upon the powers of heaven to handle crises. What is important about these experiences is that it is always very instantaneous, very clear as to what I have to do. I felt absolute oneness and confidence in what I had to do. I knew that I had as much right to ask for healing as someone else. What is thrilling in retrospect is that I knew what to do. I feel that the understanding of our possibilities in this is so limited. I have had experiences with leaders of the church which have helped me understand the priesthood. As the church moved forward in the priesthood correlation program, I sensed, through many conversations with the leaders, that they were often talking about all the power of the priesthood being available to the women in order to meet the challenges of these last days. It was said to me that the women of the church must "be clothed in the priesthood." I think that means immediate access, never being without the priesthood power. I'm never without it.

She related an experience when she and her husband had been asked to speak in a stake conference about the priesthood. At one point in her husband's talk, while he was standing at the podium, he put up an umbrella and asked her to come and stand under it with him. He said, "This umbrella represents the power of the priesthood which is protecting me and my wife."

He then asked her to grasp the handle with him and said, "As we hold on together, those powers are equally distributed." The idea of a mutual sheltering and a mutual sharing of those powers was the focus. It was not emphasized that he was the one who had the umbrella or that he had opened it. Unity was the message.

Most of the women interviewed relied heavily on one Latter-day Saint scripture, Doctrine and Covenants 121, for their understanding of the priesthood. The revelation is dated 20 March 1839. Joseph Smith and some companions who had been in Liberty Jail in Missouri for several months felt abandoned and very much alone. The section begins with a plea to the Lord not to abandon them, a plea for help in understanding the purposes of their suffering. The tone is both anguished and strident, pointing out the injustices they had suffered at the hands of their enemies. But from verse 34 to the end of the section, the tone changes. One senses that divine instruction begins at that point, explaining why things go wrong and what the role of the priesthood can be in the individual lives of its members.

"Behold, there are many called, but few are chosen. And why are they not chosen?" This opening statement makes it clear that one may be called to a position, but that the call in no way guarantees the recipient's righteousness. The scripture goes on to answer its own far-from-rhetorical question: "Because their hearts are set so much upon the things of this world, and aspire to the honors of men, that they do not learn this one lesson—that the rights of the priesthood are inseparably connected with the powers of heaven, and that the powers of heaven cannot be controlled nor handled only upon the principles of righteousness."[7] This seems to imply that priesthood power is greater than any individual who holds it and that its blessings are predicated upon an individual's righteousness, not his position or priesthood.

Verse 37 enumerates the unrighteous behavior which will cause the "heavens [to] withdraw themselves"; "When we undertake to cover our sins, or to gratify our pride, our vain ambition, or to exercise control or dominion or compulsion upon the souls of the children of men . . . the Spirit of the Lord is grieved; and when it is withdrawn, Amen to the priesthood or the authority of that man."

Verse 39 acknowledges that "it is the nature and disposition of almost all men, as soon as they get a litle authority, as they suppose, they will immediately begin to exercise unrighteous dominion."

The next four verses speak of the context in which the priesthood must be exercised:

> No power or influence can or ought to be maintained by virtue of the priesthood, only by persuasion, by long-suffering, by gentleness and meekness, and by love unfeigned;
> By kindness, and pure knowledge, which shall greatly enlarge the soul without hypocrisy, and without guile—

Reproving betimes with sharpness, when moved upon by the Holy Ghost; and then showing forth afterwards an increase of love toward him whom thou has reproved, lest he esteem thee to be his enemy;

That he may know that thy faithfulness is stronger than the cords of death.[8]

That impressive list of nouns—*persuasion, long-suffering, gentleness, meekness, love, kindness,* and *knowledge*—are all applicable to Christ-like behavior. Two final injunctions to charity and personal righteousness are added: "Let thy bowels also be full of charity towards all men, and to the household of faith, and let virtue garnish thy thoughts unceasingly."[9]

The promises accompanying these injunctions are equally impressive: "Then shall thy confidence wax strong in the presence of God; and the doctrine of the priesthood shall distil upon thy soul as the dews from heaven." It is noteworthy that an understanding of "the doctrine of the priesthood" follows obedience to its exercise in a righteous and Christ-like way. Furthermore, the manner in which this understanding comes implies that it will follow naturally ("as the dews from heaven") once the proper conditions have been met but that it is, to some extent, a gift—not completely accessible only by intellectual efforts.

The promises continue: "The Holy Ghost shall be thy constant companion, and thy scepter an unchanging scepter of righteousness and truth; and thy dominion shall be an everlasting dominion, and without compulsory means it shall flow unto thee forever and ever."[10] Part of this promise—the companionship of the Holy Ghost—is clearly a promise for this life, but the reference to "everlasting dominion" and the reference in the previous verse to "the presence of God" at least suggest an extension of priesthood blessings and promises beyond mortality, although they do not exclude the possibility of fulfillment in this life.

All of this suggests that both the end and the means of priesthood as a functioning principle is a certain type of character, a Christ-like character. The conspicuous absence of a list of priesthood tasks from this particular discussion of priesthood suggests that such tasks and assignments are some of the necessary administrative forums for such character to be developed and, in developing, to express itself. But that lack of an absolute link with administrative functions also suggests that priesthood transcends mere administration.

As with many other facets of marriage, the quality of the relationship tends both to transcend definitions and to invest them with meaning. In many families father's blessings of comfort and instruction to the children or healing blessings are initiated by the woman and administered by the man, suggesting an awareness of reciprocal and mutually supportive roles in meeting their own spiritual needs and those of their families. Evidence also suggests that many modern marriages are actually more partnership than patriarchal. Perhaps the most sensitive pressure points will come in the interface between the individual and the institution.

Meg Wheatley-Pesci, a management consultant specializing in women in organizational structure, has written an insightful extrapolation of what has happened in other organizations when women have been incorporated in large numbers. She explores two questions: (1) "What are some of the unintended consequences we experience presently because women do not hold priesthood?" and (2) "If priesthood were extended to women, would the nature of priesthood change?" She hypothesizes:

> In the present church structure, where so much is contingent upon priesthood, women suffer from a lack of opportunity. This can result in negative or diverted energy, in a loss of commitment to the Church, and in a loss of personal and even spiritual growth for large numbers of women. However, if priesthood were expanded to include women, priesthood might diminish in status, the criteria for admission to administrative office might simply change, and women might still be excluded from increased opportunities to contribute to the Church....
>
> ... For me, the dilemma does not create a sense of hopelessness for improving women's role in the Church. Instead, it points to the importance of beginning now to separate priesthood functions from administrative activity. Before priesthood can be expanded—if it ever is—a tremendous amount can be done to improve women's position within the Church and to clarify the priestly role.

She suggests such important steps as improving women's access to decision-making forums, increasing access to ward callings and duties, improving women's influence over their own organization, and developing greater visibility for women's activities.[11]

Nora agrees: "There's no doctrinal reason whatsoever why a woman couldn't be a Sunday School president, for instance, and function in many of the positions that are now completely assigned to men. No revelation is needed for that. Women could stand in the circles when their babies are blessed. No revelation would be needed for that. But I perceive a great deal of defensiveness where women are concerned. It is difficult to have a dispassionate discussion of these issues because, in my opinion, many male leaders of the church perceive any change as the opening of a floodgate and are frightened, just as men throughout our social institutions are frightened by the potential loss of their power, the loss of their comforts."

Ann, Betty, and Susan disagree, citing their personal experiences of working with men on ecclesiastical committees and in other church settings. "There is a great sensitivity to the needs of women, an awareness of their needs, a desire to give more, not to hold back or restrain or limit."

Mary points out:

I think no one would fault the intent or conscious motives of male leaders of the church. But I think that the mere fact that they are in the position of givers and the women must be in the position of suppliants and receivers tells a more forceful story than agreeing on the purity of their motives. Yes, I think it is true that individual men are experiencing great change. There is more concern for daughters as well as sons. But institutionally I do not see the same pattern. As nearly as I can tell from my reading in history, change in the church has come in three ways: (1) A charismatic leader has created a form and filled it with a concept. In experiencing the form, people have learned to accept and accommodate the new concept. (2) Massive apathy, to use Claudia Bushman's phrase, and passive aggression have finally reached such proportions that the need became apparent even on the highest level. The level of nonattendance in church meetings during the 1920s and 1930s led to a concentration on involvement, entertainment, and attendance for its own sake that redefined, in some ways, what constituted acceptable behavior for Mormons. The current emphasis on boys' programs in the church I see as a response to the low proportion of boys who went on missions a few years ago. (3) External pressures have become so painful that they upset the status quo and the leadership must provide an institutional response.

It is clear that a great deal of thinking has yet to be done on the nature and theology of priesthood. Although some women in the church have defined an aspect of the temple endowment as an endowment of priesthood (in addition to being endowed with priesthood power), others have pointed out that, in contrast to the event-centered nature of male priesthood ordination, this female version remains unhelpfully fuzzy. Furthermore, an even more important problem is that the endowment is not recognized by the church hierarchy as a "priesthood endowment," whatever individual recipients may feel about it.

To put the paradox in its most pointed form: Is priesthood more than conducting meetings, administering ordinances such as baptism, and making task-related assignments? If it is not, then the criteria for priesthood should be administrative competence. Why would half the membership of the church arbitrarily be excluded from demonstrating and/or developing such abilites? If priesthood is more than administration, then does God have no special work for women in his church? Women can, of course, pray, teach, serve, and learn. But, as several of the women pointed out, "So can men. So can men without priesthood. So can people who aren't Mormons. So can anyone who believes in Christ."

Nora summed it up this way: "If government is the chief function of priesthood, then women must confront the fact that they belong to a class of human beings who are absolutely denied any access to priesthood under that definition. What does it do to a human being to be told that the power of God is the power to change, heal, and bless, and then be told that you have no personal access to it?"

Is that, in fact, the message of the church to its women? Possibly not. Gordon B. Hinckley, First Counselor in the First Presidency, speaking at the women's fireside before October conference 1985, said: "Some are prone to complain that you are discriminated against. All of us rejoice in the enlargement of opportunities for women. Under the law, there are few opportunities afforded men that are not now also open to women. With this enlargement of opportunity, a few Latter-day Saint women are asking why they are not entitled to hold the priesthood. To that I can say that only the Lord, through revelation, could alter that situation. He has not done so, so it is profitless for us to speculate and worry about it." [12]

The women who speak of a concept of universal priesthood seem to understand it as a principle that transcends the application of priesthood function and authority on personal and organizational levels. They speak of the principle of universal priesthood as the connection between heaven and earth which facilitates all functions between God and members of the human family. How, then, does it differ from the prayer of faith that any believer, Mormon or non-Mormon, may address to God? Unlike that connection, which is initiated by mortals and directed toward deity, priesthood power originates in deity and is directed toward mortals. Mormons believe that the "restoration" of priesthood to Joseph Smith before the organization of the church in fact represents just such divine initiative. Because God is the source of that priesthood power and both grants and commands the authority to act in his name, the connection provided by priesthood is different from and elevated above all other links such as prayer. Not only does the holy priesthood facilitate ordinations and the organization of the church, but it works the same transcendent way in individual lives. How these women feel about equality, motherhood, self-esteem, and male and female relationships may depend upon the quality of the experience they have had with priesthood holders on the personal and organizational level; but how they ultimately resolve personal problems, how they deal with conflict, and how they see their possibilities comes from the knowledge they have that the universal concept of a priesthood connects them with the Lord.

The women interviewed are forging living definitions of the priesthood which are positive and strengthening. Their perceptions suggest that each woman has the prerogative to function within the priesthood on a personal, organizational, and/or universal level. They do not see themselves as "under" the priesthood or "outside" the priesthood. Even though the hierarchical structure of the church is administered by male priesthood holders, the universal concept of priesthood is not male or female. It is beyond gender. These women perceive a universal principle of the priesthood that encircles all functions, all offices, and all persons within the church.

These working definitions are limited. They come from only eight women, though they echo concerns heard from hundreds of women in dozens of settings. They are still in process and very directly related to individual experiences. The perceptions and experiences of these women have been quite different, but their understanding of priesthood potential has been similar and unifying. They appear to agree with a missionary who, 120 years ago, wrote for the *LDS Millennial Star*:

> This, then, is true Priesthood—to be images of the living God, exhibiting in our characteristics his brightness and his strength; to be girt and endowed with the purity of his nature; to be unsullied in heart and mind; to stand by the strength of redeeming, saving qualities; to bless, and bless, and bless again, notwithstanding ingratitude in some—building, sustaining, and protecting . . . the weak, the down-trodden, and the helpless, till helping becomes our natural food,—working on all principles that yield nourishment, support, and strength,—till our very presence is as the sun, cheering and blessing all. . . . And the characteristics of the holy Priesthood will grow out from us like the branches of a fruitful tree that yield shelter, shield, and fruit.[13]

NOTES

1. Joseph F. Smith, *Gospel Doctrine: Selections from the Sermons and Writings of Joseph F. Smith*, 5th ed. (Salt Lake City: Deseret Book Co., 1939), p. 139.

2. Harold B. Lee, *Stand Ye in Holy Places: Selected Sermons and Writings of President Harold B. Lee* (Salt Lake City: Deseret Book Co., 1974), p. 258.

3. John A. Widtsoe, comp., *Priesthood and Church Government in the Church of Jesus Christ of Latter-day Saints*, rev. ed. (Salt Lake City: Deseret Book Co., 1954), p. 92.

4. *The Latter-day Saint Woman: Basic Manual for Women*, Part A (Salt Lake City: Church of Jesus Christ of Latter-day Saints, 1979), p. 90.

5. Bruce R. McConkie, *Mormon Doctrine*, 2nd ed. (Salt Lake City: Bookcraft, 1966), p. 844.

6. "Why Priesthood At All?" *Improvement Era* 34 (October 1931): 735.

7. Doctrine and Covenants 121:34–36.

8. Ibid., v. 41–44.

9. Ibid., v. 45.

10. Ibid., v. 46.

11. Meg Wheatley-Pesci, "An Expanded Definition of Priesthood? Some Present and Future Consequences," *Dialogue* 18 (Fall 1985): 33, 40–42.

12. Gordon B. Hinckley, "Ten Gifts from the Lord," *Ensign* 15 (November 1985): 86.

13. E. L. T. Harrison, "A Real Representative of the Most High," *The Latter-day Saints' Millennial Star* 20 (9 October 1858): 643.

Notes on Contributors

Lavina Fielding Anderson

Lavina Fielding Anderson, a doctoral graduate of the University of Washington in American literature, wrote her dissertation on "Attitudes toward Landscape in Western Travel Narratives." After eight years as an editor of the *Ensign*, official organ of the Church of Jesus Christ of Latter-day Saints, she organized Editing, Inc., of which she is president. She is also co-associate editor of *Dialogue: A Journal of Mormon Thought*. A research interest is the Young Women's Mutual Improvement Association, and she has presented papers on aspects of Mormon women's history at professional meetings. She was a charter member of the Utah Women's History Association and has served on the Mormon History Association council, awards committee, and membership committee. She and her husband, Paul, an architect, have one son, Christian.

Maureen Ursenbach Beecher

Currently associate professor of English at Brigham Young University and research appointee with its Joseph Fielding Smith Institute for Church History, Maureen Ursenbach Beecher has been writing Mormon women's history since 1973, when she finished her dissertation at the University of Utah on the picaresque in European literatures. Once she became involved in history, she promoted the interdisciplinary study of Mormon women. She was founding president of the Association for Mormon Letters in 1976, and 1984–85 president of the Mormon History Association. She and her husband, Dale, a historian, are the parents of two children, Daniel and Bronwen, and live in Salt Lake City, where she is Relief Society president in her ward.

Melodie Moench Charles

In 1978 Melodie Moench Charles received the degree of Master of Theological Studies in Old Testament from Harvard University. Returning to

Utah, she helped prepare a commentary on the Book of Mormon for the LDS Church's Translation Department and taught Old Testament for the University of Utah's Division of Continuing Education. Besides teaching the adult Gospel Doctrine classes in her ward, Charles has published in *Dialogue* and *Sunstone* on Mormon interpretations of Old Testament scriptures. On her husband Bob Charles's graduation from law school, she moved with him and their son, Louie, to Washington, D.C., and then Colorado, where Sally and Evan were born. The family recently acquired Sandra, an adoptive daughter from Spain. They now live in the Boston area, while Bob attends Harvard for postgraduate studies.

Jill Mulvay Derr

Native to Salt Lake City, Jill Mulvay Derr earned degrees from the University of Utah and Harvard University. Following the MAT degree, she taught two years in Boston public schools, then returned to Utah, where she became affiliated with the LDS Church History Division and launched a prolific career in researching and writing the history of Mormon women. With Kenneth and Audrey Godfrey she compiled and edited *Women's Voices: An Untold History of the Latter-day Saints, 1830–1900* (Salt Lake City: Deseret Book, 1982). A history of Relief Society, co-authored with Janath R. Cannon, and study of LDS Social Services are forthcoming. Derr has served on the council of the Mormon History Association and on the editorial staff of its *Journal of Mormon History*. Recently returned from a year's stay in France, she and her husband, C. Brooklyn Derr, also an author, live with their four children in Alpine, Utah.

Maryann MacMurray

While a student at Brigham Young University, from which she graduated with a B.S. in sociology, Maryann Olsen married Val MacMurray, an administrator and, in private practice, a therapist. They have five children, ranging in age from eight to eighteen. The family has lived in Boston, where MacMurray did graduate work at Harvard, and in Calgary, Canada; they now live in Salt Lake City. Always a poet, MacMurray has published in *Dialogue* and the *Ensign*; a volume of poems is in the gathering stages.

Carol Cornwall Madsen

Even before she had completed her doctorate, Carol Cornwall Madsen, together with Susan Staker Oman, published *Sisters and Little Saints* (Salt Lake City: Deseret Book, 1978), a history of the children's organization of the Church of Jesus Christ of Latter-day Saints. Her dissertation, completed in 1985 for the University of Utah, was a biographical study, "Emmeline B. Wells: A Mormon Woman in Victorian America." Madsen has written widely on aspects of the history of Mormon women, has presented papers at several academic conferences, and is currently an associate professor of history and research appointee of the Joseph Fielding Smith Institute for Church History of Brigham Young University. She and her attorney husband, Gordon, have six children, most of them grown, and three grandchildren.

Linda King Newell

Linda King Newell was raised in the central Utah town of Fillmore and graduated from Utah State University in Logan, Utah. She married L. Jackson Newell, and they became parents of four children. They reside in Salt Lake City. Linda and Jack Newell are co-editors of *Dialogue: A Journal of Mormon Thought*. With Valeen Tippetts Avery, Linda Newell began a nine-year study of Emma Hale Smith, wife of founding Mormon Prophet Joseph Smith. Doubleday published their award-winning biography *Mormon Enigma: Emma Hale Smith* in 1984. Newell travels widely, lecturing on aspects of the history of Mormon women.

Grethe Ballif Peterson

While living in Cambridge, Massachusetts, Grethe Peterson made her first forays into publications for and about women, becoming managing editor of *Exponent II,* a periodical founded there in 1973. Moving to Utah, where her husband, Chase Peterson, is now president of the University of Utah, she served first as a member of the general board of the young Women of the LDS Church and later chaired the Utah Endowment for the Humanities. She was instrumental in organizing Women Concerned about Nuclear War. Currently she serves on the board of directors of Deseret Book Publishing Company, as well as working with her husband in university matters. She is the mother of three and grandmother of two.

Marybeth Raynes

A marriage and family therapist by profession, Marybeth Raynes writes a column on "Issues of Intimacy" for *Sunstone,* an independent magazine for the Mormon audience, and regularly gives speeches and conducts workshops on mental health matters and family topics. She holds master's degrees in family relationships and social work from both Brigham Young University and the University of Utah, the latter granted in 1979, and is now in private practice. Married to Alan Parsons, she lives in Salt Lake City with him and Teri, Nathan, and Sara.

Jolene Edmunds Rockwood

From the time of her B.A. at the University of Utah, where she was elected Associated Women Students president and Outstanding Woman, to the present, Jolene Edmunds Rockwood has been involved in community affairs as well as being active in her church responsibilities. Most recently, in her adopted city of Batesville, Indiana, she has won grants which have supported art and gifted education programs for the elementary schools, as well as teaching and coordinating challenge programs there. Her master's degree from Harvard's Divinity School in Old Testament was followed by her marriage to Fred Rockwood, now a corporate president. They have five children, the oldest just barely a teenager.

Jan Shipps

Jan Shipps, whose recent book *Mormonism: The Story of a New Religious Tradition* has pointed new directions in the study of American religion, is director of the Center for American Studies and professor of history and religious studies at Indiana University-Purdue University at Indianapolis. Methodist by persuasion, she has since 1962 been an observer and scholar of Mormonism, is frequently invited nationwide to lecture on the subject, and is a past president of the Mormon History Association. Her current works in progress are a full study of Mormonism in the twentieth century and a continuation of her work on Mormons in the media. She is married to Anthony Shipps, librarian for English at Indiana University, is mother of a musician son, and has two grandchildren.

Linda P. Wilcox

Living in Salt Lake City with her three daughters, Linda Wilcox is an administrative assistant in the county government. She is a graduate of Stanford University with a master's degree in education and of the University of Utah with another in history. She has published on Brigham Young and on Utah agriculture, as well as on women's issues. Her essay "Crying 'Change' in a Permanent World: Contemporary Mormon Women on Motherhood" won special recognition on its publication in *Dialogue* in 1985.

Index